Points of View

Readings in American Government and Politics

Points of View

Readings in American Government and Politics

NINTH EDITION

Edited by

Robert D. DiClerico
West Virginia University

Allan S. Hammock
West Virginia University

OAKTON COMMUNITY COLLEGE
DES PLAINES CAMPUS
1600 EAST GOLF ROAD
DES PLAINES, IL 60016

Boston   Burr Ridge, IL   Dubuque, IA   Madison, WI   New York
San Francisco   St. Louis   Bangkok   Bogotá   Caracas   Kuala Lumpur
Lisbon   London   Madrid   Mexico City   Milan   Montreal   New Delhi
Santiago   Seoul   Singapore   Sydney   Taipei   Toronto

McGraw-Hill Higher Education

A Division of The McGraw-Hill Companies

POINTS OF VIEW: READINGS IN AMERICAN GOVERNMENT AND POLITICS
Published by McGraw-Hill, a business unit of The McGraw-Hill Companies, Inc., 1221 Avenue
of the Americas, New York, NY, 10020. Copyright © 2004, 2001, 1998, 1995, 1992, 1989,
1986, 1983, 1980, by The McGraw-Hill Companies, Inc. All rights reserved. No part of this
publication may be reproduced or distributed in any form or by any means, or stored in a
database or retrieval system, without the prior written consent of The McGraw-Hill Companies,
Inc., including, but not limited to, in any network or other electronic storage or transmission, or
broadcast for distance learning.

Some ancillaries, including electronic and print components, may not be available to customers
outside the United States.

This book is printed on acid-free paper.

1 2 3 4 5 6 7 8 9 0 DOC/DOC 0 9 8 7 6 5 4 3

ISBN 0-07-281739-9

Publisher: *Lyn Uhl*
Senior sponsoring editor: *Monica Eckman*
Developmental editor: *Kate Scheinman*
Marketing manager: *Katherine Bates*
Senior media producer: *Sean Crowley*
Project manager: *Diane M. Folliard*
Lead production supervisor: *Randy L. Hurst*
Design coordinator: *Mary E. Kazak*
Cover design: *Aesthetic Apparatus*
Typeface: *10/12 Palatino*
Compositor: *ElectraGraphics, Inc.*
Printer: *R. R. Donnelley and Sons Inc.*

Library of Congress Cataloging-in-Publication Data

Points of view : readings in American government and politics / edited by Robert E.
  DiClerico, Allan S. Hammock.—9th ed.
    p. cm.
  ISBN 0-07-281739-9 (softcover : alk. paper)
  1. United States—Politics and government. I. DiClerico, Robert E. II. Hammock, Allan
S., 1938–
JK21.P59 2004
320.973—dc21   2003051181

www.mhhe.com

About the Editors

ROBERT E. DiCLERICO is Eberly Distinguished Professor of Political Science at West Virginia University. An Indiana University (Bloomington) Ph.D. and a Danforth fellow, he is author of *The American President,* 5th edition (2000); co-author of *Choosing Our Choices* (2000) and *Few Are Chosen* (1984); and editor of *Political Parties, Campaigns, and Elections* (2000) and *Analyzing the Presidency* (1985).

ALLAN S. HAMMOCK is an Associate Professor and Chairman of the Department of Political Science at West Virginia University. He received his Ph.D. from the University of Virginia and is co-author of *West Virginia Politics and Government* (1996). He currently serves as chairman of the West Virginia Election Commission.

Contents

Preface

Reflecting the press of events and editorial judgments, we have made a number of changes for the ninth edition of *Points of View*. Under the general subject of the Courts (Chapter 14) we have added a new topic on "Judicial Selection" and likewise added a new topic on "Gender Equity" under the general subject of Civil Rights (Chapter 15). In addition, under the general subject of Elections (Chapter 7) there are two new selections for both Campaign Finance and the Electoral College. We have also included new selections for the general subjects of Political Parties (Chapter 8) and Bureaucracy (Chapter 13), and we changed one of the selections for the chapters on Campaign and the Media (Chapter 6) and Interest Groups (Chapter 9). Finally, of the articles retained from the previous edition, two have been updated: Larry Sabato's article on PACs (Chapter 9) and John Kilwein's selection on crime and the courts (Chapter 14).

The basic goal of the book remains the same: to provide students with a manageable number of selections that present readable, succinct, thoughtful, and diverse perspectives across a broad range of issues related to American government.

Jim Hoeffler, of Dickinson College, has developed a website to accompany the ninth edition of *Points of View*. We invite readers to visit our site at http://www.mhhe.com/diclerico where Internet resources for chapter-specific topics are presented.

We would like to extend our thanks to a number of individuals who made valuable contributions to this project. A special debt of gratitude is owed to Kate Scheinman who had primary editorial responsibility for this latest edition and whose keen eye for details was instrumental in improving the style and content of the final manuscript. We would like to express our appreciation to our sponsoring editor Monica Eckman who had overall responsibility in coordinating this latest revision and did a superb job of expediting the publishing process. We would also like to thank Diane Folliard, our project manager, for her excellent guidance of our project through the production process.

In the course of revising and updating this manuscript, we repeatedly called upon the typing skills of administrative associate Lee Ann Greathouse, who cheerfully reproduced manuscripts with unfailing accuracy and in less time than we had any reason to expect.

Finally, we would like to express our deep appreciation to the following academicians who carefully read the previous edition of *Points of View* and offered the most detailed and constructive suggestions we have ever received on a revision:

Ross Baker,
Rutgers University

Christopher Borick,
Mulhenberg College

Rachel Paine Caulfield,
Drake University

Richardson Dilworth,
Drexel University

Terri Fine,
University of Central Florida

Steven Green,
Texas Tech University

James Hoeffler,
Dickinson College

Lauren Holland,
University of Utah

James King,
University of Wyoming

Mary Kweit,
University of North Dakota

Kathleen Lee,
College of Redwoods

David Mann,
College of Charleston

Kevin Smith,
University of Nebraska

Robert E. DiClerico
Allan S. Hammock
Morgantown, West Virginia

A Note to the Instructor

For some years now, we have jointly taught the introductory course to American government. Each year we perused the crop of existing readers, and while we adopted several different readers over this period, we were not wholly satisfied with any of them. It is our feeling that many of the readers currently on the market suffer from one or more of the following deficiencies: (1) Some contain selections that are difficult for students to comprehend because of the sophistication of the argument, the manner of expression, or both. (2) In many instances, readers do not cover all of the topics typically treated in an introductory American government course. (3) In choosing selections for a given topic, editors do not always show sufficient concern for how—or whether—one article under a topic relates to other articles under the same topic. (4) Most readers contain too many selections for each topic—indeed, in several cases the number of selections for some topics exceeds ten. Readers are nearly always used in conjunction with a textbook. Thus, to ask a student to read a lengthy chapter—jammed with facts—from a textbook and then to read anywhere from five to ten selections on the same topic from a reader is to demand that students read more than they can reasonably absorb in a meaningful way. Of course, an instructor need not assign all the selections under a given topic. At the same time, however, this approach justifiably disgruntles students who, after purchasing a reader, discover that they may only be asked to read one-half or two-thirds of it.

Instead of continuing to complain about what we considered to be the limitations of existing American government readers, we decided to try our own hand at putting one together. In doing so, we were guided by the following considerations.

Readability

Quite obviously, students will not read dull, difficult articles. We feel that, as well as having something important to say, each of the articles in *Points of View* is clearly written, well organized, and free of needless jargon.

Comprehensiveness

The fifteen chapters of *Points of View* cover all the major topics of concern that are typically treated in the standard introductory course on American government.

Economy of Selections

We decided, generally, to limit the number of selections to two per topic, although we did include three selections on representation in Chapter 10. The limitation on selections will maximize the likelihood that students will read them. It has been our experience that when students are assigned four, five, or more selections under a given topic, they simply do not read them all. In addition, by limiting the selections for each topic, there is a greater likelihood that students will be able to associate an argument with the author who made it.

Juxtaposition

The two selections for each topic will take *opposing* or *different* points of view on some aspect of a given topic. This approach was chosen for three reasons. First, we believe that student interest will be enhanced by playing one article off against the other. Thus, the "interest" quality of a given article will derive not only from its own content, but also from its juxtaposition with the other article. Second, we think it is important to sensitize students to the fact that one's perspective on an issue will depend upon the values that he or she brings to it. Third, by having both selections focus on a particular issue related to a given topic, the student will have a greater depth of understanding about that issue. We think this is preferable to having five or six selections under a topic, with each selection focusing on a different aspect, and with the result that the student ultimately is exposed to "a little of this and a little of that"—that is, if the student even bothers to read all five or six selections.

While the readers currently available take into account one or, in some instances, several of the considerations identified, we believe that the uniqueness of *Points of View* lies in the fact that it has sought to incorporate *all* of them.

Robert E. DiClerico

Allan S. Hammock

Points of View

Readings in American Government and Politics

chapter 1

Democracy

Defining Democracy

Any assessment of a society's democratic character will be fundamentally determined by what the observer chooses to use as a definition of democracy. Though the concept of democracy has commanded the attention of political thinkers for centuries, the following selections by Howard Zinn and Sidney Hook serve to demonstrate that there continues to be considerable disagreement over its meaning. Each of them has scanned the American scene and reached different conclusions regarding the democratic character of our society. This difference of opinion is explained primarily by the fact that each approaches his evaluation with a different conception of what democracy is.

For Zinn, the definition of democracy includes criteria that bear not only upon how decisions get made but also upon what results from such decisions. Specifically, he argues that such results must lead to a certain level of human welfare within a society. In applying these criteria of human welfare to the United States, he concludes that we fall short of the mark in several areas.

Although Sidney Hook is willing to acknowledge that democracy might indeed function more smoothly in societies where the conditions of human welfare are high, he insists that these conditions do not themselves constitute the definition of democracy. Rather, he maintains that democracy is a process—a way of making decisions. Whether such decisions lead to the conditions of human welfare that Zinn prescribes is irrelevant. The crucial test, according to Hook, is whether the people have the right, by majority rule, to make choices about the quality of their lives—whatever those choices might be.

How Democratic Is America?

Howard Zinn

To give a sensible answer to the question "How democratic is America?" I find it necessary to make three clarifying preliminary statements. First, I want to define "democracy," not conclusively, but operationally, so we can know what we are arguing about or at least what I am talking about. Second, I want to state what my criteria are for measuring the "how" in the question. And third, I think it necessary to issue a warning about how a certain source of bias (although not the only source) is likely to distort our judgments.

Our definition is crucial. This becomes clear if we note how relatively easy is the answer to our question when we define democracy as a set of formal institutions and let it go at that. If we describe as "democratic" a country that has a representative system of government, with universal suffrage, a bill of rights, and party competition for office, it becomes easy to answer the question "how" with the enthusiastic reply, "Very!" . . .

I propose a set of criteria for the description "democratic," which goes beyond formal political institutions, to the quality of life in the society (economic, social, psychological), beyond majority rule to a concern for minorities, and beyond national boundaries to a global view of what is meant by "the people," in that rough, but essentially correct view of democracy as "government of, by, and for the people."

Let me list these criteria quickly, because I will go on to discuss them in some detail later:

1. To what extent can various people in the society participate in those decisions which affect their lives: decisions in the political process and decisions in the economic structure?
2. As a corollary of the above: do people have equal access to the information which they need to make important decisions?
3. Are the members of the society equally protected on matters of life and death—in the most literal sense of that phrase?
4. Is there equality before the law: police, courts, the judicial process—as well as equality *with* the law-enforcing institutions, so as to safeguard equally

Howard Zinn is professor emeritus of political science at Boston University. This essay was originally published in Robert A. Goldwin, ed., *How Democratic Is America?* (Chicago, Rand McNally, 1971), pp. 39–60. The author revised and updated the original for *Points of View* in 1985 and again in 1997.

everyone's person, and his freedom from interference by others, and by the government?

5. Is there equality in the distribution of available resources: those economic goods necessary for health, life, recreation, leisure, growth?
6. Is there equal access to education, to knowledge and training, so as to enable persons in the society to live their lives as fully as possible, to enlarge their range of possibilities?
7. Is there freedom of expression on all matters, and equally for all, to communicate with other members of the society?
8. Is there freedom for individuality in private life, in sexual relations, family relations, the right of privacy?
9. To minimize regulation: do education and the culture in general foster a spirit of cooperation and amity to sustain the above conditions?
10. As a final safety feature: is there opportunity to protest, to disobey the laws, when the foregoing objectives are being lost—as a way of restoring them? . . .

Two historical facts support my enlarged definition of democracy. One is that the industrialized Western societies have outgrown the original notions which accompanied their early development: that constitutional and procedural tests sufficed for the "democracy" that overthrew the old order; that democracy was quite adequately fulfilled by the Bill of Rights in England at the time of the Glorious Revolution, the Constitution of the United States, and the declaration of the Rights of Man in France. It came to be acknowledged that the rhetoric of these revolutions was not matched by their real achievements. In other words, the limitations of that "democracy" led to the reformist and radical movements that grew up in the West in the middle and late nineteenth century. The other historical note is that the new revolutions in our century, in Africa, Asia, Latin America, while rejecting either in whole or in part the earlier revolutions, profess a similar democratic aim, but with an even broader rhetoric. . . .

My second preliminary point is on standards. By this I mean that we can judge in several ways the fulfillment of these ten criteria I have listed. We can measure the present against the past, so that if we find that in 2000 we are doing better in these matters than we were doing in 1860 or 1910, the society will get a good grade for its "democracy." I would adjure such an approach because it supports complacency. With such a standard, Russians in 1910 could point with pride to how much progress they had made toward parliamentary democracy; as Russians in 1985 could point to their post-Stalin progress away from the gulag; as Americans could point in 1939 to how far they had come toward solving the problem of economic equality; as Americans in the South could point in 1950 to the progress of the southern African-American. Indeed, the American government has given military aid to brutal regimes in Latin America on the ground that a decrease in the murders by semiofficial death squads is a sign of progress.

Or, we could measure our democracy against other places in the world. Given the high incidence of tyranny in the world, polarization of wealth, and lack of freedom of expression, the United States, even with very serious defects, could declare itself successful. Again, the result is to let us all off easily; some of our most enthusiastic self-congratulation is based on such a standard.

On the other hand, we could measure our democracy against an ideal (even if admittedly unachievable) standard. I would argue for such an approach, because, in what may seem to some a paradox, the ideal standard is the pragmatic one; it affects what we *do*. To grade a student on the basis of an improvement over past performance is justifiable if the intention is to encourage someone discouraged about his ability. But if he is rather pompous about his superiority in relation to other students (and I suggest this is frequently true of Americans evaluating American "democracy"), and if in addition he is a medical student about to graduate into a world ridden with disease, it would be best to judge him by an ideal standard. That might spur him to an improvement fast enough to save lives. . . .

My third preliminary point is a caution based on the obvious fact that we make our appraisals through the prism of our own status in society. This is particularly important in assessing democracy, because if "democracy" refers to the condition of masses of people, and if we as the assessors belong to a number of elites, we will tend (and I am not declaring an inevitability, just warning of a tendency) to see the present situation in America more benignly than it deserves. To be more specific, if democracy requires a keen awareness of the condition of black people, of poor people, of young people, of that majority of the world who are not American—and we are white, prosperous, beyond draft age, and American—then we have a number of pressures tending to dull our sense of inequity. We are, if not doomed to err, likely to err on the side of complacency—and we should try to take this into account in making our judgments.

1. PARTICIPATION IN DECISIONS

We need to recognize first, that whatever decisions are made politically are made by representatives of one sort or another: state legislators, congressmen, senators, and other elected officials, governors and presidents; also by those appointed by elected officials, like Supreme Court justices. These are important decisions, affecting our lives, liberties, and ability to pursue happiness. Congress and the president decide on the tax structure, which affects the distribution of resources. They decide how to spend the monies received; whether or not we go to war; who serves in the armed forces; what behavior is considered a crime; which crimes are prosecuted and which are not. They decide what limitations there should be on our travel, or on our right to speak freely. They decide on the availability of education and health services.

If representation by its very nature is undemocratic, as I would argue, this is an important fact for our evaluation. Representative government is *closer* to democracy than monarchy, and for this reason it has been hailed as one of the great political advances of modern times; yet, it is only a step in the direction of democracy, at its best. It has certain inherent flaws—pointed out by

Rousseau in the eighteenth century, Victor Considerant in the nineteenth century, Robert Michels in the beginning of the twentieth century, Hannah Arendt in our own time. No representative can adequately represent another's needs; the representative tends to become a member of a special elite; he has privileges which weaken his sense of concern at others' grievances; the passions of the troubled lose force (as Madison noted in *The Federalist 10*) as they are filtered through the representative system; the elected official develops an expertise which tends toward its own perpetuation. Leaders develop what Michels called "a mutual insurance contract" against the rest of society. . . .

If only radicals pointed to the inadequacy of the political processes in the United States, we might be suspicious. But established political scientists of a moderate bent talk quite bluntly of the limitations of the voting system in the United States. Robert Dahl, in *A Preface to Democratic Theory*, drawing on the voting studies of American political scientists, concludes that "political activity, at least in the United States, is positively associated to a significant extent with such variables as income, socio-economic status, and education." He says:

> By their propensity for political passivity the poor and uneducated disfranchise themselves. . . . Since they also have less access than the wealthy to the organizational, financial, and propaganda resources that weigh so heavily in campaigns, elections, legislative, and executive decisions, anything like equal control over government policy is triply barred to the members of Madison's unpropertied masses. They are barred by their relatively greater inactivity, by their relatively limited access to resources, and by Madison's nicely contrived system of constitutional checks.[1]

Dahl thinks that our society is essentially democratic, but this is because he expects very little. (His book was written in the 1950s, when lack of commotion in the society might well have persuaded him that no one else expected much more than he did.) Even if democracy were to be superficially defined as "majority rule," the United States would not fulfill that, according to Dahl, who says that "on matters of specific policy, the majority rarely rules."[2] After noting that "the election is the critical technique for insuring that governmental leaders will be relatively responsive to nonleaders," he goes on to say that "it is important to notice how little a national election tells us about the preferences of majorities. Strictly speaking, all an election reveals is the first preferences of some citizens among the candidates standing for office."[3] About 45 percent of the potential voters in national elections, and about 60 percent of the voters in local elections do not vote, and this cannot be attributed, Dahl says, simply to indifference. And if, as Dahl points out, "in no large nation state can elections tell us much about the preferences of majorities and minorities," this is "even more true of the interelection period." . . .

Dahl goes on to assert that the election process and interelection activity "are crucial processes for insuring that political leaders will be *somewhat* responsive to the preferences of *some* ordinary citizens."[4] I submit (the emphasized words are mine) that if an admirer of democracy in America can say no more than this, democracy is not doing very well.

Dahl tells us the election process is one of "two fundamental methods of social control which, operating together, make governmental leaders so responsive
to nonleaders that the distinction between democracy and dictatorship still makes
sense." Since his description of the election process leaves that dubious, let's look
at his second requirement for distinguishing democracy: "The other method of social control is continuous political competition among individuals, parties, or
both." What it comes down to is "not minority rule but minorities rule."[5]

If it turns out that this—like the election process—also has little democratic
content, we will not be left with very much difference—by Dahl's own admission—between "dictatorship" and the "democracy" practiced in the United
States. Indeed, there is much evidence on this: the lack of democracy within the
major political parties, the vastly disproportionate influence of wealthy groups
over poorer ones. What antismoking consumer group in the election year of
1996 could match the five million dollars donated to the Republican Party by
the tobacco interests? What ordinary citizen could have the access to President
Bill Clinton that a group of bankers had in May of that election year when they
were invited to the White House?[6] All of this, and more, supports the idea of a
"decline of American pluralism" that Henry Kariel has written about. What
Dahl's democracy comes down to is "the steady appeasement of relatively
small groups."[7] If these relatively small groups turn out to be the aircraft industry far more than the aged, the space industry far more than the poor, the
Pentagon far more than the college youth—what is left of democracy?

Sometimes the elitism of decision-making is defended (by Dahl and by others) on the ground that the elite is enacting decisions passively supported by
the mass, whose tolerance is proof of an underlying consensus in society. But
Murray Levin's studies in *The Alienated Voter* indicate how much nonparticipa-
tion in elections is a result of hopelessness rather than approval. And Robert
Wiebe, a historian at Northwestern University, talks of "consensus" becoming
a "new stereotype." He approaches the question historically.

> Industrialization arrived so peacefully not because all Americans secretly
> shared the same values or implicitly willed its success but because its millions
> of bitter enemies lacked the mentality and the means to organize an effective
> counterattack.[8]

Wiebe's point is that the passivity of most Americans in the face of elitist decision-
making has not been due to acquiescence but to the lack of resources for effective
combat, as well as a gulf so wide between the haves and have-nots that there was
no ground on which to dispute. Americans neither revolted violently nor reacted
at the polls; instead they were subservient, or else worked out their hostilities in
personal ways. . . .

Presidential nominations and elections are more democratic than monar-
chical rule or the procedures of totalitarian states, but they are far from some
reasonable expectation of democracy. The two major parties have a monopoly
of presidential power, taking turns in the White House. The candidates of minority parties don't have a chance. They do not have access to the financial
backing of the major parties, and there is not the semblance of equal attention

in the mass media; it is only the two major candidates who have free access to prime time on national television.

More important, both parties almost always agree on the fundamentals of domestic and foreign policy, despite the election-year rhetoric which attempts to find important differences. Both parties arranged for United States intervention in Vietnam in the 1950s and 1960s, and both, when public opinion changed, promised to get out (note the Humphrey-Nixon contest of 1968). In 1984, Democratic candidate Walter Mondale agreed with Republican candidate Ronald Reagan that the United States (which had ten thousand thermonuclear warheads) needed to continue increasing its arms budget, although he asked for a smaller increase than the Republicans. Such a position left Mondale unable to promise representatives of the black community (where unemployment was over 20 percent) that he would spend even a few billion dollars for a jobs program. Meanwhile, Democrats and Republicans in Congress were agreeing on a $297 billion arms bill for the 1985 fiscal year.[9]

I have been talking so far about democracy in the political process. But there is another serious weakness that I will only mention here, although it is of enormous importance: the powerlessness of the American to participate in economic decision-making, which affects his life at every moment. As a consumer, that is, as the person whom the economy is presumably intended to serve, he has virtually nothing to say about what is produced for him. The corporations make what is profitable; the advertising industry persuades him to buy what the corporations produce. He becomes the passive victim of the misallocation of resources, the production of dangerous commodities, the spoiling of his air, water, forests, beaches, cities.

2. ACCESS TO INFORMATION

Adequate information for the electorate is a precondition for any kind of action (whether electoral or demonstrative) to affect national policy. As for the voting process, Berelson, Lazarsfeld, and McPhee tell us (in their book, *Voting*) after extensive empirical research: "One persistent conclusion is that the public is not particularly well informed about the specific issues of the day." . . .

Furthermore, there are certain issues which never even reach the public because they are decided behind the scenes. . . .

Consider the information available to voters on two major kinds of issues. One of them is the tax structure, so bewilderingly complex that the corporation, with its corps of accountants and financial experts, can prime itself for lobbying activities, while the average voter, hardly able to comprehend his own income tax, stands by helplessly as the president, the Office of Management and Budget, and the Congress decide the tax laws. The dominant influences are those of big business, which has the resources both to understand and to act.

Then there is foreign policy. The government leads the citizenry to believe it has special expertise which, if it could only be revealed, would support its position against critics. At the same time, it hides the very information which would reveal its position to be indefensible. The mendacity of the government on the Bay of Pigs operation and the withholding of vital information about the Tonkin Gulf events are only two examples of the way the average person becomes a victim of government deception.*

In 1990, historian Warren Cohen resigned as adviser to the State Department in its publication of the series *Foreign Relations of the United States*, pointing out that the government was refusing to cover events less than thirty years old. And even what it did publish was not trustworthy. "The United States government is publishing blatantly fraudulent accounts of its activities in Guatemala, Iran, and Southeast Asia in the 1950s" (*World Monitor Magazine*, 1990).

When the United States invaded the tiny island of Grenada in the fall of 1983, no reporters were allowed to observe the invasion, and the American public had little opportunity to get independent verification of the reasons given by the government for the invasion. As a result, President Reagan could glibly tell the nation what even one of his own supporters, journalist George Will, admitted was a lie: that he was invading Grenada to protect the lives of American medical students on the island. He could also claim that documents found on the island indicated plans for a Cuban-Soviet takeover of Grenada; the documents showed no such thing.[10]

Furthermore, the distribution of information to the public is a function of power and wealth. The government itself can color the citizens' understanding of events by its control of news at the source: the presidential press conference, the "leak to the press," the White Papers, the teams of "truth experts" going around the country at the taxpayers' expense. As for private media, the large networks and mass-circulation magazines have the greatest access to the public mind. There is no "equal time" for critics of public policy. . . .

3. EQUAL PROTECTION

Let us go now from the procedural to the substantive, indeed to the most substantive of questions: the right of all people to life itself. Here we find democracy in America tragically inadequate. Not only Locke, one of the leading theorists of the democratic tradition, declared the ultimate right of any person to safeguard his own life when threatened by the government; Hobbes, often looked on as the foe of democratic thought, agreed. Yet, in matters of foreign policy, where the decisions involve life or death for large numbers of Americans, power rests in the hands of the president and a small group of advisers. Despite the constitutional provision that war must be declared by Congress, in reality the President can create situations (as in the Mexican War, as in both world wars) which make inevitable congressional votes for war. And in all post–World War II conflicts (Korea, Vietnam, Iraq) there was no declaration of war by Congress.

*The Bay of Pigs operation was an unsuccessful, United States–backed invasion of Cuba by Cuban exiles in 1961; the Gulf of Tonkin Resolution, passed by Congress in 1965 on the occasion of an alleged attack on U.S. ships by the North Vietnamese, authorized the deployment of thousands of U.S. troops to Vietnam—*Editors*.

It is in connection with this most basic of rights—life itself, the first and most important of those substantive ends which democratic participation is designed to safeguard—that I would assert the need for a global view of democracy. One can at least conceive of a democratic decision for martial sacrifice by those ready to make the sacrifice; a "democratic" war is thus a theoretical possibility. But that presumption of democracy becomes obviously false at the first shot because then *others* are affected who did not decide. . . . Nations making decisions to slaughter their own sons are at least theoretically subject to internal check. The victims on the other side fall without any such chance. For the United States today, this failure of democracy is total; we have the capacity to destroy the world without giving it a chance to murmur a dissent; we did, in fact, destroy a part of southeast Asia on the basis of a unilateral decision made in Washington. There is no more pernicious manifestation of the lack of democracy in America than this single fact.

4. EQUALITY BEFORE THE LAW

Is there equality before the law? At every stage of the judicial process—facing the policeman, appearing in court, being freed on bond, being sentenced by the judge—the poor person is treated worse than the rich, the black treated worse than the white, the politically or personally odd character is treated worse than the orthodox. A defendant's poverty affects his preliminary hearing, his right to bail, the quality of his counsel. The evidence is plentiful in the daily newspapers, which inform us that an African-American boy fleeing the scene of a two-dollar theft may be shot and killed by a pursuing policeman, while a wealthy man who goes to South America after a million-dollar swindle, even if apprehended, need never fear a scratch. The wealthy price-fixer for General Motors, who costs consumers millions, will get ninety days in jail, the burglar of a liquor store will get five years. An African-American youth, or a bearded white youth poorly dressed, has much more chance of being clubbed by a policeman on the street than a well-dressed white man, given the fact that both respond with equal tartness to a question. . . .

Aside from inequality among citizens, there is inequality between the citizen and his government, when they face one another in a court of law. Take the matter of counsel: the well-trained government prosecutor faces the indigent's court-appointed counsel. Four of my students did a study of the City Court of Boston several years ago. They sat in the court for weeks, taking notes, and found that the average time spent by court-appointed counsel with his client, before arguing the case at the bench, was seven minutes.

5. DISTRIBUTION OF RESOURCES

Democracy is devoid of meaning if it does not include equal access to the available resources of the society. In India, democracy might still mean poverty; in the United States, with a Gross National Product of more than $3 trillion a year, democracy should mean that every American, working a short work-week, has adequate food, clothing, shelter, health care, education for himself and his family—in short, the material resources necessary to enjoy life and freedom. Even if only 20 percent of the American population is desperately poor . . . in a country so rich, that is an inexcusable breach of the democratic principle. Even if there is a large, prosperous middle class, there is something grossly unfair in the fact that in 1995 the richest 1 percent of the population owned over 40 percent of the total wealth, a figure that, throughout our history, has rarely been under 33 percent.

Whether you are poor or rich determines the most fundamental facts about your life: whether you are cold in the winter while trying to sleep, whether you suffocate in the summer; whether you live among vermin or rats; whether the smells around you all day are sweet or foul; whether you have adequate medical care; whether you have good teeth; whether you can send your children to college; whether you can go on vacation or have to take an extra job at night; whether you can afford a divorce, or an abortion, or a wife, or another child. . . .

6. ACCESS TO EDUCATION

In a highly industrialized society, education is a crucial determinant of wealth, political power, social status, leisure, and the ability to work in one's chosen field. Educational resources in our society are not equitably distributed. Among high-school graduates of the same IQ levels, a far higher percentage of the well-to-do go on to college than the poor.[11] A mediocre student with money can always go to college. A mediocre student without money may not be able to go, even to a state college, because he may have to work to support his family. Furthermore, the educational resources in the schools—equipment, teachers, etc.— are far superior in the wealthy suburbs than in the poor sections of the city, whether white or black.

7. FREEDOM OF EXPRESSION

Like money, freedom of expression is available to all in America, but in widely varying quantities. The First Amendment formally guarantees freedom of speech, press, assembly, and petition to all—but certain realities of wealth, power, and status stand in the way of the equal distribution of these rights. Anyone can stand on a street corner and talk to ten or a hundred people. But someone with the resources to buy loudspeaker equipment, go through the necessary red tape, and post a bond with the city may hold a meeting downtown and reach a thousand or five thousand people. A person or a corporation with $100,000 can buy time on television and reach 10 million people. A rich person simply has much more freedom of speech than a poor person. The government has much more freedom of expression than a private individual, because the president can command the airwaves when he wishes, and reach 60 million people in one night.

Freedom of the press also is guaranteed to all. But the student selling an underground newspaper on the street with a nude woman on the cover may be arrested by a policeman, while the airport newsstand selling *Playboy* and ten magazines like it will remain safe. Anyone with $10,000 can put out a newspaper to reach a few thousand people. Anyone with $10 million can buy a few newspapers that will reach a few million people. Anyone who is penniless had better have a loud voice; and then he might be arrested for disturbing the peace.

8. FREEDOM FOR INDIVIDUALITY

The right to live one's life, in privacy and freedom, in whatever way one wants, so long as others are not harmed, should be a sacred principle in a democracy. But there are hundreds of laws, varying from state to state, and sometimes joined by federal laws, which regulate the personal lives of people in this country: their marriages, their divorces, their sexual relations. Furthermore, both laws and court decisions protect policemen and the FBI in their use of secret devices which listen in on private conversations, or peer in on private conduct.

9. THE SPIRIT OF COOPERATION

The maintenance of those substantive elements of democracy which I have just sketched, if dependent on a pervasive network of coercion, would cancel out much of the benefit of that democracy. Democracy needs rather to be sustained by a spirit in society, the tone and the values of the culture. I am speaking of something as elusive as a mood, alongside something as hard as law, both of which would have to substitute cooperation tinged with friendly competition for the fierce combat of our business culture. I am speaking of the underlying drive that keeps people going in the society. So long as that drive is for money and power, with no ceiling on either, so long as ruthlessness is built into the rules of the game, democracy does not have a chance. If there is one crucial cause in the failure of American democracy—not the only one, of course, but a fundamental one—it is the drive for corporate profit, and the overwhelming influence of money in every aspect of our daily lives. That is the uncontrolled libido of our society from which the rape of democratic values necessarily follows.

The manifestations are diverse and endless: the drug industry's drive for profit has led to incredible overpricing of drugs for consumers (700 percent markup, for instance, for tablets to arthritic patients). It was disclosed in 1979 that Johns-Manville, the nation's largest asbestos manufacturer, had deliberately withheld from its workers X-ray results that showed they were developing cancer. In 1984, a company making an intrauterine birth control device—the Dalkon Shield—was found by a Minnesota court to have allowed tens of thousands of women to wear this device despite knowing that it was dangerous to their health (*Minneapolis Star and Tribune*, May 18, 1984). In the mid-1990s, it was revealed that tobacco companies had concealed information showing the narcotic nature of cigarettes. All in the interest of maximizing profit.

If these were isolated cases, reported and then eliminated, they could be dismissed as unfortunate blemishes on an otherwise healthy social body. But the major allocations of resources in our society are made on the basis of money profit rather than social use. . . .

. . . News items buttress what I have said. The oil that polluted California's beautiful beaches in the 1960s . . . was produced by a system in which the oil companies' hunger for profit has far more weight than the ordinary person's need to swim in clean water. This is not to be attributed to Republicanism over-riding the concern for the little fellow of the Democratic Party. Profit is master whichever party is in power; it was the liberal Secretary of the Interior Stewart Udall who allowed the dangerous drilling to go on. . . .

In 1984, the suit of several thousand veterans against the Dow Chemical Company, claiming that they and their families had suffered terrible illnesses as a result of exposure in Vietnam to the poisonous chemical Agent Orange, was settled. The Dow corporation avoided the disclosures of thousands of doc-uments in open court by agreeing to pay $180 million to the veterans. One thing seemed clear: the company had known that the defoliant used in Vietnam might be dangerous, but it held back the news, and blamed the government for ordering use of the chemical. The government itself, apparently wanting to shift blame to the corporation, declared publicly that Dow Chemical had been motivated in its actions by greed for profit.

10. OPPORTUNITY TO PROTEST

The first two elements in my list for democracy—decision-making and infor-mation to help make them—are procedural. The next six are substantive, deal-ing with the consequences of such procedures on life, liberty, and the pursuit of happiness. My ninth point, the one I have just discussed, shows how the money motive of our society corrupts both procedures and their consequences by its existence and suggests we need a different motive as a fundamental requisite of a democratic society. The point I am about to discuss is an ultimate requisite for democracy, a safety feature if nothing else—neither procedures nor conse-quences nor motivation—works. It is the right of citizens to break through the impasse of a legal and cultural structure, which sustains inequality, greed, and murder, to initiate processes for change. I am speaking of civil disobedience, which is an essential safeguard even in a successful society, and which is an ab-solute necessity in a society which is not going well.

If the institutional structure itself bars any change but the most picayune and grievances are serious, it is silly to insist that change must be mediated through the processes of that legal structure. In such a situation, dramatic ex-pressions of protest and challenge are necessary to help change ways of think-ing, to build up political power for drastic change. A society that calls itself democratic (whether accurately or not) must, as its ultimate safeguard, allow such acts of disobedience. If the government prohibits them (as we must expect from a government committed to the existent) then the members of a society concerned with democracy must not only defend such acts, but encourage them. Somewhere near the root of democratic thought is the theory of popular sovereignty, declaring that government and laws are instruments for certain ends, and are not to be deified with absolute obedience; they must constantly be checked by the citizenry, and challenged, opposed, even overthrown, if they become threats to fundamental rights.

Any abstract assessment of *when* disobedience is justified is pointless. Proper conclusions depend on empirical evidence about how bad things are at the moment, and how adequate are the institutional mechanisms for correcting them. . . .

One of these is the matter of race. The intolerable position of the African-American, in both North and South, has traditionally been handled with a few muttered apologies and tokens of reform. Then the civil disobedience of militants in the South forced our attention on the most dramatic (southern) manifestations of racism in America. The massive African-American urban uprisings of 1967 and 1968 showed that nothing less than civil disobedience (for riots and uprisings go beyond that) could make the nation see that the race problem is an American—not a southern—problem and that it needs bold, revolutionary action.

As for poverty: it seems clear that the normal mechanisms of congressional pretense and presidential rhetoric are not going to change things very much. Acts of civil disobedience by the poor will be required, at the least, to make middle-class America take notice, to bring national decisions that begin to reallocate wealth.

The war in Vietnam showed that we could not depend on the normal processes of "law and order," of the election process, of letters to the *Times*, to stop a series of especially brutal acts against the Vietnamese and against our own sons. It took a nationwide storm of protest, including thousands of acts of civil disobedience (14,000 people were arrested in one day in 1971 in Washington, D.C.), to help bring the war to an end. The role of draft resistance in affecting Lyndon Johnson's 1968 decision not to escalate the war further is told in the Defense Department secret documents of that period. In the 1980s and 1990s civil disobedience continued, with religious pacifists and others risking prison in order to protest the arms race and the plans for nuclear war.

The great danger for American democracy is not from the protesters. That democracy is too poorly realized for us to consider critics—even rebels—as the chief problem. Its fulfillment requires us all, living in an ossified system which sustains too much killing and too much selfishness, to join the protest.

NOTES

1. Robert A. Dahl, *A Preface to Democratic Theory* (Chicago: University of Chicago Press, 1963), p. 81.

2. *Ibid.*, p. 124.

3. *Ibid.*, p. 125.

4. *Ibid.*, p. 131.

5. *Ibid.*, pp. 131–32.

6. *New York Times,* January 25, 27, 1997.

7. Dahl, *A Preface to Democratic Theory,* p. 146.

8. Robert Wiebe, "The Confinements of Consensus," *TriQuarterly,* 1966. Copyright by TriQuarterly 1966. All rights reserved.

9. *New York Times,* September 25, 1984.

10. The *New York Times* reported, November 5, 1983: "There is nothing in the documents, however, that specifically indicates that Cuba and the Soviet Union were on the verge of taking over Grenada, as Administration officials have suggested."

11. See the Carnegie Council on Children study, *Small Futures,* by Richard de-Lore, 1979.

How Democratic Is America?
A Response to Howard Zinn
Sidney Hook

Charles Peirce, the great American philosopher, once observed that there was such a thing as the "ethics of words." The "ethics of words" are violated whenever ordinary terms are used in an unusual context or arbitrarily identified with another concept for which other terms are in common use. Mr. Zinn is guilty of a systematic violation of the "ethics of words." In consequence, his discussion of "democracy" results in a great many methodological errors as well as inconsistencies. To conserve space, I shall focus on three.

I

First of all, he confuses democracy as a political *process* with democracy as a political *product* or state of welfare; democracy as a *"free society"* with democracy as a *"good society,"* where good is defined in terms of equality or justice (or both) or some other constellation of values. One of the reasons for choosing to live under a democratic political system rather than a nondemocratic system is our belief that it makes possible a better society. That is something that must be empirically established, something denied by critics of democracy from Plato to Santayana. The equality which is relevant to democracy as a *political process* is, in the first instance, political equality with respect to the rights of citizenship. Theoretically, a politically democratic community could vote, wisely or unwisely, to abolish, retain, or establish certain economic inequalities. Theoretically, a benevolent despotism could institute certain kinds of social and even juridical equalities. Historically, the Bismarckian political dictatorship introduced social welfare legislation for the masses at a time when such legislation would have been repudiated by the existing British and American political democracies. Some of Mr. Zinn's proposed reforms could be introduced under a dictatorship or benevolent despotism. Therefore, they are not logically or organically related to democracy.

Sidney Hook (1902–1989) was head of the department of philosophy at New York University from 1934 to 1969 and was a senior research fellow at the Hoover Institution on War, Revolution, and Peace at Stanford University from 1973 to 1989. This essay was originally published in *How Democratic Is America?* edited by Robert A. Goldwin (Chicago, Rand McNally, 1971), pp. 62–75. The author revised and updated the original for *Points of View* in 1985.

The second error in Mr. Zinn's approach to democracy is "to measure our democracy against an ideal (even if admittedly unachievable) standard . . . even if utopian . . ." without *defining* the standard. His criteria admittedly are neither necessary nor sufficient for determining the presence of democracy since he himself admits that they are applicable to societies that are not democratic. Further, even if we were to take his criteria as severally defining the presence of democracy—as we might take certain physical and mental traits as constituting a definition of health—he gives no operational test for determining whether or not they have been fulfilled. For example, among the criteria he lists for determining whether a society is democratic is this: "Are the members of the society equally protected on matters of life and death—in the most literal sense of that phrase?" A moment's reflection will show that here—as well as in other cases where Zinn speaks of equality—it is impossible for all members to be equally protected on matters of life and death—certainly not in a world in which men do the fighting and women give birth to children, where children need *more* protection than adults, and where some risk-seeking adults require and deserve less protection (since resources are not infinite) than others. As Karl Marx realized, "in the most literal sense of that phrase," there cannot be absolute equality even in a classless society. . . .

The only sensible procedure in determining the absence or presence of equality from a democratic perspective is comparative. We must ask whether a culture is more or less democratic in comparison to the past with respect to some *desirable* feature of equality (Zinn ignores the fact that not all equalities are desirable). It is better for some people to be more intelligent and more knowledgeable than others than for all to be unintelligent and ignorant. There never is literally equal access to education, to knowledge and training in any society. The question is: Is there more access today for more people than yesterday, and how can we increase the access tomorrow?

Mr. Zinn refuses to take this approach because, he asserts, "it supports complacency." It does nothing of the sort! On the contrary, it shows that progress is possible, and encourages us to exert our efforts in the same direction if we regard the direction as desirable.

It will be instructive to look at the passage in which Mr. Zinn objects to this sensible comparative approach because it reveals the bias in his approach:

"With such a standard," he writes, "Russia in 1910 could point with pride to how much progress they had made toward parliamentary democracy; as Russians in 1985 could point to their post-Stalin progress away from the gulag; as Americans could point in 1939 to how far they had come in solving the problem of economic equality; as Americans in the South could point in 1950 to the progress of the southern African-American."

a. In 1910 the Russians were indeed moving toward greater progress in local parliamentary institutions. Far from making them complacent, they moved towards more inclusive representative institutions which culminated in elections to the Constituent Assembly in 1918, which was bayoneted out of existence by Lenin and the Communist Party, with a minority party dictatorship established.

b. Only Mr. Zinn would regard the slight diminution in terror from the days of Stalin to the regime of Chernenko as progress toward democracy. Those who observe the ethics of words would normally say that the screws of repression had been slightly relaxed. Mr. Zinn seems unaware that as bad as the terror was under Lenin, it was not as pervasive as it is today.* But no one with any respect for the ethics of words would speak of "the progress of democracy" in the Soviet Union from Lenin to Stalin to Khrushchev to Chernenko. Their regimes were varying degrees of dictatorship and terror.

c. Americans could justifiably say that in 1939 progress had been made in giving workers a greater role, not as Mr. Zinn says in "solving the problem of economic equality" (a meaningless phrase), but in determining the conditions and rewards of work that prevailed in 1929 or previously because the existence of the Wagner Labor Relations Act made collective bargaining the law of the land. They could say this *not* to rest in complacency, but to use the organized force of their trade unions to influence further the political life of the country. And indeed, it was the organized labor movement in 1984 which in effect chose the candidate of the Democratic Party.

d. Americans in the South in 1950 could rightfully speak of the progress of the southern African-American over the days of unrestricted Jim Crow and lynching bees of the past, *not* to rest in complacency, but to agitate for further progress through the Supreme Court decision of *Brown v. Board of Education in Topeka* and through the Civil Rights Act of Congress. This has not made them complacent, but more resolved to press further to eliminate remaining practices of invidious discrimination.

Even Mr. Zinn should admit that with respect to some of his other criteria this is the only sensible approach. Otherwise we get unhistorical answers, the hallmark of the doctrinaire. He asks—criterion 1—"To what extent can various people in the society participate in those decisions which affect their lives?" and—criterion 7—"Is there freedom of expression on all matters, and equally for all, to communicate with other members of the society?" Why doesn't Mr. Zinn adopt this sensible comparative approach? Because it would lead him to inquire into the extent to which people are free to participate in decisions that affect their lives *today,* free to express themselves, free to organize, free to protest and dissent today, *in comparison with the past.* It would lead him to the judgment *which he wishes to avoid at all costs,* to wit, that despite the grave problems, gaps, and tasks before us, the United States is more democratic today than it was a hundred years ago, fifty years ago, twenty years ago, five years ago with respect to every one of the criteria he has listed. To recognize this is *not* an invitation to complacency. On the contrary, it indicates the possibility of broadening, deepening, and using the democratic political process to improve the quality of human life, to modify and redirect social institutions in order to

---

*These words and subsequent references to the Soviet Union preceded the reforms initiated under Mikhail Gorbachev and continued under Boris Yeltsin and Vladimir Putin—*Editors.*

realize on a wider scale the moral commitment of democracy to an equality of concern for all its citizens to achieve their fullest growth as persons. This commitment is to a process, not to a transcendent goal or a fixed, ideal standard.

In a halting, imperfect manner, set back by periods of violence, vigilantism, and xenophobia, the political democratic process in the United States has been used to modify the operation of the economic system. The improvements and reforms won from time to time make the still-existing problems and evils more acute in that people become more aware of them. The more the democratic process extends human freedoms, and the more it introduces justice in social relations and the distribution of wealth, the greater grows the desire for *more* freedom and justice. Historically and psychologically, it is false to assume that reforms breed a spirit of complacency. . . .

The third and perhaps most serious weakness in Mr. Zinn's view is his conception of the nature of the formal political democratic process. It suffers from several related defects. First, it overlooks the central importance of majority rule in the democratic process. Second, it denies in effect that majority rule is possible by defining democracy in such a way that it becomes impossible. . . .

"Representation by its very nature," claims Mr. Zinn, "is undemocratic." This is Rousseauistic nonsense. For it would mean that no democracy—including all societies that Mr. Zinn ever claimed at any time to be democratic—could possibly exist, not even the direct democracies or assemblies of Athens or the New England town meetings. For all such assemblies must elect officials to carry out their will. If no representative (and an official is a representative, too) can adequately represent another's needs, there is no assurance that in the actual details of governance, the selectmen, road commissioners, or other town or assembly officials will, in fact, carry out their directives. No assembly or meeting can sit in continuous session or collectively carry out the common decision. In the nature of the case, officials, like representatives, constitute an elite and their actions *may* reflect their interests more than the interests of the governed. This makes crucial the questions whether and how an elite can be removed, whether the consent on which the rule of the officials or representatives rests is free or coerced, whether a minority can peacefully use these mechanisms, by which freely given consent is registered, to win over or become a majority. The existence of representative assemblies makes democracy difficult, not impossible.

Since Mr. Zinn believes that a majority never has any authority to bind a minority as well as itself by decisions taken after free discussion and debate, he is logically committed to anarchy. Failing to see this, he confuses two fundamentally different things—the meaning or definition of democracy, and its justification.

1. A democratic government is one in which the general direction of policy rests directly or indirectly upon the freely given consent of a majority of the adults governed. Ambiguities and niceties aside, that is what democracy means. It is not anarchy. The absence of a unanimous consensus does not entail the absence of democracy.

2. One may reject on moral or religious or personal grounds a democratic society. Plato, as well as modern totalitarians, contends that a majority of mankind is either too stupid or vicious to be entrusted with self-government, or to be given the power to accept or reject their ruling elites, and that the only viable alternative to democracy is the self-selecting and self-perpetuating elite of "the wise," or "the efficient," or "the holy," or "the strong," depending upon the particular ideology of the totalitarian apologist. The only thing they have in common with democrats is their rejection of anarchy.

3. No intelligent and moral person can make an *absolute* of democracy in the sense that he believes it is always, everywhere, under any conditions, and no matter what its consequences, ethically legitimate. Democracy is obviously not desirable in a head-hunting or cannibalistic society or in an institution of the feeble-minded. But wherever and whenever a principled democrat accepts the political system of democracy, he must accept the binding authority of legislative decisions, reached after the free give-and-take of debate and discussion, as binding upon him whether he is a member of the majority or minority. Otherwise the consequence is incipient or overt anarchy or civil war, the usual preface to despotism or tyranny. Accepting the decision of the majority as binding does not mean that it is final or irreversible. The processes of freely given consent must make it possible for a minority to urge amendment or repeal of any decision of the majority. Under carefully guarded provisions, a democrat may resort to civil disobedience of a properly enacted law in order to bear witness to the depths of his commitment in an effort *to reeducate* his fellow citizens. But in that case he must voluntarily accept punishment for his civil disobedience, and so long as he remains a democrat, voluntarily abandon his violation or noncompliance with law at the point where its consequences threaten to destroy the democratic process and open the floodgates either to the violent disorders of anarchy or to the dictatorship of a despot or a minority political party.

4. That Mr. Zinn is not a democrat but an anarchist in his views is apparent in his contention that not only must a democracy allow or tolerate civil disobedience within limits, but that "members of a society concerned with democracy must not only defend such acts, but encourage them." On this view, if southern segregationists resort to civil disobedience to negate the long-delayed but eminently just measures adopted by the government to implement the amendments that outlaw slavery, they should be encouraged to do so. On this view, any group that defies any law that violates its conscience—with respect to marriage, taxation, vaccination, abortion, education—should be encouraged to do so. Mr. Zinn, like most anarchists, refuses to generalize the principles behind his action. He fails to see that if all fanatics of causes deemed by them to be morally just were encouraged to resort to civil disobedience, even our imperfect existing political democracy would dissolve in chaos, and that civil disobedience would soon become quite uncivil. He fails to see that *in a democracy the processes of intelligence, not individual conscience, must be supreme.*

II

I turn now to some of the issues that Mr. Zinn declares are substantive. Before doing so I wish to make clear my belief that the most substantive issue of all is the procedural one by which the inescapable differences of interests among men, once a certain moral level of civilization has been reached, are to be negotiated. The belief in the validity of democratic procedures rests upon the conviction that where adult human beings have freedom of access to relevant information, they are, by and large, better judges of their own interests than are those who set themselves up as their betters and rulers, that, to use the homely maxim, those who wear the shoes know best where they pinch and therefore have the right to change their political shoes in the light of their experience. . . .

Looking at the question "How democratic is America?" with respect to the problems of poverty, race, education, etc., we must say "Not democratic enough!", but not for the reasons Mr. Zinn gives. For he seems to believe that the failure to adopt *his* solutions and proposals with respect to foreign policy, slum clearance, pollution, etc., is evidence of the failure of the democratic process itself. He overlooks the crucial difference between the procedural process and the substantive issues. When he writes that democracy is devoid of meaning if it does not include "equal access to the available resources of the society," he is simply abusing language. Assuming such equal access is desirable (which some might question who believe that access to *some* of society's resources—for example, to specialized training or to scarce supplies—should go not equally to all but to the most needful or sometimes to the most qualified), a democracy may or may not legislate such equal access. The crucial question is whether the electorate has the power to make the choice, or to elect those who would carry out the mandate chosen. . . .

When Mr. Zinn goes on to say that "in the United States . . . democracy should mean that every American, working a short work-week, has adequate food, clothing, shelter, health care, . . ." he is not only abusing language, he is revealing the fact that the procedural processes that are essential to the meaning of democracy, in ordinary usage, are not essential to his conception. He is violating the basic ethics of discourse. If democracy "should mean" what Zinn says it should, then were Huey Long or any other dictator to seize power and introduce a "short work-week" and distribute "adequate food, clothing, shelter, health care" to the masses, Mr. Zinn would have to regard his regime as democratic.

After all, when Hitler came to power and abolished free elections in Germany, he at the same time reduced unemployment, increased the real wages of the German worker, and provided more adequate food, clothing, shelter, and health care than was available under the Weimar Republic. On Zinn's view of what democracy "should mean," this made Hitler's rule more democratic than that of Weimar. . . .

Not surprisingly, Mr. Zinn is a very unreliable guide even in his account of the procedural features of the American political system. In one breath he maintains that not enough information is available to voters to make intelligent choices on major political issues like tax laws. (The voter, of course, does not vote on such laws but for representatives who have taken stands on a number of complex issues.) "The dominant influences are those of big business, which has the resources both to understand and to act." In another breath, he complains that the electorate is at the mercy of the propagandist. "The propagandist does not need to lie; he overwhelms the public with so much information as to lead it to believe that it is all too complicated for anyone but the experts."

Mr. Zinn is certainly hard to please! The American political process is not democratic because the electorate hasn't got enough information. It is also undemocratic because it receives too much information. What would Zinn have us do so that the public gets just the right amount of information and propaganda? Have the government control the press? Restrict freedom of propaganda? But these are precisely the devices of totalitarian societies. The evils of the press, even when it is free of government control, are many indeed. The great problem is to keep the press free and responsible. And as defective as the press and other public media are today, surely it is an exaggeration to say that with respect to tax laws "the dominant influences are those of big business." If they were, how can we account for the existence of the income tax laws? If the influence of big business on the press is so dominant and the press is so biased, how can we account for the fact that although 92 percent of the press opposed Truman's candidacy in 1948, he was reelected? How can we account for the profound dissatisfaction of Vice President Agnew with the press and other mass media?* And since Mr. Zinn believes that big business dominates our educational system, especially our universities, how can we account for the fact that the universities are the centers of the strongest dissent in the nation to public and national policy, that the National Association of Manufacturers bitterly complained a few years ago that the economics of the free enterprise system was derided, and often not even taught, in most Departments of Economics in the colleges and universities of the nation?

Mr. Zinn's exaggerations are really caricatures of complex realities. Far from being controlled by the monolithic American corporate economy, American public opinion is today marked by a greater scope and depth of dissent than at any time in its history, except for the days preceding the Civil War. The voice and the votes of Main Street still count for more in a democratic polity than those of Wall Street. Congress has limited, and can still further limit, the influence of money on the electoral process by federal subsidy and regulations. There are always abuses needing reforms. By failing to take a comparative approach and instead focusing on some absolute utopian standard of perfection, Mr. Zinn gives an exaggerated, tendentious, and fundamentally false picture of the United States. There is hardly a sentence in his essay that is free of some serious flaw in perspective, accuracy, or emphasis. Sometimes they have a comic effect, as when Mr. Zinn talks about the lack of "equal distribution of the right of freedom of expression." What kind of "equal distribution" is he talking about? Of course, a person with more money can talk to more people than one

---

*Spiro Agnew, former governor of Maryland and vice president of the United States before being forced to resign in 1973 during the second term of President Richard Nixon, was a frequent and vociferous critic of the "liberal" press—*Editors.*

with less, although this does not mean that more persons will listen to him, agree with him, or be influenced by him. But a person with a more eloquent voice or a better brain can reach more people than you or I. What shall we do to insure equal distribution of the right of freedom of expression? Insist on equality of voice volume or pattern, and equality of brain power? More money gives not only greater opportunity to talk to people than less money but the ability to do thousands of things barred to those who have less money. Shall we then decree that all people have the same amount of money all the time and forbid anyone from depriving anyone else of any of his money even by fair means? "The government," writes Mr. Zinn, "has much more freedom of expression than a private individual because the president can command the airwaves when he wishes, and reach 60 million people in one night."

Alas! Mr. Zinn is not joking. Either he wants to bar the president or any public official from using the airwaves or he wants all of us to take turns. One wonders what country Mr. Zinn is living in. Nixon spoke to 60 million people several times, and so did Jimmy Carter. What was the result? More significant than the fact that 60 million people hear the president is that 60 million or more can hear his critics, sometimes right after he speaks, and that no one is compelled to listen.

Mr. Zinn does not understand the basic meaning of equality in a free, open democratic society. Its philosophy does not presuppose that all citizens are physically or intellectually equal or that all are equally gifted in every or any respect. It holds that all enjoy a *moral* equality, and that therefore, as far as is practicable, given finite resources, the institutions of a democratic society should seek to provide an equal opportunity to all its citizens to develop themselves to their full desirable potential.

Of course, we cannot ever provide complete equal opportunity. More and more is enough. For one thing, so long as children have different parents and home environments, they cannot enjoy the same or equal opportunities. Nonetheless, the family has compensating advantages for all that. Let us hope that Mr. Zinn does not wish to wipe out the family to avoid differences in opportunity. Plato believed that the family, as we know it, should be abolished because it did not provide equality of opportunity, and that all children should be brought up by the state.

Belief in the moral equality of men and women does not require that all individuals be treated identically or that equal treatment must be measured or determined by equality of outcome or result. Every citizen should have an equal right to an education, but that does not mean that, regardless of capacity and interest, he or she should have the same amount of schooling beyond the adolescent years, and at the same schools, and take the same course of study. With the increase in national wealth, a good case can be made for an equal right of all citizens to health care or medical treatment. But only a quack or ideological fanatic would insist that therefore all individuals should have the same medical regimen no matter what ails them. This would truly be putting all human beings in the bed of Procrustes.

This conception of moral equality as distinct from Mr. Zinn's notions of equality is perfectly compatible with intelligent recognition of human inequalities and relevant ways of treating their inequalities to further both the individual and common good. Intelligent and loving parents are equally concerned with the welfare of all their children. But precisely because they are, they may provide different specific strategies in health care, education, psychological motivation, and intellectual stimulation to develop the best in all of them. The logic of Mr. Zinn's position—although he seems blissfully unaware of it—leads to the most degrading kind of egalitarian socialism, the kind which Marx and Engels in their early years denounced as "barracks socialism."

It is demonstrable that democracy is healthier and more effective where human beings do not suffer from poverty, unemployment, and disease. It is also demonstrable that to the extent that property gives power, private property in the means of social production gives power over the lives of those who must live by its use, and, therefore, that such property, whether public or private, should be responsible to those who are affected by its operation. Consequently one can argue that political democracy depends not only on the extension of the franchise to all adults, not only on its active exercise, but on programs of social welfare that provide for collective bargaining by free trade unions of workers and employees, unemployment insurance, minimum wages, guaranteed health care, and other social services that are integral to the welfare state. It is demonstrable that although the existing American welfare state provides far more welfare than was ever provided in the past—my own lifetime furnishes graphic evidence of the vast changes—it is still very far from being a genuine welfare state. Political democracy can exist without a welfare state, but it is stronger and better with it.

The basic issue that divides Mr. Zinn from others no less concerned about human welfare, but less fanatical than he, is how a genuine welfare state is to be brought about. My contention is that this can be achieved by the vigorous exercise of the existing democratic process, and that by the same coalition politics through which great gains have been achieved in the past, even greater gains can be won in the future.

For purposes of economy, I focus on the problem of poverty, or since this is a relative term, hunger. If the presence of hunger entails the absence of the democratic political process, then democracy has never existed in the past—which would be an arbitrary use of words. Nonetheless, the existence of hunger is always a threat to the continued existence of the democratic process because of the standing temptation of those who hunger to exchange freedom for the promise of bread. This, of course, is an additional ground to the even weightier moral reasons for gratifying basic human needs.

That fewer people go hungry today in the United States than ever before may show that our democracy is better than it used to be but not that it is as good as it can be. Even the existence of one hungry person is one too many. How then can hunger or the extremes of poverty be abolished? Certainly not by the method Mr. Zinn advises: "Acts of civil disobedience by the poor will be required, at the least, to make middle-class America take notice, to bring national decisions that begin to reallocate wealth."

This is not only a piece of foolish advice, it is dangerously foolish advice. Many national decisions to reallocate wealth have been made through the political process—what else is the system of taxation if not a method of reallocating wealth?—without resort to civil disobedience. Indeed, resort to civil disobedience on this issue is very likely to produce a backlash among those active and influential political groups in the community who are aware that normal political means are available for social and economic reform. The refusal to engage in such normal political processes could easily be exploited by demagogues to portray the movement towards the abolition of hunger and extreme poverty as a movement towards the confiscation and equalization of all wealth.

The simplest and most effective way of abolishing hunger is to act on the truly revolutionary principle, enunciated by the federal government, that it is responsible for maintaining a standard of relief as a minimum beneath which a family will not be permitted to sink. . . .

For reasons that need no elaboration here, the greatest of the problems faced by American democracy today is the race problem. Although tied to the problems of poverty and urban reconstruction, it has independent aspects exacerbated by the legacy of the Civil War and the Reconstruction period.

Next to the American Indians, African-Americans have suffered most from the failure of the democratic political process to extend the rights and privileges of citizenship to those whose labor and suffering have contributed so much to the conquest of the continent. The remarkable gains that have been made by African-Americans in the last twenty years have been made primarily through the political process. If the same rate of improvement continues, the year 2000 may see a rough equality established. The growth of African-American suffrage, especially in the South, the increasing sense of responsibility by the white community, despite periodic setbacks resulting from outbursts of violence, opens up a perspective of continuous and cumulative reform. The man and the organization he headed chiefly responsible for the great gains made by African-Americans, Roy Wilkins and the NAACP, were convinced that the democratic political process can be more effectively used to further the integration of African-Americans into our national life than by reliance on any other method. . . .

The only statement in Mr. Zinn's essay that I can wholeheartedly endorse is his assertion that the great danger to American democracy does not come from the phenomena of protest as such. Dissent and protest are integral to the democratic process. The danger comes from certain modes of dissent, from the substitution of violence and threats of violence for the mechanisms of the political process, from the escalation of that violence as the best hope of those who still have grievances against our imperfect American democracy, and from views such as those expressed by Mr. Zinn which downgrade the possibility of peaceful social reform and encourage rebellion. It is safe to predict that large-scale violence by impatient minorities will fail. It is almost as certain that attempts at violence will backfire, that they will create a climate of repression that may reverse the course of social progress and expanded civil liberties of the last generation. . . .

It is when Mr. Zinn is discussing racial problems that his writing ceases to be comic and silly and becomes irresponsible and mischievous. He writes:

> The massive African-American urban uprisings of 1967 and 1968 showed that nothing less than civil disobedience (for riots and uprisings go beyond that)

could make the nation see that the race problem is an American—not a southern—problem and that it needs bold, revolutionary action.

First of all, every literate person knows that the race problem is an American problem, not exclusively a southern one. It needs no civil disobedience or "black uprisings" to remind us of that. Second, the massive uprisings of 1967 and 1968 were violent and uncivil, and resulted in needless loss of life and suffering. The Civil Rights Acts, according to Roy Wilkins, then head of the NAACP, were imperiled by them. They were adopted despite, not because, of them. Third, what kind of "revolutionary" action is Mr. Zinn calling for? And by whom? He seems to lack the courage of his confusions. Massive civil disobedience when sustained becomes a form of civil war.

Despite Mr. Zinn and others, violence is more likely to produce reaction than reform. In 1827 a resolution to manumit slaves by purchase (later, Lincoln's preferred solution) was defeated by three votes in the House of Burgesses of the State of Virginia. It was slated to be reintroduced in a subsequent session with excellent prospects of being adopted. Had Virginia adopted it, North Carolina would shortly have followed suit. But before it could be reintroduced, Nat Turner's rebellion broke out. Its violent excesses frightened the South into a complete rejection of a possibility that might have prevented the American Civil War—the fiercest and bloodiest war in human history up to that time, from whose consequences American society is still suffering. Mr. Zinn's intentions are as innocent as those of a child playing with matches.

III

One final word about "the global" dimension of democracy of which Mr. Zinn speaks. Here, too, he speaks sympathetically of actions that would undermine the willingness and capacity of a free society to resist totalitarian aggression.

The principles that should guide a free democratic society in a world where dictatorial regimes seek to impose their rule on other nations were formulated by John Stuart Mill, the great defender of liberty and representative government, more than a century ago:

> To go to war for an idea, if the war is aggressive not defensive, is as criminal as to go to war for territory or revenue, for it is as little justifiable to force our ideas on other people, as to compel them to submit to our will in any other aspect. . . . *The doctrine of non-intervention, to be a legitimate principle of morality, must be accepted by all governments.* The despots must consent to be bound by it as well as the free states. Unless they do, the profession of it by free countries comes but to this miserable issue, that the wrong side may help the wrong side but the right may not help the right side. Intervention to enforce non-intervention is always right, always moral *if not always prudent.* Though it may be a mistake to give freedom (or independence—S.H.) to a people who do not value the boon, it cannot be right to insist that if they do value it, they shall not be hindered from the pursuit of it by foreign coercion (*Fraser's Magazine,* 1859, emphasis mine).

Unfortunately, these principles were disregarded by the United States in 1936 when Hitler and Mussolini sent troops to Spain to help Franco overthrow the legally elected democratic Loyalist regime. The U.S. Congress, at the behest of the administration, adopted a Neutrality Resolution which prevented the democratic government of Spain from purchasing arms here. This compelled the Spanish government to make a deal with Stalin, who not only demanded its entire gold supply but the acceptance of the dread Soviet secret police, the NKVD, to supervise the operations. The main operation of the NKVD in Spain was to engage in a murderous purge of the democratic ranks of anti-Communists which led to the victory of Franco. The story is told in George Orwell's *Homage to Catalonia*. He was on the scene.

The prudence of American intervention in Vietnam may be debatable but there is little doubt that [UN ambassador] Adlai Stevenson, sometimes referred to as the liberal conscience of the nation, correctly stated the American motivation when he said at the UN on the very day of his death: "My hope in Vietnam is that resistance there may establish the fact that changes in Asia are not to be precipitated by outside force. This was the point of the Korean War. This is the point of the conflict in Vietnam."

. . . Mr. Zinn's remarks about Grenada show he is opposed to the liberal principles expressed by J. S. Mill in the passage cited above. His report of the facts about Grenada is as distorted as his account of present-day American democracy. On tiny Grenada, whose government was seized by Communist terrorists, were representatives of every Communist regime in the Kremlin's orbit, Cuban troops, and a Soviet general. I have read the documents captured by the American troops. They conclusively establish that the Communists were preparing the island as part of the Communist strategy of expansion.[1]

It is sad but significant that Mr. Zinn, whose heart bleeds for the poor Asians who suffered in the struggle to prevent the Communist takeover in Southeast Asia, has not a word of protest, not a tear of compassion for the hundreds of thousands of tortured, imprisoned, and drowned in flight after the victory of the North Vietnamese "liberators," not to mention the even greater number of victims of the Cambodian and Cuban Communists. . . .

NOTE

1. *The Grenada Papers: The Inside Story of the Grenadian Revolution—and the Making of a Totalitarian State as Told in Captured Documents* (San Francisco: Institute of Contemporary Studies, 1984).

Making Democracy Work: Civic Involvement

In this second pair of articles, we turn our attention from the question of how democracy should be defined to the matter of how to make it work. In this connection, there is a considerable amount of evidence to suggest that democracy functions more effectively in societies characterized by a high level of civic participation; that is to say, where citizens join with others in pursuit of some community-related goal or purpose. Although the propensity for Americans to form and join civic associations has long been remarked upon as a salient feature of our society, Robert Putnam, in the first selection, argues that several indicators point to a significant decline in civic engagement over the last twenty-five years. He then identifies what he believes to be the major factor responsible for producing this decline and explains why it has had this effect.

Michael Schudson, however, is unpersuaded by Putnam's analysis. In response, he asserts that the alleged decline in civic participation might not be real at all, but rather an artifact of how Putnam defines civic participation, how he measures it, and what he selects as a baseline for comparison. Moreover, even if we assume for the sake of argument that there has been such a decline, the culprit that Putnam points to does not fit his own evidence very well; and besides, there are, according to Schudson, other culprits that are equally plausible.

Tuning In, Tuning Out
The Strange Disappearance of Social Capital in America
Robert D. Putnam

BOWLING ALONE: AMERICA'S DECLINING SOCIAL CAPITAL

Many students of the new democracies that have emerged over the past decade and a half have emphasized the importance of a strong and active civil society to the consolidation of democracy. Especially with regard to the postcommunist countries, scholars and democratic activists alike have lamented the absence or obliteration of traditions of independent civic engagement and a widespread tendency toward passive reliance on the state. To those concerned with the weakness of civil societies in the developing or postcommunist world, the advanced Western democracies and above all the United States have typically been taken as models to be emulated. There is striking evidence, however, that the vibrancy of American civil society has notably declined over the past several decades.

Ever since the publication of Alexis de Tocqueville's *Democracy in Ameria,* the United States has played a central role in systematic studies of the links between democracy and civil society. Although this is in part because trends in American life are often regarded as harbingers of social modernization, it is also because America has traditionally been considered unusually "civic" (a reputation that, as we shall later see, has not been entirely unjustified).

When Tocqueville visited the United States in the 1830s, it was the Americans' propensity for civic association that most impressed him as the key to their unprecedented ability to make democracy work. "Americans of all ages, all stations in life, and all types of disposition," he observed, "are forever form-

Robert D. Putnam is the Peter and Isabel Professor of Public Policy and Director of the Saguaro Seminar at the Kennedy School of Government. He has written numerous books including one best-selling *Bowling Along: The Collapse and Revival of American Community* (May 2000). This article is a composite of two articles written by Robert D. Putnam. The first section of the article, "Bowling Alone: America's Declining Social Capital," is from Robert D. Putnam "Bowling Alone: America's Declining Social Capital" *Journal of Democracy* (January, 1995), pp. 65–78; the second section, beginning with "Bowling Alone: Trends in Civic Engagement," is from Robert D. Putnam "Tuning In Tuning Out: The Strange Disappearance of Social Capital in America," *PS: Political Science & Politics* (December, 1995), pp. 664–666, 677–683. Notes and references have been changed to correspond with edited text. Reprinted by permission of the author.

ing associations. There are not only commercial and industrial associations in which all take part, but others of a thousand different types—religious, moral, serious, futile, very general and very limited, immensely large and very minute. . . . Nothing, in my view, deserves more attention than the intellectual and moral associations in America."

Recently, American social scientists of a neo-Tocquevillean bent have unearthed a wide range of empirical evidence that the quality of public life and the performance of social institutions (and not only in America) are indeed powerfully influenced by norms and networks of civic engagement. Researchers in such fields as education, urban poverty, unemployment, the control of crime and drug abuse, and even health have discovered that successful outcomes are more likely in civically engaged communities. Similarly, research on the varying economic attainments of different ethnic groups in the United States has demonstrated the importance of social bonds within each group. These results are consistent with research in a wide range of settings that demonstrates the vital importance of social networks for job placement and many other economic outcomes. . . .

The norms and networks of civic engagement also powerfully affect the performance of representative government. That, at least, was the central conclusion of my own 20-year, quasi-experimental study of subnational governments in different regions of Italy. Although all these regional governments seemed identical on paper, their levels of effectiveness varied dramatically. Systematic inquiry showed that the quality of governance was determined by longstanding traditions of civic engagement (or its absence). Voter turnout, newspaper readership, membership in choral societies and football clubs—these were the hallmarks of a successful region. In fact, historical analysis suggested that these networks of organized reciprocity and civic solidarity, far from being an epiphenomenon of socioeconomic modernization, were a precondition for it.

No doubt, the mechanisms through which civic engagement and social connectedness produce such results—better schools, faster economic development, lower crime, and more effective government—are multiple and complex. . . . Social scientists in several fields have recently suggested a common framework for understanding these phenomena, a framework that rests on the concept of *social capital*. By analogy with notions of physical capital and human capital—tools and training that enhance individuals' productivity—"social capital" refers to features of social organization such as networks, norms, and social trust that facilitate coordination and cooperation for mutual benefit.

Civic Engagement

For a variety of reasons life is easier in a community blessed with a substantial stock of social capital. In the first place, networks of civic engagement foster sturdy norms of generalized reciprocity and encourage the emergence of social trust. Such networks facilitate coordination and communication, amplify reputations, and thus allow dilemmas of collective action to be resolved. When economic and political

negotiation is embedded in dense networks of social interaction, incentives for op-
portunism are reduced. At the same time, networks of civic engagement embody
past success at collaboration, which can serve as a cultural template for future collaboration. Finally, dense networks of interaction probably broaden the participants'
sense of self developing the "I". . . into the "we." . . .

* * *

BOWLING ALONE: TRENDS IN CIVIC ENGAGEMENT

Evidence from a number of independent sources strongly suggests that America's stock of social capital has been shrinking for more than a quarter century.

- Membership records of such diverse organizations as the PTA, the Elks
  club, the League of Women Voters, the Red Cross, labor unions, and even
  bowling leagues show that participation in many conventional voluntary
  associations has declined by roughly 25 percent to 50 percent over the last
  two to three decades (Putnam 1995, 1996).
- Surveys of the time budgets of average Americans in 1965, 1975, and 1985,
  in which national samples of men and women recorded every single activity undertaken during the course of a day, imply that the time we spend on
  informal socializing and visiting is down (perhaps by one quarter) since
  1965, and that the time we devote to clubs and organizations is down even
  more sharply (probably by roughly half) over this period.[1]
- While Americans' interest in politics has been stable or even growing over
  the last three decades, and some forms of participation that require moving
  a pen, such as signing petitions and writing checks, have increased significantly, many measures of collective participation have fallen sharply
  (Rosenstone and Hansen 1993; Putnam 1996), including attending a rally or
  speech (off 36 percent between 1973 and 1993), attending a meeting on
  town or school affairs (off 39 percent), or working for a political party (off
  56 percent).
- Evidence from the General Social Survey demonstrates, at all levels of education and among both men and women, a drop of roughly one-quarter
  in group membership since 1974 and a drop of roughly one-third in social
  trust since 1972.[2] . . . slumping membership has afflicted all sorts of groups,
  from sports clubs and professional associations to literary discussion
  groups and labor unions.[3] Only nationality groups, hobby and garden
  clubs, and the catch-all category of "other" seems to have resisted the
  ebbing tide. Furthermore, Gallup polls report that church attendance fell by
  roughly 15 percent during the 1960s and has remained at that lower level
  ever since, while data from the National Opinion Research Center suggests
  that the decline continued during the 1970s and 1980s and by now amounts
  to roughly 30 percent (Putnam 1996). . . .

A fuller audit of American social capital would need to account for apparent countertrends.[4] Some observers believe, for example, that support groups and neighborhood watch groups are proliferating, and few deny that the last several decades have witnessed explosive growth in interest groups represented in Washington. The growth of "mailing list" organizations, like the American Association of Retired People or the Sierra Club, although highly significant in political (and commercial) terms, is not really a counterexample to the supposed decline in social connectedness, however, since these are not really associations in which members meet one another. Their members' ties are to common symbols and ideologies, but not to each other. These organizations are sufficiently different from classical "secondary" associations as to deserve a new rubric—perhaps "tertiary" associations. Similarly, although most secondary associations are not-for-profit, most prominent nonprofits (from Harvard University to the Metropolitan Opera) are bureaucracies, not secondary associations, so the growth of the "Third Sector" is not tantamount to a growth in social connectedness. With due regard to various kinds of counterevidence, I believe that the weight of the available evidence confirms that Americans today are significantly less engaged with their communities than was true a generation ago.

Of course, lots of civic activity is still visible in our communities. American civil society is not moribund. Indeed, evidence suggests that America still outranks many other countries in the degree of our community involvement and social trust (Putnam 1996). But if we compare ourselves, not with other countries but with our parents, the best available evidence suggests that we are less connected with one another.

This prologue poses a number of important questions that merit further debate:

- Is it true that America's stock of social capital has diminished?
- Does it matter?
- What can we do about it?

The answer to the first two questions is, I believe, "yes," but I cannot address them further in this setting. Answering the third question—which ultimately concerns me most—depends, at least in part, on first understanding the causes of the strange malady afflicting American civic life. This is the mystery I seek to unravel here: Why, beginning in the 1960s and accelerating in the 1970s and 1980s, did the fabric of American community life begin to fray? Why are more Americans bowling alone?

Explaining the Erosion of Social Capital

Many possible answers have been suggested for this puzzle:

- Busyness and time pressure
- Economic hard times (or, according to alternative theories, material affluence)
- Residential mobility

- Suburbanization
- The movement of women into the paid labor force and the stresses of two-career families
- Disruption of marriage and family ties
- Changes in the structure of the American economy, such as the rise of chain stores, branch firms, and the service sector
- The sixties (most of which actually happened in the seventies), including
  - –Vietnam, Watergate, and disillusion with public life
  - –The cultural revolt against authority (sex, drugs, and so on)
- Growth of the welfare state
- The civil rights revolution
- Television, the electronic revolution, and other technological changes

The Puzzle Reformulated

To say that civic disengagement in contemporary America is in large measure generational merely reformulates our central puzzle. We . . . know that much of the cause of our lonely bowling probably dates to the 1940s and 1950s, rather than to the 1960s and 1970s. What could have been the mysterious anti-civic "X-ray" that affected Americans who came of age after World War II and whose effects progressively deepened at least into the 1970s?[5] . . .

I have discovered only one prominent suspect against whom circumstantial evidence can be mounted, and in this case, it turns out, some directly incriminating evidence has also turned up. This is not the occasion to lay out the full case for the prosecution, nor to review rebuttal evidence for the defense. However, I want to illustrate the sort of evidence that justifies indictment. The culprit is television.

First, the timing fits. The long civic generation was the last cohort of Americans to grow up without television, for television flashed into American society like lightning in the 1950s. In 1950 barely 10 percent of American homes had television sets, but by 1959, 90 percent did, probably the fastest diffusion of a technological innovation ever recorded. The reverberations from this lightning bolt continued for decades, as viewing hours per capita grew by 17–20 percent during the 1960s and by an additional 7–8 percent during the 1970s. In the early years, TV watching was concentrated among the less educated sectors of the population, but during the 1970s the viewing time of the more educated sectors of the population began to converge upward. Television viewing increases with age, particularly upon retirement, but each generation since the introduction of television has begun its life cycle at a higher starting point. By 1995, viewing per TV household was more than 50 percent higher than it had been in the 1950s.[6]

Most studies estimate that the average American now watches roughly four hours per day.[7] Robinson (1990b), using the more conservative time-budget technique for determining how people allocate their time, offers an estimate closer to three hours per day, but concludes that as a primary activity, television absorbs 40 percent of the average American's free time, an increase of about one-third since 1965. Moreover, multiple sets have proliferated; by the late 1980s, three-quarters of all U.S. homes had more than one set (Comstock 1989), and these numbers too are rising steadily, allowing ever more private viewing. In short, as Robinson and Godbey 1995 conclude, "television is the 800-pound gorilla of leisure time." This massive change in the way Americans spend our days and nights occurred precisely during the years of generational civic disengagement.

Evidence of a link between the arrival of television and the erosion of social connections is, however, not merely circumstantial. The links between civic engagement and television viewing can instructively be compared with the links between civic engagement and newspaper reading. The basic contrast is straightforward: newspaper reading is associated with high social capital, TV viewing with low social capital. . . .

. . . [E]ach hour spent viewing television is associated with less social trust and less group membership, while each hour reading a newspaper is associated with more. An increase in television viewing of the magnitude that the United States has experienced in the last four decades might directly account for as much as one-quarter to one-half of the total drop in social capital, even without taking into account, for example, the indirect effects of television viewing on newspaper readership or the cumulative effects of "life-time" viewing hours.[8]

How might television destroy social capital?

- *Time displacement.* Even though there are only 24 hours in everyone's day, most forms of social and media participation are positively correlated. People who listen to lots of classical music are more likely, not less likely, than others to attend Cubs games. Television is the principal exception to this generalization—the only leisure activity that seems to inhibit participation outside the home. TV watching comes at expense of nearly every social activity outside the home, especially social gatherings and informal conversations (Comstock et al. 1978; Comstock 1989; Bower 1985; and Robinson and Godbey 1995). TV viewers are homebodies.

  Most studies that report a negative correlation between television watching and community involvement . . . are ambiguous with respect to causality, because they merely compare different individuals at a single time. However, one important quasi-experimental study of the introduction of television in three Canadian towns (Williams 1986) found the same pattern at the aggregate level across time: a major effect of television's arrival was the reduction in participation in social, recreational, and community activities among people of all ages. In short, television is privatizing our leisure time.

- *Effects on the outlooks of viewers.* An impressive body of literature, gathered under the rubric of the "mean world effect," suggests that heavy watchers of TV are unusually skeptical about the benevolence of other people—overestimating crime rates, for example. This body of literature has generated much debate about the underlying causal patterns, with skeptics suggesting that misanthropy may foster couch-potato behavior rather than the reverse. While awaiting better experimental evidence, however, a reasonable interim judgment is that heavy television watching may well increase pessimism about human nature (Gerbner et al. 1980; Dobb and MacDonald 1979; Hirsch 1980; Hughes 1980; and Comstock 1989, 265–69). Perhaps, too, as social critics have long argued, both the medium and the message have more basic effects on our ways of interacting with the world and with one another. Television may induce passivity, as Postman (1985) has claimed, and it may even change our fundamental physical and social perceptions, as Meyrowitz (1985) has suggested.

- *Effects on children.* TV occupies an extraordinary part of children's lives—consuming about 40 hours per week on average. Viewing is especially high among pre-adolescents, but it remains high among younger adolescents: time-budget studies (Carnegie Council on Adolescent Development 1993, 5, citing Timmer et al. 1985) suggest that among youngsters aged 9–14 television consumes as much time as *all other discretionary activities combined,* including playing, hobbies, clubs, outdoor activities, informal visiting, and just hanging out. The effects of television on childhood socialization have, of course, been hotly debated for more than three decades. The most reasonable conclusion from a welter of sometimes conflicting results appears to be that heavy television watching probably increases aggressiveness (although perhaps not actual violence), that it probably reduces school achievement, and that it is statistically associated with "psychosocial malfunctioning," although how much of this effect is self-selection and how much causal remains much debated (Condry 1993). The evidence is, as I have said, not yet enough to convict, but the defense has a lot of explaining to do.

Conclusion

Ithiel de Sola Pool's posthumous book, *Technologies Without Borders* (1990), is a prescient work, astonishingly relevant to our current national debates about the complicated links among technology, public policy, and culture. Pool defended what he called "soft technological determinism." Revolutions in communications technologies have profoundly affected social life and culture, as the printing press helped bring on the Reformation. Pool concluded that the electronic revolution in communications technology, whose outlines he traced well before most of us were even aware of the impending changes, was the first major technological advance in centuries that would have a profoundly decentralizing and fragmenting effect on society and culture.

Pool hoped that the result might be "community without contiguity." As a classic liberal, he welcomed the benefits of technological change for individual freedom, and, in part, I share that enthusiasm. Those of us who bemoan the decline of community in contemporary America need to be sensitive to the liberating gains achieved during the same decades. We need to avoid an uncritical nostalgia for the Fifties. On the other hand, some of the same freedom-friendly technologies whose rise Pool predicted may indeed be undermining our connections with one another and with our communities. I suspect that Pool would have been open to that argument, too, for one of Pool's most talented protégés, Samuel Popkin (1991, 226–31) has argued that the rise of television and the correlative decline of social interaction have impaired American political discourse. The last line in Pool's last book (1990, 262) is this: "We may suspect that [the technological trends that we can anticipate] will promote individualism and will make it harder, not easier, to govern and organize a coherent society."

Pool's technological determinism was "soft" precisely because he recognized that social values can condition the effects of technology. In the end this perspective invites us not merely to consider how technology is privatizing our lives—if, as it seems to me, it is—but to ask whether we entirely like the result, and if not, what we might do about it. But that is a topic for another day.

NOTES

1. The 1965 sample, which was limited to nonretired residents of cities between 30,000 and 280,000 population, was not precisely equivalent to the later national samples, so appropriate adjustments need to be made to ensure comparability. For the 1965–1975 comparison, see Robinson (1981, 125). For the 1975–1985 comparison (but apparently without adjustment for the 1965 sampling peculiarities), see Cutler (1990). Somewhat smaller declines are reported in Robinson and Godbey (1995), although it is unclear whether they correct for the sampling differences. Additional work to refine these cross-time comparisons is required and is currently underway.

2. Trust in political authorities—and indeed in many social institutions—has also declined sharply over the last three decades, but that is conceptually a distinct trend. As we shall see later, the etiology of the slump in social trust is quite different from the etiology of the decline in political trust.

3. . . . [C]ontrolling for the respondent's education level.

4. Some commentaries on "Bowling Alone" have been careless, however, in reporting apparent membership growth. *The Economist* (1995, 22), for example, celebrated a recent rebound in total membership in parent-teacher organizations, without acknowledging that this rebound is almost entirely attributable to the growing number of children. The fraction of parents who belong to PTAs has regained virtually none of the 50 percent fall that this metric registered between 1960 and 1975. Despite talk about the growth of "support groups," another oft-cited counterexample, I know of no statistical substantiation for this claim. One might even ask whether the vaunted rise in neighborhood watch groups might not represent only a partial,

artificial replacement for the vanished social capital of traditional neigh-borhoods—a kind of sociological Astroturf, suitable only where you can't grow the real thing. See also Glenn (1987, S124) for survey evidence of "an increased tendency for individuals to withdraw allegiance from . . . any-thing outside of themselves."

5. I record here one theory attributed variously to Robert Salisbury (1985), Gerald Gamm, and Simon and Garfunkel. Devotees of our national pas-time will recall that Joe Dimaggio signed with the Yankees in 1936, just as the last of the long civic generation was beginning to follow the game, and he turned center field over to Mickey Mantle in 1951, just as the last of "the suckers" reached legal maturity. Almost simultaneously, the Braves, the Athletics, the Browns, the Senators, the Dodgers, and the Giants deserted cities that had been their homes since the late nineteenth century. By the time Mantle in turn left the Yankees in 1968, much of the damage to civic loyalty had been done. This interpretation explains why Mrs. Robinson's plaintive query that year about Joltin' Joe's whereabouts evoked such widespread emotion. A deconstructionist analysis of social capital's decline would highlight the final haunting lamentation, "our nation turns its *lonely* eyes to you" [emphasis added].

6. For introductions to the massive literature on the sociology of television, see Bower (1985), Comstock et al. (1978), Comstock (1989), and Grabner (1993). The figures on viewing hours in the text are from Bower (1985, 33) and *Public Perspective* (1995, 47). Cohort differences are reported in Bower 1985, 46.

7. This figure excludes periods in which television is merely playing in the back-ground. Comstock (1989, 17) reports that "on any fall day in the late 1980s, the set in the average television owning household was on for about eight hours."

8. Newspaper circulation (per household) has dropped by more than half since its peak in 1947. To be sure, it is not clear which way the tie between newspaper reading and civic involvement works, since disengagement might itself dampen one's interest in community news. But the two trends are clearly linked.

REFERENCES

Bower, Robert T. 1985. *The Changing Television Audience in America.* New York: Columbia University Press.

Carnegie Council on Adolescent Development. 1993. *A Matter of Time: Risk and Opportunity in the Nonschool House: Executive Summary.* New York: Carnegie Corporation of New York.

Coleman, James. 1990. *Foundations of Social Theory.* Cambridge, MA: Harvard University Press.

Comstock, George, Steven Chaffee, Natan Katzman, Maxwell McCombs, and Donald Roberts. 1978. *Television and Human Behavior.* New York: Columbia University Press.

Comstock, George. 1989. *The Evolution of American Television.* Newbury Park, CA: Sage.

Condry, John. 1993. "Thief of Time. Unfaithful Servant: Television and the American Child." *Daedalus* 122 (Winter): 259–78.

Cutler, Blaine. 1990. "Where Does the Free Time Go?" *American Demographics* (November): 36–39.

Dobb, Anthony N., and Glenn F. Macdonald. 1979. "Television Viewing and Fear of Victimization: Is the Relationship Causal?" *Journal of Personality and Social Psychology* 37: 170–79.

Gerbner, George, Larry Gross, Michael Morgan, and Nancy Signorielli. 1980. "The 'Mainstreaming' of America: Violence Profile No. 11." *Journal of Communication* 30 (Summer): 10–29.

Glenn, Norval D. 1987. "Social Trends in the United States: Evidence from Sample Surveys."*Public Opinion Quarterly* 51: S109–S126.

Grabner, Doris A. 1993. *Mass Media and American Politics.* Washington, DC: CQ Press.

Hirsch, Paul M. "The 'Scary World' of the Nonviewer and Other Anomalies: A Reanalysis of Gerbner et al.'s Findings on Cultivation Analysis. Part I." *Communication Research* 7 (October): 403–56.

Hughes, Michael. 1980. "The Fruits of Cultivation Analysis: A Re-examination of the Effects of Television Watching on Fear of Victimization, Alienation, and the Approval of Violence." *Public Opinion Quarterly* 44: 287–303.

Meyrowitz, Joshua. 1985. *No Sense of Place: The Impact of Electronic Media on Social Behavior.* New York: Oxford University Press.

Pool, Ithiel de Sola. 1990. *Technologies Without Boundaries: On Telecommunications in a Global Age.* Cambridge, MA: Harvard University Press.

Popkin, Samuel L. 1991. *The Reasoning Voter.* Chicago: University of Chicago Press.

Postman, Neil. 1985. *Amusing Ourselves to Death: Public Discourse in the Age of Show Business.* New York: Viking-Penguin Books.

Putnam, Robert D. 1993. *Making Democracy Work: Civic Traditions in Modern Italy.* Princeton, NJ: Princeton University Press.

Putnam, Robert D. 1995. "Bowling Alone. Revisited." *The Responsive Community* (Spring): 18–33.

Putnam, Robert D. 1996. "Bowling Alone: Democracy in America at the End of the Twentieth Century," forthcoming in a collective volume edited by Axel Hadenius, New York: Cambridge University Press.

Robinson, John. 1981. "Television and Leisure Time: A New Scenario." *Journal of Communication* 31 (Winter): 120–30.

Robinson, John. 1990b. "I Love My TV." *American Demographics* (September): 24–27.

Robinson, John, and Geoffrey Godbey. 1995. *Time for Life.* College Park, MD: University of Maryland. Unpublished manuscript.

Rosenstone, Steven J., and John Mark Hansen. 1993. *Mobilization Participation and Democracy in America.* New York: Macmillan.

Salisbury, Robert H. 1985. "Blame Dismal World Conditions on . . . Baseball." *Miami Herald* (May 18): 27A.

Timmer, S. G., J. Eccles, and I. O'Brien. 1985. "How Children Use Time." In *Time, Goods, and Well-Being,* ed. F. T. Juster and F. B. Stafford. Ann Arbor: University of Michigan, Institute for Social Research.

Williams, Tannis Macbeth, ed. 1986. *The Impact of Television: A Natural Experiment in Three Communities.* New York: Academic Press.

What If Civic Life Didn't Die?

Michael Schudson

Robert Putnam's important and disturbing work on civic participation . . . (*TAP* Winter 1996) has led him to conclude that television is the culprit behind civic decline. But lest we be *too* disturbed, we ought to consider carefully whether the data adequately measure participation and justify his conclusions and whether his conclusions fit much else that we know about recent history. I suggest that his work has missed some key contrary evidence. If we could measure civic participation better, the decline would be less striking and the puzzle less perplexing. If we looked more carefully at the history of civic participation and the differences among generations, we would have to abandon the rhetoric of decline. And if we examined television and recent history more closely, we could not convict TV of turning off civic involvement.

Consider, first, the problem of measuring whether there has been civic decline. Putnam has been ingenious in finding multiple measures of civic engagement, from voter turnout to opinion poll levels of trust in government to time-budget studies on how people allocate their time to associational membership. But could it be that even all of these measures together mask how civic energy is deployed?

Data collected by Sidney Verba, Kay Lehman Schlozman, and Henry Brady suggest the answer is yes. In 1987, 34 percent of their national sample reported active membership in a community problem-solving organization compared to 31 percent in 1967; in 1987, 34 percent reported working with others on a local problem compared to 30 percent in 1967. Self-reports should not be taken at face value, but why does this survey indicate a slight increase in local civic engagement? Does it capture something Putnam's data miss?

Putnam's measures may, in fact, overlook several types of civic activity. First, people may have left the middling commitment of the League of Women Voters or the PTA for organized activity both much less and much more involving. As for much more: Churches seem to be constantly reinventing themselves, adding a variety of groups and activities to engage members, from singles clubs to job training to organized social welfare services to preschools. An individual who reports only one associational membership—say, a church or

Michael Schudson is professor of communication and sociology, University of California–San Diego. Reprinted from Michael Schudson, "What If Civic Life Didn't Die?" Reprinted with permission from *The American Prospect* Volume 7, Number 25: March 1, 1996–April 1, 1996. The American Prospect, 5 Broad Street, Boston, MA 02109. All rights reserved.

synagogue—may be more involved in it and more "civic" through it than someone else who reports two or three memberships.

Second, people may have left traditional civic organizations that they used for personal and utilitarian ends for commercial organizations. If people who formerly joined the YMCA to use the gym now go to the local fitness center, Putnam's measures will show a decrease in civic participation when real civic activity is unchanged.

Third, people may be more episodically involved in political and civic activity as issue-oriented politics grows. For instance, in California, motorcycle riders have become influential political activists since the 1992 passage of a law requiring bikers to wear helmets. According to the *San Diego Union*, of 800,000 licensed motorcyclists, 10,000 are now members of the American Brotherhood Aimed Toward Education (ABATE), which has been credited as decisive in several races for the state legislature. Members do not meet on a regular basis, but they do periodically mobilize in local political contests to advance their one legislative purpose. Would Putnam's data pick up on this group? What about the intense but brief house-building activity for Habitat for Humanity?

Fourth, Putnam notes but leaves to the side the vast increase in Washington-based mailing list organizations over the past 30 years. He ignores them because they do not require members to do more than send in a check. This is not Tocquevillian democracy, but these organizations may be a highly efficient use of civic energy. The citizen who joins them may get the same civic payoff for less personal hassle. This is especially so if we conceive of politics as a set of public policies. The citizen may be able to influence government more satisfactorily with the annual membership in the Sierra Club or the National Rifle Association than by attending the local club luncheons.

Of course, policy is a limited notion of government. Putnam assumes a broader view that makes personal investment part of the payoff of citizenship. Participation is its own reward. But even our greatest leaders—Jefferson, for one—complained about the demands of public life and, like Dorothy in liberating Oz, were forever trying to get back home. Getting government off our backs was a theme Patrick Henry evoked. And who is to say that getting back home is an unworthy desire?

The concept of politics has broadened enormously in 30 years. Not only is the personal political (the politics of male-female relations, the politics of smoking and not smoking), but the professional or occupational is also political. A woman physician or accountant can feel that she is doing politics—providing a role model and fighting for recognition of women's equality with men—every time she goes to work. The same is true for African American bank executives or gay and lesbian military officers.

The decline of the civic in its conventional forms, then, does not demonstrate the decline of civic-mindedness. The "political" does not necessarily depend on social connectedness: Those membership dues to the NRA are political. Nor does it even depend on organized groups at all: Wearing a "Thank you for not smoking" button is political. The political may be intense and transient: Think of the thousands of people who have joined class action suits against producers of silicone breast implants or Dalkon shields or asbestos insulation.

Let us assume, for argument's sake, that there has been a decrease in civic involvement. Still, the rhetoric of decline in American life should send up a red flag. For the socially concerned intellectual, this is as much off-the-rack rhetoric as its mirror opposite, the rhetoric of progress, is for the ebullient technocrat. Any notion of "decline" has to take for granted some often arbitrary baseline. Putnam's baseline is the 1940s and 1950s when the "long civic generation"—people born between 1910 and 1940—came into their own. But this generation shared the powerful and unusual experience of four years of national military mobilization on behalf of what nearly everyone came to accept as a good cause. If Putnam had selected, say, the 1920s as a baseline, would he have given us a similar picture of decline?

Unlikely. Intellectuals of the 1920s wrung [sic] their hands about the fate of democracy, the decline of voter turnout, the "eclipse of the public," as John Dewey put it or "the phantom public" in Walter Lippmann's terms. They had plenty of evidence, particularly in the record of voter turnout, so low in 1920 and 1924 (49 percent each year) that even our contemporary nadir of 1988 (50.3 percent)* does not quite match it. Putnam himself reports that people born from 1910 to 1940 appear more civic than those born before as well as those born after. There is every reason to ask why this group was so civic rather than why later groups are not.

The most obvious answer is that this group fought in or came of age during World War II. This is also a group that voted overwhelmingly for Franklin D. Roosevelt and observed his leadership in office over a long period. Presidents exercise a form of moral leadership that sets a norm or standard about what kind of a life people should lead. A critic has complained that Ronald Reagan made all Americans a little more stupid in the 1980s—and I don't think this is a frivolous jibe. Reagan taught us that even the president can make a philosophy of the principle, "My mind's made up, don't confuse me with the facts." He taught us that millions will pay deference to someone who regularly and earnestly confuses films with lived experience.

The "long civic generation" had the advantages of a "good war" and a good president. Later generations had no wars or ones about which there was less massive mobilization and much less consensus—Korea and, more divisively, Vietnam. They had presidents of dubious moral leadership—notably Nixon, whom people judged even in the glow of his latter-day "rehabilitation" as the worst moral leader of all post–World War II presidents. So if there has been civic disengagement in the past decades, it may be not a decline but a return to normalcy.

If the rhetoric of decline raises one red flag, television as an explanation raises another. Some of the most widely heralded "media effects" have by now been thoroughly discredited. The yellow press had little or nothing to do with getting us into the Spanish-American War. Television news had little or nothing

---

*48.9 percent in 1996—*The Editors.*

to do with turning Americans against the Vietnam War. Ronald Reagan's mastery of the media did not make him an unusually popular president in his first term (in fact, for his first 30 months in office he was unusually unpopular).

Indeed, the TV explanation doesn't fit Putnam's data very well. Putnam defines the long civic generation as the cohort born from 1910 to 1940, but then he also shows that the downturn in civic involvement began "rather abruptly" among people "born in the early 1930s." In other words, civic decline began with people too young to have served in World War II but too old to have seen TV growing up. If we take 1954 as a turning-point year—the first year when more than half of American households had TV sets—Americans born from 1930 to 1936 were in most cases already out of the home and the people born the next four years were already in high school by the time TV is likely to have become a significant part of their lives. Of course, TV may have influenced this group later, in the 1950s and early 1960s when they were in their twenties and thirties. But this was a time when Americans watched many fewer hours of television, averaging five hours a day rather than the current seven, and the relatively benign TV fare of that era was not likely to induce fearfulness of the outside world.

All of my speculations here and most of Putnam's assume that one person has about the same capacity for civic engagement as the next. But what if some people have decidedly more civic energy than others as a function of, say, personality? And what if these civic spark plugs have been increasingly recruited into situations where they are less civically engaged?

Putnam accords this kind of explanation some attention in asking whether women who had been most involved in civic activities were those most likely to take paying jobs, "thus lowering the average level of civic engagement among the remaining homemakers and raising the average among women in the workplace." Putnam says he "can find little evidence" to support this hypothesis, but it sounds plausible.

A similar hypothesis makes sense in other domains. Since World War II, higher education has mushroomed. Of people born from 1911 to 1920, 13.5 percent earned college or graduate degrees; of those born during the next decade, 18.8 percent; but of people born from 1931 to 1950, the figure grew to between 26 and 27 percent. A small but increasing number of these college students have been recruited away from their home communities to elite private colleges; some public universities also began after World War II to draw from a national pool of talent. Even colleges with local constituencies increasingly have recruited faculty nationally, and the faculty have shaped student ambitions toward national law, medical, and business schools and corporate traineeships. If students drawn to these programs are among the people likeliest in the past to have been civic spark plugs, we have an alternative explanation for civic decline.

Could there be a decline? Better to conceive the changes we find as a new environment of civic and political activity with altered institutional openings for engagement. Television is a part of the ecology, but in complex ways. It is a significant part of people's use of their waking hours, but it may be less a substitute for civic engagement than a new and perhaps insidious form of it. TV has been more politicized since the late 1960s than ever before. In 1968, *60 Minutes* began as the first moneymaking entertainment news program, spawning a dozen imitators. *All In The Family* in 1971 became the first prime-time sitcom to routinely take on controversial topics, from homosexuality to race to women's rights. *Donahue* was first syndicated in 1979, *Oprah* followed in 1984, and after them, the deluge.

If TV does nonetheless discourage civic engagement, what aspect of TV is at work? Is it the most "serious," civic-minded, and responsible part—the news? The latest blast at the news media, James Fallow's *Breaking the News*, picks up a familiar theme that the efforts of both print and broadcast journalists since the 1960s to get beneath the surface of events has led to a journalistic presumption that no politician can be trusted and that the story behind the story will be invariably sordid.

All of this talk needs to be tempered with the reminder that, amidst the many disappointments of politics between 1965 and 1995, this has been an era of unprecedented advances in women's rights, gay and lesbian liberation, African American opportunity, and financial security for the elderly. It has witnessed the first consumers' movement since the 1930s, the first environmental movement since the turn of the century, and public health movements of great range and achievement, especially in antismoking. It has also been a moment of grassroots activism on the right as well as on the left, with the pro-life movement and the broad-gauge political involvement both locally and nationally of the Christian right. Most of this activity was generated outside of political parties and state institutions. Most of this activity was built on substantial "grassroots" organizing. It is not easy to square all of this with an account of declining civic virtue.

Robert Putnam has offered us a lot to think about, with clarity and insight. Still, he has not yet established the decline in civic participation, let alone provided a satisfying explanation for it. What he has done is to reinvigorate inquiry on a topic that could scarcely be more important.

Internet Resources
Visit our website at http://www.mhhe.com/diclerico for links and resources related to Democracy.

chapter 2

The Constitution

Of the many books that have been written about the circumstances surrounding the creation of our Constitution, none generated more controversy than Charles Beard's An Economic Interpretation of the Constitution of the United States *(1913). An historian by profession, Beard challenged the belief that our Constitution was fashioned by men of democratic spirit. On the contrary, in what appeared to be a systematic marshaling of evidence, Beard sought to demonstrate (1) that the impetus for a new constitution came from individuals who saw their own economic interests threatened by a growing trend in the population toward greater democracy; (2) that the Founding Fathers themselves were men of considerable "personalty" (i.e., holdings other than real estate), who were concerned not so much with fashioning a democratic constitution as with protecting their own financial interests against the more democratically oriented farming and debtor interests within the society; and (3) that the individuals charged with ratifying the new Constitution also represented primarily the larger economic interests within the society. Although space limitations prevent a full development of Beard's argument, the portions of his book that follow should provide some feel for both the substance of his argument and his method of investigation.*

Beard's analysis has been subject to repeated scrutiny over the years. The most systematic effort in this regard came in 1956 with the publication of Robert Brown's Charles Beard and the Constitution: A Critical Analysis of "An Economic Interpretation of the Constitution." *Arguing that the rigor of Beard's examination was more apparent than real, Brown accuses him of citing only the facts that supported his case while ignoring those that did not. Moreover, he contends that even the evidence Beard provided did not warrant the interpretation he gave to it. Brown concludes that the best evidence now available does not support the view that "the Constitution was put over undemocratically in an undemocratic society by personal property."*

An Economic Interpretation
of the Constitution of the United States
Charles A. Beard

Suppose it could be shown from the classification of the men who supported and opposed the Constitution that there was no line of property division at all; that is, that men owning substantially the same amounts of the same kinds of property were equally divided on the matter of adoption or rejection—it would then become apparent that the Constitution had no ascertainable relation to economic groups or classes, but was the product of some abstract causes remote from the chief business of life—gaining a livelihood.

Suppose, on the other hand, that substantially all of the merchants, money lenders, security holders, manufacturers, shippers, capitalists, and financiers and their professional associates are to be found on one side in support of the Constitution and that substantially all or the major portion of the opposition came from the nonslaveholding farmers and the debtors—would it not be pretty conclusively demonstrated that our fundamental law was not the product of an abstraction known as "the whole people," but of a group of economic interests which must have expected beneficial results from its adoption? Obviously all the facts here desired cannot be discovered, but the data presented in the following chapters bear out the latter hypothesis, and thus a reasonable presumption in favor of the theory is created.

Of course, it may be shown (and perhaps can be shown) that the farmers and debtors who opposed the Constitution were, in fact, benefited by the general improvement which resulted from its adoption. It may likewise be shown, to take an extreme case, that the English nation derived immense advantages from the Norman Conquest and the orderly administrative processes which were introduced, as it undoubtedly did; nevertheless, it does not follow that the vague thing known as "the advancement of general welfare" or some abstraction known as "justice" was the immediate, guiding purpose of the leaders in either of these great historic changes. The point is, that the direct, impelling

Charles A. Beard (1874–1948) was professor of history and political science at Columbia University and former president of the American Political Science Association. Reprinted with the permission of Scribner, an imprint of Simon & Schuster Adult Publishing Group, from *An Economic Interpretation of the Constitution of the United States* by Charles A. Beard. Copyright 1935 by The Macmillan Publishing Company; copyright renewed © 1963 by William Beard and Mrs. Miriam Beard Vagts.

motive in both cases was the economic advantages which the beneficiaries expected would accrue to themselves first, from their action. Further than this,
economic interpretation cannot go. It may be that some larger world process is
working through each series of historical events: but ultimate causes lie beyond
our horizon. . . .

THE FOUNDING FATHERS: AN ECONOMIC PROFILE

A survey of the economic interests of the members of the Convention presents
certain conclusions:

A majority of the members were lawyers by profession.

Most of the members came from towns, on or near the coast, that is, from
the regions in which personalty was largely concentrated.

Not one member represented in his immediate personal economic interests
the small farming or mechanic classes.

The overwhelming majority of members, at least five-sixths, were immediately, directly, and personally interested in the outcome of their labors at
Philadelphia, and were to a greater or less extent economic beneficiaries from
the adoption of the Constitution.

1. Public security interests were extensively represented in the Convention.
   Of the fifty-five members who attended no less than forty appear on the
   Records of the Treasury Department for sums varying from a few dollars
   up to more than one hundred thousand dollars. . . .

   It is interesting to note that, with the exception of New York, and possibly Delaware, each state had one or more prominent representatives in the
   Convention who held more than a negligible amount of securities, and who
   could therefore speak with feeling and authority on the question of providing in the new Constitution for the full discharge of the public debt. . . .
2. Personalty invested in lands for speculation was represented by at least
   fourteen members. . . .
3. Personalty in the form of money loaned at interest was represented by at
   least twenty-four members. . . .
4. Personalty in mercantile, manufacturing, and shipping lines was represented by at least eleven members. . . .
5. Personalty in slaves was represented by at least fifteen members. . . .

It cannot be said, therefore, that the members of the Convention were "disinterested." On the contrary, we are forced to accept the profoundly significant
conclusion that they knew through their personal experiences in economic affairs the precise results which the new government that they were setting up
was designed to attain. As a group of doctrinaires, like the Frankfort assembly
of 1848, they would have failed miserably; but as practical men they were able
to build the new government upon the only foundations which could be stable:
fundamental economic interests.[1] . . .

RATIFICATION

New York

There can be no question about the predominance of personalty in the contest over the ratification in New York. That state, says Libby, "presents the problem in its simplest form. The entire mass of interior counties . . . were solidly anti-Federal, comprising the agricultural portion of the state, the last settled and the most thinly populated. There were however in this region two Federal cities (not represented in the convention [as such]), Albany in Albany county and Hudson in Columbia county. . . . The Federal area centred about New York city and county: to the southwest lay Richmond county (Staten Island); to the southeast Kings county, and the northeast Westchester county; while still further extending this area, at the northeast lay the divided county of Dutchess, with a vote in the convention of 4 to 2 in favor of the Constitution, and at the southeast were the divided counties of Queens and Suffolk. . . . These radiating strips of territory with New York city as a centre form a unit, in general favorable to the new Constitution; and it is significant of this unity that Dutchess, Queens, and Suffolk counties, broke away from the anti-Federal phalanx and joined the Federalists, securing thereby the adoption of the Constitution."[2]

Unfortunately the exact distribution of personalty in New York and particularly in the wavering districts which went over to the Federalist party cannot be ascertained, for the system of taxation in vogue in New York at the period of the adoption of the Constitution did not require a state record of property.[3] The data which proved so fruitful in Massachusetts are not forthcoming, therefore, in the case of New York; but it seems hardly necessary to demonstrate the fact that New York City was the centre of personalty for the state and stood next to Philadelphia as the great centre of operations in public stock.

This somewhat obvious conclusion is reinforced by the evidence relative to the vote on the legal tender bill which the paper money party pushed through in 1786. Libby's analysis of this vote shows that "no vote was cast against the bill by members of counties north of the county of New York. In the city and county of New York and in Long Island and Staten Island, the combined vote was 9 to 5 against the measure. Comparing this vote with the vote on the ratification in 1788, it will be seen that of the Federal counties 3 voted against paper money and 1 for it; of the divided counties 1 (Suffolk) voted against paper money and 2 (Queens and Dutchess) voted for it. Of the anti-Federal counties none had members voting against paper money. The merchants as a body were opposed to the issue of paper money and the Chamber of Commerce adopted a memorial against the issue."[4]

Public security interests were identified with the sound money party. There were thirty members of the New York constitutional convention who voted in favor of the ratification of the Constitution and of these no less than sixteen were holders of public securities. . . .

South Carolina

South Carolina presents the economic elements in the ratification with the utmost simplicity. There we find two rather sharply marked districts in antagonism over the Constitution. "The rival sections," says Libby, "were the coast or lower district and the upper, or more properly, the middle and upper country. The coast region was the first settled and contained a larger portion of the wealth of the state; its mercantile and commercial interests were important; its church was the Episcopal, supported by the state." This region, it is scarcely necessary to remark, was overwhelmingly in favor of the Constitution. The upper area, against the Constitution, "was a frontier section, the last to receive settlement; its lands were fertile and its mixed population was largely small farmers. . . . There was no established church, each community supported its own church and there was a great variety in the district."[5]

A contemporary writer, R. G. Harper, calls attention to the fact that the lower country, Charleston, Beaufort, and Georgetown, which had 28,694 white inhabitants, and about seven-twelfths of the representation in the state convention, paid £28,081:5:10 taxes in 1794, while the upper country, with 120,902 inhabitants, and five-twelfths of the representation in the convention, paid only £8390:13:3 taxes.[6] The lower districts in favor of the Constitution therefore possessed the wealth of the state and a disproportionate share in the convention—on the basis of the popular distribution of representation.

These divisions of economic interest are indicated by the abstracts of the tax returns for the state in 1794 which show that of £127,337 worth of stock in trade, faculties, etc. listed for taxation in the state, £109,800 worth was in Charleston, city and county—the stronghold of Federalism. Of the valuation of lots in towns and villages to the amount of £656,272 in the state, £549,909 was located in that city and county.[7]

The records of the South Carolina loan office preserved in the Treasury Department at Washington show that the public securities of that state were more largely in the hands of inhabitants than was the case in North Carolina. They also show a heavy concentration in the Charleston district.

At least fourteen of the thirty-one members of the state-ratifying convention from the parishes of St. Philip and Saint Michael, Charleston (all of whom favored ratification) held over $75,000 worth of public securities. . . .

Conclusions

At the close of this long and arid survey—partaking of the nature of catalogue—it seems worthwhile to bring together the important conclusions for political science which the data presented appear to warrant.

The movement for the Constitution of the United States was originated and carried through principally by four groups of personalty interests which had been adversely affected under the Articles of Confederation: money, public securities, manufactures, and trade and shipping.

The first firm steps toward the formation of the Constitution were taken by a small and active group of men immediately interested through their personal possessions in the outcome of their labors.

No popular vote was taken directly or indirectly on the proposition to call the Convention which drafted the Constitution.

A large propertyless mass was, under the prevailing suffrage qualifications, excluded at the outset from participation (through representatives) in the work of framing the Constitution.

The members of the Philadelphia Convention which drafted the Constitution were, with a few exceptions, immediately, directly, and personally interested in, and derived economic advantages from, the establishment of the new system.

The Constitution was essentially an economic document based upon the concept that the fundamental private rights of property are anterior to government and morally beyond the reach of popular majorities.

The major portion of the members of the Convention are on record as recognizing the claim of property to a special and defensive position in the Constitution.

In the ratification of the Constitution, about three-fourths of the adult males failed to vote on the question, having abstained from the elections at which delegates to the state conventions were chosen, either on account of their indifference or their disfranchisement by property qualifications.

The Constitution was ratified by a vote of probably not more than one-sixth of the adult males.

It is questionable whether a majority of the voters participating in the elections for the state conventions in New York, Massachusetts, New Hampshire, Virginia, and South Carolina, actually approved the ratification of the Constitution.

The leaders who supported the Constitution in the ratifying conventions represented the same economic groups as the members of the Philadelphia Convention; and in a large number of instances they were also directly and personally interested in the outcome of their efforts.

In the ratification, it became manifest that the line of cleavage for and against the Constitution was between substantial personalty interests on the one hand and the small farming and debtor interests on the other.

The Constitution was not created by "the whole people" as the jurists have said; neither was it created by "the states" as southern nullifiers long contended; but it was the work of a consolidated group whose interests knew no state boundaries and were truly national in their scope.

NOTES

1. The fact that a few members of the Convention, who had considerable economic interests at stake, refused to support the Constitution does not invalidate the general conclusions here presented. In the cases of Yates, Lansing, Luther Martin, and Mason, definite economic reasons for their action are forthcoming; but this is a minor detail.

2. O. G. Libby, *Geographical Distribution of the Vote of the Thirteen States on the Federal Constitution,* p. 18. Libby here takes the vote in the New York convention, but that did not precisely represent the popular vote.

3. *State Papers: Finance,* vol. 1, p. 425.

4. Libby, *Geographical Distribution,* p. 59.

5. *Ibid.,* pp. 42–43.

6. "Appius," *To the Citizens of South Carolina* (1794), Library of Congress, Duane Pamphlets, vol. 83.

7. *State Papers: Finance,* vol. 1, p. 462. In 1783 an attempt to establish a bank with $100,000 capital was made in Charleston, S.C., but it failed. "Soon after the adoption of the funding system, three banks were established in Charleston whose capitals in the whole amounted to twenty times the sum proposed in 1783." D. Ramsey, *History of South Carolina* (1858 ed.), vol. 2, p. 106.

Charles Beard and the Constitution

A Critical Analysis

Robert E. Brown

At the end of Chapter XI [of *An Economic Interpretation of the Constitution of the United States*], Beard summarized his findings in fourteen paragraphs under the heading of "Conclusions." Actually, these fourteen conclusions merely add up to the two halves of the Beard thesis. One half, that the Constitution originated with and was carried through by personalty interests—money, public securities, manufactures, and commerce—is to be found in paragraphs two, three, six, seven, eight, twelve, thirteen, and fourteen. The other half—that the Constitution was put over undemocratically in an undemocratic society—is expressed in paragraphs four, five, nine, ten, eleven, and fourteen. The lumping of these conclusions under two general headings makes it easier for the reader to see the broad outlines of the Beard thesis.

Before we examine these two major divisions of the thesis, however, some comment is relevant on the implications contained in the first paragraph. In it Beard characterized his book as a long and arid survey, something in the nature of a catalogue. Whether this characterization was designed to give his book the appearance of a coldly objective study based on the facts we do not know. If so, nothing could be further from reality. As reviewers pointed out in 1913, and as subsequent developments have demonstrated, the book is anything but an arid catalogue of facts. Its pages are replete with interpretation, sometimes stated, sometimes implied. Our task has been to examine Beard's evidence to see whether it justifies the interpretation which Beard gave it. We have tried to discover whether he used the historical method properly in arriving at his thesis.

If historical method means the gathering of data from primary sources, the critical evaluation of the evidence thus gathered, and the drawing of conclusions consistent with this evidence, then we must conclude that Beard has done great violation to such method in this book. He admitted that the evidence had not been collected which, given the proper use of historical method, should have precluded the writing of the book. Yet he nevertheless proceeded on the assumption that a valid interpretation could be built on secondary writings whose authors had likewise failed to collect the evidence. If we accept Beard's own maxim, "no evidence, no history," and his own admission that the data had never been collected, the answer to whether he used historical method properly is self-evident.

Neither was Beard critical of the evidence which he did use. He was accused in 1913, and one might still suspect him, of using only that evidence which appeared to support his thesis. The amount of realty in the country compared with the personalty, the vote in New York, and the omission of the part of *The Federalist*, No. 10, which did not fit his thesis are only a few examples of the uncritical use of evidence to be found in the book. Sometimes he accepted secondary accounts at face value without checking them with the sources; at other times he allowed unfounded rumors and traditions to color his work.

Finally, the conclusions which he drew were not justified even by the kind of evidence which he used. If we accepted his evidence strictly at face value, it would still not add up to the fact that the Constitution was put over undemocratically in an undemocratic society by personalty. The citing of property qualifications does not prove that a mass of men were disfranchised. And if we accept his figures on property holdings, either we do not know what most of the delegates had in realty and personalty, or we know that realty outnumbered personalty three to one (eighteen to six). Simply showing that a man held public securities is not sufficient to prove that he acted only in terms of his public securities. If we ignore Beard's own generalizations and accept only his evidence, we have to conclude that most of the country, and that even the men who were directly concerned with the Constitution, and especially Washington, were large holders of realty.

Perhaps we can never be completely objective in history, but certainly we can be more objective than Beard was in this book. Naturally, the historian must always be aware of the biases, the subjectivity, the pitfalls that confront him, but this does not mean that he should not make an effort to overcome these obstacles. Whether Beard had his thesis before he had his evidence, as some have said, is a question that each reader must answer for himself. Certain it is that the evidence does not justify the thesis.

So instead of the Beard interpretation that the Constitution was put over undemocratically in an undemocratic society by personal property, the following fourteen paragraphs are offered as a possible interpretation of the Constitution and as suggestions for future research on that document.

1. The movement for the Constitution was originated and carried through by men who had long been important in both economic and political affairs in their respective states. Some of them owned personalty, more of them owned realty, and if their property was adversely affected by conditions under the Articles of Confederation, so also was the property of the bulk of the people in the country, middle-class farmers as well as town artisans.

2. The movement for the Constitution, like most important movements, was undoubtedly started by a small group of men. They were probably interested personally in the outcome of their labors, but the benefits which they expected were not confined to personal property or, for that matter, strictly to things economic. And if their own interests would be enhanced by a new government, similar interests of other men, whether agricultural or commercial, would also be enhanced.

3. Naturally there was no popular vote on the calling of the convention which drafted the Constitution. Election of delegates by state legislatures was the constitutional method under the Articles of Confederation, and had been the method long established in this country. Delegates to the Albany Congress, the Stamp Act Congress, the First Continental Congress, the Second Continental Congress, and subsequent congresses under the Articles were all elected by state legislatures, not by the people. Even the Articles of Confederation had been sanctioned by state legislatures, not by popular vote. This is not to say that the Constitutional Convention should not have been elected directly by the people, but only that such a procedure would have been unusual at the time. Some of the opponents of the Constitution later stressed, without avail, the fact that the Convention had not been directly elected. But at the time the Convention met, the people in general seemed to be about as much concerned over the fact that they had not elected the delegates as the people of this country are now concerned over the fact that they do not elect our delegates to the United Nations.

4. Present evidence seems to indicate that there were no "propertyless masses" who were excluded from the suffrage at the time. Most men were middle-class farmers who owned realty and were qualified voters, and, as the men in the Convention said, mechanics had always voted in the cities. Until credible evidence proves otherwise, we can assume that state legislatures were fairly representative at the time. We cannot condone the fact that a few men were probably disfranchised by prevailing property qualifications, but it makes a great deal of difference to an interpretation of the Constitution whether the disfranchised comprised 95 percent of the adult men or only 5 percent. Figures which give percentages of voters in terms of the entire population are misleading, since less than 20 percent of the people were adult men. And finally, the voting qualifications favored realty, not personalty.

5. If the members of the Convention were directly interested in the outcome of their work and expected to derive benefits from the establishment of the new system, so also did most of the people of the country. We have many statements to the effect that the people in general expected substantial benefits from the labors of the Convention.

6. The Constitution was not just an economic document, although economic factors were undoubtedly important. Since most of the people were middle class and had private property, practically everybody was interested in the protection of property. A constitution which did not protect property would have been rejected without any question, for the American people had fought the Revolution for the preservation of life, liberty, and property. Many people believed that the Constitution did not go far enough to protect property, and they wrote these views into the amendments to the Constitution. But property was not the only concern of those who wrote and ratified the Constitution, and we would be doing a grave injustice to the political sagacity of the Founding Fathers if we assumed that property or personal gain was their only motive.

7. Naturally the delegates recognized that protection of property was important under government, but they also recognized that personal rights were

equally important. In fact, persons and property were usually bracketed together as the chief objects of government protection.

8. If three-fourths of the adult males failed to vote on the election of delegates to ratifying conventions, this fact signified indifference, not disfranchisement. We must not confuse those who could *not* vote with those who *could* vote but failed to exercise their right. Many men at the time bewailed the fact that only a small portion of the voters ever exercised their prerogative. But this in itself should stand as evidence that the conflict over the Constitution was not very bitter, for if these people had felt strongly one way or the other, more of them would have voted.

    Even if we deny the evidence which I have presented and insist that American society was undemocratic in 1787, we must still accept the fact that the men who wrote the Constitution believed that they were writing it for a democratic society. They did not hide behind an iron curtain of secrecy and devise the kind of conservative government that they wanted without regard to the views and interests of "the people." More than anything else, they were aware that "the people" would have to ratify what they proposed, and that therefore any government which would be acceptable to the people must of necessity incorporate much of what was customary at the time. The men at Philadelphia were practical politicians, not political theorists. They recognized the multitude of different ideas and interests that had to be reconciled and compromised before a constitution would be acceptable. They were far too practical, and represented far too many clashing interests themselves, to fashion a government weighted in favor of personalty or to believe that the people would adopt such a government.

9. If the Constitution was ratified by a vote of only one-sixth of the adult men, that again demonstrates indifference and not disfranchisement. Of the one-fourth of the adult males who voted, nearly two-thirds favored the Constitution. Present evidence does not permit us to say what the popular vote was except as it was measured by the votes of the ratifying conventions.

10. Until we know what the popular vote was, we cannot say that it is questionable whether a majority of the voters in several states favored the Constitution. Too many delegates were sent uninstructed. Neither can we count the towns which did not send delegates on the side of those opposed to the Constitution. Both items would signify indifference rather than sharp conflict over ratification.

11. The ratifying conventions were elected for the specific purpose of adopting or rejecting the Constitution. The people in general had anywhere from several weeks to several months to decide the question. If they did not like the new government, or if they did not know whether they liked it, they could have voted *no* and there would have been no Constitution. Naturally the leaders in the ratifying conventions represented the same interests as the members of the Constitutional Convention—mainly realty and some personalty. But they also represented their constituents in these same interests, especially realty.

12. If the conflict over ratification had been between substantial personalty interests on the one hand and small farmers and debtors on the other, there

would not have been a constitution. The small farmers comprised such an overwhelming percentage of the voters that they could have rejected the new government without any trouble. Farmers and debtors are not synonymous terms and should not be confused as such. A town-by-town or county-by-county record of the vote would show clearly how the farmers voted.

13. The Constitution was created about as much by the whole people as any government could be which embraced a large area and depended on representation rather than on direct participation. It was also created in part by the states, for as the *Records* show, there was strong state sentiment at the time which had to be appeased by compromise. And it was created by compromising a whole host of interests throughout the country, without which compromises it could never have been adopted.

14. If the intellectual historians are correct, we cannot explain the Constitution without considering the psychological factors also. Men are motivated by what they believe as well as by what they have. Sometimes their actions can be explained on the basis of what they hope to have or hope that their children will have. Madison understood this fact when he said that the universal hope of acquiring property tended to dispose people to look favorably upon property. It is even possible that some men support a given economic system when they themselves have nothing to gain by it. So we would want to know what the people in 1787 thought of their class status. Did workers and small farmers believe that they were lower class, or did they, as many workers do now, consider themselves middle class? Were the common people trying to eliminate the Washingtons, Adamses, Hamiltons, and Pinckneys, or were they trying to join them?

As did Beard's fourteen conclusions, these fourteen suggestions really add up to two major propositions: the Constitution was adopted in a society which was fundamentally democratic, not undemocratic; and it was adopted by a people who were primarily middle-class property owners, especially farmers who owned realty, not just by the owners of personalty. At present these points seem to be justified by the evidence, but if better evidence in the future disproves or modifies them, we must accept that evidence and change our interpretation accordingly.

After this critical analysis, we should at least not begin future research on this period of American history with the illusion that the Beard thesis of the Constitution is valid. If historians insist on accepting the Beard thesis in spite of this analysis, however, they must do so with the full knowledge that their acceptance is founded on "an act of faith," not an analysis of historical method, and that they were indulging in a "noble dream," not history.

Internet Resources
Visit our website at http://www.mhhe.com/diclerico for links and resources relating to the Constitution.

Federalism

The Tenth Amendment to the U.S. Constitution states, "The powers not delegated to the United States by the Constitution, nor prohibited by it to the States, are reserved to the States respectively, or to the people." Although this brief amendment, containing just slightly more than twenty-five words, seems simple and uncomplicated, it has, in fact, constituted the basis for one of the more protracted debates in U.S. history—namely, the extent of the national government's powers versus the powers of the states.

Few critics of the contemporary political scene have been more vociferous in their criticism of national government power than have Douglas Seay and Wesley Smith of the Heritage Foundation, a Washington, D.C. think tank known for its anti-federal government, pro–states' rights views. In the first selection in this chapter, Seay and Smith present a litany of what they believe to be wrong with the current balance of power between the states and federal government—everything from the national government assuming powers not granted to it by the Constitution to the government forcing the states to do what the people of the states might not wish to do. Lamenting the erosion of state powers and the democratic process, as well as the heavy economic price paid as a result of the emergence of an all powerful national government, the authors propose several reforms to get at the "root causes" of what they perceive as today's imbalance of governmental powers. These suggested reforms go beyond simply creating a bit more balance in the federal system; they call for a radical shift in power away from Washington to the states and communities.

Writing in defense of the current relationship between the states and the federal government is Milton Esman, a professor of political science at Cornell University. Esman argues that, far from preempting the states, the national government has only acted to solve problems when it has been appropriate to do so; and the truth is that states are far from being subject to the will and pleasure of the federal government, and thus there is no great need to turn back the clock to an earlier time when the national government was not so prominent in our national affairs.

Fed Up with the Feds: Whatever Happened to the Federal System?

Douglas Seay and Wesley Smith

THE ISSUES

With frustrated Americans focusing their anger increasingly on Washington and gridlock, many political candidates have successfully run against Washington, appealing to voters to "throw the bums out" and replace them with individuals who are more honest and more devoted to the public welfare.

One result has been that ideas such as devolution and federalism, ignored for decades, are back in the forefront of public debate. Because Washington is seen as cumbersome, rigid, and distant from the people, Congress has attempted to give the states and local governments more autonomy and responsibility in areas such as welfare. The assumption is that this will result in greater experimentation, increased efficiency, and government that once again is closer to the people. However, although devolution in its many forms may produce benefits in selected programs, by itself it will not address the root cause of the many problems plaguing American society. . . . The fundamental problem is systemic: The Constitutional system established by the Framers has been largely dismantled, releasing government, especially the national government, from virtually all restraint. Unconstrained government inevitably has swept aside civil society, replacing it with political decisionmaking and bureaucratic administration unaccountable to the public. . . .

This has resulted in four dilemmas, all of which require action:

First, the central purpose of the Constitution—limiting the power of government—has been forgotten, and many of the mechanisms for enforcing those limits have been dismantled.

Douglas Seay was a policy analyst and program director from 1989 to 1997 at the Heritage Foundation, a government and public policy research organization in Washington, D.C. He currently is a staff member of the International Relations Committee of the U.S. House of Representatives. Wesley Smith also served as a policy analyst with the Heritage Foundation and currently is a partner in WaterDance Pictures, a film company engaged in the production of feature dramatic and documentary films. From Douglas Seay and Wesley R. Smith, "Federalism," in *Issues '96: The Candidate's Briefing Book,* edited by Stuart M. Butler and Kim R. Holmes (Washington, D.C.: The Heritage Foundation, 1996), pp. 411–436.

Second, the states—the key element in the American constitutional system—have been stripped of the ability to carry out their constitutional responsibility of checking and balancing the national government, and this has allowed Washington to assume an unlimited and unchallengeable role in the economy, in society, and in the lives of individuals.

Third, the resulting centralization of power in Washington and the unchecked expansion of its reach have undermined the institutions of civil society and thereby severely weakened the ability of the people to exercise self-government. Washington has replaced civil society with bureaucratic rulemaking and administration from above, and has made decisionmaking in all areas of public and private life more responsive to political factors and ideologies than to empirical results and the preferences of the citizenry. In addition, centralization has insulated decisionmaking from participation by the very people most directly affected by government programs.

Fourth, the federal judiciary has permitted, even mandated, an open-ended expansion of power by the national government, arrogating to itself the role of legislature of last resort and imposing a liberal agenda explicitly and repeatedly rejected by the electorate.

THE FACTS

What the Framers Intended

A fundamental assumption of the Framers of the Constitution was that the American people were and would continue to be largely self-governing, running their own affairs by means of the network of social relationships and voluntary organizations collectively known as civil society, such as families, communities, and churches. Government, especially local government controlled directly by the community, was seen as a necessary ally of civil society. But it was restricted to those limited functions which civil society could not easily perform for itself, such as defense, the police, and the coining of money. The purpose of government was to secure an environment within which free people would control their own affairs: in other words, an environment that makes possible the individual "pursuit of happiness." . . .

Trusting neither the written word of the Constitution nor self-restraint on the part of office-holders to enforce the necessary limits, the Framers devised a complex system of checks and balances in which various political actors were placed deliberately in permanent opposition to one another. This tension was intended to ensure that the energies and ambitions of the respective groups would be directed against one another, thereby protecting civil society from unwanted interference. The best known of these safeguards—the division of the national government into three competing branches: executive, legislative, and judicial—has proven both effective and durable despite two centuries of change.

The Central Role of Federalism

Even more essential to the intent of the Constitution were the several checks and balances between the national government and the states, and the division of power between them, a wholly new system which came to be called federalism. . . .

. . . The national and state governments were intended to constrain one another, not to work hand-in-glove or parcel out functions to that level of government which will perform them best. Thus, the new government was given the power to prevent the states from abusing their authority through such actions as erecting trade barriers against one another, and national legislation was given preeminence over state and local law in those limited areas reserved to the national government. In turn, the states were expected to constrain Washington, as they were regarded as the only effective means of doing so.

So crucial was the role of the states in limiting the national government's power that the Framers provided them with several safeguards, including:

- **A direct role** in the making of all laws and the appointment of all federal officials, including federal judges, through a Senate composed of members appointed by the states;
- **The ability to block** all constitutional amendments proposed by Congress and to bypass an out-of-touch national government altogether by means of a constitutional convention; and
- **A written guarantee** against Washington's assumption of additional powers in the form of the blunt and sweeping language of the Tenth Amendment, which reserved all powers not delegated to the national government by the Constitution either to the states or to the people.

How the Safeguards Were Dismantled

This carefully constructed system remained largely intact for over 100 years; but beginning in the early part of this century, the ability of the states to perform their constitutional role of limiting the national government has been progressively reduced to the point that it has been virtually eliminated.

The process was a lengthy and complex one, but its principal landmarks were:

- **The ratification in 1913 of the 16th and 17th Amendments,** which removed key restraints on the national government by giving it unlimited taxing authority and by mandating that Senators were to be elected by popular vote rather than selected by state legislatures. As a result, Washington secured the resources necessary for an open-ended expansion of its functions even as the states were removed from the making of national policy and eliminated as the principal bulwark against expansion by the national government.
- **The national emergencies of the Depression, World War II, and the Cold War,** which legitimized political forces arguing for greater power at the

national level to deal with domestic and international problems. The powers and functions assumed by Washington in times of emergency have remained long after their original justification has passed. In fact, many of the emergency powers of the 1930s were vastly expanded in the 1960s and 1970s in such programs as the Great Society and the War on Poverty, each of which further increased Washington's power by giving it an activist leading role in areas of the economy and society never before assumed by any level of government.

- **Beginning in 1937, the Supreme Court's abandonment of its traditional role of enforcing limits** laid out in the Constitution through a series of decisions that have removed virtually all constitutional restraints on the national government. The power of the national government to regulate interstate commerce, for example, has been interpreted as being virtually unlimited, extending to virtually every area of the economy and society; the Tenth Amendment, in effect, has been gutted.
- **Beginning in the 1950s, in pursuit of what its advocates have called a "judicial revolution,"** the Supreme Court's radical alteration of established interpretations of rights guaranteed by the Constitution, with some vastly expanded, others restricted, and still others simply invented. This judicial activism has transformed the Court into an unelected "super legislature," effectively unbound by any restraints.

Judicial Activism

Judicial activism now extends to all areas of public and private life because the Supreme Court and the federal judiciary have succeeded in granting themselves virtually unlimited power. Federal, state, and local laws, duly enacted by elected officials, have been struck down; state and local government functions such as schools and prisons have been taken over by the federal courts and subjected to their increasingly minute direction; and state constitutions have been rewritten at will. Referenda passed with overwhelming public support are annulled. The courts even order that taxes be imposed directly on populations deemed incompetent to govern themselves.

The courts have engaged in highly subjective and selective interpretations of the Constitution, creating rights by locating them in previously unnoticed "penumbras" and "invisible radiations" even as they ignore other, clearly expressed constitutional provisions. . . .

- **The First Amendment's guarantee of "speech"** has been interpreted to include aggressive panhandling, while the provision that Congress "shall make no law respecting an establishment of religion" has been interpreted to mean that the Ten Commandments may not be used in classrooms but that prisoners demanding pornography must be accommodated.[1]
- **The Second Amendment** is regularly circumscribed with the permission of the federal courts despite the fact that it states explicitly that "the right of the people to keep and bear Arms, shall not be infringed."

- **The language of the Tenth Amendment,** which states with magnificent clarity that "the powers not delegated to the United States by the Constitution . . . are reserved to the States respectively, or to the people," has been dismissed as a mere "truism" with no real application to the national government's authority.

In short, unelected, unrepresentative, and ideologically driven courts have dispensed with democratic choice and constitutional procedure to impose sweeping changes in the law. Intended as a clear and agreed-upon set of rules, the Constitution has become a document subject to the most arbitrary revision by the federal courts. . . .

THE COST OF RUNAWAY NATIONAL GOVERNMENT

The central purpose of the Constitution was to ensure that government remained limited, but the system established to police those limits has been undone. As a direct result:

- Government has expanded its reach into all areas of American life;
- All major governmental decisionmaking has been centralized in Washington; and
- A self-governing society has been replaced by distant, bureaucratic, and all-powerful government.

Advocates of the concentration of power in Washington usually have pointed to some pressing national need for action. However, the costs associated with these changes have rarely been given more than passing consideration. The centralization of power in the hands of the national government has *exacted a heavy economic price, weakened the democratic process,* and *helped to undermine civil society.*

I. The High Cost to Taxpayers

Calculating the economic costs stemming from the demise of federalism and the expansion of the national government is difficult, if only because of the enormity of the task. These costs include reduced economic growth for the nation as a whole through heavy taxation, burdensome regulation of businesses, and the skewed investment of resources.

- As programs have expanded to cover all areas of national life, the federal budget has grown commensurately, both in terms of taxpayer dollars and as a percentage of the national economy. In 1934, the national government accounted for 10 percent of gross domestic product (GDP). In 1948, it was still only 12 percent. By 1960, however, it had ballooned to 18 percent, and by 1994, to 22 percent.
- The tax burden also has necessarily expanded. In 1914, the first year of the federal income tax, Americans making from $4,000 to $20,000 were taxed 1 percent of their incomes. The rate gradually increased to 7 percent for

Americans making over $500,000. Because those making over $4,000 in 1914 accounted for less than 1 percent of the population, the average family paid no income tax. Even by 1950, following the expansion of the national government during and after the New Deal, the average American family with two children paid only 3 percent of its income to the federal government. In 1994, federal taxes accounted for 24 percent of a typical family's income.

- Though taxation has increased dramatically since World War II, spending has grown even faster. A 1991 study prepared for the Joint Economic Committee found that for every $1 increase in taxes since the end of World War II, expenditures have grown $1.59. The national debt now stands at $4.9 trillion, representing more than $18,500 for every man, woman, and child in the country—an obligation that will be paid by every individual and family through higher taxes and lower living standards. . . .

Overregulation

An enormous regulatory bureaucracy has been created in Washington to oversee every area of public and private life. Although the public manifests high levels of support for many regulatory objectives, such as clean air and water, access for the disabled, and other social goals, one reason for this popularity is that these goals are commonly portrayed as having little or no economic cost, at least for the average citizen. The reach and inflexibility of the regulatory agencies lead to frequent absurdities.

- The typical American business must sort through and fill out 100 forms and booklets of information on how to comply with federal regulations.
- "A Louisiana family applied for permits to build a crawfish pond on eighty acres of land it owned. The EPA denied permission stating 'High quality habitats such as these provide food, shelter, nesting and spawning areas to a wide variety of game and non-game fish . . . including the red swamp crawfish.' "[2]
- "Environmental and other regulations can increase start-up costs for a single dry cleaner as much as $138,000."[3]
- An Orange County development expected to inject $500 million into the . . . local economy was halted when the Fish and Wildlife Service placed the Pacific Pocket Mouse on the endangered species list. Before continuing the project, regulators will have to be convinced development will not harm the mouse population.[4]
- The state of Arizona must regulate and monitor the Salt River to comply with fishing and swimming standards set by the Clean Water Act of 1977, even though the river is dry 50 weeks of the year.
- In 1991, a federal district judge found San Diego was not in compliance with certain Clean Water Act regulations dealing with pretreatment of sewage by industrial users and sewage spills in the collection system. In-

stead of confining himself to ordering the city to rectify the noncompliance, the judge mandated that the city require the public at large to install smaller toilets and shower heads.[5]

Unfunded Mandates on the States

Unfunded federal mandates on state and local governments are particularly burdensome. The costs are substantial and fall not just on state and local governments, but also on private businesses and individuals.

Federal mandates are requirements laid down by Washington, through legislation, executive regulation or order, or judicial fiat, which force state and local governments to undertake certain programs or provide certain services at their own cost.

- The National Conference of State Legislatures (NCSL) has identified 192 unfunded mandates on the states, including Medicaid, regulations governing the use of underground storage tanks, the Clean Water Act, the Clean Air Act, the Resource Conservation and Recovery Act, the Safe Drinking Water Act, requirements to remove lead paint and asbestos from schools and other areas, the Endangered Species Act, the Americans with Disabilities Act, and the Fair Labor Standards Act, to name only a few.
- The U.S. Conference of Mayors and Price Waterhouse estimate the 1994–1998 cost of these mandates (excluding Medicaid) on 314 cities at $54 billion, or the equivalent of 11.7 percent of all local taxes.[6]
- The EPA estimates that environmental mandates cost state and local governments $30 billion to $40 billion annually. Other studies have produced much higher numbers. The city of Columbus, Ohio, estimates that it will spend $1.3 billion from 1991 to 2001 to comply with EPA regulations; a companion study estimates that the annual cost of federal mandates to each household in Columbus will be $856 by the year 2000.[7]
- State and local governments will spend an estimated $137 billion to ensure safe drinking water under the Clean Water Act, according to the EPA.[8]
- In 1991, the National School Board surveyed 670 school systems and revealed that the costs of complying with the Asbestos Hazard Emergency Response Act of 1986 had totaled $6 billion in the five years since the Act was passed. Estimates of the cost of full compliance for all schools reach $200 billion. These costs are mandated in spite of mounting evidence that asbestos removal programs actually may increase the exposure of children to asbestos.
- Even though immigration is solely the responsibility of the national government, extensive judicial and legislative mandates require states and local governments to provide services to illegal immigrants. The current data are inconclusive on whether illegal immigrants are a drain or benefit to the economy as a whole, but federal mandates that require the states to provide education, health services, and other services to illegal aliens still cost the states billions each year. . . .

II. The High Cost to Democracy

More difficult to calculate, but nevertheless far-reaching, are the high costs to democracy that stem from the demise of federalism. An oft-repeated description of the American system of government is that it is a "government of laws, not of men," meaning that the rules which govern society are openly formulated, apply equally to all, and are reliably stable over time. Laws are made by citizens and their elected representatives; they are not supposed to be subject to the whims of individuals.

However, this characterization is no longer accurate. Even as federal power over the economy, society, and all facets of public policy has grown, the concentration of decisionmaking in Washington has radically reduced the ability of the public to affect it. Whereas the American people once were described routinely as self-governing and self-reliant, it is now virtually impossible for individuals or communities to influence the decisions which directly affect them. Distant rule-making bureaucracies are immune from local pressure; Congress is overrun with powerful and well-heeled interest groups; and enormous coalitions of citizens are required to get even rudimentary attention from Washington. . . .

The Untethered Judiciary

Even if elected officials could be made more responsive to the public's preferences, however, they would remain subject to the unelected judges of the federal courts. The Supreme Court and the federal judiciary as a whole have arrogated to themselves a dominant role in every public and private institution in society. Federal judges have taken charge of wide areas of state and local jurisdiction and imposed on them their own dictates, from which there is little appeal. Individual judges overturn and rewrite laws, suspend whole sections of state constitutions, impose detailed mandates, order actions by officials at all levels, and even mandate the imposition of taxes on populations which refuse to vote for them.

- Thirty-nine states and 300 of the nation's largest jails operate under some form of federal court direction. Federal court orders cover the administration of entire prison systems in nine states down to such details as supervising magazine subscription lists, mandating the wattage of light bulbs, and specifying the number of basketballs, Ping-Pong tables, and pianos to be kept on hand.
- In November 1995, a federal court struck down California's Proposition 187, which limited the rights of illegal immigrants to free health, welfare, and education benefits at the state's expense and which had been passed in November 1994 with overwhelming public support. The judge ruled that the state has no right to limit benefits for illegal immigrants; nor can it even question applicants about their immigration status.
- Also in November 1995, a federal judge in New York City blocked a fare increase by the New York Transit Authority, saying that the increase violated the U.S. Civil Rights Act because it discriminated against ethnic minorities who use the subway system more heavily than the rest of the public.

III. The High Costs to Civil Society

Of all the costs produced by the demise of federalism, the greatest have been those associated with the breakdown of civil society: the individuals, families, communities, and voluntary organizations and institutions which together enable individuals to control the environment in which they, their families, and their communities live and operate.

For the Framers, the purpose of government was to establish and secure the general environment within which civil society could operate essentially unmolested. Within this environment, the array of social institutions would regulate the public aspects of the community and intrude in the lives of individuals and families as little as possible. Government, especially local government controlled by the adult citizenry, was essential to maintaining this order, but only if its power was limited to narrow purposes. It was well understood that the more distant the government, the less control the citizens would have over its actions, and thus the more damage it could do.

Once the national government had freed itself from its constitutional restraints, however, its rapid expansion inevitably undermined civil society, because the purpose of expanded government is to substitute itself for civil society. The national government, in centralizing power, inevitably has taken control away from citizens and communities and replaced it with political decisionmaking and bureaucratic administration. It also has forcibly replaced civil society's homegrown workings with its own political and bureaucratic vision of how society should be structured and run, and with devastating costs. Unconstrained government and civil society cannot coexist; their respective resources are too unequal to permit competition. When government expands, society must retreat.

The result has been a broad decline in civilized life, especially in the nation's cities where government activism has been greatest. Among the results: vastly increased crime and violence, a breakdown of public order, a decline in community life, erosion of the family, the rise of illegitimacy, and the pervasive mediocrity of public education, among other ills.

Social scientists profess bafflement at the emergence and continuation of these developments. Among the most common explanations: America is an inherently violent society, there has been a "war on the poor" stemming from hard-hearted budget cutters, or endemic racism prevents progress. The true source, however, can be located directly in the engineered demise of civil society and its replacement by the federal government. Individuals, families, and communities have been stripped of the ability to control either their environment or the behavior of individuals within it.

WHAT TO DO

Correcting the many problems confronting American society will involve more than isolated reforms; a lasting solution will require dealing with their root causes, especially the federal government's crushing impact on civil society. This means more than merely resurrecting the past. Too much has changed to permit a simple repeal of the many constitutional innovations of the preceding decades, and powerful and well-entrenched groups with economic, political, and ideological interests at stake are certain to resist any change which diminishes the power of Washington to reward them from the public treasury and impose their agendas on the rest of the country. Instead, new approaches must be developed that draw on the lessons learned in this century about Washington's ability to free itself, Houdini-like, from almost any constraint.

1. Devolve Power to the States by Returning Taxes, Not Just Programs

. . . Under current plans, the principal funding for programs devolved to the states will continue to be through block grants from Washington. Although the states gain flexibility, this formula undermines accountability because the federal government collects the money but state and local governments spend it. As a result, the public is less able to connect the collection of taxes with the provision of services, and neither level of government has sufficient incentive to ensure that the money is spent wisely and frugally. A far better approach would be for Washington to bow out of the picture entirely and return the money to the people in the form of a tax cut. The states could collect the taxes themselves—and thereby assure a direct connection between taxes and services—or allow individuals to retain the money for their own use. . . .

2. Hold a Constitutional Convention on Federalism

Calling a convention to propose amendments to the Constitution is the route most favored by those who seek a quick and comprehensive solution to the problem of Washington's overreaching. Two-thirds of the state legislatures may call a constitutional convention by petitioning Congress to do so, a provision the Framers included both to deny Congress a monopoly on proposing amendments and to prevent it from insulating itself from the public will.

In the two centuries since the Constitution's adoption, there have been several efforts to call a convention. The most notable attempts in recent decades include an effort in the 1960s to overturn the Supreme Court's revision of state constitutions regarding the structure of state legislatures and several efforts concerning a balanced budget amendment, the most successful of which reached 32 states by 1983.

The principal reason these and other efforts have not succeeded is fear that a "runaway" convention might lead to an extensive rewriting of the Constitution. But opponents generally do not take into account the fact that any amendment proposed by a convention is exactly that: merely a proposal. To become part of the Constitution, it must be ratified by the same three-fourths of the state legislatures required for the approval of any amendment put forth by Congress. . . .

3. Revive the Tenth Amendment

Efforts to revive the Tenth Amendment occupy a special place in the movement to restore federalism. The Tenth Amendment is the "federalism amendment," a written contractual guarantee against the expansion of federal power. It has not performed as intended because the political and other mechanisms designed to make it effective have been removed and because the Supreme Court has been allowed to render it null and void. . . .

A grass-roots movement to revive the Tenth Amendment has been gathering strength. Several state legislatures have passed resolutions stating their view that the Amendment remains fully in effect, with several going further to demand that the federal government abide by its provisions. However, this has occurred in a largely uncoordinated and low-key manner, and little political pressure has been brought to bear on Washington.

4. Implement Federalism Legislation

. . . Unwilling to part with its own money, Congress often has resorted to requiring state and local governments to pay for programs that Washington enacts and for which it takes the credit. Faced with a growing revolt in the states because of the unsustainable burden these mandates impose on state budgets, Congress in 1994 passed the Unfunded Mandates Act, advertised as largely solving the problem. However, the scope of the Act is very limited, covering only new mandates while leaving the truly burdensome existing ones in place. More important, the legislation puts no real restraints on Congress at all, as it requires Congress merely to label an unfunded mandate as such before enactment. . . .

Among the actions the next Congress should take:

- **Restore constitutional authority**. At present, Congress may legislate on virtually any subject it chooses, regardless of the Constitution's actual provisions. Legislation sponsored by Senator Spencer Abraham (R-MI) and Representative John Shadegg (R-AZ) seeks to restrict this unlimited power by requiring that each bill specifically cite Congress's constitutional authority to act in the affected area, including grants of authority to the executive branch. . . .
- **Curb the federal judiciary.** Article III of the Constitution gives Congress virtually unlimited power to regulate the federal judiciary through legislation; Congress should use this power to limit the abuses of the federal courts. Areas of possible congressional action include, among others, limiting the ability of federal courts to force state and local governments into burdensome and open-ended consent decrees; restricting the ability of the federal courts to take over state and local administrative functions for decades at a time; directing that the measures federal courts impose to rectify problems at the state and local levels be appropriate to the specific situation; limiting the federal courts' appellate review power in order to help restore the autonomy of the individual states as originally guaranteed by the Constitution; and prohibiting courts from ordering the imposition of taxes.

5. Propose Constitutional Amendments through Congress

Since it is unlikely that a constitutional convention will be called within the next few years, members of Congress should propose several amendments that can be presented to the states for debate and ratification. The following are among the measures needed to restore a balance between the state and federal governments:

- **A balanced budget amendment.** The last proposal for a balanced budget amendment passed the House but failed by one vote to achieve the necessary two-thirds majority in the Senate. Passage of such an amendment must remain one of the highest priorities for the 104th Congress or its successors.
- **A "states' veto" amendment.** There are several versions of amendments which would allow a majority of the state legislatures to veto or recommit federal legislation. . . .
- **An amendment to allow states to propose amendments.** Under the amending formulas of Article V, the states may not propose constitutional amendments except by calling a constitutional convention. Since there are a host of perceived and real dangers in calling such a convention, this route has proven unusable, and Congress retains its monopoly on proposing amendments to the Constitution. However, amending Article V to allow the states to propose amendments without calling a convention, but subject to a congressional veto on such amendments, could overcome this obstacle. . . .

The domination of the national government by the states under the Articles of Confederation produced such chaos that the Framers of the Constitution sought to permanently redress the balance. As a result, the Constitution lists several powers reserved to the national government and makes its laws superior to those of the states in these areas. That grant of power, however, is strictly limited. The Constitution specifies procedures for amending the document to alter that list should a sufficient majority of the country desire it, but it does not sanction federal action simply because it may be efficient or expedient. Under the system established by the Founders, state governments and the national government were to have distinct and limited powers in order to serve as a check on one another.

The presumption throughout much of this century, however, has been that the national government is progressive and the states regressive, and therefore that progress requires a centralization of power in Washington. Once achieved, however, the result has been not only to shift most decisionmaking to the federal government, but to make possible the vast expansion of government throughout every area of society, with decidedly negative results. Whatever the past failings of the states, they pale in comparison with those of the federal government. Federalism is not based on the assumption that one level of government is necessarily better than another; instead, it holds that limited, constitutional government is the goal and that the different levels are needed to restrain one another.

NOTES

1. See Dirk Johnson, "In Prison, Pornography Becomes a Rights Issue," *The New York Times,* February 6, 1989, p. A12: Ronald Brownstein, "Taming the Mean Streets," *The Los Angeles Times,* May 4, 1994, p. A1.
2. James Bovard, *Lost Rights: The Destruction of American Liberty* (New York: St. Martins Press, 1994), p. 35.
3. Representative John Mica (R-FL), in Representative Tom DeLay, "Reducing the Regulatory Maze," *Congressional Record,* May 12, 1994, p. H3336.
4. See Len Hall, "Dana Point Approves Headlands Resort Plan: More Hurdles to $500-Million Bluff Development Remain," *The Los Angeles Times,* April 6, 1994, p. A1.
5. *United States v. City of San Diego,* 1991 U.S. Dist. LEXIS 5429 (S.D. Ca. April 17, 1991).
6. Robert S. Stein, "Decentralizing American Government: People, Politicians Seek Power Closer to Home," *Investors Business Daily,* November 21, 1994, p. A1.
7. "Environmental Legislation: The Increasing Costs of Regulatory Compliance to the City of Columbus," *Report of the Environmental Law Review Committee,* City of Columbus, Ohio, May 13, 1991.
8. National Governors Association, "Unfunded Federal Mandates: The Cost for States," *Backgrounder,* October 18, 1993, p. 5.

Government Works:

Why Americans Need the Feds

Milton J. Esman

Despite rightist rhetoric that ambitious federal politicians and bureaucrats, prompted by "interest groups," have, since the era of the New Deal, reached out through taxation, regulation, and spending to usurp activities from the states or markets, the very opposite has been the case. The federal government has assumed functions only when states and the private sector have proved unable or unwilling to undertake them. Neither party has, during this century, challenged a fundamental premise of American economic culture: that the production and distribution of marketable goods and services should be the province of private enterprise. Even as security sensitive a field as nuclear energy and the actual manufacturing of nuclear weapons have been entrusted from the outset, beginning with the Truman administration, to private enterprise.

The bicameral structure of Congress, the lengthy committee hearings, and the public debate that precedes every new initiative guarantee that new responsibilities will be undertaken by federal authority only when other possibilities are unavailable. The federal government took over the operation of the eastern freight and passenger rail services (Conrail and Amtrak) only after their private owners had abandoned these essential services. The federal role in environmental regulation became inevitable as citizen pressures impressed the issue of air and water pollution on the public agenda, while corporate and local government polluters declined to limit their emissions voluntarily and the fifty state governments proved unable or unwilling to cope with a problem that had become regional and national in scale.

* * *

FEDERALISM FOR THE TWENTY-FIRST CENTURY

The American state is organized as a federal structure. Functions that are necessary to maintain the United States as an integrated security, political, economic,

Milton J. Esman is John S. Knight Professor Emeritus of International Studies at Cornell University. From Milton J. Esman, *Government Works: Why Americans Need the Feds*. (Ithaca and London: Cornell University Press, 2000), pp. 62–63, 93–99. Notes have been changed to correspond with edited text.

and cultural community are assigned to the federal government; residual activities, including those that are distinctively regional and local, are reserved for the states and their local subdivisions. The boundaries between federal and state powers are deliberately flexible and ambiguous, permitting adjustments to changing circumstances and needs. During periods of crisis—wars, economic depressions, and natural disasters—federal powers expand to cope with national emergencies. As the economy has become increasingly integrated and the society has become bound by a common culture, as economic, environmental, informational, and social relationships have become national and even transnational in scope, new functions have been assumed by the federal government, usually in default of the ability of states and localities to deal with them effectively. Thus, during the twentieth century, as the United States has evolved into a more perfect union and assumed a larger role in international affairs, the scale of federal activities has expanded greatly.

It is a mistake, however, to assume a zero-sum relationship between federal and state authority. To the contrary, as federal activities have expanded, so have those of state and local governments. Throughout the twentieth century the states have maintained unchallenged control over a vast array of responsibilities that affect the daily lives of their residents. These include the bulk of civil, criminal, and domestic relations law; most phases of law enforcement; elementary and secondary education; most roads, water supply systems, and other public works; regulation of and assistance to all units of local government, including cities; social services; and state police powers, which include the protection of public health, safety, welfare, and morals. The size and scope of state governments have expanded in tandem with those of the federal government. Many functions are shared, financially and administratively, in dense networks involving Washington, the states, local authorities, and often private enterprise in what has been termed by many scholars "twentieth-century cooperative federalism."[1] There is no danger that state governments are about to wither away or that they are being hobbled by federal action.

Economic integration, population growth, technological complexity, and urbanization have imposed greater demands on state governments as well. Since the end of the conservative Eisenhower administration in 1960, federal civilian employment has grown by 20 percent. State and local government employment during these same years has expanded by 160 percent. Federal expenditures have increased by 317 percent, mainly for Medicare, Social Security, defense, and debt servicing, while state and local expenditures together have grown by 341 percent. State and local governments are more active and vigorous than at any time in their history; contrary to rightist jeremiads, their powers have not been usurped, nor have they withered away, nor have they been reduced to mere administrative agents of Washington.

Much cant is abroad in today's public discourse about the remoteness of Congress and federal administrators ("inside the Beltway") from the diverse needs and concerns of the American public and the much greater understanding, sympathy, competence, and accountability of state governments. Little evidence is ever submitted to confirm this populist maxim, and it deserves to be treated with skepticism as a theme of rightist propaganda. The notion that California's state government enjoys an intimate relationship with its 36 million citizens or Texas with its 20 million, different in kind from their citizens' relationships with, say, the U.S. Postal Service, Social Security system, FBI, veterans hospitals, or park service, is far from self-evident.[2] More than 90 percent of federal employees live and work outside the Washington area in the fifty states. . . .

The needs and interests of the various states, which are often at odds with one another, are articulated and negotiated by vigorous lobbying in the processes of congressional deliberation and administrative implementation and by day-to-day interstate and federal-state exchanges among professional colleagues. Far from being passive or helpless by-standers, state governments are active participants in both the legislative and administrative phases of their relationships with the federal government. The notion that federal politicians and bureaucrats have ridden roughshod over the states, reaching out and grabbing functions that are properly within the purview of states and localities is a myth hallowed by rightist ideology and rhetoric. Most such functions have been assumed by Washington after considerable hesitation and open hearings in which members of the federal House and Senate, all with local roots and subject to local pressures, decide that the federal government is the proper locus for the effective management of that particular program.

Progressives are committed to maintaining a sound and vigorous balance between federal and state powers and between state and local government. The federal government must not encroach on legitimate state authority, nor should it be stripped of its constitutional responsibilities in the name of states' rights, including its powers to "raise and collect taxes to provide for the common defense and promote the general welfare" and to regulate interstate commerce. Any fair reading of American history demonstrates the abuses and the retrograde practices that have been associated with the doctrine of states' rights, from slavery to the century-long denial of civil rights and constitutional protections of African-American citizens, from repressing labor unions and applying subhuman welfare standards, to gerrymandering legislative seats in violation of the one person one vote principle, and tolerating grossly unequal educational facilities for children from affluent and low-income districts. Many of the landmark victories scored by progressives and their allies for expanded civil rights and social welfare have been bitterly resisted in the name of states' rights.

It is no surprise that the present generation of rightist leaders has rediscovered and attempted to rehabilitate the tattered doctrine of states' rights as a weapon in their ideological crusade for minimal government. During the 1980s President Reagan succeeded in decentralizing a number of federal programs by eliminating federal standards for grants-in-aid to the states and expanding the discretion of state agencies through the device of block grants.[3] Several programs were eliminated entirely, leaving the states with the option of abandoning the programs or financing them from their own resources. The consequent reduction in state services is compatible with the rightist commitment to laissez-faire, low and regressive taxes, minimal regulation, and a social Darwinist morality.

The current enthusiasm for states' rights is manifested in pressures for "devolution" of federal programs, from welfare, housing, and health to environment, labor standards, and civil rights, from the federal to state governments on a much larger scale than those attempted by President Reagan. As with the 1996 welfare reform, reduced federal funds are allocated through block grants to the states to administer under much laxer federal standards. Though states may supplement these funds to improve services, the expectation is that few will do so, resulting thereby in a net reduction of government services and regulation in all activities for which Republicans successfully implement their strategy of devolution. Progressives readily agree that some activities undertaken by Washington, for example, vocational education and the promotion of local economic development, might be transferred to state governments because they are local in scope and the states are competent to deal with them. But these transfers should be deliberated on a case by case basis, not as a mindless, wholesale process. The claim that devolution will increase administrative efficiency is unpersuasive, since there is no evidence that fifty sets of state bureaucracies, individually or collectively, are administratively more competent than the agencies of the federal government.

The diffusion of political power from the federal government to the fifty states, without a concomitant diffusion of economic power, results in the direct transfer of power to giant corporations. The 1990s have witnessed a frenzied rush of mergers among financial and industrial firms, leading to an unprecedented concentration of economic power, with diminishing market competition. The scale of these combinations precludes any serious efforts of regulation by state governments. To the extent the federal government yields functions to the states, it sacrifices the only countervailing power that might protect the public against the abuses of economic concentration.

Republicans have dusted off the Tenth Amendment to the Constitution, which reserves to the states and the people those powers not conferred on the federal government. Since the time of Chief Justice John Marshall (1800–1835), the courts have held that in addition to those powers specifically mentioned in Article I, other powers can reasonably be implied (*McCullough v. Maryland*, 4 Wheat 316–1819). In the exercise of these powers, the federal government cannot be constrained by the reserve clause of the Tenth Amendment (*U.S. v. Jones and Laughlin*, 300 U.S. 1, 1937). Congressional Republicans, with help from a Supreme Court dominated by Reagan and Bush appointees, are attempting to reverse this principle, in pursuit of their ideology of minimal government.

Yet, despite their solicitude for the Tenth Amendment, congressional Republicans attempted in 1995 to shift jurisdiction in tort liability cases from state courts, where it has resided since the birth of the Republic, to the federal judiciary. This occurred at the same time that Republicans were demonizing the federal government and glorifying the states, proclaiming their intention to devolve numerous functions. It was promoted in deference to their corporate constituency, which has objected to large awards granted by juries to plaintiffs in product liability suits in state courts, expecting that the Republican Congress would place limits on the amounts that plaintiffs could claim in such cases once jurisdiction had been transferred. When their agenda requires it and the interests of influential supporters dictate, contemporary rightists seem quite willing to enhance federal powers—to practice devolution in reverse! (Congressional Democrats and President Clinton blocked the enactment of this initiative.)

The Republican right believes that in promoting devolution they are responding to popular sentiment.[4] This can be understood both as an element of American political culture and as the fruits of a half century of concentrated anti-federal government propaganda and bureaucrat bashing. It is perhaps for this reason that neither Democratic politicians nor progressive opinion leaders have found it expedient to take a principled position against the drive for devolution, including stripping the federal government of functions it has performed for many decades. Federal-state relations are a dynamic process, reflecting shifting political forces and changing perceptions about the needs of American society. In the absence of national emergencies, wars, or economic depressions, there are strong pressures promoted mainly in business circles to cut taxes, reduce the regulatory activities of the federal government, and transfer functions to the states. The post–Cold War decade of the 1990s has been such an era. The role of progressives during such periods is to remind attentive publics of emergent national needs that cannot be met by unregulated markets or by the uncoordinated efforts of fifty state governments. . . .

Federalism in the United States remains very much alive and well, dynamic and flourishing. There have been some abuses by Congress in imposing financial obligations (unfunded mandates) on the states when the latter are called upon to implement federal legislation, including health and safety standards for workers, environmental practices, and civil rights laws. The Republican Congress has, however, brought this process to an abrupt halt.[5] The presumption generally applied in the past has been that functions that can be better handled by the states should remain in their hands. Beginning in the 1930s, the courts have ruled that the reserve powers of the states under the Tenth Amendment cannot limit the federal government in the exercise of its constitutional powers, including its power to spend federal tax dollars to "provide for the common defense and general welfare" (Article I, section 8); Congress and the president are the judges of what the general welfare requires. In the exercise of its powers Congress can determine that an activity should be directly administered by the federal government (e.g., Social Security), by the states under federal standards (e.g., unemployment compensation), or by the states with joint funding by the federal government and the states (e.g., Medicaid). The number of possible patterns is infinite, subject to political and administrative feasibility and bargaining.

Under Chief Justice William Rehnquist, the current Supreme Court, the majority of whose members were selected on ideological grounds by recent Republican presidents, is increasingly employing the federal judiciary to circumscribe the implied powers of Congress and to reassert the autonomy of state governments.[6] A major target of rightist think tanks are conservatively oriented young lawyers, several of whom have already been appointed to federal judgeships and are available for promotion to the Supreme Court. The election of a Republican president in 2000 would almost certainly result in capture of the highest court by jurists determined to cut back the role of the federal government and expand the powers of the states. This could have crippling long-term effects on the ability of progressives to enact their legislative program.

With the populist revival of states' rights, progressives should bear in mind and remind the public that, as its preamble proclaims, the Constitution of the United States was ordained and established by "we, the people of the United States," not by the state governments, and that among the objectives of this historic project were to "form a more perfect union" and "to promote the general welfare." Contrary to the anti-federalists of the 1780s, who vainly opposed the constitutional project in their time and whose thinking inspires the Republican right two centuries later, the government of the United States is not a confederal union of fifty sovereignties; that issue was decided by the Civil War.[7]

NOTES

1. On cooperative federalism, see David B. Walker, *Toward a Functioning Federalism* (Cambridge, Mass.: Winthrop Publishers, 1981). See also Morton Grodzins, *The American System: A New View of the Government of the United States* (Chicago: Rand-McNally, 1966). Steuerle et al. briefly outlines a pattern for allocating functions between the federal and state governments (177–81).
2. For example, labor union members in South Carolina and Alabama, Mexican Americans in California, and African Americans in Texas may consider their interests better served by the federal government than by their state governments.
3. Richard S. Williamson, *Reagan's Federalism: His Efforts to Decentralize Government* (Lanham, Md.: University Press of America, 1990).
4. Surveys conducted in 1995 and 1997 by Peter Hart and Robert Teeter for the Council for Excellence in Government, Washington, D.C. revealed a consistent pattern of greater confidence in local and state rather than the federal government. However, "Americans are optimistic that government could be more effective and work better for them, but at present is not living up to their expectations."
5. The Unfunded Mandates Reform Act of 1995 (PL No. 104–4).

6. For example, *United States v. Lopez*, 115 S CT 1624, 1995.
7. Herbert Storing, *What the Anti-Federalists Were For* (Chicago: University of Chicago Press, 1981).

Internet Resources
Visit our website at http://www.mhhe.com/diclerico for links and resources relating to Federalism.

chapter 4

Public Opinion

At a time when a substantial number of Americans see government as increasingly re-mote and excessively influenced by organized interests, it is not surprising that "re-formers" are seeking new ways to reconnect the American people to their government. Some reformers have turned to new technology to help provide that connection. Com-puter enthusiasts, for example, foresee the use of the Internet as a means to energize cit-izens, to get them to vote, and to get them to express their opinions on a whole range of issues. Thus, in the year 2000, candidates for president communicated directly with voters via the Internet, and Democratic primary elections in Arizona were held on-line. If this trend continues, voting on policy issues will no doubt be on-line, and the poten-tial for the Internet to provide citizens with information on a whole array of topics will be virtually unlimited.

The two selections that follow present contrasting arguments on the potential for us-ing the new computer technology to improve the public discourse and government decision-making. In the first selection, political consultant Dick Morris sees the Internet as revolutionizing politics. An unabashed advocate of the Internet, Morris views the technology of cyberspace as a means to energize the electorate and to connect citizens to their government in a way not possible with any other medium. Indeed, in his judgment politics via the Internet is about as close as one can get to direct democracy, literally al-lowing millions of Americans to share their opinions one-on-one with representatives and with each other. In the second selection, two Washington, D.C., commentators, Norman Ornstein and Amy Schenkenberg Mitchell, raise very serious questions about the new technology and the role the public should play in our representative system of govern-ment. Ornstein and Schenkenberg ask, will "cyberdemocracy" improve our system of rep-resentation? Will voters take seriously their responsibilities in this new system of direct participation? Moreover, what controls, if any, will be placed on these new systems? And, most importantly, do we really want a sometimes disinterested and ill-formed public to exert that much control over policy making? These are profound questions that once again cause us to reflect on the proper role of citizens in our still evolving democracy.

Vox Populi in Cyberspace
Dick Morris

Thomas Jefferson would have loved to see the Internet. His utopian vision of a democracy based on town meetings and direct popular participation is about to become a reality. In the era of the Fifth Estate, the massive, uncontrolled, and unregulated interaction of tens of millions of people will be the central political reality. Ideas, opinions, viewpoints, and perspectives will race back and forth over the Internet instantly and continuously, weaving together to create new national fabric of democracy.

Input from a multiplicity of sources will make it impossible for any organization or agency to control the flow of information or the shaping of opinion. As Matt Drudge, the Internet investigative reporter, puts it, "Everybody will be a publisher, disseminating his views to all who choose to log on to read them." News organizations and opinion leaders will spring up all over in a wonderfully chaotic and anarchic freedom. Limitations imposed by capital, paper, and ink, or the unavailability of bands and frequencies, will no longer screen out the opinions of the less connected and less powerful.

Only a few years ago, the voting records of our elected officials were inaccessible, the identities of large campaign donors were obscured, and the expenditures by government and by campaigns were concealed by layers of bureaucracy. Only by joining one of the few public interest organizations, such as Public Interest Research Group (PIRG) or Common Cause, could we find some of this data. Even then, it was slow to reach us through monthly newsletters, annual reports, or pre-election mailings. All of that is in the past. Now we are able to get instantaneous and comprehensive reports of the activities of political figures. Through a wide array of documents placed on the Internet by organizations, individuals, and the press, we are inundated with the tools of effective citizenship.

The incredible speed and interactivity of the Internet will inevitably return our country to a de facto system of direct democracy by popular referendums. The town-meeting style of government will become a national reality. Eventually the 1990s contrived "town meetings" popularized by Bill Clinton will be obsolete, as voters will reject the idea of specially handpicked, agreeable partici-

Dick Morris is a political consultant, TV commentator for *Fox News Channel,* and newspaper columnist for the *New York Post.* Copyright © 1999 by Dick Morris. From *VOTE.com* by Dick Morris. Reprinted by permission of St. Martin's Press, L.L.C./Renaissance Books.

pants who, in fact, don't reflect our towns. Instead, the real town meetings will occur on the Internet, with real people, and the politicians will have to listen.

Ad hoc, nonbinding voting over the Internet is starting to transform our democracy. A proliferation of political Web sites soon will offer voters the chance to be heard at the instant that an issue becomes important. Whether it is in response to a random act of violence such as Columbine, the death of an American icon like John F. Kennedy Jr., or a court decision such as O. J. Simpson's acquittal, American voters are already finding an outlet for their emotions and political views that has never before been available.

Through interactive political and news Web sites, people will be able to vote on any issue they wish. We will all be more like the citizens in California and other states where voters can take matters into their own hands through direct referendums and initiatives in each year's balloting. Internet referendums will not, in the beginning, have any legally binding effect, but they will be politically binding. As the number of people participating in these votes grows from the thousands well into the millions, they will acquire a political force that will compel our elected representatives, anxious to keep their jobs, to heed their message. No congressman, senator, or president would dare fly in the face of so massive an expression of public sentiment.

In all likelihood these Internet referendums will be staged without the slightest government participation. Private Web sites like Vote.com will provide the ballot boxes. Financed by advertising, these nongovernmental means of expressing voter opinion, in effect, mean the end of a government monopoly on the process of registration and voting.

When will voters be consulted on important issues? Whenever they want to be. Anytime enough Internet users want to have a referendum they will simply have one. There will likely be hundreds of referendums each year. Of course only a few will attract the attention of enough voters to matter politically, but, by the self-correcting increase or decrease in turnout, voters will indicate how important they feel a given issue to be. Some issues will arouse sufficient public attention to generate a huge outpouring of public opinion and tens of millions of votes. These referendums, on the key issues of the day, will have an enormous impact on governmental decision-making at all levels. Others will, undoubtedly, be flaky or unimportant. Then few will vote or participate and they will be ignored.

Elections will still be run by government bureaucracies. We'll still choose our president and Congress by the old election system, but the influence the public can bring to bear will make it far less important whom we elect. It is the public's will, not theirs, that will most often be controlling.

Is this a good thing? Our legislators and leaders, with their addiction to special-interest money and power, have forfeited their right to our trust. A little direct democracy might dilute the power of these self-interested and well-funded organizations and restore a measure of popular sovereignty. The insider system, with its focus on partisan combat and subservience to powerful lobbyists, could use a bit of fresh air now and then. Thomas Jefferson recommended a revolution every twenty years to "refresh . . . the tree of liberty." As revolutions go, this one is likely to be both more pacific and more constructive than most.

Of course voters make mistakes and are often turned from good sense by racism, bigotry, and prejudice. Demagogues make a good living off the gullible. Ultimately our experience with direct democracy will lead voters to see the wisdom of ceding back to those who are more experienced a measure of the power the Internet has given the general public. Eventually, chastened and humbled, our elected leaders may find the pendulum swinging back in their direction. But not anytime soon.

Whether direct Internet democracy is good or bad is, however, quite beside the point. It is inevitable. It is coming and we had better make our peace with it. We have to better educate ourselves so that we can make good decisions. Restricting the power of the people is no longer a viable option. The Internet made it obsolete.

People are yearning for some way to express their views on political issues, beyond talking back to an unresponsive television screen or muttering into their coffee over the morning newspaper. (As we shall see, this frustration with the limited opportunities for political self-expression is a basic reason for the popularity of talk radio's call-in format.)

How popular would Internet referendums become? An April 1999 survey by Dresner, Wickers and Associates, taken for the Vote.com website, predicts that upwards of 40 percent of people over sixteen years of age would be interested in participating. The survey asked respondents on which issues they would like to vote. The answer is that significant numbers would like to vote on practically anything.

Interest in Voting on the Internet

Topic	% of Internet Users Who Are Interested		
	Very	Somewhat	Total
General interest in participating in referendums	25	19	44
. . . In presidential primaries	35	19	54
How should budget surplus be spent?	48	20	68
Should Hillary run for the senate?	20	9	29
Should the U.S. grant more trade concessions to China?	20	14	34
Should sales over the Internet be taxed?	24	12	36

Source: Dresner, Wickers and Associates Survey, April 1999. 1,000 Internet users.

How are we to reconcile this predicted quantum leap in voter interest with the depressing spectacle of annually dropping election-day turnout? While turnout has indeed decreased, the falloff is more illusory than real. As political consultant Richard Dresner puts it, the drop in voter turnout is "more a generational thing than anything else." Dresner notes that turnout among those reared during the Depression and amid World War II has always been very high, higher than that of any other generation. "Much of the drop in turnout," Dresner says, "is due to this generation dying out. Turnout among all other generations has been roughly the same over the past twenty or thirty years." The sole exception, he notes, is that there is a very low turnout among young adults who have not been to college.

As turnout drops, how will participation through the Internet rise? Will the X Generation, skilled in the Internet but indifferent to politics, remain online but continue to ignore the ballot box? Probably this is exactly what will happen.

Participation is a simple matter of logging on. There is no trip through the rain to the polling place. No authority-figure inspectors are there to look up your name in the Doomsday Book to verify your status as a legal voter.

Internet users may not elect public officials, but they will tell those officials what to do. Indeed, referendum voting over the Internet will likely become as habitual as reading a newspaper or using e-mail. Instantly the voter will see his or her vote counted and can log on to follow the progress of the referendum. Those who vote will soon learn how their representative in Congress, the state legislature, or the city council voted on the issue at hand. Feedback will be instantaneous and responsive.

Will the resulting vote-count truly mirror the opinions of those who will really vote to select their senators and congressmen on election day? At first, probably not. But in a society where only about half of voting-age adults actually participates in presidential elections, and only about 40 percent in off-year congressional contests, why should this national canvass of opinion exclude the other half to two-thirds? Indeed, as nonvoters get used to voting over the Internet, they will find themselves more involved in the political process and may well become interested enough to make the journey to the polls on election day.

* * *

Internet use is disproportionately concentrated among those under fifty, but contrary to popular wisdom, its use among minorities is extensive. While the proportion of Internet users who are Black or Hispanic is somewhat less than that of the general population, it does approximate their proportion of those who actually vote. The following table compares the proportion of Internet users from each age and race group with their percentage of the general population.

Internet Use by Age and Race

Age or Racial Group	% of Net Users	% of Population over 16
16–30	39	27
31–50	46	40
51–65	11	17
Over 65	4	16
Black	11	12
Hispanic	5	11

Only Hispanics and those over sixty-five are grossly underrepresented on the Internet. The former is likely due, in part, to linguistic problems, which will be overcome as the years pass. As Internet use grows, the participation of Americans over sixty-five is certain to increase. The Internet population is more and more likely to be a reflection of America.

Obviously, a fair number of people under the age of eighteen will also vote in Internet referendums. While these young people would not be able to vote in actual elections, they will likely still want to use the Internet to send messages to the adult leadership of their country. As teen habits go, voting is relatively less pernicious than smoking, drinking, or drug use, so why not encourage it? The Internet will redefine citizenship.

Will Internet voting be subject to fraud or abuse? Technology can, or soon will, likely be able to stop multiple voting. Every once in a while, a dedicated hacker will be up to the challenge of invading the system and recording multiple votes, but systems can be put in place to prevent any substantial abuse of the process. The validity of an Internet referendum will depend mainly on the verification system of the Web site.

As Internet voting becomes widespread and the turnout for Internet referendum mounts, the energies of our political system will flow into the Internet and further increase its impact. Candidates will campaign over the Internet. Lobbying groups will use Internet voting to animate their positions. Special-interest organizations will adapt themselves to using Internet referendums to make their political points. A new arena will be created that will absorb more and more of the kinetic energy of our political process.

The Promise and Perils
of Cyberdemocracy

Norman Ornstein and Amy Schenkenberg Mitchell

In 1992, Ross Perot promised that if elected president he would use electronic town hall meetings to guide national decisions. Perot lost the election (and never made clear how those meetings would operate), but the idea of "cyberdemocracy" aroused much interest and is spreading quickly as technology advances. Every U.S. senator and 190 representatives currently have World Wide Web pages, as do all . . . major . . . presidential contenders. In 1995, the Library of Congress, under the leadership of Newt Gingrich, established an on-line system offering all legislation considered and passed by Congress.

On the local level, the city government of Colorado Springs has a non-commercial electronic bulletin board called Citylink. Established in 1990 to allow citizens to communicate with city managers and city council members, it's available free of charge. In 1994, the Minnesota Electronic Democracy Project conducted on-line debates among candidates in the gubernatorial and senate races.

States have begun fashioning their governmental processes around this direct-democracy ideal. Twenty-four states permit citizen initiatives that place legislation or constitutional amendments on the ballot. Oregon has held local vote-by-mail elections since 1981, and in 1995 initiated its first state-wide mail ballot to replace Senator Bob Packwood. North Dakota's 1996 presidential primary [was conducted] by mail ballot.

All this may be just the beginning. As new technologies emerge, many futurists paint rosy scenarios of more direct roles for individuals in law-making. Some prophesy that legislators will vote and debate from their home state through computers and televisions, eliminating the need for the actual houses of Congress in Washington. Lawrence Grossman, former president of PBS and NBC, imagines Congress evolving into a body that discusses issues and disseminates information, but only makes decisions after being instructed by the

Norman Ornstein is a resident scholar and Amy Schenkenberg Mitchell is a former research associate at the American Enterprise Institute, a government and public policy research organization in Washington, D.C. Reprinted from Norman Ornstein and Amy Schenkenberg Mitchell, "The Promise & Perils of Cyberdemocracy," *American Enterprise* (March/April 1996): 53–54. Reprinted with the permission of The American Enterprise Institute for Public Policy Research, Washington, D.C.

public. Futurist Christine Slaton questions the need for elected legislators at all. She envisions using technology to create a participatory democracy where representatives are selected by lot and rotated regularly. Alvin and Heidi Toffler of "third wave" fame predict that today's political parties will disappear, replaced by fluid coalitions that vary according to changing legislative interests. The Tofflers also envision representatives chosen by lot, or at a minimum, elected officials casting 50 percent of a vote and a random sampling of the public casting the other 50 percent. In this scenario, individuals will not only vote on more things than they do now, they'll vote on more complex questions, as simple yes/no votes are replaced by if-then referenda. Nor will voters have to inconvenience themselves by traveling to the local polling station. They probably won't even have to lick a stamp. Instead, voters will simply punch in their vote from their TV remote control, never leaving the house, never having to speak with another individual, not even having to spend more than a few seconds thinking about their choice.

Enchanting as these innovations may sound to Americans grown weary of Washington ways, several questions arise: Would cyberdemocracy in fact be more representative? Would voters take seriously their new responsibilities? Would they even be interested? Who will determine the exact questions the public will decide? And most importantly, what sort of deliberation, if any, will exist under this new regime?

A cyberdemocracy based on personal computers and upscale television systems will not be equally open to all citizens. Twenty-two percent of college graduates go on line at least weekly, while only 1 percent of those with a high school diploma do, a recent Times Mirror survey reports. Men are twice as likely as women to be daily on-line users. Twenty-seven percent of families with incomes of $50,000 or greater have gone on line, but only 6 percent of those with incomes under $20,000 have. Indeed, the Colorado Springs information systems manager reported that in 1995 there were only 250 active Citylink users in a city of over 300,000. No doubt the popularity of comparable information systems will increase substantially over time, and costs will come down, but a skew toward the highly educated and well-to-do is inevitable.

Even if the technology were made available to everyone equally, how would interest be sustained? Lloyd Morrisett, president of the Markle Foundation, recently wrote that he envisions the early fascination with cyberdemocracy ebbing until cybervoting falls into the same predicament as current voting rights: treasured but not necessarily used. Studying California's experience with referenda, Morrisett found that "the ballot has become so loaded with complex initiatives that it seems to discourage people from going to the polls, rather than motivating them to express their judgment." If the average voter tuned out complex items flashing across his screen, "voting" would be much less representative than it is today.

Cyberdemocracy's greatest danger lies in the way it would diminish deliberation in government. Everyone applauds technology's capacity to inform voters and to improve communications between them and their representatives. But we must also recall that the Founders expressly rejected "pure" democracies where citizens "assemble and administer the government in person," because they usually end in the tyranny of the majority. The Constitution instead establishes a republic where voters select representatives to make and execute the laws. The Founders designed this process to produce a public *judgment*, enlarging upon and refining popular opinions. That judgment, as opposed to public emotions, can only arise through deliberation. In the slow process of debate, give-and-take, and face-to-face contact among representatives, all perspectives and interests can be considered. The need to persuade an informed group of representatives with diverse concerns should, the Founders thought, result in decisions that are more just and more likely to meet the test of time with citizens.

Deliberation even figures in our political campaigns. Over weeks and months, campaigns provide a larger deliberative canvas, an opportunity for voters to consider issues, governing philosophies, and questions of leadership, resulting in a great appreciation of the choices that will face Congress and the President. Of course, our governing system does not always live up to the challenges of serious deliberation, but it still remains our foundation.

What happens to deliberation with the ascent of cyberdemocracy? Consider elections. For all the understandable criticism of never-ending campaigns, negative advertising, and demagoguery, campaigns still work, at least sometimes, as deliberative processes. Voters' initial inclination, not to mention their priorities on issues, often change as they receive more information. Early polls rarely reflect the actual voting. Citizens striving for informed judgments usually make them in the final, most intense days of a campaign. Instantaneous electronic voting would destroy whatever is left of this deliberative process. In Oregon most voters return their mail ballots within five days, casting their votes well before the final days (or even weeks) of intense campaigning.

Mail or electronic balloting also removes the symbolic quality of voting as an act where voters make a private judgment in a public place, surrounded by their fellow citizens, acknowledging simultaneously our individuality and our collective responsibility and common purpose. Compare standing in line at a polling place, going into a private booth, and making individual choices with the alternative of vote-by-mail—the political equivalent of filling out a Publishers Clearing House ballot—or electronic voting, where elections would resemble the Home Shopping Network.

Voting by mail or electronically is only one challenge cyberpolitics presents to deliberative democracy. Consider the difference between laws passed by referenda and laws passed in legislatures. Legislative deliberation encourages informed debate among somewhat-informed individuals with different interests. It allows a proposal to change, often dramatically, as it goes through the gantlet of hearings, floor debate, and amendment in both houses of Congress.

To be sure, some debate can occur during a state referendum campaign, through ads and media analysis, but that is no substitute for face-to-face debate involving not just two sides, but sometimes dozens or hundreds, reflected in representatives from various areas and constituencies. Mail or electronic balloting would short-circuit campaigns even further. And referenda have no amendment process, no matter how complex the issue. Their outcome relies on voters who have many other things to do besides study the issues, much less read the bills or provisions.

Could electronic town meetings provide a popular equivalent to traditional legislating? Theoretically, a broad mass of voters could be part of a different deliberative process. That's the thesis of political scientist James Fishkin, whose "deliberative poll" brought a random sample of 600 citizens together in late January [1996] at considerable expense for three days of expert-guided discussion in Austin, Texas. Even if the Fishkin experiment were scrupulously fair, such enterprises generally seem susceptible to undemocratic manipulation by "experts" and agenda-setters. And "deliberative polls" are unlikely to win out over the allure of a quick, trigger-like vote on the TV or computer. Cyberdemocratic meetings would likely turn into fancier versions of "Talk Back Live." And most deliberation would be reduced—as now in California and other initiative-prone states—to high-tech public relations campaigns by powerful interests with the resources to put their issues on the ballot—making for more special interest influence, not more democracy.

Cyberspace offers wonderful possibilities for citizens to discuss issues. New electronic alliances based on similar interests can be enjoyed. And every day, citizens and legislators can download more information. But the combination of cynical distrust of political institutions, a rising tide of populism glorifying "pure" democracy, and the increased speed of information technology, is a highly dangerous one. While Newt Gingrich has benefited from the political cynicism and populism that drove voters in 1994, he knows the dangers facing deliberative democracy. As he told one of his college classes, "Direct democracy says, Okay, how do we feel this week? We all raise our hand. Let's rush off and do it. The concept of republican representation, which is very clear in the Founding Fathers, is you hire somebody who you send to a central place. . . . They, by definition, learn things you don't learn, because you don't want to—you want to be able to live your life. They are supposed to use their judgment to represent you. . . . [The Founders] feared the passion of the moment."

Newt is right. But preserving the Founders' vision as the "third wave" of cybertechnology approaches won't be easy.

Internet Resources

Visit our website at http://www.mhhe.com/diclerico for links and resources relating to Public Opinion.

Voting

*D*espite the fact that our population is better educated and faces fewer procedural impediments to voting than ever before, a significant portion of the American electorate does not participate in elections. Indeed, from 1960 through 1996 voting turnout in presidential elections declined some 14 percentage points, and the turnout figure of just over 49 percent in 1996 was the lowest in seventy-two years. Although the turnout rate edged up to 51.2% in 2000, to many observers the turnout rate is shockingly low. Low voter turnout, it is argued, is just one more sign of a general deterioration in the quality of political life in the United States as citizens increasingly opt out of the political system. Indeed, citizen trust in government is at an all-time low just as voting for president barely exceeds the 50 percent mark.

Should we be alarmed by the decline in voting? In the following selections, two distinguished political commentators address this question. In the first selection, a former president of the American Political Science Association, Arend Lijphart, argues that low voter turnout is indeed a serious problem about which citizens ought to be concerned, for the level of voter participation has important implications for the legitimacy of government, as well as its policies. Indeed, so concerned is Lijphart about low voter turnout in the United States that he proposes what some might regard as a radical solution—compulsory voting.

The author of the second article, political scientist Austin Ranney, argues that we need not fear the fact that many persons choose not to vote. Ranney bases his argument on two main propositions: First, he contends that because voters and nonvoters do not differ significantly in policy and candidate preferences, no great harm is done to our system of representation if a sizable percentage of people do not vote; and second, nonvoting does not offend any basic democratic principle, for the right not to vote is every bit as precious as the right to vote.

Compulsory Voting Is the Best Way to Keep Democracy Strong

Arend Lijphart

Voting is the commonest and most basic way of participating in a democracy, but far too many citizens do not exercise their right to vote, especially in the United States. In the 1988 and 1992 Presidential elections, the turnout of registered voters was only 50 and 55 percent, respectively, and in the midterm Congressional elections in 1990 and 1994, it was only 33 and 36 percent. Four years later, the turnout in the Presidential election was 49 percent, while for the 1998 off-year Congressional election it was 36 percent.

This is a serious problem for two reasons. One is democratic legitimacy: Can a government that has gained power in a low-turnout election really claim to be a representative government? For instance, some Americans questioned President Clinton's mandate because he received only 43 percent of the votes cast and because only 55 percent of those registered to vote actually did so—which meant that he received the support of fewer than 25 percent of all eligible voters in 1992. The other, even more serious problem is that low turnout almost inevitably means that certain groups vote in greater numbers than other groups and hence gain disproportionate influence on the government and its policies.

The only way to solve these problems is to maximize turnout. It may not be realistic to expect everyone to vote, but a turnout of, say, 90 percent is a feasible goal, as the experience of quite a few democracies shows.

On the basis of studies ranging from the 1920s work of Harold F. Gosnell at the University of Chicago to the 1990s research of Robert W. Jackman of the University of California at Davis and Mark N. Franklin of the University of Houston, we know a great deal about the institutional mechanisms that can increase turnout. They include voter-friendly registration procedures; voting on the weekend instead of during the week; easy access to absentee ballots; proportional representation, with multiple lawmakers representing electoral districts instead of the current U.S. system of winner-takes-all elections; and scheduling as many elections as possible—national, state, and local—on the same day.

Arend Lijphart is a professor of political science at the University of California at San Diego and a former president of the American Political Science Association. From "Compulsory Voting Is the Best Way to Keep Democracy Strong," *The Chronicle of Higher Education* (October 18, 1996): B3–4. Reprinted by permission.

The evidence suggests that using all of these measures together can produce a voter turnout of around 90 percent. But adopting all of them is a tall order. Only a handful of states have even managed to introduce the minor reform of allowing citizens to register to vote on the same day as the election.

Fortunately, one other reform, by itself, can maximize turnout as effectively as all of the other methods combined: compulsory voting. In Australia, Belgium, Brazil, Greece, Italy, Venezuela, and several other Latin American democracies, mandatory voting has produced near-universal voter turnout.

It is somewhat surprising that making voting compulsory is so effective, because the penalties for failing to vote are typically minor, usually involving a fine roughly equal to that for a parking violation. Moreover, enforcement tends to be very lax; because of the large numbers of people involved, compulsory voting simply cannot be strictly enforced. (Parking rules tend to be enforced much more strictly.)

For instance, with 10 million eligible voters in Australia, even a typical turnout of 95 percent means that half a million people did not vote, and it obviously is not practical to issue such a large number of fines. Australia is actually among the strictest enforcers of compulsory voting, but even there, only about 4 percent of nonvoters end up having to pay the small fines. In Belgium, fewer than one-fourth of 1 percent of nonvoters are fined.

Mandatory-voting requirements produce large turnouts, however, even though a government technically cannot compel an actual vote. A government can require citizens to show up at the polls, or even to accept a ballot and then drop it into the ballot box, but it cannot require its citizens to cast a valid vote; secret ballots mean that nobody can be prevented from casting an invalid or blank one.

It is worth emphasizing why low voter turnout is such a serious problem for democracies—one that deserves our attention. Low turnout typically means that privileged citizens (those with better education and greater wealth) vote in significantly larger numbers than less-privileged citizens. This introduces a systematic bias in favor of well-off citizens, because, as the old adage has it, "If you don't vote, you don't count." The already-privileged citizens who vote are further rewarded with government policies favoring their interests.

The socio-economic bias in voter turnout is an especially strong pattern in the United States, where turnout is extremely low. In Presidential elections from 1952 to 1988, turnout among the college-educated was 26 percentage points higher than that among the population as a whole; the turnout for people without a high-school diploma was 16 percentage points lower. Unless turnout is very high—about 90 percent—socio-economic biases in voting tend to be a major problem. For instance, low and unequal voter turnout is a major reason why politicians find it so much easier to reduce government aid to the poor than to cut entitlement programs that chiefly benefit the middle class.

The low levels of voter turnout in the United States are often contrasted with turnouts as high as 95 percent in a few other countries. But when we measure turnout in other democracies in the way we usually measure it in the United States—as a percentage of the *voting-age population,* rather than as a percentage of *the registered electorate*—we find very few countries with turnouts above 90 percent, and most of those nations have compulsory voting. According to a study by G. Bingham Powell of the University of Rochester, half of the world's democracies have turnout levels below about 75 percent of the voting-age population. This half includes most of the larger democracies; not only the United States, but also Britain, France, Japan, and India, none of which require citizens to vote.

Even these figures cast turnouts in a deceptively favorable light, because they measure voting in what political scientists call first-order elections—that is, national-level parliamentary or presidential elections. But the vast majority of elections are second-order elections—for lesser posts—which attract less attention from citizens and lower turnouts. In the United States, only Presidential elections produce turnouts of more than 50 percent of the voting-age population; turnout in midterm Congressional elections has been only about 35 percent in recent years, and in local elections is closer to 25 percent.

Low turnout is typical for second-order elections in other countries, too. For local elections in Britain, it is only about 40 percent. Even in Australia, it is only about 35 percent, because voting at the local level is not mandatory, as it is for national elections. In the 1994 elections for the European Parliament, another example of a second-order contest, the average turnout in the 12 nations of the European Union was 58 percent. The power of mandatory voting is highlighted by the fact that when it is applied to local elections—as it is in all nations with compulsory voting except Australia—turnout levels are almost the same as those for presidential and parliamentary contests.

It is time that we paid more attention to the issue of voter turnout, because the already low levels of voting in many countries around the world are declining even more. In the United States, voting in Presidential elections has fallen to 50 to 55 percent of the voting-age population in the 1980s and '90s, from 60 to 65 percent during the 1950s and '60s. . . .

The biggest advantage of compulsory voting is that, by enhancing voter turnout, it equalizes participation and removes much of the bias against less-privileged citizens. It also has two other significant advantages. One is that mandatory voting can reduce the role of money in politics, since it does away with the need for candidates and political parties to spend large sums on getting voters to the polls. Second, it reduces the incentives for negative advertising.

As the political scientists Stephen Ansolabehere of the Massachusetts Institute of Technology and Shanto Iyengar of the University of California at Los Angeles have shown in *Going Negative: How Attack Ads Shrink and Polarize the Electorate* (Free Press, 1995), attack ads work—indeed, they work all too well. They are effective not because they persuade people to vote *for* the candidate making the attack and *against* the candidate attacked in the ads, but because they raise enough doubts in voters' minds that they decide not to vote at all. So the candidate making the attack has lowered his or her opponent's total vote.

Moreover, attack ads breed general distrust of politicians and cynicism about politics and government. Under mandatory voting, it would be so much harder for attack ads to depress turnout that I believe they would no longer be worth the effort.

The main objection to compulsory voting is that it violates the individual's freedom—the freedom not to vote. This was the main reason it was abolished in the Netherlands in 1970, for example. It is unlikely, however, that the Dutch would have made this decision had they foreseen the disastrous plunge in their voter turnouts, from about 90 percent in all elections to only 50 percent and 36 percent, respectively, in the most recent elections for provincial offices and for seats in the European Parliament.

In any case, the individual-freedom argument is extremely weak, because—as I've noted—compulsory voting does not actually require a citizen to cast a valid ballot. Besides, mandatory voting entails an extremely small decrease in freedom compared with many other, more onerous tasks that democracies require their citizens to perform, such as serving on juries, paying taxes, and serving in the military.

Some scholars argue that U.S. courts might rule compulsory voting unconstitutional because it restricts individual freedom. Richard L. Hasen, of the Chicago-Kent College of Law at the Illinois Institute of Technology, . . . has argued, in "Voting Without Law?" (*University of Pennsylvania Law Review*, May 1996), that the only plausible ground for such a ruling would be the First Amendment's guarantee of freedom of speech. But the Supreme Court has explicitly rejected the notion that voting can be regarded as a form of speech. For instance, in 1992, in *Burdick v. Takushi*, the Court upheld Hawaii's ban on write-in votes, ruling against a voter's claim that the ban deprived him of the right to cast a protest vote for Donald Duck. The Court said an election is about choosing representatives, not about expressing oneself. Of course, even if mandatory voting were to be found unconstitutional, a constitutional amendment permitting it could be adopted—a difficult, but not impossible, prospect.

Probably the most important practical obstacle to compulsory voting in countries that do not have it is the opposition of conservative parties, like the Republican Party in the United States. High turnout is clearly not in their partisan self-interest, because unequal turnout favors privileged voters, who tend to be conservative. But conservative parties generally were also opposed to universal suffrage, which eventually was accepted by all democracies, because it was recognized to be a basic democratic principle. Compulsory voting should be seen as an extension of universal suffrage—which we now all take for granted.

Nonvoting Is Not a Social Disease

Austin Ranney

In 1980 only 53 percent of the voting-age population in the United States voted for president, and in 1982 only 38 percent voted for members of the House.* As the statistics are usually presented, this rate is, on the average, from 10 to 40 points lower than in the democratic nations of Western Europe, Scandinavia, and the British Commonwealth—although such numbers involve major technical problems of which we should be aware.[1] We also know that the level of voter participation has [declined] since the early 1960s.

All forms of *in*voluntary nonvoting—caused by either legal or extralegal impediments—are violations of the most basic principles of democracy and fairness. Clearly it is a bad thing if citizens who want to vote are prevented from doing so by law or intimidation. But what about *voluntary* nonvoters—the 30 percent or so of our adult citizens who *could* vote if they were willing to make the (usually minimal) effort, but who rarely or never do so? What does it matter if millions of Americans who could vote choose not to?

We should begin by acknowledging that suffrage and voting laws, extralegal force, and intimidation account for almost none of the nonvoting. A number of constitutional amendments, acts of Congress, and court decisions since the 1870s—particularly since the mid-1960s—have outlawed all legal and extralegal denial of the franchise to African-Americans, women, Hispanics, people over the age of 18, and other groups formerly excluded. Moreover, since the mid-1960s most states have changed their registration and voting laws to make casting ballots a good deal easier. Many states, to be sure, still demand a somewhat greater effort to register than is required by other democratic countries. But the best estimates are that even if we made our voting procedures as undemanding as those in other democracies, we would raise our average turnouts by only nine or so percentage points. That would still leave our voter partici-

*The 2000 presidential election turnout was 51.2 percent; the 2002 congressional election turnout was 39.3 percent—*Editors.*

Austin Ranney is professor emeritus of political science at the University of California–Berkeley and a former president of the American Political Science Association. This selection was adapted from a paper delivered to the ABC/Harvard Symposium on Voter Participation on October 1, 1983. From Austin Ranney, "Nonvoting Is Not a Social Disease," *Public Opinion* (October/November 1983): pp. 16–19. Reprinted with permission of The American Enterprise Institute for Public Policy Research, Washington, D.C.

pation level well below that of all but a handful of the world's democracies, and far below what many people think is the proper level for a healthy democracy.

Throughout our history, but especially in recent years, many American scholars, public officials, journalists, civic reformers, and other people of good will have pondered our low level of voting participation and have produced a multitude of studies, articles, books, pamphlets, manifestoes, and speeches stating their conclusions. On one point they agree: All start from the premise that voluntary, as well as involuntary, nonvoting is a bad thing for the country and seek ways to discourage it. Yet, despite the critical importance of the question, few ask *why* voluntary nonvoting is a bad thing.

Voluntary nonvoting's bad name stems from one or a combination of three types of arguments or assumptions. Let us consider these arguments in turn.

WHAT HARM DOES IT DO?

One of the most often-heard charges against nonvoting is that it produces unrepresentative bodies of public officials. After all, the argument runs, if most of the middle-class WASPs vote and most of the African-Americans, Hispanics, and poor people do not, then there will be significantly lower proportions of African-Americans, Hispanics, and poor people in public office than in the general population. Why is that bad? For two reasons. First, it makes the public officials, in political theorist Hanna Pitkin's term, "descriptively unrepresentative." And while not everyone would argue that the interests of African-Americans are best represented by African-American officials, the interests of women by women officials, and so on, many people believe that the policy preferences of the underrepresented groups will get short shrift from the government. Second, this not only harms the underrepresented groups but weakens the whole polity, for the underrepresented are likely to feel that the government cares nothing for them and they owe no loyalty to it. Hence it contributes greatly to the underclasses' feelings of alienation from the system and to the lawlessness that grows from such alienation.

This argument seems plausible enough, but a number of empirical studies comparing voters with nonvoters do not support it. They find that the distributions of policy preferences among nonvoters are approximately the same as those among voters, and therefore the pressures on public officials by constituents for certain policies and against others are about the same as they would be if everyone, WASPs and minorities, voted at the same rate.

Moreover, other studies have shown that the level of cynicism about the government's honesty, competence, and responsiveness is about the same among nonvoters as among voters, and an increased level of nonvoting does not signify an increased level of alienation or lawlessness. We can carry the argument a step further by asking if levels of civic virtue are clearly higher and levels of lawlessness lower in Venezuela (94 percent average voting turnout), Austria (94 percent), and Italy (93 percent) than in the United States (58 percent), Switzerland (64 percent), and Canada (76 percent). If the answer is no, as surely it is, then at least we have to conclude that there is no clear or strong relationship between high levels of voting turnout and high levels of civic virtue.

Another argument concerns future danger rather than present harm to the Republic. Journalist Arthur Hadley asserts that our great and growing number of "refrainers" (his term for voluntary nonvoters) constitutes a major threat to the future stability of our political system. In his words:

> These growing numbers of refrainers hang over the democratic process like a bomb, ready to explode and change the course of our history as they have twice in our past. . . . Both times in our history when there have been large numbers of refrainers, sudden radical shifts of power have occurred. As long as the present gigantic mass of refrainers sits outside of our political system, neither we nor our allies can be certain of even the normally uncertain future. This is why creating voters, bringing the refrainers to the booth, is important.

Hadley's argument assumes that if millions of the present nonvoters suddenly voted in some future election, they would vote for persons, parties, and policies radically different from those chosen by the regular voters. He asserts that that is what happened in 1828 and again in 1932, and it could happen again any time. Of course, some might feel that a sudden rush to the polls that produces another Andrew Jackson or Franklin Roosevelt is something to be longed for, not feared, but in any case his assumption is highly dubious. We have already noted that the policy preferences of nonvoters do not differ greatly from those of voters, and much the same is true of their candidate preferences. For example, a leading study of the 1980 presidential election found that the five lowest voting groups were African-Americans, Hispanics, whites with family incomes below $5,000 a year, whites with less than high school educations, and working-class white Catholics. The study concluded that if all five groups had voted at the same rate as the electorate as a whole, they would have added only about one-and-a-half percentage points to Carter's share of the vote, and Reagan would still have been elected with a considerable margin. So Hadley's fear seems, at the least, highly exaggerated.

WHAT SOCIAL SICKNESS DOES NONVOTING MANIFEST?

Some writers take the position that, while a high level of voluntary nonvoting may not in itself do harm to the nation's well-being, it is certainly a symptom of poor civic health. Perhaps they take their inspiration from Pericles, who, in his great funeral oration on the dead of Marathon, said:

> . . . Our ordinary citizens, though occupied with the pursuits of industry, are still fair judges of public matters; for, unlike any other nation, regarding him who takes no part in these duties not as unambitious but as useless. . . .

One who holds a 20th-century version of that view is likely to believe that our present level of voluntary nonvoting is a clear sign that millions of Americans are civically useless—that they are too lazy, too obsessed with their own selfish affairs and interests, and too indifferent to the welfare of their country and the quality of their government to make even the minimum effort required to vote. A modern Pericles might ask, How can such a nation hope to defend itself in war and advance the public welfare in peace? Are not the lassitude and indifference manifested by our high level of nonvoting the root cause of our country's declining military strength and economic productivity as well as the growing corruption and bungling of our government?

Perhaps so, perhaps not. Yet the recent studies of nonvoters have shown that they do not differ significantly from voters in the proportions who believe that citizens have a civic duty to vote or in the proportions who believe that ordinary people have a real say in what government does. It may be that nonvoters are significantly less patriotic citizens, poorer soldiers, and less productive workers than voters, but there is no evidence to support such charges. And do we accept the proposition that the much higher turnout rates for the Austrians, the French, and the Irish show that they are significantly better on any or all of these counts than the Americans? If not, then clearly there is no compelling reason to believe that a high level of nonvoting is, by itself, a symptom of sickness in American society.

WHAT BASIC PRINCIPLES DOES IT OFFEND?

I have asked friends and colleagues whether they think that the high level of voluntary nonvoting in America really matters. Almost all of them believe that it does, and when I ask them why they usually reply not so much in terms of some harm it does or some social illness it manifests but rather in terms of their conviction that the United States of America is or should be a democracy, and that a high level of voluntary nonvoting offends some basic principles of democracy.

Their reasoning goes something like this: The essential principle of democratic government is government by the people, government that derives its "just powers from the consent of the governed." The basic institution for ensuring truly democratic government is the regular holding of free elections at which the legitimate authority of public officials to govern is renewed or terminated by the sovereign people. Accordingly, the right to vote is the basic right of every citizen in a democracy, and the exercise of that right is the most basic duty of every democratic citizen.

Many have made this argument. For example, in 1963 President John F. Kennedy appointed an 11-member Commission on Registration and Voting Participation. Its report, delivered after his death, began:

> Voting in the United States is the fundamental act of self-government. It provides the citizen in our free society the right to make a judgment, to state a choice, to participate in the running of his government. . . . The ballot box is the medium for the expression of the consent of the governed.

In the same vein the British political philosopher Sir Isaiah Berlin declares, "Participation in self-government is, like justice, a basic human requirement, *an end in itself.*"

If these views are correct, then any nominal citizen of a democracy who does not exercise this basic right and fulfill this basic duty is not a full citizen, and the larger the proportion of such less-than-full citizens in a polity that aspires to democracy, the greater the gap between the polity's low realities and democracy's high ideals.

Not everyone feels this way, of course. The late Senator Sam Ervin, for example, argues:

> I'm not going to shed any real or political or crocodile tears if people don't care enough to vote. I don't believe in making it easy for apathetic, lazy people. I'd be extremely happy if nobody in the United States voted except for the people who thought about the issues and made up their own minds and wanted to vote. No one else who votes is going to contribute anything but statistics, and I don't care that much for statistics.

The issues between these two positions are posed most starkly when we consider proposals for compulsory voting. After all, if we are truly convinced that voluntary nonvoting is a violation of basic democratic principles, and a major social ill, then why not follow the lead of Australia, Belgium, Italy, and Venezuela and enact laws *requiring* people to vote and penalizing them if they do not?

The logic seems faultless, and yet most people I know, including me, are against compulsory voting laws for the United States. All of us want to eradicate all vestiges of *in*voluntary nonvoting, and many are disturbed by the high level of voluntary nonvoting. Yet many of us also feel that the right to abstain is just as precious as the right to vote, and the idea of legally compelling all citizens to vote whether they want to or not is at least as disturbing as the large numbers of Americans who now and in the future probably will not vote without some compulsion.

THE BRIGHT SIDE

In the light of the foregoing considerations, then, how much should we worry about the high level of voluntary nonvoting in our country? At the end of his magisterial survey of voting turnout in different democratic nations, Ivor Crewe asks this question and answers, "There are . . . reason[s] for *not* worrying—too much."

I agree. While we Americans can and probably should liberalize our registration and voting laws and mount register-and-vote drives sponsored by political parties, civic organizations, schools of government, and broadcasting companies, the most we can realistically hope for from such efforts is a modest increase of 10 or so percentage points in our average turnouts. As a college professor and political activist for 40 years, I can testify that even the best reasoned and most attractively presented exhortations to people to behave like good democratic citizens can have only limited effects on their behavior, and most get-out-the-vote drives by well-intentioned civic groups in the past have had disappointingly modest results.

An even more powerful reason not to worry, in my judgment, is that we are likely to see a major increase in our voting turnouts to, say, the 70 or 80 percent levels, only if most of the people in our major nonvoting groups—African-Americans, Hispanics, and poor people—come to believe that voting is a powerful instrument for getting the government to do what they want it to do. The . . . register-and-vote drives by the NAACP and other African-American-mobilization organizations have already had significant success in getting formerly inactive African-American citizens to the polls. . . . Organizations like the Southern Voter Registration Education Project have had some success with Hispanic nonvoters in Texas and New Mexico and may have more. Jesse Helms and Jerry Falwell may also have success in their . . . efforts to urge more conservatives to register and vote. But hard evidence that voting brings real benefits, not exhortations to be good citizens, will be the basis of whatever success any of these groups enjoy.

If we Americans stamp out the last vestiges of institutions and practices that produce *in*voluntary nonvoting, and if we liberalize our registration and voting laws and procedures to make voting here as easy as it is in other democracies, and if the group-mobilization movements succeed, then perhaps our level of voting participation may become much more like that of Canada or Great Britain. (It is unlikely ever to match the levels in the countries with compulsory voting or even those in West Germany or the Scandinavian countries.)

But even if that does not happen, we need not fear that our low voting turnouts are doing any serious harm to our politics or our country, or that they deprive us of the right to call ourselves a democracy.

NOTE

1. European and American measures of voting and nonvoting differ significantly. In all countries the numerator for the formula is the total number of votes cast in national elections. In most countries the denominator is the total number of persons on the electoral rolls—that is, people we would call "registered voters"—which includes almost all people legally eligible to vote. In the United States, on the other hand, the denominator is the "voting-age population," which is the estimate by the Bureau of the Census of the number of people in the country who are 18 or older at the time of the election. That figure, unlike its European counterpart, includes aliens and inmates of prisons and mental hospitals as well as persons not registered to vote. One eminent election analyst, Richard M. Scammon, estimates that if voting turnout in the United States were computed by the same formula as that used for European countries, our average figures would rise by 8 to 10 percentage points, a level that would exceed Switzerland's and closely approach those of Canada, Ireland, Japan, and the United Kingdom.

Internet Resources
Visit our website at http://www.mhhe.com/diclerico for links and resources relating to Voting.

chapter 6

Campaigns and the Media

*P*robably nothing has so revolutionized American politics as the emergence of television as the principal means of communicating with voters. What used to be the experience of only a few people—hearing and seeing a candidate at a campaign rally, for example—is now an experience shared by many millions of Americans. Because television enables political candidates to be seen and heard in every living room of the country, it is no wonder that politicians devote so much time and resources to producing television advertisements and other political programming.

The advent of TV advertising also has led to shorter and shorter campaign spots, in which candidates in thirty-second or shorter sound and picture bites "bash" their opponents or attempt to communicate key word messages to the sometimes uninformed, unsuspecting, and undecided voters. These political advertisements are most often referred to as "negative ads," though exactly what constitutes a negative ad is often in dispute.

The thirty-second or less campaign TV spots, particularly those deemed "negative," are roundly criticized by "good government" advocates. Critics claim that such ads do not simply present a negative view of specific candidates for office, but also damage the political system itself. Such a view is taken by the author of the first selection in this chapter— Fred Wertheimer—who argues that the effect of negative ads is to breed public distrust of the political process. According to Wertheimer, the damage done by negative ads makes it very difficult to govern in a world increasingly beset with public cynicism and distrust, that cynicism being fed by negative campaigning. To remedy this, Wertheimer suggests a number of reforms to make those who sponsor negative ads more accountable.

There are those, however, who defend TV spots, be they negative or not, arguing that political ads actually are highly beneficial. Such a point of view is presented by the authors of our second selection—Stephen Bates and Edwin Diamond. Bates and Diamond, while recognizing that TV spots have their negative aspects, are not convinced that such spots are as bad as the critics allege. Indeed, they see such ads as contributing greatly to political "discourse," leaving the voter better informed than would otherwise be the case. To Bates and Diamond, then, reforming TV campaign spots is like trying to remove politics from campaigns. TV is the modern medium of politics; it cannot and should not be "turned off" for the sake of satisfying the critics.

TV Ad Wars: How to Cut Advertising Costs in Political Campaigns

Fred Wertheimer

[Television,] like the colossus of the ancient world, stands astride our political system, demanding tribute from every candidate for major public office, incumbent or challenger. Its appetite is insatiable, and its impact is unique.

—SENATOR EDWARD KENNEDY, Senate Committee
on Commerce, Hearings, 92nd Congress, 1971

. . . Television advertising is the principal means by which candidates publicly define for the voters their opponents and themselves and the government in which they serve or hope to serve. Television advertising is characterized in the public's mind by one word: negative.

Every two years during the fall, and much earlier in presidential election years, a focused, intense, negative message goes out to the American people over the airwaves about how bad the candidates are, how dangerous their ideas are, how their programs don't work, how problems cannot be solved. Obviously, discussing and disagreeing with your opponent's record and views is a normal and necessary part of our political process. It is a key part of informing and educating voters on the choice they have to make. However, our political TV ad campaigns go far beyond traditional comparative advertising.

Although many candidates have some positive things to say in their TV ads, these messages are overwhelmed by the negative attack ads that set the tone and dominate the debate. Because television appeals to our emotions and magnifies and intensifies what it communicates, the impact of the negative message is much more powerful and damaging on television than if the same message were being communicated through print.

Most politicians and their media handlers focus their TV advertising exclusively on one goal: winning on election day. If winning on election day means undermining your own credibility or damaging your ability to govern or breeding public distrust and cynicism or turning large segments of the public away from voting, so be it. Thus we end up with the perverse result that

Fred Wertheimer is President of *Democracy 21* and served as President of Common Cause from 1981 to 1995. From Fred Wertheimer, "TV Ad Wars: How to Cut Advertising Costs in Political Campaigns," by Fred Wertheimer from *The Harvard International Journal of Press/Politics* 2 (Summer 1997): pp. 93–101.

many politicians use TV advertising in their campaigns in ways that ultimately do as much damage to their own credibility as they do to their opponents'.

Regardless of what politicans may believe about negative advertising "working" in their campaigns, it certainly does not work when it comes to doing their jobs and serving the American people as effective and credible representatives. As Stephen Ansolabehere and Shanto Iyengar find in their book, *Going Negative*, "Negative advertising demoralizes the electorate . . . eats away at the individual's sense of civic duty . . . and contribute[s] to the general antipathy towards politicians and parties and the high rates of disapproval and distrust of political institutions" (1996).

Although the candidates bear the principal responsibility for this happening, we cannot underestimate how important the role played by media consultants is in bringing about these enormously damaging results. As a result of the perceived need for consultant expertise to design and produce TV ad campaigns, many candidates abdicate much of the power to define themselves and their opponents to their media consultants. The media consultants have only one objective—winning the election—and this is often equated with negative attack ads. The carnage that is left after the election is over and it is time to govern is someone else's problem.

Media consultants, furthermore, normally receive as part of their fee a percentage of the amount spent to purchase TV advertising time for the campaign, such as 15 percent. This can involve hundreds of thousands of dollars—sometimes even millions of dollars—in fees. It also means that media consultants have a strong personal economic incentive to spend as much money as they can to conduct the negative TV ad campaigns they devise.

Although the thirty-second negative ad has a preeminent role in U.S. politics today, it hasn't always been this way, in terms of either the length or the content of our political ads. During the first twenty years of presidential ads, for example, sixty-second spots were the dominant form of TV advertising. In the 1970s, ads of four minutes and twenty seconds played the dominant role, and starting in the 1980s, the thirty-second spot became dominant in presidential campaigns. Presidential ads also went through a transition, over time, from positive to negative. According to one study, for example, from 1960 to 1988, ads in presidential campaigns were 72 percent positive and 29 percent negative. In 1992, 63 percent of Bill Clinton's ads and 56 percent of George Bush's ads were negative, representing a high-water mark, as of that time, in negative ad emphasis in a presidential campaign (Kaid and Holtz-Bacha 1995).

A PROPOSED SOLUTION

A number of proposals have been offered to challenge and break out of the grip of the thirty-second negative attack ad. The most radical proposal would bar all political advertising on TV. Other proposals include requiring that candidates appear on screen the whole time in their campaign TV ads, that whenever a negative charge is made in a campaign TV ad that it be made on screen by the candidate, that all campaign TV ads be five minutes or more in length, and that candidates take greater personal responsibility for their campaign ads.

The issues and choices involved here are very difficult. On the one hand, there is great value to our political process and our democracy in moving away from the political culture embedded in the thirty-second attack ad. On the other hand, regulating, through mandatory requirements, the use and content of political ads raises fundamental First Amendment and policy concerns regarding the ability of citizens to exercise free speech in presenting their candidacies to the American people.

Although TV ad campaigns are causing deep problems for our political system today, it is also important to keep in mind how valuable communicating on TV can be. TV campaign ads allow candidates to communicate their views to mass audiences and to do so unfiltered by any intermediaries, such as the media. Ansolabehere and Iyengar point out the real problem: "It's not the pervasiveness of broadcast advertising that spawns public cynicism; it is instead the tone of the advertising campaign. If campaigns were to become more positive, people would be less embittered about politics as usual and more willing to vote" (1996).

Congress should require that candidates appear on screen at the end of their political ads and state they are responsible for the ads. This would provide clearer public accountability for candidates regarding the messages they present to voters on TV. By having to take personal responsibility for their ads, visually, candidates may become less interested in and less likely to run the kinds of negative attack ads that are common practice today.

Congress should also require TV stations to provide a designated amount of free TV time to political parties for use either by their candidates for their campaigns or by party officials to present party views. The free TV time to the parties could be conditioned on the candidates and party officials appearing on screen to present their messages. Broadcasters could be provided financial relief for this free TV time through tax credits or deductions. (Most democracies provide free TV time for campaigns, and since most of these countries involve parliamentary systems, the free time is given to the political parties.) This would strengthen the role of political parties, providing them with new clean campaign resources to use to support their candidates or present their views. It would also provide the parties with the opportunity to focus new resources on underfinanced challengers, to the extent the parties are willing to assist them as opposed to their incumbent candidates.

CONCLUSION

There *are* ways to reduce the financial and social costs of TV advertising in U.S. campaigns. The policy changes proposed here would greatly reduce the current financial costs to federal candidates of communicating through TV. The changes would also challenge the basic premise that currently drives TV political ad campaigns. Through a combination of incentives and requirements, they would help move us away from the thirty-second negative attack ad without intruding on the candidates' First Amendment free-speech rights.

Changing the culture of American political campaigns is no easy task, needless to say. Citizens, however, are rightly fed up with the current system. The stakes involved here for our politics, our governance, and our country are enormous. Now is the time to begin changing our TV ways.

REFERENCES

Ansolabehere, Stephen, and Shanto Iyengar. 1996. *Going Negative: How Political Advertisements Shrink and Polarize the Electorate.* New York: Free Press.
Kaid, Lynda Lee, and Christiana Holtz-Bacha, eds. 1995. *Political Advertising in Western Democracies: Parties and Candidates on Television.* London: Sage.

Damned Spots
A Defense of Thirty-Second Campaign Ads
Stephen Bates and Edwin Diamond

. . . [E]veryone denounc[es] 30-second spots as demeaning, manipulative, and responsible for all that's wrong with American politics. David Broder, the mandarin of the op-ed page, admits he's "a crank on the subject." Otherwise staunch First Amendment champions, including *Washington Monthly* and, yes, *The New Republic,* want Congress to restrict the content of political ads. In fact, such commercials are good for the campaign, the voter, and the republic.

To cite the most common complaints:

1. TV Spots Make Campaigns Too Expensive.   The problem is nearly as old as television itself. William Benton, an ad-agency founder and a U.S. senator from Connecticut, talked of the "terrifying" cost of TV back in 1952. Campaign spending has risen sharply since then, and television advertising has contributed disproportionately. Whereas total political spending, adjusted for inflation, has tripled since 1952, the amount spent on television has increased at least fivefold. In some races, nine out of ten campaign dollars go to TV.

The important question is what candidates get in return. Quite a lot: a dollar spent on TV advertising may reach as many voters as $3 worth of newspaper ads or $50 worth of direct mail. Banning spots would probably *increase* campaign spending, by diverting candidates to less efficient forms of communication. In addition, spots reach supporters, opponents, and fence-sitters alike. This mass auditing imposes a measure of accountability that other media, particularly direct mail, lack.

2. A Candidate Can't Say Anything Substantive in 30 Seconds.   Referring to sound bites as well as spots, Michael Dukakis* sourly concluded that the 1988 campaign was about "phraseology," not ideology. But a lot can be said in thirty seconds. John Lindsay's 1972 presidential campaign broadcast a 30-

*Dukakis was 1988 Democratic candidate for president—*Editors.*

Stephen Bates is a Senior Fellow with the Annenberg Washington Program in Communication Policy Studies, Washington, D.C. Edwin Diamond is professor of journalism at New York University and a media columnist for *The New Yorker* magazine. From "Damned Spots," *New Republic* (September 7 and 14, 1992): pp. 14–18. Reprinted by permission of the *New Republic,* © 1992, The New Republic, Inc.

second spot in Florida that gave the candidate's positions on, among other issues, gun control (for), abortion rights (for), and school prayer (against). Lindsay's media manager, David Garth, later joked that the spot "probably lost the entire population of Florida."

A candidate can even make his point in 10 seconds. In California's 1992 Republican primary for U.S. Senate, one spot said simply: "I'm Bruce Herschensohn. My opponent, Tom Campbell, was the only Republican congressman opposing the 1990 anti-crime bill. He's liberal and wrong." Campbell replied in kind: "Bruce Herschensohn is lying, Tom Campbell voted to extend the death penalty to twenty-seven crimes, and was named Legislator of the Year by the California Fraternal Order of Police."

Though hardly encyclopedic, these spots reveal something about the candidates' priorities. They assert facts that can be checked and conclusions that can be challenged. If nothing else, they improve on what may have been the first ten-second spot, broadcast in 1954: "Minnesota needs a wide-awake governor! Vote for Orville Freeman and bring wide-awake action to Minnesota's problems!"

Brief ads do have one shortcoming. In 30 seconds, a candidate cannot hope to answer a half-true attack spot. In Bush's [Willie Horton] "revolving door" prison ad of 1988,* for instance, the voice-over says that Dukakis "gave weekend furloughs to first-degree murderers not eligible for parole," while the text on the screen tells viewers that "268 escaped" and "many are still at large." But as reporters discovered, only 4 of the 268 escapees were first-degree murderers, and only three escapees—none of them a murderer—were still at large. The Willie Horton example was an aberration.

This point might have been hard for the Dukakis team to convey in 30 seconds. What kept them from responding to Hortonism, however, was not the constraints of brevity; it was their decision to try to get public attention off the furlough program—a subject that, even without the Bush campaign's factual finagling, was bound to cost them votes. No sensible candidate will defend himself by saying he's only half as bad as his opponent charges.

Just as short spots aren't invariably shallow, long telecasts aren't invariably thoughtful. The 1960 John F. Kennedy campaign aired a two-minute spot with a bouncy jingle; it conveyed youth and vitality, but scarcely any information (except for a musical reference to Kennedy's Catholicism: "Can you deny to any man/The right he's guaranteed/To be elected president/No matter what his creed?"). As Ross Perot demonstrated, a candidate determined to be evasive can do so in a 30-second spot or in a two-hour live Q&A session.

3. Political Ads Are Responsible for the Low-Down-and-Dirty State of Political Discourse.   According to Arthur Schlesinger Jr., television is "draining content out of campaigns." But that assertion romanticizes the past. In the

---

*The "revolving door" ad became associated with convicted murderer Willie Horton, who, under a Massachusetts furlough program, was released from prison in 1986 for 48 hours, but never returned. He subsequently assaulted and raped a woman in Maryland, for which he was convicted and sentenced to prison in 1987—*Editors.*

1890s James Bryce, a Briton, decried American political campaigns in 1990s terms. Campaigns devote less attention to issues, he fretted, than to "questions of personal fitness," such as any "irregularity" in the candidate's relations with women. These issueless campaigns diminish the "confidence of the country in the honor of its public men."

Sleazy ads hardly raise the level of political discourse, but they aren't the superweapon that critics claim. "When a client of ours is attacked," boasts Democratic consultant Bob Squier, "the people of that state are going to get some kind of response the next day." These responses are invariably revealing. In a 1988 Dukakis ad, the candidate watches a TV set showing a Bush ad. "I'm fed up with it," Dukakis says. "Never seen anything like it in twenty-five years of public life—George Bush's negative television ads, distorting my record. . . ." But instead of presenting a sharp reply, Dukakis only turns off the set—a metaphor for his entire campaign.

4. TV Ads Keep the Potatoes on the Couch.   Barely half of eligible citizens voted in 1988, the lowest turnout in 40 years.* In fact, turnout has declined steadily since 1960. During the same period campaign-TV expenditures have tripled in constant dollars. Many of the TV dollars have been diverted from doorbell pushing, rallies, and other activities that involve citizens in politics. And, according to critics, simplistic, unfair spots discourage people from voting.

It is nearly impossible to untangle the factors that influence voter turnout. Some consultants, like Republican Eddie Mahe, argue that the decline in voting is a passing consequence of demographics. In the 1960s and 1970s the baby-boom generation reached voting age and lowered voting figures (so did the 26th Amendment, which changed the voting age from 21 to 18). No surprises there: turnout is traditionally lower among the young. So, as the boomer generation ages, turnout will increase.

As for how spots affect turnout in particular elections, the evidence goes both ways. In the 1990 race for U.S. Senate in North Carolina, early polls showed blue-collar whites inclined to stay home. But many of them turned out to vote for Jesse Helms after his anti-quotas spot received heavy air play and news coverage.

Are spots, then, blameless for the parlous state of voter participation? Well, no. Even if they don't cloud the mind, they may in some sense sap the political will. To the extent that spots resemble lifestyle commercials—It's Miller Time, It's Morning in America—they may be taken no more seriously than other TV advertising. This is especially so when no other campaign is visible to the viewer. Today's political rally, as Democratic consultant Robert Shrum has said, consists of three people around the TV set.

But the doomsayers' solution—to try to divorce politics from TV—won't work. Since the 1950s the voting classes have increasingly stayed home to be entertained, a trend encouraged by demographics (the suburban migration), by

---

*Turnout in 1996 was even lower—49 percent—*Editors.*

new at-home options (cable, VCRs), and at least partly by fear (crime in the streets). Banning political spots, as some cranks in the press and Congress would do, wouldn't bring voters outdoors. It would deprive the couch-potato/citizen of a sometimes abused but ultimately unmatched source of electoral information. As Dukakis discovered, melodramatically turning off the TV resolves nothing.

Internet Resources

Visit our website at http://www.mhhe.com/diclerico for links and resources relating to Campaigns and the Media.

Elections

Campaign Finance

It was the magnitude of money scandals in the 1972 presidential election that spurred Congress to act, producing by 1974 the most comprehensive campaign finance reforms enacted in our nation's history. These included contribution limits, spending limits, public financing, more rigorous disclosure requirements, and a newly created Federal Election Commission to oversee the financing of federal elections. The 1996 presidential election, however, brought with it renewed concern about the role of money in elections as unprecedented sums were raised and spent—much of it legal, and some not. In the 2000 race for the presidential nomination, the issue of financing campaigns continued to receive considerable attention, not only because it appeared that spending levels would outdistance even the record set in 1996, but also because presidential candidates spoke to the issue. The parties' two nominees, Al Gore and George W. Bush, went on record as favoring some changes in the current law, and Senator John McCain (R-Ariz.) went so far as to make campaign finance reform the very centerpiece of his unsuccessful bid for the Republican presidential nomination.

Congress finally decided to act in 2002, passing reform legislation known as the McCain-Feingold bill. Among other things, it raised from $1,000 to $2,000 the contribution an individual may make to a candidate running for federal office (nomination and general election campaigns were defined as separate elections). In addition, the new legislation prohibited the national political parties from accepting any "soft money" contributions—a form of giving that had allowed individuals, groups, labor unions, and corporations to contribute unlimited sums of money to political parties for activities defined as party building.

As often happens, however, the best of intentions led to consequences not intended—a point made by authors Thomas Edsall and Juliet Eilperin in the first selection. Although identifying two positive effects that will follow from the new campaign finance legislation, they fear that the legislation is also destined to increase the influence of special interest money, diminish the role of public financing, and frustrate public disclosure of contributions—all consequences that campaign finance reformers would presumably want to avoid.

In the second selection, Bruce Ackerman and Ian Ayres view with a jaundiced eye efforts to curb the influence of money by such conventional practices as limiting contribution and spending amounts, providing for public financing of campaigns, and full disclosure. Thinking outside the box and taking their cue from principles underlying the vote, they offer two highly novel proposals for campaign finance reform—proposals that, they assert, will serve to offset the impact of special interest contributions, foster political expression by enabling all the citizenry to play a more active role in financing candidates, and eliminate the purchase with large contributions of access and influence.

PAC Attack II

Why Some Groups Are Learning to Love Campaign
Finance Reform

Thomas B. Edsall and *Juliet Eilperin*

Campaign finance reform . . . [took] effect . . . Nov. 6, 2002, and political consultant Bob Doyle is ready. Rather than relying on the Democratic Party to help bankroll his candidates, he is going directly to Jewish organizations, unions, even gun-rights groups.

Steering candidates toward special interest groups isn't new, but Doyle—a Democrat who runs his own fundraising and strategy firm, Sutter's Mill—predicts it will soon be more important than ever. "We're going to see explosive growth in the role of interest groups when it comes to campaigns," Doyle says.

That's because of the . . . McCain-Feingold bill. The biggest change in campaign finance law in 25 years, it is transforming the way candidates, major parties and political action committees (PACs) operate—but not exactly the way the legislation's sponsors had in mind. Instead of reducing the power wielded by special interest groups in American elections, the McCain-Feingold reform bill is magnifying that power and making PACs, the *betes noires* of Common Cause and other good government groups, key players in campaign finance once again.

And that isn't the only unintended consequence of the campaign finance measure President Bush signed in March 2002. The public financing of presidential primaries, a centerpiece of 1974 reform legislation, may soon go the way of the whistle-stop tour. Without an infusion of federal money or changes in federal regulations—steps Congress is unlikely to take—public financing for presidential primaries will be dealt a setback in 2004, and could disappear altogether by 2008 as candidates opt to rely solely on private support to free themselves from spending ceilings.

Public disclosure could suffer too. Political operatives of all ideological persuasions are scrambling to find new places to put the "soft money" that had been going to the political parties. When soft money was channeled through the parties, laws required full disclosure of both contributors and expenditures. But the new vehicles for this money are almost certain to be more secretive, with little or no obligation to reveal their activities.

Thomas Edsall covers money and politics and Juliet Eilperin covers Congress for *The Washington Post*. From Thomas B. Edsall and Juliet Eilperin, "PAC Attack II: Why Some Groups Are Learning to Love Campaign Finance Reform," *The Washington Post* (August 18, 2002): B-2. © 2002, *The Washington Post*. Reprinted with permission.

Reformers still defend McCain-Feingold as the first step in a long process, and in fairness, it does appear likely to achieve at least two significant goals.

- The curtailment, if not the full elimination, of "soft money" raising and spending by the national political parties. "Soft money" is made up of large donations, generally $25,000 to well in excess of $1 million, made by corporations, unions and rich people.
- An expansion of direct mail and e-mail fundraising—a method of campaign financing viewed as among the least corrupting since the contributions are mostly small, reducing the danger of quid pro quo relationships between givers and recipients.

On the other side of the ledger, however, the legislation—named after chief sponsors Sens. John McCain (R-Ariz.) and Russell Feingold (D-Wis.)—is pushing the political system in directions that members of the self-described "reform community" say they find very troubling.

The strengthening of businesses, trade associations and single-issue PACs is one of those trends.

For years, these groups epitomized, in the eyes of campaign reformers, special interests and a system that overwhelmingly favored incumbents. In preelection periods, legislative leaders felt compelled to attend three or more "Washington fundraisers" a day. In the early and mid-1990s, most campaign finance reform proposals included provisions that would have either reduced the amount of money PACs can give to candidates—now set at $5,000 in a primary and $5,000 in the general election—or banned PACs altogether. After repeated failures, however, the anti-PAC movement faded, and no tighter limits were included in McCain-Feingold.

Now, the McCain-Feingold ban on the use of soft money by the national parties has abruptly made "hard money"—smaller contributions of up to a maximum $2,000 by an individual—crucial to the survival of politicians. That favors PACs and business groups, which can act as "bundlers" of individual contributions by gathering like-minded people from around the country to give the maximum amount permitted to many different campaigns. Well-connected lobbyists and trade associations with large Rolodexes will be among the best equipped to capitalize on the new law, which places a premium on the ability to raise tens, if not hundreds, of $1,000 to $2,000 donations.

One group that immediately recognized this was the Business and Industry PAC (BIPAC), an organization supported by corporations and trade associations who want to flex their political muscles. On June 6, 2002, BIPAC held a strategy session with 110 business and trade association executives where there was immediate agreement "that PACs have become the coin of the realm," according to Greg Casey, BIPAC president and CEO. "Now we are back to where PACs are not only important, but good."

Envisioning a similar strategy, albeit with different aims, Ellen Malcolm, who runs EMILY's List, a PAC devoted to electing Democratic women who favor abortion rights, said at a recent panel session on McCain-Feingold at Georgetown Law School: "Nothing has changed for PACs. . . . We are going to do an awful lot to elect people. And the changes of the new law are not going to get in the way of our doing that."

Though some reformers fear this could strengthen incumbents, it could also bolster challengers from within party ranks. Challengers will be at less of a disadvantage in primaries now that parties can no longer reward loyal incumbents with soft money support. Special interests could have greater impact in primaries, where turnout is lower.

"It's a bigger bang for your buck," says Stephen Moore, senior fellow at the Cato Institute and head of the pro-freemarket Club for Growth, which has funded conservative challengers in GOP primaries. "You can get almost ten times for your money what you could in a general election."

Meanwhile, McCain-Feingold seems likely to put a stake through the heart of public financing. Since 1974, major political candidates have been able to receive taxpayer money in exchange for accepting ceilings on their overall primary and general election spending. Now, operatives for almost all the prospective Democratic presidential candidates say that they would prefer to abandon public financing to free themselves from the spending limits, both overall and state-by-state. For the 2004 presidential campaign, candidates can receive taxpayer money to match the first $250 of every contribution from an individual, if they agree to an overall primary spending limit of about $44 million.

It is a near certainty that President Bush will reject public financing in the primaries, as he did in 2000. Most GOP and Democratic political operatives expect Bush to be able to at least double the $101 million he raised in 2000, meaning he will have more than $200 million to spend before the GOP's September convention even though he will probably not face any serious opposition for the nomination.

A Democratic candidate who takes public money, in contrast, faces the daunting prospect of having to spend most or all of the estimated $44 million allotted to him or her to fight multiple opponents for the nomination. With early primaries, a winning candidate could well emerge by mid-March 2004 virtually broke, with no way to pay for staff, travel or even token commercials. Under earlier rules, the Democratic National Committee would have been able to step in and temporarily hire and house campaign staff, and air "issue" ads, thinly cloaked campaign commercials, all paid for with soft money. Under the new legislation, the party standard bearer might have to wait four months, until the Democratic convention in late July or early August, before spending more money—while Bush floods the television airwaves.

McCain-Feingold has added to this incentive to abandon public financing. First, the new law doubled to $2,000 the amount an individual can give a candidate. This makes it easier to raise more than the $44 million ceiling that comes with public financing. At the same time, the higher limit on individual contributions reduces the relative value of the public subsidy. Under the $1,000 limit, a candidate could get $250, or 25 percent, of top contributions matched by the government; under a $2,000 limit, the $250 match, which was not changed, amounts to only 12.5 percent of the maximum individual gift.

So why did campaign finance reformers back this legislation? Basically, they say it was the best they could get.

Tom Mann, a senior fellow at the Brookings Institution and a leading proponent of McCain-Feingold, says that the framers of the legislation wanted to make public financing more attractive, "but the fact was, it could not be done. It was politically impossible." Faced with what Mann calls a political system "collapsing" under the weight of soft money, reformers backed McCain-Feingold "with full awareness" that it "would further increase incentives to opt out of the system."

Fred Wertheimer, who has devoted much of his adult life to campaign finance reform, says McCain-Feingold was "the first battle in a series of battles that have to take place. The fact that all could not be done at once was not of our choosing." . . .

Wertheimer argues that as much as anything, passage of McCain-Feingold has broken a 28-year logjam blocking congressional action on campaign finance. It remains to be seen what, and who, will be washed away now.

Voting with Dollars
A New Paradigm for Campaign Finance
Bruce Ackerman and Ian Ayres

Campaign finance lives in a time warp, untouched by the regulatory revolution of the past generation. Reformers suppose that they can adapt well-established models to fix the problem of big money in politics. But they are wrong. Real progress requires us to rethink the very foundations of the enterprise.

The old paradigm has three elements. The first confronts big money as if it raised a problem similar to the one posed by polluters dumping garbage into a waterway. The Environmental Protection Agency not only restricts the garbage each polluter can dump but places an overall limit on the amount of junk in the river. Why not do the same when big money pollutes democratic politics?

To be sure, the Supreme Court has resisted this analogy in the name of the First Amendment—repeatedly striking down efforts to restrict overall campaign spending. But judicial intervention manages only to precipitate predictable boos from the left, and cheers from the right, with no serious efforts at reappraisal from either side.

The debate is no less pre-scripted when we turn to a second basic remedy. Why not reduce or eliminate the flood of private money by providing for publicly subsidized campaigns? Reformers invariably understand the injection of "clean money" as a centralized process—replete with heavy-handed requirements that favor incumbents, entrench existing parties, and alienate citizens from funding decisions. . . .

[T]he third reform plank . . . [is] . . . full publicity for all contributions. The public has a right to know who is paying whom when. With every deal open and aboveboard, let the voters decide whether a big gift or giver taints the candidate's integrity. This full-information plank has gained increasing prominence over the past decade. Even strict conservatives concede that secret transfers of cash look suspicious.[1] If the public keeps demanding reform, the best way to channel protest is by insisting on full information. Still more recently, leading liberals have been coming to the same conclusion.[2] . . .

These standard responses systematically mislead when we turn to our present subject. Command and control [i.e., contribution and spending limits],

Bruce Ackerman is Sterling Professor of Law and Political Science, and Ian Ayres is William K. Townsend Professor of Law at Yale University. From Bruce Ackerman and Ian Ayres, *Voting with Dollars: A New Paradigm for Campaign Finance.* (New Haven and London: Yale University Press, 2002), pp. 3–9.

bureaucratic subsidies [i.e., public subsidies], and full information are part of the problem, not part of the solution. We . . . build on a more democratic tradition centered on the franchise. When dealing with the ballot, Americans do not champion the virtues of full information. We make it a crime for anybody to penetrate the sanctity of the voting booth. Nor do we suppose that votes . . . may be sold to the highest bidder. Each citizen expects his ballot to have equal weight in the final decision.

THE PATRIOT DOLLAR PLAN

Why not think of campaign finance in similar ways? It isn't enough to count every vote equally on election day. The American citizen should also be given a more equal say in funding decisions. Just as he receives a ballot on election day, he should also receive a special credit card to finance his favorite candidate as she makes her case to the electorate. Call it a Patriot card, and suppose that Congress seeded every voter's account with fifty "patriot dollars." If the 100 million Americans who came to the polls in 2000 had also "voted" with their patriot cards during the campaign, their combined contributions would have amounted to $5 billion—overwhelming the $3 billion provided by private donors.[3] Under this scenario, would George W. Bush and Al Gore—two heirs of political dynasties—have emerged as the leading candidates? If so, would they have made different issues central to their campaigns?

Our patriotic initiative avoids many of the difficulties associated with traditional "clean money" proposals. The old paradigm creates a special bureaucracy charged with the delicate task of doling out funds to qualifying candidates and parties. But the Patriot program does not keep ordinary Americans on the sidelines while bureaucrats give politicians handouts. Our new paradigm makes campaign finance into a new occasion for citizen sovereignty—encouraging Americans to vote with their dollars as well as their ballots, giving renewed vitality to their democratic commitments.

We have only begun to tap the potential of voting with dollars. Our paradigm also points in a new direction for the regulation of private contributions. Liberals and conservatives have increasingly converged on the "full information" plank of the traditional reform agenda—to the point where it is fast becoming a Motherhood issue. Who could possibly complain about requiring candidates to reveal who is bankrolling their campaigns, and how much they are giving?[4]

THE SECRET DONATION PLAN

We do. Full publicity makes sense only under one assumption—that the candidates themselves know the identity of their contributors. Because candidates will naturally be grateful to big givers, shouldn't they be obliged to share this knowledge with the public? Otherwise, ordinary voters can't subject political rhetoric to a basic reality test—matching each politician's words against the list of contributors who will come around after election day to assert, however discreetly, their claims to official favor.

But this argument begs a big question—why *should* candidates know how much money their contributors have provided? . . .

A victorious politician is guilty of corruption if he delivers the goods to his campaign contributors in too obvious a fashion. The analogy with the ballot box provides a sounder guide for policy. The secret ballot came to America only during the late nineteenth century. Voters previously cast their ballots in full view of the contesting parties, who carefully monitored each decision. Within this framework, corrupt vote-buying was commonplace. Party hacks could readily determine whether they got what they were paying for. No voter could receive his election day turkey without casting his ballot before the watchful eyes of the turkey's provider.

It was the secret ballot, not some sudden burst of civic virtue, that transformed the situation. Once a voter could promise to vote one way, and actually vote another, it was no longer easy for him to sell his vote. Even if he sincerely intended to perform his side of the bargain, vote-buyers could no longer verify the credibility of his commitment. Suddenly, the promise of a voter to sell his franchise for money became worthless—and as a consequence, vote-buying declined dramatically.[5]

We use the same logic in dealing with private contributions. On analogy with the secret ballot, we propose the "secret donation booth." Contributors will be barred from giving money directly to candidates. They must instead pass their checks through a blind trust. Candidates will get access to all money deposited in their account with the blind trust. But we will take steps to assure that they won't be able to identify who provided the funds. To be sure, lots of people will come up to the candidate and say they have given vast sums of money. And yet none of them will be able to prove it. As a consequence, lots of people who *didn't* give gifts will also claim to have provided millions of dollars.

The resulting situation will be structurally similar to the one created by the secret ballot. Protected by the privacy of the voting booth, you are free to go up to George W. Bush and tell him that you voted for him enthusiastically in 2000 even though you actually voted for Al Gore. Knowing this, neither the president nor you will be prone to take such protestations seriously.

The same "cheap talk" regime will disrupt the special-interest dealing we now take for granted. Just as the secret ballot makes it more difficult for candidates to *buy* votes, a secret donation booth makes it harder for candidates to *sell* access or influence. The voting booth disrupts vote-buying because candidates are uncertain how a citizen actually voted; anonymous donations disrupt influence peddling because candidates are uncertain whether givers actually gave what they say they gave. Just as vote-buying plummeted with the secret ballot, campaign contributions would sink with the secret donation booth.

But not to zero. There are lots of reasons for contributing to campaigns, and the new regime undercuts only one of them—the desire to obtain a quid pro quo from a victorious candidate. It would no longer make much business sense for a group of trial lawyers or oil barons to contribute big bucks to a candidate to encourage special-interest legislation. But the secret donation booth will not deter gifts from citizens who simply wish to express their ideological commitment to a candidate's causes without any expectation of special access or influence. These ideological gifts may well be very substantial, depending on the candidate's charisma and the attractiveness of her positions.[6] Nevertheless, the overall volume of private donations will generally be much lower.

Especially when Patriot is taken into account. Each voter already has 50 Patriot dollars at his disposal to support candidates and political organizations during the campaign. Only those who find this sum inadequate to express their convictions will dip into their private funds. Cumulating our two initiatives, it seems safe to predict that our new paradigm will generate a big change in the prevailing public-private mix of financing. During the last campaign more than $3 billion flowed into the campaign coffers of all aspirants for federal office, but we would be surprised if half this sum were generated under the new regime; in contrast, $5 billion or so would be coming into the campaign through the patriotic system. On conservative assumptions, public funds would dominate by a ratio of 2 to 1, and probably much more. At the same time, the total resources available for political speech would be much greater under the reformed system—in contrast to the $3-plus billion under the ancien régime, politicians would have more than $6 billion with which to engage the voters. The new paradigm, in short, promises an effective increase in both political equality *and* political expression. It achieves this result without compromising any of the basic liberties of citizens—even the freedom to give private contributions. As long as givers channel money through blind trusts, they should be free to give substantial amounts to the causes they favor. . . .

SUMMING UP

To sum up the new paradigm: We reject centralized campaign subsidies in favor of massive democratization through Patriot dollars; we reject full disclosure of private contributions in favor of the secret donation booth; we reject comprehensive controls on private money in favor of selective restrictions imposed only as a last resort.

We call this "voting with dollars" because it mimics two core attributes of the franchise: Citizens are given equal voting power, but they must exercise this power anonymously. The basic equality of citizens is expressed by their equal access to Patriot dollars. The secrecy of the ballot box is expanded to disrupt special-interest dealing in campaign finance.

We refuse, in short, to view the problem of campaign finance as if it represents the all-or-nothing choice of suppressing private contributions or leaving them unregulated. Our new paradigm uses anonymity to cleanse private giving of its worst abuses while allowing it to serve as a valuable supplementary support to the robust public debate fostered by billions of Patriot dollars allocated by millions of concerned citizens.

NOTES

1. See Doug Bandow, Best Campaign-Finance Reform Is No Limits, *USA Today,* Aug. 11, 2000, at 15A; James Bopp, Jr., Campaign Finance "Reform": The Good, the Bad and the Unconstitutional, Heritage Foundation, Backgrounder no. 1308, July 19, 1999, pp. 3, 20, 21–22 (found on www.heritage.org); Pete du Pont, Campaign Finance Defies a Complicated Solution, *Tampa Trib.,* Sept. 7, 1997, at 6. This theme is taken up by Justices Kennedy and Thomas in their separate opinions—both dissenting—in *Nixon v. Shrink Missouri Government PAC,* 528 U.S. 377, 408, 428–29 (2000). Representative John Doolittle has proposed "The Citizen Legislature and Political Freedom Act," which essentially repeals all limits on contributions and requires their immediate disclosure to the public. H.R. 1922, 106th Cong. §§ 2 and 4 (1999).

2. See, e.g., Kathleen M. Sullivan, Political Money and Freedom of Speech, 30 *U.C. Davis L. Rev.* 663, 688–89 (1997); Samuel Issacharoff and Pamela S. Karlan, The Hydraulics of Campaign Finance Reform, 77 *Tex. L. Rev.* 1705, 1736–37 (1999); Testimony of Ira Glasser, Executive Director of the American Civil Liberties Union, before the United States Senate Committee on Rules and Administration, Mar. 22, 2000, FDCH Congressional Testimony; Kathleen Sullivan, Against Campaign Finance Reform, 1998 *Utah L. Rev.* 311, 326–27; Joel M. Gora, *Buckley v. Valeo:* A Landmark of Political Freedom, 33 *Akron L. Rev.* 7, 35–36 (1999).

3. See www.fec.gov/finance (contributions to federal candidates and parties of federal "hard" monies were in excess of $2.9 billion). See also Don Van Natta, Jr., Dough Gets Little Rise Out of Voters: The 2000 Campaigns for President and Congress Might Cost a Record $3 Billion, but People Don't Seem to Care, *Portland Oregonian,* Jan. 30, 2000, at D-3 ("Never have so many given so much in so little time. . . . [C]ampaign finance experts estimate that the 2000 elections for president and Congress will end up costing a total of $3 billion, an amount that would dwarf the $2.1 billion spent in 1996").

4. There is one obvious constitutional problem generated by a regime of mandatory disclosure. Publicity may have a chilling effect on contributions to unpopular groups. See, e.g., *NAACP v. Alabama,* 357 U.S. 449 (1958) (finding production order issued in connection with litigation over qualification of NAACP to do business in state unconstitutional to extent it required disclosure of members within the state, because of potential chilling effect on affiliation with NAACP). *Buckley* accordingly exempts from the disclosure requirement minor parties that can show "a reasonable probability that the compelled disclosure of a party's contributors' names will subject them to threats, harassment, or reprisals from either Government officials or private parties." *Buckley v. Valeo,* 424 U.S. 1, 73. See also *Brown v. Socialist Workers '74 Campaign Comm. (Ohio),* 459 U.S. 87, 93–98 (1982) (finding that Ohio could compel the disclosure of neither campaign contributors nor recipients of campaign disbursements when the people so identified would likely be subject to harassment).

This is a very serious problem, but it need not detain us because we will be arguing against the entire notion of mandatory disclosure.

5. See, e.g., Jack C. Heckelman, The Effect of the Secret Ballot on Voter Turnout Rates, 82 *Pub. Choice* 107, 119 (1995) (estimating a 6.9 percent drop in voting in states utilizing the secret ballot and attributing drop to the elimination of bribery).

6. Ideological giving raises the question of democratic fairness, because ideologies favored by the rich will have an obvious advantage. In Chapter 3 we shall suggest ways of ameliorating this problem—it can never be magically "solved"—within the framework of a free society.

The Electoral College

No feature of our Constitution has been the subject of more constitutional amendments than the Electoral College. The primary impetus behind these proposals has been to correct what is widely regarded as the most fundamental flaw in the Electoral College—the possibility that presidents can be elected with fewer votes than their opponents. This outcome has in fact been visited upon us three times (excluding the 1824 election decided by the House) in American history. The most recent, of course, was the 2000 presidential election in which Vice President Al Gore outran George W. Bush by more than half a million votes nationwide, while losing to Bush by five votes (271–266) in the Electoral College.

It should come as no surprise that this latest "misfiring" of the Electoral College has renewed the debate over what to do about it. In the first selection, historian Arthur Schlesinger Jr. minces no words, arguing that the Electoral College as it currently functions is simply incompatible with the theory of democracy. Although insisting that change is imperative, he rejects as inadequate a number of alternatives, including direct election which, while guaranteeing victory to the candidate with the most votes, could be harmful to the political process in other ways. The solution, he suggests, is a simple and workable proposal advanced back in 1978 by the Twentieth Century Fund Task Force on Reform of the Presidential Election Process. Known as the "national bonus" plan, it retains the Electoral College arrangement while at the same time insuring that the candidate with the most popular votes wins.

Political scientist Robert Weissberg is little moved by Schlesinger's call for action. Not only does he question exactly what "majority" Schlesinger has in mind for presidential elections, but he also finds the historian to be highly selective in his concern for majority rule. Although readily acknowledging that the Electoral College is a flawed institution, Weissberg also cautions us against expecting too much from attempts to reform the system. Any changes will, after all, be fashioned by human beings, all having their own agendas, which may well result in substituting one set of biases for another, or even more likely—deadlock. And as for the particular fix advanced by Schlesinger, Weissberg is dismissive, insisting that the purpose behind the national bonus plan can easily be corrupted and make much worse some of the problems that already attend our electoral process.

Not the People's Choice

How to Democratize American Democracy

Arthur M. Schlesinger Jr.

The true significance of the disputed 2000 election has thus far escaped public attention. This was an election that made the loser of the popular vote the president of the United States. But that astounding fact has been obscured: first by the flood of electoral complaints about deceptive ballots, hanging chads, and so on in Florida; then by the political astuteness of the court-appointed president in behaving as if he had won the White House by a landslide; and now by the effect of September 11 in presidentializing George W. Bush and giving him commanding popularity in the polls.

"The fundamental maxim of republican government," observed Alexander Hamilton in the 22d Federalist, "requires that the sense of the majority should prevail." A reasonable deduction from Hamilton's premise is that the presidential candidate who wins the most votes in an election should also win the election. That quite the opposite can happen is surely the great anomaly in the American democratic order.

Yet the National Commission on Federal Election Reform, a body appointed in the wake of the 2000 election and co-chaired (honorarily) by former Presidents Gerald Ford and Jimmy Carter, virtually ignored it. [In] August 2001, in a report optimistically entitled *To Assure Pride and Confidence in the Electoral Process*, the commission concluded that it had satisfactorily addressed "most of the problems that came into national view" in 2000. But nothing in the ponderous 80-page document addressed the most fundamental problem that came into national view: the constitutional anomaly that permits the people's choice to be refused the presidency.

Little consumed more time during our nation's Constitutional Convention than debate over the mode of choosing the chief executive. The framers, determined to ensure the separation of powers, rejected the proposal that Congress elect the president. Both James Madison and James Wilson, the "fathers" of the Constitution, argued for direct election by the people, but the convention, fear-

Arthur M. Schlesinger, Jr. is a former special assistant to President John F. Kennedy and the recipient of two Pulitzer Prizes. This article is adapted from his contribution to *A Badly Flawed Election*, edited by Ronald Dworkin (New Press 2002). From "Not the People's Choice: How to Democratize American Democracy." Reprinted with permission from *The American Prospect*, Volume 13, Number 6: March 25, 2002. The American Prospect, 5 Broad Street, Boston, MA 02109. All rights reserved.

ing the parochialism of uninformed voters, also rejected that plan. In the end, the framers agreed on the novel device of an electoral college. Each state would appoint electors equal in number to its representation in Congress. The electors would then vote for two persons. The one receiving a majority of electoral votes would then become president; the runner-up, vice president. And in a key sentence, the Constitution stipulated that of these two persons at least one should not be from the same state as the electors. . . .

"The mode of appointment of the Chief Magistrate [President] of the United States," wrote Hamilton in the 68th Federalist, "is almost the only part of the system, of any consequence, which has escaped without severe censure." This may have been true when Hamilton wrote in 1788; it was definitely not true thereafter. According to the Congressional Research Service, legislators since the First Congress have offered more than a thousand proposals to alter the mode of choosing presidents.

No legislator has advocated the election of the president by Congress. Some have advocated modifications in the electoral college—to change the electoral units from states to congressional districts, for example, or to require a proportional division of electoral votes. In the 1950s, the latter approach received considerable congressional favor in a plan proposed by Senator Henry Cabot Lodge, Jr., and Representative Ed Gossett. The Lodge-Gossett amendment would have ended the winner-take-all electoral system and divided each state's electoral vote according to the popular vote. In 1950 the Senate endorsed the amendment, but the House turned it down. Five years later, Senator Estes Kefauver revived the Lodge-Gossett plan and won the backing of the Senate Judiciary Committee. A thoughtful debate ensued, with Senators John F. Kennedy and Paul H. Douglas leading the opposition and defeating the amendment.

Neither the district plan nor the proportionate plan would prevent a popular-vote loser from winning the White House. To correct this great anomaly of the Constitution, many have advocated the abolition of the electoral college and its replacement by direct popular elections. . . .

The most recent president to propose a direct-election amendment was Jimmy Carter in 1997. The amendment, he said, would "ensure that the candidate chosen by the votes actually becomes President. Under the Electoral College, it is always possible that the winner of the popular vote will not be elected." This had already happened, Carter said, in 1824, 1876, and 1888. . . .

Over the last half-century, many other eminent politicos and organizations have also advocated direct popular elections: Presidents Richard Nixon and Gerald Ford; Vice Presidents Alben Barkley and Hubert Humphrey; Senators Robert A. Taft, Mike Mansfield, Edward Kennedy, Henry Jackson, Robert Dole, Howard Baker, and Everett Dirksen; the American Bar Association, the League of Women Voters, the AFL-CIO, and the U.S. Chamber of Commerce. Polls have shown overwhelming public support for direct elections.

In the late 1960s, the drive for a direct-election amendment achieved a certain momentum. Led by Senator Birch Bayh of Indiana, an inveterate and persuasive constitutional reformer, the campaign was fueled by the fear that Governor George Wallace of Alabama might win enough electoral votes in 1968 to throw the election into the House of Representatives. In May 1968, a Gallup poll recorded 66 percent of the U.S. public in favor of direct election—and in November of that year, an astonishing 80 percent. But Wallace's 46 electoral votes in 1968 were not enough to deny Nixon a majority, and complacency soon took over. "The decline in one-party states," a Brookings Institution study concluded in 1970, "has made it far less likely today that the runner-up in popular votes will be elected President."

Because the danger of electoral-college misfire seemed academic, abolition of the electoral college again became a low-priority issue. Each state retained the constitutional right to appoint its electors "in such manner as the legislature thereof directs." And all but two states, Maine and Nebraska, kept the unit rule.

Then came the election of 2000. For the fourth time in American history, the winner of the popular vote was refused the presidency. And Albert Gore, Jr., had won the popular vote not by Grover Cleveland's dubious 100,000 but by more than half a million. Another nearly three million votes had gone to the third-party candidate Ralph Nader, making the victor, George W. Bush, more than ever a minority president.

Nor was Bush's victory in the electoral college unclouded by doubt. The electoral vote turned on a single state, Florida. Five members of the Supreme Court, forsaking their usual deference to state sovereignty, stopped the Florida recount and thereby made Bush president. Critics wondered: If the facts had been the same but the candidates reversed, with Bush winning the popular vote (as indeed observers had rather expected) and Gore hoping to win the electoral vote, would the gang of five have found the same legal arguments to elect Gore that they used to elect Bush?

I expected an explosion of public outrage over the rejection of the people's choice. But there was surprisingly little in the way of outcry. It is hard to imagine such acquiescence in a popular-vote-loser presidency if the popular-vote winner had been, say, Adlai Stevenson or John F. Kennedy or Ronald Reagan. Such leaders attracted do-or-die supporters, voters who cared intensely about them and who not only would have questioned the result but would have been ardent in pursuit of fundamental reform. After a disappointing campaign, Vice President Gore simply did not excite the same impassioned commitment.

Yet surely the 2000 election put the Republic in an intolerable predicament—intolerable because the result contravened the theory of democracy. Many expected that the election would resurrect the movement for direct election of presidents. Since direct elections have obvious democratic plausibility and since few Americans understand the electoral college anyway, its abolition seems a logical remedy.

The resurrection has not taken place. Constitutional reformers seem intimidated by the argument that a direct-election amendment would antagonize small-population states and therefore could not be ratified. It would necessarily eliminate the special advantage conferred on small states by the two electoral votes handed to all states regardless of population. Small-state opposition, it is claimed, would make it impossible to collect the two-thirds of Congress and the three-fourths of the states required for ratification.

This is an odd argument, because most political analysts are convinced that the electoral college in fact benefits large states, not small ones. Far from being hurt by direct elections, small states, they say, would benefit from them. The idea that "the present electoral-college preserves the power of the small states," write Lawrence D. Longley and Alan G. Braun in *The Politics of Electoral Reform,* ". . . simply is not the case." The electoral-college system "benefits large states, urban interests, white minorities, and/or black voters." So, too, a Brookings Institution report: "For several decades liberal, urban Democrats and progressive, urban-suburban Republicans have tended to dominate presidential politics; they would lose influence under the direct-vote plan."

Racial minorities holding the balance of power in large states agree. "Take away the electoral college," said Vernon Jordan as president of the Urban League, "and the importance of being black melts away. Blacks, instead of being crucial to victory in major states, simply become 10 percent of the electorate, with reduced impact."

The debate over whom direct elections would benefit has been long, wearisome, contradictory, and inconclusive. Even computer calculations are of limited use, since they assume a static political culture. They do not take into account, nor can they predict, the changes wrought in voter dynamics by candidates, issues, and events.

As Senator John Kennedy said during the Lodge-Gossett debate: "It is not only the unit vote for the Presidency we are talking about, but a whole solar system of governmental power. If it is proposed to change the balance of power of one of the elements of the solar system," Kennedy observed, "it is necessary to consider all the others. . . . What the effects of these various changes will be on the Federal system, the two-party system, the popular plurality system and the large-State-small-State checks and balances system, no one knows."

Direct elections do, however, have the merit of correcting the great anomaly of the Constitution and providing an escape from the intolerable predicament. "The electoral college method of electing a President of the United States," said the American Bar Association when an amendment was last seriously considered, "is archaic, undemocratic, complex, ambiguous, indirect, and dangerous." In contrast, as Birch Bayh put it, "direct popular election of the president is the only system that is truly democratic, truly equitable, and can truly reflect the will of the people."

The direct-election plan meets the moral criteria of a democracy. It would elect the people's choice. It would ensure equal treatment of all votes. It would reduce the power of sectionalism in politics. It would reinvigorate party competition and combat voter apathy by giving parties the incentive to get out their votes in states that they have no hope of carrying.

The arguments for abolishing the electoral college are indeed powerful. But direct elections raise troubling problems of their own—especially their impact on the two-party system and on JFK's "solar system of governmental power." . . .

The two-party system has been a source of stability; FDR called it "one of the greatest methods of unification and of teaching people to think in common terms." The alternative is a slow, agonized descent into an era of what Walter Dean Burnham has termed "politics without parties." Political adventurers might roam the countryside like Chinese warlords, building personal armies equipped with electronic technologies, conducting hostilities against various rival warlords, forming alliances with others, and, if they win elections, striving to govern through ad hoc coalitions. Accountability would fade away. Without the stabilizing influences of parties, American politics would grow angrier, wilder, and more irresponsible.

There are compelling reasons to believe that the abolition of state-by-state, winner-take-all electoral votes would hasten the disintegration of the party system. Minor parties have a dim future in the electoral college. Unless third parties have a solid regional base, like the Populists of 1892 or the Dixiecrats of 1948, they cannot hope to win electoral votes. Millard Fillmore, the Know-Nothing candidate in 1856, won 21.6 percent of the popular vote and only 2 percent of the electoral vote. In 1912, when Theodore Roosevelt's candidacy turned the Republicans into a third party, William Howard Taft carried 23 percent of the popular vote and only 1.5 percent of the electoral votes.

But direct elections, by enabling minor parties to accumulate votes from state to state—impossible in the electoral-college system—would give them a new role and a new influence. Direct-election advocates recognize that the proliferation of minor candidates and parties would drain votes away from the major parties. Most direct-election amendments therefore provide that if no candidate receives 40 percent of the vote the two top candidates would fight it out in a runoff election.

This procedure would offer potent incentives for radical zealots (Ralph Nader, for example), freelance media adventurers (Pat Buchanan), eccentric billionaires (Ross Perot), and flamboyant characters (Jesse Ventura) to jump into presidential contests; incentives, too, to "green" parties, senior-citizen parties, nativist parties, right-to-life parties, pro-choice parties, anti-gun-control parties, homosexual parties, prohibition parties, and so on down the single-issue line.

Splinter parties would multiply not because they expected to win elections but because their accumulated vote would increase their bargaining power in the runoff. Their multiplication might well make runoffs the rule rather than the exception. And think of the finagling that would take place between the first and second rounds of a presidential election! Like J. Q. Adams in 1824, the victors would very likely find that they are a new target for "corrupt bargains."

Direct election would very likely bring to the White House candidates who do not get anywhere near a majority of the popular votes. The prospect would be a succession of 41 percent presidents or else a succession of double national elections. Moreover, the winner in the first round might often be beaten in the second round, depending on the deals the runoff candidates made with the splinter parties. This result would hardly strengthen the sense of legitimacy that the presidential election is supposed to provide. And I have yet to mention the problem, in close elections, of organizing a nationwide recount.

In short, direct elections promise a murky political future. They would further weaken the party system and further destabilize American politics. They would cure the intolerable predicament—but the cure might be worse than the disease.

Are we therefore stuck with the great anomaly of the Constitution? Is no remedy possible?

There is a simple and effective way to avoid the troubles promised by the direct-election plan and at the same time to prevent the popular-vote loser from being the electoral-vote winner: Keep the electoral college but award the popular-vote winner a bonus of electoral votes. This is the "national bonus" plan proposed in 1978 by the Twentieth Century Fund Task Force on Reform of the Presidential Election Process. . . .

Under the bonus plan, a national pool of 102 new electoral votes—two for each state and the District of Columbia—would be awarded to the winner of the popular vote. This national bonus would balance the existing state bonus—the two electoral votes already conferred by the Constitution on each state regardless of population. This reform would virtually guarantee that the popular-vote winner would also be the electoral-vote winner.

At the same time, by retaining state electoral votes and the unit rule, the plan would preserve both the constitutional and the practical role of the states in presidential elections. By insulating recounts, it would simplify the consequences of close elections. By discouraging multiplication of parties and candidates, the plan would protect the two-party system. By encouraging parties to maximize their vote in states that they have no chance of winning, it would reinvigorate state parties, stimulate turnout, and enhance voter equality. The national-bonus plan combines the advantages in the historic system with the assurance that the winner of the popular vote will win the election, and it would thus contribute to the vitality of federalism.

The national-bonus plan is a basic but contained reform. It would fit comfortably into the historic structure. It would vindicate "the fundamental maxim of republican government . . . that the sense of the majority should prevail." It would make the American democracy live up to its democratic pretensions.

How many popular-vote losers will we have to send to the White House before we finally democratize American democracy?

The Electoral College Didn't Do It
Robert Weissberg

That Al Gore out-polled George W. Bush in the 2000 presidential election is in-contestable. That many Gore supporters, notably Professor Arthur Schlesinger, feel that Gore was robbed of a deserved victory is equally indisputable. And, as typical when a serious crime is alleged, the question is, "Who did it?" The likely suspects include malicious Florida election officials, cunning GOP lawyers, and "the gang" of five conservative Supreme Court Justices. But, at least for Profes-sor Schlesinger, this compilation omits the Arch Foe, the Mother of All tribula-tions: the Electoral College. In legal language, these other miscreants were merely willing accomplices. The rickety old anti-democratic Electoral College was the true mastermind perpetrating the most heinous crime—subverting a genuine popular majority. Worse, the troublemaker is still at large, and who knows when it will strike again. Surely the good democratic town folk must act swiftly, abolish this Evil, and replace it with an electoral system that will honor majority rule. Anything less, it appears, denies the very legitimacy of American democracy.

This is nonsense, a view better understood as sour grapes that comes when an immense, just-within-reach victory is denied by a disputed few hundred votes. That the popular vote winner and the Electoral College vote victor are different people does not constitute smoking gun evidence that this presiden-tial selection system is antithetical to majority rule and should therefore be abolished. The equivalent is to insist that Oakland "really" won the 2003 Super Bowl against Tampa Bay since the rules (somehow) gave Tampa Bay an unfair advantage and the rulebook needs a major overhaul. Fantasizing about im-proved outcomes under alternative rules is a therapeutic exercise, not a method for implementing reform.

A MAJORITY OF WHOM?

Let's begin simply. Even had Gore prevailed in 2000, he could not properly have claimed a popular majority verdict. Since only about half of all those eli-gible actually voted, this "mandate" arrives from about only a little more than a quarter of all those permitted to vote, and voters typically differ from non-

Robert Weissberg is a professor of political science at the University of Illinois—Urbana. This arti-cle was written especially for *Points of View* in 2003.

voters. Who knows, these stay-at-homes might have loved Bush. And even this "eligible voter" category does not comprise "the people." The list of those excluded from this "people" is substantial: non-citizens, felons, the mentally incompetent, and countless others legally denied access. Significantly, those who insist that a majority of "the people" elect the president are oddly silent about the banished outsiders, all of whom can be incorporated via simple statute, not a Constitutional amendment. If a "real" majority is so vital, why the silence regarding compulsory voting, same day registration, Sunday elections, polling places in malls, and all the other mechanisms readily available to boost turnout? Surely these enhancements are as relevant as junking an antique, difficult-to-change system. The hush on these expansion possibilities suggests that achieving "real" popular majorities may not be that pressing.

In reality, uncovering a Platonically true popular majority is a hopeless task, save in dictatorial regimes favoring compulsory voting (and hanging chads are seldom a problem there). Taking a cue from those wanting to replace census enumerations with random sampling, why not use an opinion poll to elect the president? And do we really want "all the people" taking part? Certainly some people should be disqualified, so incompleteness is not a lethal defect. What about the millions of permanent foreign residents who are virtually identical to those permitted to vote save their allegiance to overseas governments? Or temporary, even illegal, foreign workers? In actual practice, *no* rendered collective judgment will be a "real" popular majority. Each alleged definitive mechanism inevitably yields contradictory outcomes depending on minor details except when the division is lopsided. To insist upon this lofty standard is fantasy, a tactic more useful for damning the sturdy status quo than achieving perfection.

Moreover, if a *bona fide* popular majority (regardless of how "the people" are defined) is the non-negotiable gold standard, where was Professor Schlesinger when Bill Clinton was "undemocratically" elected in 1992 and 1996 with less than a popular majority? What was wrong with the Electoral College back then? Did he complain in 1992 when Bush senior was the real victor and Clinton was the usurper since, quite reasonably, most Perot voters would have chosen Bush in a two-way contest? Did Clinton represent, as Alexander Hamilton intoned in *Federalist 22*, "the sense of the majority"? Would our fretful professor argue that Lincoln, Truman, Kennedy were similarly illegitimate since each failed to gain popular majorities? Maybe the Confederacy was right about Lincoln being a false claimant since a majority *clearly* opposed him. Perhaps for Professor Schlesinger only Richard Nixon's victory in 1968 contravened the "will of the people" and therefore subverted democratic governance. Judgments here are obviously flavored by who wins and loses, grandiloquence aside.

Let's put this all into a broader context. We admit that the Electoral College is flawed, prone to what may appear anti-majority outcomes, and what transpired in 2000 is only minor compared to what might happen eventually—for example, the U.S. House of Representatives selecting the third-place finisher to avoid deadlock. Garbling the enigmatic "public will" is not, however, a death sentence that requires returning to the drawing boards. *Every* electoral system is blemished when the standard is faithfully translating votes into political power. For decades proponents of proportional representation (PR)—which awards legislative seats according to votes for party lists—have tinkered with mechanisms to eliminate disproportional outcomes, but to no avail. Connoisseurs of PR know all too well that slight administrative details—for example, assembling "wasted" votes when calculating final seat awards—can be critical, and PR-created coalition governments result from elite negotiations, not mechanically implementing voting totals. Those who have labored for this elusive perfection usually embrace some system of multiple, cumulative voting having zero to do with the Electoral College (these add second and third choices to the official tally to achieve a broad consensus). Runoff systems designed to force majorities to emerge are notorious for undesirable outcomes—two conservatives in a field of six candidates where everyone else is a liberal can easily be the final choices, though clear majorities oppose both. Runoffs have also been attacked for de facto disenfranchising of racial minorities. Demonstrating "unpopular" outcomes of every conceivable election arrangement, complete with concrete examples, is a well-established scholarly industry.

The upshot of this inescapable bias is that every proposed reform is assessed not as gradually moving toward democratic perfection, but in terms of electoral advantage. To imagine Congress reflecting on Electoral College alternatives as disinterested Philosopher Kings displays a remarkable disconnect from grubby real world politics. Without question, each party would microscopically scan alternatives, and recommendations would surely seek to maximize subsequent electoral advantage under the guise of "making democracy work." The relevant parallel is periodic redistricting. Though the Supreme Court has seemingly provided strict criteria (e.g., compactness, equal population) partisans have become boundary-making geniuses to exploit the smallest gain.

THE NATIONAL BONUS SYSTEM

Subverting the professor's "national bonus" system to "guarantee" a popular presidential majority would be a snap and may make matters worse. Since it puts a premium on total votes, regardless of where secured, it differs not one iota from the potentially troublesome direct election proposal for choosing presidents. It adds nothing new in the way of safeguards or disincentives to prevent skullduggery. It will surely encourage each party to mobilize—by hook or crook—its supports while immobilizing foes. Predicting the likely outcomes is not rocket science. Savvy Republicans and Democrats will keep third parties off the ballot in their strongholds while encouraging them in their enemy's backyard. Envision Democrats faced with Republicans quietly funding a Black Nationalist party in California while fundamentalist Christian parties "mysteriously" arise in Texas. Multiple voting, voting by non-citizens, ballot box tampering, and all the other well-practiced scurrilous tricks will become a national epidemic, not just limited to a few corrupt localities.

Democratic elections comprise more than simple majorities. A manufactured statistical majority cannot, in and of itself, bestow democratic legitimacy if the outcome is widely perceived as being rigged, and rigging may entail opportunistically manipulating the rules in addition to securing bogus votes. Legitimacy comes from heeding long established conventions—even rules putting one at a disadvantage—not merely achieving 50% plus one. Better to win fair and square with a popular minority than manufacture a counterfeit margin with make-it-up-as-you-go-along laws. That the 2000 outcome *was* judged legitimate by nearly everyone should not be forgotten. A newfangled system may not be so lucky.

At best, this "national bonus" plan is uncertain in its impact, a stellar instance of the "perfect is the enemy of the good" adage. This is no small liability given the horrendous political obstacles awaiting constitutional ratification. It is preposterous to assume that once "tinkering with the Electoral College" is put into play, this particular reform—of the dozens of available options—will prevail. Much depends on who dominates when reform is afloat, and any successful plan must garner multiple super-majorities, a difficult task in the face of nervous minorities intent on exercising veto power. If Las Vegas betting parlors were to put odds on this amendment enterprise, the safest bet would probably be "no change." This is certainly consistent with past countless failed efforts to "improve" the Electoral College or abolish it altogether. Inertia is not catastrophic—partisans can still play politics with clear-cut rules, even if these rules are archaic.

Is this a defense of preserving the Electoral College against all critiques? Hardly, though compared to what often transpires elsewhere, the arrangement seems sturdy enough. Multiple, differing electoral arrangements perform admirably in other democracies, and, conceivably, modifications or outright abandonment might improve matters, though it is not clear what, precisely, would bring net improvement. Our point is more modest—beware of those hawking novel contrivances to "rescue" democracy. Changing the rules means shifting the odds on likely winners, and this is the likely aim here. Had Gore prevailed by a razor thin plurality (when taking into account minor party votes), and captured the Electoral vote, today's disgruntled Democrats would have probably celebrated the Electoral College's power to diminish divisive nation-wide recounts. Bush won, and he did not gain the presidency by administrative accident. The Electoral College is not guilty of subverting the popular will.

Internet Resources

Visit our website at http://www.mhhe.com/diclerico for links and resources relating to Elections.

chapter 8

Political Parties

*O*ver the course of our nation's history, the political process has periodically experienced the equivalent of an earthquake, whereby the reigning majority party in the electorate is replaced by a newly dominant party. This party then runs with the ball until finally losing its appeal, only to return the other party to power. Referred to as "political realignments" such events occurred in 1800, 1828, 1860, 1896, and 1932, suggesting to some that they are likely to happen every thirty-two to thirty-six years.

In a much discussed book (The Emerging Republican Majority), political writer Kevin Phillips predicted back in 1969 that the New Deal Democratic party coalition, which had dominated American politics since 1932, was in the process of breaking down and about to be replaced by a new Republican Party majority. That prediction, however, has never been fully realized, leaving political observers to speculate on when the next, long overdue, political realignment will occur. Karl Rove, one such observer and key political advisor to President George W. Bush, has argued that his boss's ascension to the presidency will in fact lead to just such a realignment, thereby cementing the Republican Party's grip on a majority of Americans.

In the first selection, John Judis and Ruy Teixeira fully agree with Rove that a realignment is occurring, but they insist that he has mistakenly made the Republican Party the beneficiary of this realignment when, in actuality, it is the Democrats who are emerging as the new majority party. More precisely, they argue that geography, demography, and ideology favor the Democrats. Why? For one thing, those parts of the country where Republicans dominate are in decline, while those areas most closely tied into the postindustrial economy are growing in population and tilting Democratic. They likewise contend that on moral and economic issues it is the Democrats, not the Republicans, who are most in tune with a majority of voters, and finally, that the movement of certain key groups—all growing in numbers—into the Democratic column ensures that the Democratic Party will dominate American politics for years to come.

Not so fast, says Michael Barone, author of the second selection. He suggests that Judis and Teixeira put too much stock in the results of the 2000 presidential election—one that, according to Barone, provided the Democrats with advantages they are not likely to enjoy in subsequent presidential contests. Moreover, those Democratic areas of *the country that Judis and Teixeira claim are growing may not do so for very long, according to Barone. Nor, he insists, are the blocks of voters that Judis and Teixeira identify as key to an emerging Democratic majority likely to be as reliably Democratic as they seem to believe. Accordingly, to suggest that the Democrats will be the winners in the next political realignment is, in Barone's judgment, premature to say the least.*

The Coming Democratic Majority

John B. Judis and Ruy Teixeira

Long before George W. Bush won the 2000 presidential election, his chief polit-ical adviser, Karl Rove, was predicting to reporters that a Bush victory would produce a historic political realignment. This new Republican majority would resemble the one William McKinley built roughly one century ago. "I look at this time as 1896, the time where we saw the rise of William McKinley and his vice president, Teddy Roosevelt," Rove declared. "That was the last time we had a shift in political paradigm." Just as McKinley exploited America's shift from an agrarian to an industrial economy to build his majority, Bush would exploit America's "transformational" shift from an industrial to a postindus-trial economy to build his. Bush would be the candidate and the president of the "new economy."

In Rove's mind, September 11 has reinforced the parallel: Bush's war on terrorism is the political equivalent of McKinley's Spanish-American War. . . .

Rove is half right. He's correct that we are in a transformational political era that displays marked similarities to 1896. And he is correct that this era will produce a majority party that dominates American politics for years to come. It just won't be the GOP. To the contrary, ever since the collapse of the Reagan conservative majority, which enjoyed its final triumph in November 1994, American politics has been turning slowly, but inexorably, toward a new Dem-ocratic majority. It was evident in Al Gore's popular-vote victory in 2000 (made more significant by the overhang of the Bill Clinton scandals and Gore's inep-titude as a campaigner) and in Bush's and the Republicans' sinking fortunes in the first two-thirds of 2001. It was obscured by the patriotic rush of support for Bush after September 11, which to some extent carried over to the Republican Party as a whole. But it has resurfaced in recent months. . . . Far from being a temporary distraction from a long-term shift toward the GOP, popular anger at the business scandals and the plummeting Dow heralds the resumption of a long-term shift toward the Democrats.

If this emerging Democratic majority has eluded many observers, perhaps it is because it differs substantially from the New Deal Democratic coalition that dominated American politics from 1932 to 1968. Today the Democrats are

John B. Judis is a senior editor at *The New Republic*. Ruy Teixeira is a senior fellow at The Century Foundation. Adapted from their book *The Emerging Democratic Majority* (Scribner, 2002), which first appeared as "Majority Rules: The Coming Democratic Dominance," in *The New Republic* (August 5 and 12, 2002): 18–23.

increasingly a party of professionals, women, and minorities rather than of blue-collar workers. They are based in post-industrial metropolitan areas rather than in the small-town South and the Rust Belt North. And they are a party of the progressive center rather than the Great Society left or the laissez-faire right. The new Democratic Party's true historical antecedent is, ironically, that same progressive Republican Party of the early twentieth century that Rove identifies with the Bush Republicans. It, and not Bush's GOP, will oversee America's postindustrial transition because it, and not Bush's GOP, embodies the demographic and cultural changes that this new America will bring.

THE ROVE-BARONE THESIS

It is difficult to assess Rove's theory of Republican realignment because, although he refers to it often, he has never publicly spelled it out in detail. For that, one must turn to *U.S. News*'s Barone, who in the 2002 edition of *The Almanac of American Politics* uses Rove's categories and his assumptions to argue that an America evenly divided between Bush and Gore in 2000 is gradually but unavoidably becoming what he calls the "Bush nation." Bush and Gore voters, Barone writes, represent "two nations of different faiths. One is observant, tradition-minded, moralistic. The other is unobservant, liberation-minded, relativist." Barone also depicts Bush and Gore supporters as divided in their view of the free market: Bush voters want "more choice" in economics, Gore voters "more government." The GOP's ace in the hole, argues Barone, is that Bush's voters are growing far more quickly than Gore's. According to Barone, Republicans enjoy an advantage in "the fastest-growing parts of the United States." The United States, he writes, is "moving, slowly, toward the Bush nation."

But Barone's—and by extension, perhaps, Rove's—reading of the nation's changing demography is dead wrong. His argument about the GOP's advantage in the "fastest-growing parts" rests on a simple confusion between the *rate* of growth and the *size* of growth. Yes, Bush did better than Gore in the 50 counties that grew the fastest during the '90s, averaging 62 percent of the vote, compared with 33 percent for Gore. But these pro-Bush counties are relatively small—averaging just 109,000 inhabitants—so their high growth rates translate into only modest increases in actual Bush voters. By contrast, in the 50 counties with the *largest* overall population growth—metropolitan counties averaging 1.46 million inhabitants—Gore won by a decisive 54 percent to 42 percent.

What Barone's numbers really reveal is that Bush and the Republicans enjoy an advantage in rural areas and in the "collar" counties on the edge of metropolitan areas being formed primarily by white émigrés from rural areas. If history were running in reverse, and if the United States were becoming a primarily rural nation, the GOP would enjoy a distinct demographic advantage. But rural America is shrinking—its share of the country's population has declined 17 percent over the last 40 years—while densely populated metropolitan America is growing and, with it, Democratic prospects.

A closer look at Barone and Rove's other categories reveals similar flaws. Take Barone's "observant, tradition-minded, moralistic" believers—a group Rove has cited in pep talks with Republican operatives as the basis for an expanding GOP majority. According to exit polls, Bush beat Gore among voters who say they attend church more than once weekly by 63 percent to 36 percent and among voters who say they attend church weekly by 57 percent to 40 percent. If these groups were growing as a percentage of the electorate, so would Bush's and the Republicans' political fortunes. But they're not; the number of Americans who rarely or never attend church is growing far faster. According to the National Opinion Research Center biennial survey, the number of Americans who said they never attended church or attended less than once per year rose from 18 percent in 1972 to 30 percent in 1998. In 2000 the National Election Study found that nonattenders—who overwhelmingly vote Democratic—represented 27 percent of the electorate. By contrast, voters who identify themselves as members of the religious right fell from 17 percent of the electorate in 1996 to 14 percent in 2000. And according to Notre Dame political scientist David Leege, the proportion of observant Catholics—another Rove-targeted group—also dropped during the '90s.

Barone and Rove's contention that Republicans better represent the public on economics also lacks basis in fact. Popular support for deregulation and privatization (what Barone calls "more choice") peaked between 1978 and 1984 in the wake of Jimmy Carter-era stagflation, but it has been in retreat ever since. Newt Gingrich learned that the hard way in 1995 when he mistook the public's discomfort with Clinton's overly ambitious health plan for public opposition to regulation and social programs like Medicare. If anything, the public now wants more spending on social programs and more regulation of business. Bush and Rove have admitted as much by co-opting Democratic rhetoric on key domestic issues—from prescription drugs to evironmental enforcement to corporate reform—rather than arguing, as Ronald Reagan did in the early '80s and Gingrich did in the mid-'90s, against greater government regulation. From geography to demography to ideology, the structural forces in American politics—the ones that endure the idiosyncrasies of any given election—are trending the Democrats' way.

THE EMERGING DEMOCRATIC MAJORITY

The most straightforward evidence that the American electorate is trending Democratic is actual election results. Since losing Congress in November 1994, the Democrats have gained seats in three successive congressional elections; Democrat Bill Clinton easily won reelection in 1996; and Al Gore won the popular vote against George W. Bush in 2000. . . .

By itself, of course, the string of recent Democratic successes does not prove a Democratic majority is emerging. But demographic trends suggest something deeper is at hand. Over the past decade not only have Democrats won back some white, working-class voters who deserted them during the '70s and '80s, but they have forged a new coalition that includes three groups: women (especially working, single, and highly educated women), minorities, and professionals—all of whom are growing as a portion of the electorate. These groups overlap in composition, but each entered the party in different stages over the last 40 years for different reasons.

Given the GOP's well-known "gender gap," it's easy to forget that not long ago American women voted disproportionately Republican. In 1960, for instance, women supported Richard Nixon over John F. Kennedy 53 percent to 46 percent. But starting with Barry Goldwater's nomination in 1964, and accelerating after Reagan's nomination in 1980, the GOP's growing social conservatism began driving away women voters. That led, by the '90s, to women regularly supporting Democrats by absolute majorities. In 2000, women backed Gore 54 percent to 43 percent.

This change in women's voting reflects the convergence of an economic trend and a social movement. For at least 50 years working women have supported the Democratic Party at much higher rates than have homemakers. But until recently, most women *were* homemakers. As more and more women have entered the workforce, however—from 37.7 percent of adult women in 1960 to 57.5 percent in 1990—women have begun voting more Democratic. Their entrance into the workforce has been accelerated by the rise of modern feminism, which has produced a spate of contested political issues, from abortion to child care to Title IX. Before 1980, Republicans and Democrats were largely indistinguishable on these issues. But in that election, the first in which gender issues like abortion and the Equal Rights Amendment played a major role, a gap opened that has not closed since—as working women began to suspect that Republican social policy was undergirded by the belief that society would be better off if women returned home.

Making matters worse for the GOP, the subcategories of women who trend most strongly Democratic are also the ones growing the fastest. Single, working women—who have grown from 19 percent of the adult, female population in 1970 to 29 percent today—backed Gore 67 percent to 29 percent. College-educated women—who have grown from just 8 percent of the 25-and-older female population in 1970 to 24 percent today—backed Gore over Bush by 57 percent to 39 percent. By contrast, those groups of women who still vote Republican—for instance, white homemakers who live outside metropolitan areas—comprise a steadily diminishing proportion of American women and of the American electorate.

Then there is the "minority vote"—a catchall for a range of groups with varying political histories. African Americans have been voting heavily Democratic since the New Deal and voting overwhelmingly Democratic since the 1964 Civil Rights Act; barring a radical change in Republican social attitudes and economic priorities, they will continue to do so. Among Hispanics, only Cuban-Americans vote Republican, and they make up just 4 percent of the overall Hispanic population. Most Hispanics are either Mexican-American (59 percent) or Puerto Rican (10 percent), and both groups have voted strongly Democratic since the '30s. Although President Bush has, on Rove's advice, loudly courted Hispanic voters, they don't seem particularly receptive. In 2000, for instance, Bush pursued California's Hispanics extensively while Gore neglected the state; but Bush still received only 28 percent of the Golden State's Hispanic vote. Bush did better in his home state of Texas, winning 43 percent of its Hispanic vote. But even there, the broader political trend suggests Hispanics are making the Democratic party their political home. . . .

Until the '90s, Republicans could at least count on Asian American voters. While Japanese immigrants voted for the Democrats as the party of civil rights and Filipinos backed Democrats as the party of the working class, the largest Asian group, Chinese-Americans, favored Republicans as the party of anti-communism and of small business. But over the past decade even Chinese-Americans have also moved to the Democratic Party—thanks to the end of the cold war, the party's move to the center, the GOP's opposition to immigration, and its nativist attacks on Asian donors during the 1996 fund-raising scandals. According to the National Asian American Political Survey, Asian Americans favored Gore over Bush by more than two to one.

All in all, Democrats can now count on about 75 percent of the minority vote in national elections. And like other Democratic-leaning groups, minorities are growing rapidly. Nationally, minorities made up about one-tenth of the electorate in 1972; by 2000 they were almost one-fifth. By 2010, if present trends continue, that could rise to one-quarter. If you don't think that strikes fear in Republican hearts, just look at California, where a rapidly growing Hispanic and Asian population has helped decimate the state GOP.

THE PROFESSIONAL EDGE

The most surprising component of the emerging Democratic majority is professionals. Professionals are highly skilled, white-collar workers, typically with a college education, who produce ideas and services. They include academics, architects, engineers, scientists, computer analysts, lawyers, physicians, registered nurses, teachers, social workers, therapists, fashion designers, interior decorators, graphic artists, writers, editors, and actors. In the 1950s they made up about 7 percent of the workforce. But as the United States has moved away from a blue-collar, industrial economy toward a postindustrial one that produces ideas and services, the professional class has expanded. Today it constitutes more than 15 percent of the workforce.

As the professional class has grown, its politics have shifted. Typically self-employed or working for small firms, professionals once saw themselves as proof of the virtues of laissez-faire capitalism. They disdained unions and opposed the New Deal and "big government." In the 1960 presidential election, professionals supported Nixon over Kennedy 61 percent to 38 percent. Since then, however, their views have changed dramatically. In the last four presidential elections, professionals have supported the Democratic candidate by an average of 52 percent to 40 percent. Meanwhile, counties disproportionately populated by professionals—such as New Jersey's Bergen County, the Philadelphia suburb of Montgomery County, and California's Santa Clara County—have gone from Republican to Democratic. . . .

Of all occupational groups, professionals were also the most affected by the political movements that took root on college campuses during the '60s. As a result, they are far more culturally liberal than their occupational forefathers—sympathetic to feminism, minority rights, and gay rights and hostile to the religious right. These are the people Barone derisively refers to as "liberation-minded"; they value tolerance as an end in itself. In the 2000 election 55 percent backed affirmative action as a response to discrimination, and 62 percent—more than any other occupational group—supported allowing homosexuals to serve in the military. . . .

Though the movement of professionals toward the Democrats was evident as early as the 1972 Nixon-McGovern election, it was not until 1988 that a majority of professionals backed a Democratic presidential nominee: former Massachusetts Governor Michael Dukakis. Unlike Walter Mondale, a party man with deep roots in the labor movement, Dukakis looked like them—a suburban reformer who said the 1988 election wasn't "about ideology, it's about competence." Since then, professional support has become vital to Democratic success. Professionals may only make up 15 percent of the workforce, but they vote at higher rates than any other occupational group. Nationally, they account for about 21 percent of voters; in many Northeastern and Far Western states, they form probably one-quarter of the electorate. . . .

THE IDEOPOLIS

Just as the McKinley majority was closely tied to the onset of industrialization, the emerging Democratic majority is closely linked to the spreading postindustrial economy. Democrats are strongest in areas where the production of ideas and services has either redefined or replaced assembly-line manufacturing, particularly the Northeast, the upper Midwest through Minnesota, and the Pacific Coast—including the Sunbelt prize of California—but also including parts of Southern states like Florida, Virginia, and North Carolina. Republicans, meanwhile, are strongest in states like Mississippi, Wyoming, and South Carolina (as well as in former Democratic enclaves like Kentucky), where the transition to postindustrial society has lagged.

The Democratic vote is anchored in postindustrial metropolises, or "ideopolises." Because postindustrial society is not organized around a rigid separation between city and suburb, these ideopolises comprise entire metropolitan areas, not merely central cities. Some ideopolises contain significant manufacturing facilities—as in Silicon Valley or Colorado's Boulder area—but it is the kind of manufacturing (whether of pharmaceuticals or semiconductors) that relies on the application of complex ideas to physical objects. This has become true even of automobile production in eastern Michigan. While much of the actual production of cars and trucks has moved south to middle Tennessee, Alabama, and Oklahoma, much of the research, development, and engineering of automobiles (which now make extensive use of computer technology) is conducted in Michigan by college-trained professionals. This is one reason Democrats now win elections in once-Republican suburbs like Oakland County outside Detroit.

Some of these ideopolises specialize in what Joel Kotkin and Ross C. DeVol call "soft technology"—entertainment, media, fashion, design, and advertising—and in providing databases, legal counsel, and other business services. New York City and Los Angeles are both premier postindustrial metropolises that specialize in soft technology. Most of these postindustrial metro areas also include a major university or several major universities, which funnel ideas and, more importantly, people into hard- or soft-technology industries. Boston's Route 128 feeds off Harvard and MIT; Silicon Valley is closely linked to Stanford and the University of California, Berkeley; Dane County's biomedical research is tied to the University of Wisconsin at Madison. And all of them have a flourishing service sector—computer learning centers, ethnic and vegetarian restaurants, children's museums, bookstore/coffee shops, and health clubs. To borrow David Brooks's phrase, this is where Bobos (i.e., "bourgeois bohemians") live.

In the most advanced ideopolises, like the San Francisco Bay or the Chicago metro areas, the work and culture of the ideopolis pervades the entire metropolitan area and its occupants. Many of the same people, the same businesses, and the same coffee shops or bookstores can be found in the central city and in the suburbs. The racial conflict that used to define such areas politically, with heavily minority cities voting Democratic and overwhelmingly white suburbs voting Republican partly in response, is fading. Indeed, the more fully a metropolitan area has entered the postindustrial economy, the more the suburbs and the city vote alike. In the 2000 election Gore didn't campaign in Colorado but still carried the Denver-Boulder area 56 percent to 35 percent. He won Portland's Multnomah County 64 percent to 28 percent. Seattle's King County went 60 percent to 34 percent for Gore; and Gore carried Cook County, whose suburbs used to be Republican, 69 percent to 29 percent. And while such ideopolises generally boast a large quotient of new Democratic groups—professionals, minorities, working women—their political ethos is not restricted to these groups. In King County, white, working-class voters backed Gore 50 percent to 42 percent; in Multnomah County, it was by 71 percent to 24 percent. (By comparison, working-class whites nationwide supported Bush by 57 percent to 40 percent.)

If you look at the 263 "ideopolis counties"—counties that are part of metro areas with high concentrations of high-tech economic activity or that contain a front-rank research university—most of them voted for Republican presidential candidates in 1980 and 1984. But in 2000 Gore garnered 54 percent of the vote in these areas, compared with 41 percent for Bush. By contrast, Democrats have continued to lose rural areas (it was Bush's dominance in rural sections of swing states like Missouri that propelled him to victory there) and low-tech metropolitan areas such as Greenville, South Carolina, and Muncie, Indiana. In all, Gore lost non-ideopolis counties 53 percent to 44 percent. Indeed, if you compare 1980—the beginning of the Reagan era—to today, it is clear that virtually the entire political shift toward the Democrats has taken place in ideopolis counties.

These counties, moreover, represent some of the fastest-growing parts of the country. Together, ideopolis counties currently account for 44 percent of the vote nationally. But between 1990 and 2000, the average ideopolis county grew by over 22 percent, compared with 10 percent for the average non-ideopolis county. And ideopolis counties start from a far larger population base—an average of 475,000 inhabitants, compared with just 54,000 for the typical non-ideopolis county. It is these areas—their demography, their culture, and their politics—that Barone and Rove discount at their peril.

None of these trends are inevitable, of course. If the Democrats move too quickly to embrace the culture of the new Bohemia—say, by pressing civil unions or gun prohibition—they could lose much of their still-vital, white, working-class support. Or if they fall back into the bad pre-Clinton habit of wooing interest-group constituents with bloated spending programs, some professionals might start moving back toward the GOP. And if Ralph Nader and the Greens begin regularly pulling in more than 5 percent of the vote in ideopolis counties, Republicans could continue winning elections even as a center-left majority emerges. But as long as the Democrats maintain a fiscally moderate, socially liberal, reformist, and egalitarian outlook, they will enjoy a structural edge in national and most state elections. The Bush administration can scour the coal pits of West Virginia or the boarded up steel mills of Youngstown for converts, but America's future lies in places like Silicon Valley and North Carolina's Research Triangle. The party that most clearly embodies the culture and beliefs of these areas will dominate political discourse in postindustrial America at the dawn of the new century, just as the McKinley Republicans dominated nascent industrial America at the dawn of the last. Today only one party does—and Karl Rove isn't in it.

Whose Majority?
Democratic Wishful Thinking
Michael Barone

A RISING TIDE?

John Judis and Ruy Teixeira are liberal optimists. . . . Their thesis is that the ingredients of a Democratic national majority have been accumulating since 1990, and that that majority will emerge, apparent to all, sometime between 2004 and 2008. This is likely to happen, they say, because Democrats have been running well and making gains among three important segments of the electorate; professionals, minorities, and women. Their most original discussion is of the professionals. Once solidly Republican, professionals voted for Al Gore over George W. Bush in 2000, and by a significant margin. They are moved to do so, the authors say, by cultural issues, notably abortion—the proxy for a bundle of such issues, which correlate far more closely with voting behavior than do economic factors like income or wealth. Professionals are increasingly likely to be women, they point out, and they are also more likely than Americans generally to be government employees (think of the teachers). All this is quite right, and helps to explain the 1988–2000 trend in affluent suburbs toward the Democrats. Professionals also like the Clintons' brand of New Democratic policies, with its embrace of cultural liberalism and its eschewing of the rhetoric of class warfare.
. . .

The second group Judis and Teixeira identify is women. Here they are necessarily less original; the press, one of the most heavily feminist institutions in the country, is always telling us how women are overwhelmingly Democratic, and a good thing too. Actually, the percentages are not overwhelming, and you could just as well say Republicans are doing well because of their strong support from men. But some sexes are more equal than others.

Minorities are the third group identified by Judis and Teixeira. They are aware that Latinos do not vote the same as blacks and that Asians do not vote the same as either of the other two. And they recognize that there are significant political differences among different kinds of Latinos and Asians. . . .

But all this does not add up to an inevitable emerging Democratic majority. Judis and Teixeira seem to take the 2000 vote—48 percent for Gore, or 51

Michael Barone is a senior writer for *U.S. News & World Report* and co-author of *The Almanac of American Politics.* From Michael Barone, "Whose Majority? A Democratic Thesis and (a Dollop of) Wishful Thinking," *National Review* (December 9, 2002); 30–34.

percent for Gore-plus-Nader—as a floor. This might be called the Brezhnev Doctrine of political analysis: "What we have we keep" (no imputation of totalitarianism intended). But Democrats will not be fighting elections anytime soon—certainly they did not fight the 2002 election—with all the advantages they had in 2000. In 1996 and 2000 the Democrats were the incumbent party in a time of apparent peace and prosperity. Each time they failed to win a majority of the vote: Bill Clinton got 49 percent, Al Gore 48 percent. No Democratic presidential nominee will run from this advantageous position until 2008 at the earliest, more likely not until 2012, maybe not then: Clinton was the first Democrat to do so since Lyndon Johnson in 1964, 32 years before, when Clinton and Gore were not old enough to vote. The Democrats' 48 percent in 2000 might turn out to be not a floor but a ceiling.

My own view, enunciated in the introduction to *The Almanac of American Politics 2002*, was that from 1995 to 2000 neither party had a majority, that it has been unclear how either party will build a majority coalition in the near future, and that Republicans may have a slightly better chance than the Democrats to do so. I called this introduction "The 49 Percent Nation" and noted that we have had three straight presidential elections and three straight House elections in which neither party has gotten a majority of the popular vote, something that hasn't happened since the 1880s. In 1996, 1998, and 2000 Republicans carried the popular vote for the House by 49–48.5, 49–48, and 49–48 percent margins.

Judis and Teixeira take issue with some points I made in that introduction and elsewhere. I argued that while Democrats made substantial gains in the nation's largest metro areas—especially the very largest, which cast about one-quarter of the nation's votes—Republicans made some partially offsetting gains in rural areas and in some of the nation's fast-growing areas at the edges of large metro areas. Absent those partially offsetting gains, George W. Bush would have lost by a decisive electoral-vote margin, and we all would have gone to bed much earlier on Election Night 2000. Judis and Teixeira don't really disagree; they just say that these areas are not likely by themselves to produce an emerging Republican majority. Maybe, maybe not: In 2002 fast-growing counties produced sharply higher turnouts and huge majorities for Republican candidates in critical races in which Republicans were not initially favored—for Sen. Wayne Allard in Colorado, Sen.-elect Saxby Chambliss in Georgia, Sen.-elect Jim Talent in Missouri, and Gov.-elect Bob Ehrlich in Maryland. . . .

TRENDS . . . AND COUNTER-TRENDS

But what about Judis and Teixeira's three groups of increasingly Democratic voters?

Professionals are indeed a growing segment of the electorate, and the Democrats do run much better among them than when I was a teenager living in a professional-and-executive suburban Detroit precinct that voted 92 percent for Republican George Romney for governor in 1962. And they may get a little more Democratic as older Republican professionals are replaced by younger Democratic professionals.

But maybe not. For the issue environment—specifically, the posture of the tax issue—can change. In 1984 and 1988 Republicans had cut taxes; Democrats wanted to increase them. In 1984 Walter Mondale promised to raise taxes and in 1988 George Bush famously said, "Read my lips, no new taxes." Reagan and Bush ran well enough in the suburbs that Reagan carried—and Bush ran even in—metro Boston, metro New York, metro Philadelphia, metro Detroit, and metro Chicago. By 2000 the posture of the tax issue had changed: Republicans promised to cut taxes, a promise that is often discounted by voters, while Democrats promised, credibly after their thrashing in 1994, to keep them the same. Professionals were free to vote on cultural issues, notably abortion, and these metro areas all produced large majorities for Al Gore.

Now the posture of the tax issue is likely to change again. The Bush tax cuts in the high brackets will start to kick in seriously in 2004 and 2005. Voters know that most Democrats are itching to rescind those tax cuts, and many say so out loud. So once again the situation is likely to be that Republicans have cut taxes and Democrats want to increase them. It is at least possible that many suburban professionals will not vote to preserve abortion rights (which don't seem very threatened anyhow) when it will cost them so much money to do so. Such voters in Massachusetts, Connecticut, and New York were willing to vote for Republican (admittedly, pro-choice Republican) governors in order to stop Democrats from raising taxes. My own hunch is that the Democratic percentages among professionals reached their ceiling in 2000.

Judis and Teixeira also write glowingly about the new "ideopolises," areas with a lot of high-tech and academic professionals, and say that these areas tend to be heavily Democratic. Most do, but some don't. And I think they define their ideopolises a little broadly: Johnston County, N.C., southeast of Raleigh, is barbecue-conservative country, quite unlike Starbucks-laden Chapel Hill. And of course it's not clear now whether high-tech centers are going to increase as a percentage of the electorate. They tend to pass low-growth ordinances that doom them to be a smaller percentage every year.

And then women. It is not at all clear that women will become more feminist unto eternity. There is some evidence that movement is in the opposite direction. More women today choose to stay at home with young children than did a few years ago. An in-depth Kaiser Family Foundation–*Washington Post*–Harvard University survey this year focusing on different age groups found that voters under 30 were the most Republican age group, and that among these young voters there was almost no gender gap: Young women were just about as Republican as men. . . .

Now, minorities. Why do liberal analysts, and many others, lump together blacks, Latinos, and Asians—so many different peoples, with such different experiences and heritages? Because there is an underlying assumption that this is still a country full of white racists and that people whom we classify as being of a different race will share a common experience of racial discrimination. But this is not a racist country anymore, and the discrimination blacks and Latinos most commonly encounter is discrimination in their favor, thanks to racial quotas and preferences and to employers' preferences for hardworking Latino and high-talent Asian workers.

Politically, blacks are already just about as heavily Democratic as can be, and are not a growing segment of the electorate: no significant gains for Democrats here. Latinos vote differently in different places, depending on where they came from and the politics they encountered in different parts of America. If no Latinos had voted in America, George W. Bush would have won a popular-vote plurality; but if no Latinos had voted in Florida, Al Gore would be president. Latinos are less likely than blacks to look to the public sector for help: Their experience in Latin America has been that the public sector is unreliable and corrupt, something to be avoided. They tend to work overwhelmingly in private-sector jobs and are more likely than blacks to stay off welfare when eligible. They are slightly more conservative on cultural issues than the national average. They flock to Catholic and evangelical Protestant churches—which does not suggest they will become more Democratic. George W. Bush is making a concerted effort to win over Latinos, and seems to have had some success. Non-VNS exit polls show that Republican governor Jeb Bush carried non-Cuban Hispanics (and, of course, Cubans, by a huge margin) in Florida, and Republican governor George Pataki and Republican mayor Michael Bloomberg carried Hispanics in New York in 2002 and 2001 respectively. Republican governor Rick Perry won 35 percent of Latinos' votes in Texas when opposed by a Latino who spent $60 million on his campaign. Other Republicans did not do so well.

The point is, Latinos are never going to be anything like blacks electorally. They will not be a 9–1 Democratic bloc. They will be voters for whom both parties will compete vigorously, with different proclivities in different states. And what will happen if George W. Bush appoints a Latino chief justice of the United States?

Asians—a far less homogeneous group—are an even more uncertain matter. Judis and Teixeira cite polls of Chinese and Vietnamese voters that show Democratic percentages among them rising in the 1990s. Certainly the Clinton team made efforts to win over Asian voters—remember Al Gore at the Buddhist temple? But George W. Bush is making such efforts as well, and they may pay off too. It is risky to generalize about Asians, since we are talking about people from so many different cultures and countries, but some political operatives have noted a tendency for at least some Asians to vote for incumbents: Stay in good with the powers that be and show your loyalty by backing the president. In any case, Asians do not seem to be an overwhelmingly Democratic group. The VNS exit poll said that Al Gore won among Asians by a 54 to 41 percent margin, as the candidate of the incumbent party. But that was mainly due to Hawaii, where Asians (a majority group there) backed Gore 61 to 35 percent. In California, with more than one-third of the nation's Asian voters, the vote was 48 percent for Gore and 47 percent for Bush—a reasonable facsimile of the national average. Such a margin is not going to produce a national Democratic majority. . . .

THE PROPHECY BIZ

This, again, is not to say that the Democratic majority Judis and Teixeira envisage can never come into existence. Visible failure in the war against terrorism, a move to Japanese-style deflation in the economy: These could make the Democrats a majority without their having to do much to bring it about. If Al Gore had won 10,000 more votes in Florida and if he had responded as well as Bush to September 11, then Democrats might have been on their way to a Judis-Teixeira majority right now. But 2000 was not a floor for Democrats. George W. Bush has come up with a carefully prepared set of policies and has responded to emergencies for which he could not have prepared, in a way that has moved Republicans ahead from the 49–49 percent deadlock that prevailed from 1995 to 2001 and put them in the way of winning a majority in 2004 that could conceivably turn out to be permanent. The Democrats have not come up with such policies. . . . The creation of a national Democratic majority today looks like a far harder and longer task than it did when Judis and Teixeira sent their book to press, and even then it was not as likely a thing as they thought.

Internet Resources
Visit our website at http://www.mhhe.com/diclerico for links and resources relating to Political Parties.

chapter 9

Interest Groups

*O*ne *of the most significant political developments over the last thirty years has been the emergence and spectacular growth of political action committees, or PACs. PACs are specially organized political campaign finance groups, functioning outside the traditional political parties, whose primary purpose is to raise and spend money on behalf of candidates running for office. Modern PACs, with members numbering in the thousands, represent all sorts of special interests, from organized labor to professional and business organizations, to liberal and conservative ideological groups.*

Although PACs clearly have every right to exist in a democratic political system and contribute significantly to our free system of elections, there are those who allege that PACs have come to exercise too much political and governmental power—that they affect electoral and legislative outcomes far more than they should, often to the detriment of the public interest.

PAC critics begin with the proposition that campaign contributions corrupt the legislative process. Pointing to what they believe to be a close connection between campaign contributions and congressional voting, these critics allege that legislative outcomes are very directly tied to PAC money. Thus, one of these critics, the Center for Responsive Politics, in the first of the articles in this chapter, details the large number of occasions when they believe PACs seem to "cash in" on bills passed by Congress.

The selection offered in rebuttal to the Center is written by political scientist Larry Sabato, considered one of the nation's leading authorities on PACs. While admitting some faults of PACs, Sabato strongly defends their existence and the contributions they make to our system of democracy. In Sabato's view, PACs have been the victim of a bum rap, neither causing the current excesses in campaign finance nor unduly influencing individual legislators or the Congress as a whole.

PACs: Cashing in from A to Z
Center for Responsive Politics

In late September 1995, all 535 members of Congress mobilized quickly for the mortgage banking industry.

It all started with a Florida widow named Martha Rodash. After she refinanced her home, she fell behind on her payments. Her attorneys then discovered that her mortgage company, AIB Mortgage, Co., had made errors in the loan papers, of a sort that lenders contend are minor. Rodash filed a lawsuit under the Truth in Lending Act. In 1994, the U.S. Court of Appeals ruled in her favor.

Seeing the success of the Rodash case, attorneys filed some 50 class action lawsuits against mortgage lenders. Lenders argued they needed relief, and fast. Congress passed a six-month moratorium on Rodash-type lawsuits, but it was due to expire on October 1.

Congress came to the rescue. On September 27, the House unanimously passed a bill that weakened the Truth in Lending Act. The Senate followed suit the next day. President Clinton signed the bill into law on September 30, a Saturday, just one day before the moratorium was due to expire.

"Consumers certainly didn't win anything," says Mary Griffin, a lobbyist for Consumers Union. While earlier proposals by the mortgage lenders were more extreme, they still got much of what they wanted. For example, the lenders are now allowed to make errors of up to $100 on loan papers; previously they were allowed only a $10 error. The law also has a clause which retroactively excuses many of the Rodash-type lawsuits.

Why was Congress so responsive to the mortgage lenders' plight? Part of the reason may lie in the financial support they receive from the banking industry. During the first half of 1995, banking interests distributed nearly $3 million in political contributions. Rep. Bill McCollum (R-Fla.), the bill's lead sponsor, collected more of his campaign money from financial interests than any other industry during the first half of 1995.

The new law did not exactly dominate headlines. And it is not the only example . . . of a legislative favor granted to generous campaign contributors that largely escaped public scrutiny. Much of what the monied interests won in the first session of the 104th Congress occurred at the margins—in obscure riders on

The Center for Responsive Politics is a non-profit, non-partisan research organization in Washington, D.C., specializing in the study of Congress and campaign finance. From *Cashing in from A to Z* (Washington, D.C.: Center for Responsive Politics, 1995), pp. 2–3, 5–6, 8–9, 15–16, 18, and 20–22. Center for Responsive Politics (OpenSecrets.org). Used by permission.

appropriations bills, little-noticed legislation approved without recorded votes or much controversy, and items buried in the vast budget reconciliation bill.

For example, the insurance and HMO industries, which contributed over $3 million through PACs and individuals during the first half of 1995, won extension of the Medicare Select program, which encourages senior citizens to adopt managed care plans. Timber companies, which gave $301,153 through PACs and individual contributions from January to June 1995, won the right to harvest more trees in national forests. And thanks to the championship of Rep. Bud Shuster (R-Pa.), who received over $57,000 in PAC and individual contributions from the billboard industry in his 1994 campaign, a new law confirms that states can allow billboards on scenic byways. Northrop Grumman, which gave $206,250 through PACs and individuals during the first six months of the year, won $493 million that could go to new B-2 bombers, even though the Department of Defense doesn't want them.

Many "interested" campaign contributors achieved multiple goals. Consider the oil and gas industry, which gave $1.6 million in PAC and individual contributions during the first half of 1995. In November, Charles J. DiBona, president of the American Petroleum Institute, gave an interview to the trade journal *Petroleum Finance Week*. He said he liked what the 104th Congress had done. And no wonder. He named five issues at the top of the oil industry's legislative wish list: royalty relief in the Gulf of Mexico, opening the Arctic National Wildlife Refuge to oil drilling, repeal of the Alaska oil export ban, alternative minimum tax relief, and Superfund reform. Of those, the first and third became law, the second and fourth are included in the budget reconciliation bill, and the fifth saw a vote by a House subcommittee.

Campaign contributions may not explain everything about lawmakers' actions, but all too often they provide a good place to start. At worst, lawmakers have a vested interest in helping the people who finance their election campaigns. At best, they try to avoid offending their financial supporters. And much of the time, campaign contributors have a big say setting the terms of a debate.

Before lawmakers introduced major telecommunications reform legislation in 1995, they first huddled with the CEOs of major communications companies at a series of private dinners. When they set about drafting reforms to the Clean Water Act, they consulted a task force of industry representatives. When a controversy developed over the future of the federal sugar support program, the agriculture committee invited sugar producers and their foes from the candy, ice cream, and soft drink industries to meetings on the Hill—but not the consumer and environmental groups that were also working on the issue.

The way of life on Capitol Hill was perhaps best described by [the late] Gerald B. H. Solomon (R-N.Y.), chairman of the House Rules Committee. "This morning I had breakfast with the cable industry. Last week, it was the chemical manufacturers. The week before that, it was the insurance industry. Tomorrow, it's the milk industry," he . . . told *The New York Times*.

The Center for Responsive Politics' Cashing In Project . . . [tracked] what campaign contributors wanted from the 104th Congress. The list grew so long that we decided to compile it. In the interest of keeping the list manageable, we included only examples that saw significant legislative action during the 104th Congress' first session. . . .

Under each entry a summary provides background on a particular issue, how much money the interests involved contributed, and a status line that explains where the issue is in the legislative process. All told, we include 55 examples, from accountants to Zantac. [What follows are a few examples.]

ARCHER-DANIELS-MIDLAND

Ethanol: the subsidy that won't die . . . Manufacturers of ethanol, a gasoline additive manufactured from corn, earn about $684 million a year from a 54-cent-a-gallon excise tax break on ethanol. One of the largest beneficiaries is Archer-Daniels-Midland and its politically active chairman, Dwayne O. Andreas. The company, which had $11.4 billion in sales in 1994, has the capacity to produce more than half of the ethanol in the U.S. In September, the House Ways and Means Committee voted to end the 17-year-old tax break. But after heavy lobbying by the ethanol industry and intervention by Senate Majority Leader Bob Dole (R-Kan.), Ways and Means Chairman Bill Archer (R-Texas) backed down.

Status: Ethanol tax break remains.

Archer-Daniels-Midland

1993–1994
Total $230,170   PAC Only
Percent to Republicans   31%

January–June 1995
Total $68,450   PAC and Individuals
Percent to Republicans   47%
Percent from PACs   91%

1991–1994
Soft Money $2,136,268
Percent to Republicans   66%

B-2 BOMBER

The B-2 bomber's payload . . . Northrop Grumman's campaign for its B-2 bomber was anything but stealthy. The company orchestrated a lobbying campaign that included personalized letters to lawmakers detailing B-2 subcontractors in their districts, advertisements in newspapers and on television—and campaign contributions. The company triumphed despite opposition by the Department of Defense and two attempts on the House floor to strip funding from the program.

During the first seven months of 1995, Northrop Grumman's PAC distributed $230,950 to congressional candidates, nearly half of what Northrop and

Grumman's PACs combined to give over two previous years. (The two companies merged in 1994.) In the six weeks after the close House vote in June to retain additional funding for the bomber, Northrop Grumman distributed $50,400 to House members who voted for funding while just $1,500 went to members who voted against it. The company's PAC gave the highest post-vote contributions to supportive lawmakers hailing from California, where Northrop has its headquarters: Democrats Jane Harman ($5,000) and Vic Fazio ($4,500), and Republicans Jerry Lewis ($4,500) and Howard "Buck" McKeon ($4,000).

Status: Defense appropriations bill, H.R. 2126, became law 12/1/95 without President Clinton's signature. FINAL.

Northrop Grumman[1]

1993–1994
Total $481,294   PACs Only
Percent to Republicans   41%

January–June 1995
Total $206,250   PAC and Individuals
Percent to Republicans   73%
Percent from PACs   99%

BILLBOARDS

Billboards on scenic highways . . . Some 35,000 miles of scenic byways meander through the country, from the Dakotas and the Old West Trail to Louisiana and the Mississippi River Valley. A 1991 law effectively banned billboards from new byways. This year, the billboard industry lobbied hard to eliminate the ban. They had a champion in Bud Shuster (R-Pa.), the new chairman of the House Transportation and Infrastructure Committee. In the 1994 election cycle alone, Shuster took $57,415 in PAC and individual contributions from the billboard industry. Shuster fought hard for a provision in the House highway bill that would allow more billboards on scenic byways. The item proved so contentious that it became one of the key items stalling negotiations between the House and Senate on the final bill. In the end, the billboard industry did not get everything it wanted. But it did get a change in the law that makes permanent a Department of Transportation policy of allowing states certain exceptions to the billboard ban.

Status: National Highway System Designation Act, S. 440, House passed, 11/18/95, Senate passed, 11/17/95, President Clinton signed, 11/28/95. FINAL.

Billboards

1993–1994
Total $180,126   PACs Only
Percent to Republicans   43%
Percent from PACs in 1991–1992   37%

January–June 1995
Total $104,643   PACs and Individuals
Percent to Republicans   60%
Percent from PACs   48%

DAIRY PRODUCERS

Milk money . . . Consumers pay about $2.5 billion more a year for milk, ice cream, cheese, and other dairy products than they would without a federal dairy price support program, according to the consumer group Public Voice for Food and Health Policy. The Depression-era dairy program involves a complex system of marketing orders and price supports. These guarantee both minimum prices and a market for milk products—the government buys the surplus.

This year, milk processors represented by the International Dairy Foods Association mounted a campaign to reform the dairy program, since they could profit from cheaper milk. They found an ally in retiring Rep. Steve Gunderson (R-Wis.), chairman of the House Agriculture Subcommittee on Livestock, Dairy and Poultry. Gunderson crafted a bill that would reform the dairy program in such a way that would protect dairy farmers in his own state. A battle ensued between different regional dairy factions. After weeks of wrangling, the House leadership dropped the Freedom to Milk Act from the budget reconciliation bill.

One key opponent of the Gunderson plan was [the late] Rep. Gerald B. H. Solomon (R-N.Y.), chairman of the House Rules Committee. In mid-November, the same time that the dairy reform provisions were pulled from the budget bill, the National Milk Producers Federation rewarded him with a fundraiser at Le Mistral, a posh Washington restaurant. "To show your appreciation to Mr. Solomon, please join us. . . . PACs throughout the industry are asked to contribute $1,000. Mr. Solomon would prefer that the checks be made to his leadership fund, 'Leadership for America Committee.' If your PAC is unable to comply with this request, please make your PAC check to 'Solomon for Congress,'" read the invitation, as reported in *The New York Times*.

Status: Dairy reform provisions dropped from budget reconciliation bill, H.R. 2491.

Dairy Producers[2]

1993–1994
Total $1,562,905   PACs Only
Percent to Republicans   27%
Percent from PACs in 1991–1992   83%

January–June 1995
Total $343,163   PACs and Individuals
Percent to Republicans   58%
Percent from PACs   91%

OIL & GAS

Ending the Alaska oil export ban . . . Just three days after President Clinton signed a bill that ended a 22-year ban on international oil exports from Alaska, Taiwan announced plans to buy 10,000 barrels a day from British Petroleum (BP), which owns half the trans-Alaska pipeline. Taiwan's announcement confirmed predictions that BP, whose PAC distributed $112,950 from January 1993 to June 1995, stands to profit handsomely from the repeal of the ban. Environmentalists opposed the repeal, arguing that it would increase the chance of oil spills and other oil-related damage. But their arguments did not hold sway this Congress. At least part of the reason BP was successful this time was that they secured the support of a longtime foe—the AFL-CIO's Seafarers Union. The union signed on after BP agreed to a provision that requires the use of U.S.-flagged ships. The Seafarers' PACs, which distributed $887,794 from January 1993 to June 1995, dramatically changed their party orientation this year, giving 52 percent of their contributions to Republicans, compared with 10 percent in 1994.

Status: Repeal Alaska oil export ban, S. 395, House passed 7/25/95, Senate passed, 5/16/95, President Clinton signed, 11/28/95. FINAL.

Oil & Gas

1993–1994
Total $6,144,329   PACs Only
Percent to Republicans   61%
Percent from PACs in 1991–1992   55%

January–June 1995
Total $1,598,001   PACs and Individuals
Percent to Republicans   83%
Percent from PACs   73%

TELECOMMUNICATIONS

Deregulation for one and all . . . The wheeling and dealing over telecommunications reform this session was largely an inside deal, fought out between the long distance telephone, Baby Bells, broadcasting, and other companies. The tone was set early in the session, when Republican members of the House Commerce Committee held a series of private dinners with CEOs of major communications companies.

CEOs also had entree to the Senate. "How do you say 'no' to the CEO?" Sen. Larry Pressler (R-S.D.) told *USA Today*. Pressler, who is chairman of the Senate Commerce Committee, was by far the top Senate recipient of telecommunications PAC funds during the first half of this year, collecting $103,165.

(The next highest recipient in the Senate was Sen. Fred Thompson (R-Tenn.), with $37,000.) Rep. Jack Fields (R-Texas), chairman of the House Commerce Subcommittee on Telecommunications and Finance, received $97,500.

Clearly telecommunications PACs were directing funds where they would matter most. Lawmakers sitting on the conference committee to resolve the Senate and House versions of the telecommunications bill received a total of $640,000, or almost a third of the more than $2 million distributed by telecommunications PACs from January to June 1995.

Consumer groups following the bill, such as the Consumer Federation of America, charged that it would lead to higher rates for consumers for many services and would likely increase concentration in the broadcast industry. "Allowing a few large corporations to own most of the media is bad for consumers, bad for diversity, bad for program quality, and fundamentally dangerous for our democracy," said Jeff Chester, director of the Center for Media Education.

Status: H.R. 1555, House passed, 8/4/95, S. 652, Senate passed, 6/15/95. President Clinton signed, 2/8/96. FINAL.

Telecommunications[3]

1993–1994
Total	$8,042,183	PACs Only
Percent to Republicans		45%
Percent from PACs in 1991–1992		57%

January–June 1995
Total	$2,655,852	PACs and Individuals
Percent to Republicans		71%
Percent from PACs		75%

TOBACCO

No discussion is good discussion . . . Tobacco interests survived unscathed this year. Their subsidy program, financed primarily through user fees, enjoys permanent authorization under a 1938 law. That relieved the pressure on lawmakers from discussing it along with other farm programs this year. There was one attempt, by Rep. Richard Durbin (D-Ill.), to prohibit federal funds from going to crop insurance or extension services for tobacco. On July 20, House members rejected his amendment, 199 to 223, when he introduced it as part of debate on the agriculture appropriations bill. Tobacco PAC contributions explain at least part of the industry's hold on Congress. Members who voted for tobacco received, on average, $1,916 from the top five tobacco PACs during the first six months of 1995. That's four times the average amount received by members who voted against tobacco: $480. Meanwhile, Rep. Lewis Payne (D-Va.) introduced a bill to prevent the Food and Drug Administration from regulating tobacco as a drug. With $19,500, Payne was the top House recipient of tobacco dollars during the first six months of 1995. And freshman Rep. David Funderburk (R-N.C.), who ranked third, with $12,700, introduced a bill forbidding the government from regulating advertising by tobacco sponsors at professional auto races.

Status: Amendment to strip funding failed in agriculture appropriations bill, H.R. 1976, President Clinton signed 10/21/95. FINAL.

Tobacco

1993–1994
Total	$2,265,216	PACs Only
Percent to Republicans		49%
Percent from PACs in 1991–1992		81%

January–June 1995
Total	$792,524	PACs and Individuals
Percent to Republicans		79%
Percent from PACs		94%

NOTES

1. For 1993–1994, includes PAC contributions from Northrop Corp. and from Grumman Corp. The two companies merged in May 1994. For 1995, includes PAC contributions from the company's single PAC.
2. Milk & dairy producers as coded by the Center, excluding the Milk Industry Foundation and other groups that are solely dairy processors.
3. Media & entertainment, broadcasting, motion pictures, cable television, telephone utilities, long-distance telephone, and other communications services as coded by the Center.

The Misplaced Obsession with PACs

Larry J. Sabato

The disturbing statistics and the horror stories about political action commit-tees seem to flow like a swollen river, week after week, year in and year out. Outrage extends across the ideological spectrum: the liberal interest group Common Cause has called the system "scandalous," while the late conserva-tive senator Barry Goldwater (R-Ariz.) has bluntly declared, "PAC money is de-stroying the election process. . . ."[1]

PAC-bashing is undeniably a popular campaign sport,[2] but the "big PAC attack" is an opiate that obscures the more vital concerns and problems in cam-paign finance. PAC excesses are merely a symptom of other serious maladies in the area of political money, but the near-obsessive focus by public interest groups and the news media on the PAC evils has diverted attention from more fundamental matters. The PAC controversy, including the charges most fre-quently made against them, can help explain why PACs are best described as agents of pseudo corruption.[3]

THE PAC ERA

While a good number of PACs of all political persuasions existed prior to the 1970s, it was during that decade of campaign reform that the modern PAC era began. Spawned by the Watergate-inspired revisions of the campaign finance laws, PACs grew in number from 113 in 1972 to 4,567 in 2002, and their contri-butions to congressional candidates multiplied nearly thirty-fold from $8.5 mil-lion in 1971–72 to $245.3 million in 1999–2000.

The rapid rise of PACs has engendered much criticism, yet many of the charges made against political action committees are exaggerated and dubious. While the widespread use of the PAC structure is new, special interest money of all types has always found its way into politics. Before the 1970s it simply did so in less traceable and far more disturbing and unsavory ways. And while, in absolute terms, PACs contribute a massive sum to candidates, it is not clear that

Larry Sabato is a professor and director of the Center for Politics (*www.centerforpolitics.org*) at the University of Virginia. Reprinted from Chapter 1 by Larry J. Sabato, *Paying for Elections: The Cam-paign Finance Thicket,* A Twentieth Century Fund Paper. © 1989 by the Twentieth Century Fund, New York. Used with permission of the Twentieth Century Fund, New York. The author revised and updated the original for *Points of View* in 2003.

there is proportionately more interest-group money in the system than before. As political scientist Michael Malbin has argued, we will never know the truth because the earlier record is so incomplete.[4]

The proportion of House and Senate campaign funds provided by PACs has certainly increased since the early 1970s, but individuals, most of whom are unaffiliated with PACs, together with the political parties, still supply about three-fifths of all the money spent by or on behalf of House candidates and three-quarters of the campaign expenditures for Senate contenders. So while the importance of PAC spending has grown, PACs clearly remain secondary as a source of election funding. PACs, then, seem rather less awesome when considered within the entire spectrum of campaign finance.

Apart from the argument over the relative weight of the PAC funds, PAC critics claim that political action committees are making it more expensive to run for office. There is some validity to this assertion. Money provided to one candidate funds the purchase of campaign tools that the other candidate must match in order to stay competitive.

In the aggregate, American campaign expenditures seem huge. In 2002, the total amount spent by all U.S. House of Representatives candidates taken together was about $500 million, and the campaign cost of the winning House nominee averaged over $860,000. Will Rogers's 1931 remark has never been more true: "Politics has got so expensive that it takes lots of money to even get beat with."

Yet $500 million is far less than the annual advertising budgets of many individual commercial enterprises. These days it is expensive to communicate, whether the message is political or commercial. Television time, polling costs, consultants' fees, direct-mail investment, and other standard campaign expenditures have been soaring in price, over and above inflation.[5] PACs have been fueling the use of new campaign techniques, but a reasonable case can be made that such expenses are necessary, and that more and better communication is required between candidates and an electorate that often appears woefully uninformed about politics. PACs therefore may be making a positive contribution by providing the means to increase the flow of information during elections.

PACs are also accused of being biased toward the incumbent, and except for the ideological committees, they do display a clear and overwhelming preference for those already in office. But the same bias is apparent in contributions from individuals, who ask the same reasonable, perhaps decisive, economic question: Why waste money on contenders if incumbents almost always win? On the other hand, the best challengers—those perceived as having fair-to-good chances to win—are usually generously funded by PACs. Well-targeted PAC challenger money clearly helped the GOP win a majority in the U.S. Senate in 1994, for instance, and in turn aided the Democrats in their big 2000 gains.

The charge that PACs limit the number of strong challengers is true, because by giving so much money so early in the race to incumbents, they deter potential opponents from declaring their candidacies. On the other hand, the money that PACs channel to competitive challengers late in the election season may actually help increase the turnover of officeholders on election day. PAC money also tends to invigorate competitiveness in open-seat congressional races where there is no incumbent. . . .

PAC MONEY AND CONGRESSIONAL "CORRUPTION"

The most serious charge leveled at PACs is that they succeed in buying the votes of legislators on issues important to their individual constituencies. It seems hardly worth arguing that many PACs are shopping for congressional votes and that PAC money buys access, or opens doors, to congressmen. But the "vote-buying" allegation is generally not supported by a careful examination of the facts.[6] PAC contributions do make a difference, at least on some occasions, in securing access and influencing the course of events, but those occasions are not nearly as frequent as anti-PAC spokesmen, even congressmen themselves, often suggest.

PACs affect legislative proceedings to a decisive degree only when certain conditions prevail. First, the less visible the issue, the more likely that PAC funds can change or influence congressional votes. A corollary is that PAC money has more effect in the early stages of the legislative process, such as agenda setting and votes in subcommittee meetings, than in later and more public floor deliberations. Press, public, and even "watchdog" groups are not nearly as attentive to initial legislative proceedings.

PAC contributions are also more likely to influence the legislature when the issue is specialized and narrow, or unopposed by other organized interests. PAC gifts are less likely to be decisive on broad national issues such as American policy in Iraq or the adoption of a space-based missile defense system. But the more technical measures seem tailor-made for the special interests. Additionally, PAC influence in Congress is greater when large PACs or groups of PACs (such as business and labor PACs) are allied. In recent years, despite their natural enmity, business and labor have lobbied together on a number of issues, including defense spending, trade policy, environmental regulation, maritime legislation, trucking legislation, and nuclear power.[7] The combination is a weighty one, checked in many instances only by a tendency for business and labor in one industry (say, the railroads) to combine and oppose their cooperating counterparts in another industry (perhaps the truckers and teamsters).

It is worth stressing, however, that most congressmen are not unduly influenced by PAC money on most votes. The special conditions simply do not apply to most legislative issues, and the overriding factors in determining a legislator's votes include party affiliation, ideology, and constituents' needs and desires. Much has been made of the passage of large tax cuts for oil and business interests in the 1981 omnibus tax package. The journalist Elizabeth Drew said there was a "bidding war" to trade campaign contributions for tax breaks benefiting independent oil producers.[8] Ralph Nader's Public Citizen group charged that the $280,000 in corporate PAC money accepted by members of the House Ways and Means Committee helped to produce a bill that "contained everything business ever dared to ask for, and more."[9] Yet as Robert Samuelson has convincingly argued, the "bidding war" between Democrats and Republicans was waged not for PAC money but for control of a House of Representatives sharply divided between Reaganite Republicans and liberal Democrats, with conservative "boll weevil" Democrats from the southern oil states as the crucial swing votes.[10] The Ways and Means Committee actions cited by Nader were also more correctly explained in partisan terms. After all, if these special interests were so influential in writing the 1981 omnibus tax package, how could they fail so completely to derail the much more important (and, for them, threatening) tax reform legislation of 1986? Similarly, President George W. Bush's tax cut plan passed Congress in May 2001 because the electorate had delivered both houses of Congress and the presidency to the GOP. Almost all Republican candidates ran for office supporting the tax cuts, and they were fulfilling a campaign promise, not giving in to the "special interests" by voting for the cuts.

If party loyalty can have a stronger pull than PAC contributions, then surely the views of a congressman's constituents can also take precedence over those of political action committees. If an incumbent is faced with the choice of either voting for a PAC-backed bill that is very unpopular in his district or forgoing the PAC's money, the odds are that any politician who depends on a majority of votes to remain in office is going to side with his constituency and vote against the PAC's interest. PAC gifts are merely a means to an end: reelection. If accepting money will cause a candidate embarrassment, then even a maximum donation will likely be rejected. The flip side of this proposition makes sense as well: if a PAC's parent organization has many members or a major financial stake in the congressman's home district, he is much more likely to vote the PAC's way— not so much because he receives PAC money but because the group accounts for an important part of his electorate. Does a U.S. senator from a dairy state vote for dairy price supports because he received a significant percentage of his PAC contributions from agriculture, or because the farm population of his state is relatively large and politically active? When congressmen vote the National Rifle Association's preferences is it because of the money the NRA's PAC distributes, or because the NRA, unlike gun-control advocates, has repeatedly demonstrated the ability to produce a sizable number of votes in many legislative districts?

If PACs have appeared more influential than they actually are, it is partly because many people believe legislators are looking for opportunities to exclaim (as one did during the Abscam scandal) "I've got larceny in my blood!" It is certainly disturbing that the National Republican Congressional Committee believed it necessary to warn its PAC-soliciting candidates: "Don't *ever* suggest to the PAC that it is 'buying' your vote, should you get elected."[11] Yet knowledgeable Capitol Hill observers agree that there are few truly corrupt congressmen. Simple correlations notwithstanding, when most legislators vote for a PAC-supported bill, it is because of the *merits* of the case, or the entreaties of their party leaders, peers, or constituents, and not because of PAC money.

When the PAC phenomenon is viewed in the broad perspective of issues, party allegiance, and constituent interests, it is clear that *merit* matters most in the votes most congressmen cast. It is naive to contend that PAC money never influences decisions, but it is unjustifiably cynical to believe that PACs always, or even usually, push the voting buttons in Congress.

PACS IN PERSPECTIVE

As the largely unsubstantiated "vote-buying" controversy suggests, PACs are often misrepresented and unfairly maligned as the embodiment of corrupt special interests. Political action committees are a contemporary manifestation of what James Madison called "factions." In his *Federalist, No. 10,* Madison wrote that through the flourishing of these competing interest groups, or factions, liberty would be preserved.[12]

In any democracy, and particularly in one as pluralistic as the United States, it is essential that groups be relatively unrestricted in advocating their interests and positions. Not only is that the mark of a free society, it also provides a safety valve for the competitive pressures that build on all fronts in a capitalistic democracy. And it provides another means to keep representatives responsive to legitimate needs.

This is not to say that all groups pursue legitimate interests, or that vigorously competing interests ensure that the public good prevails. The press, the public, and valuable watchdog groups such as Common Cause must always be alert to instances in which narrow private interests prevail over the commonweal—occurrences that generally happen when no one is looking.

Besides the press and various public interest organizations, there are two major institutional checks on the potential abuses wrought by factions, associations, and now PACs. The most fundamental of these is regular free elections with general suffrage. As Tocqueville commented:

> Perhaps the most powerful of the causes which tend to mitigate the excesses of political association in the United States is Universal Suffrage. In countries in which universal suffrage exists, the majority is never doubtful, because neither party can pretend to represent the portion of the community which has not voted.
>
> The associations which are formed are aware, as well as the nation at large, that they do not represent the majority: this is, indeed, a condition inseparable from their existence; for if they did represent the prepondering power, they would change the law instead of soliciting its reform.[13]

[Former] Senator Robert Dole (R-Kan.) has said, "There aren't any Poor PACs or Food Stamp PACs or Nutrition PACs or Medicare PACs,"[14] and PAC critics frequently make the point that certain segments of the electorate are underrepresented in the PAC community. Yet without much support from PACs, there are food stamps, poverty and nutrition programs, and Medicare. Why? Because the recipients of governmental assistance constitute a hefty slice of the electorate, and *votes matter more than dollars to politicians.* Furthermore, many citizens *outside* the affected groups have also made known their support of aid to the poor and elderly—making yet a stronger electoral case for these PAC-less programs.

The other major institution that checks PAC influence is the two-party system. While PACs represent particular interests, the political parties build coalitions of groups and attempt to represent a national interest. They arbitrate among competing claims, and they seek to reach a consensus on matters of overriding importance to the nation. The parties are one of the few unifying forces in an exceptionally diverse country. . . .

However limited and checkmated by political realities PACs may be, they are still regarded by a skeptical public as thoroughly unsavory. PACs have become the embodiment of greedy special interest politics, rising campaign costs, and corruption. It does not seem to matter that most experts in the field of campaign finance take considerable exception to the prevailing characterization of political action committees. PACs have become, in the public's mind, a powerful symbol of much that is wrong with America's campaign process, and candidates for public office naturally manipulate this symbol as well as others for their own ends. It is a circumstance as old as the Republic.

PACs, however, have done little to change their image for the better. Other than the business-oriented Public Affairs Council, few groups or committees have moved to correct one-sided press coverage or educate the public on campaign financing's fundamentals. In fact, many PACs fuel the fires of discontent by refusing to defend themselves while not seeming to care about appearances. Giving to both candidates in the same race, for example—an all-too-common practice—may be justifiable in theory, but it strikes most people as unprincipled, rank influence purchasing. Even worse, perhaps, are PACs that "correct their mistakes" soon after an election by sending a donation to the winning, but not originally PAC-supported, candidate. In the seven 1986 U.S. Senate races where a Democratic challenger defeated a Republican incumbent, there were 150 instances in which a PAC gave to the GOP candidate *before* the election and to the victorious Democrat once the votes were counted.[15] These practices PACs themselves should stop. Every PAC should internally ban double giving, and there should be a moratorium on gifts to previously opposed candidates until at least the halfway point of the officeholder's term.

Whether PACs undertake some necessary rehabilitative steps or not, any fair appraisal of their role in American elections must be balanced. PACs are neither political innocents nor selfless civic boosters. But, neither are they cesspools of corruption and greed, nor modern-day versions of Tammany Hall.

PACs will never be popular with idealistic reformers because they represent the rough, cutting edge of a democracy teeming with different peoples and conflicting interests. Indeed, PACs may never be hailed even by natural allies; it was the business-oriented *Wall Street Journal,* after all, that editorially referred to Washington, D.C., as "a place where politicians, PACs, lawyers, and lobbyists for unions, business or you-name-it, shake each other down full time for political money and political support."[16]

Viewed in perspective, the root of the problem in campaign finance is not PACs; it is money. Americans have an enduring mistrust of the mix of money (particularly business money) and politics, as Finley Peter Dunne's Mr. Dooley revealed:

I niver knew a pollytician to go wrong ontil he'd been contaminated be contact with a business man. . . . It seems to me that th' only thing to do is to keep pollyticians an' business men apart. They seem to have a bad infloonce on each other. Whiniver I see an alderman an' a banker walkin' down th' street together I know th' Recordin' Angel will have to ordher another bottle iv ink.[17]

As a result of the new campaign finance rules of the 1970s, political action committees superseded the "fat cats" of old as the public focus and symbol of the role of money in politics, and PACs inherited the suspicions that go with the territory. Those suspicions are valuable because they keep the spotlight on PACs and guard against undue influence. It may be regrettable that such supervision is required, but human nature—not PACs—demands it.

NOTES

1. Quotations from Common Cause direct-mail package to members, January 1987.
2. *The New Republic*, May 28, 1984, p. 9.
3. For a much more extended discussion of these subjects, see Larry Sabato, *PAC POWER: Inside the World of Political Action Committees*, rev. ed. (New York: Report of the Twentieth Century Fund Task Force on Political Action Committees, 1984).
4. Michael J. Malbin, "The Problem of PAC-Journalism," *Public Opinion*, December/January 1983, pp. 15–16, 59.
5. See Larry Sabato, *The Rise of Political Consultants* (New York: Basic Books, 1981); see also *National Journal*, April 16, 1983, pp. 780–81.
6. See Sabato, *PAC POWER*, pp. 122–59, 222–28.
7. See, for example, Edwin M. Epstein, "An Irony of Electoral Reform," *Regulation*, May/June 1979, pp. 35–44; and Christopher Madison, "Federal Subsidy Programs Under Attack by Unlikely Marriage of Labor and Right," *National Journal*, December 31, 1983, pp. 2682–84.
8. Elizabeth Drew, "Politics and Money, Part I" *The New Yorker*, December 6, 1982, pp. 38–45.
9. Herbert E. Alexander, *Financing the 1980 Election* (Lexington, Mass.: D. C. Heath, 1983), p. 379.
10. Robert J. Samuelson, "The Campaign Reform Failure," *The New Republic*, September 5, 1983, pp. 32–33.
11. From the NRCC publication "Working with PACs" (1982).
12. See *The Federalist*, No. 10, for a much fuller discussion of the role of factions in a democratic society.
13. Alexis de Tocqueville, *Democracy in America*, vol. 1 (New York: Vintage Books, 1954), p. 224.
14. As quoted in Drew, "Politics and Money," p. 147.
15. Common Cause "If at First You Don't Succeed, Give, Give Again" (Press release, Washington, D.C., March 20, 1987).
16. "Cleaning Up Reform," *The Wall Street Journal*, November 10, 1983, p. 26.

17. Finley Peter Dunne, *The World of Mr. Dooley,* edited with an introduction by Louis Filler (New York: Collier Books, 1962), pp. 155–56.

Internet Resources

Visit our website at http://www.mhhe.com/diclerico for links and resources relating to Interest Groups.

chapter 10

Congress

Representation

*The three selections in this section are illustrative of a long-standing debate among po-
litical theorists and elected officials alike: namely, whose views should prevail on a
given issue—the constituents' or the representatives'? In the first selection, taken from
an early debate in the General Assembly of Virginia, the argument is made that legislators are obliged to act as instructed delegates—that is, they must vote in accordance
with the will of their constituents. In the second selection, former Massachusetts senator and president John F. Kennedy, writing in 1956, argues that legislators should act
as trustees, voting according to their own conscience, regardless of whether their
choices reflect the sentiments of their constituents. Finally, George Galloway, a former
staff assistant in Congress, contends that on some occasions legislators must follow
public opinion, while on others they are obliged to vote according to their own conscience. This view, which combines both the delegate and the trustee approach, is characterized as the politico role.*

The Legislator as Delegate
General Assembly of Virginia

There can be no doubt that the scheme of a representative republic was derived to our forefathers from the constitution of the English House of Commons; and that that branch of the English government . . . was in its origin, and in theory always has been, purely republican. It is certain, too, that the statesmen of America, in assuming that as the model of our own institutions, designed to adopt it here in its purest form, and with its strictest republican tenets and principles. It becomes, therefore, an inquiry of yet greater utility than curiosity, to ascertain the sound doctrines of the constitution of the English House of Commons in regard to this right of the constituent to instruct the representative. For the position may safely be assumed that the wise and virtuous men who framed our constitutions deigned, that, in the United States, the constituent should have at least as much, if not a great deal more, influence over the representative than was known to have existed from time immemorial in England. Let us then interrogate the history of the British nation; let us consult the opinions of their wise men.

Instances abound in parliamentary history of formal instructions from the constituent to the representative, of which . . . the following may suffice: In 1640, the knights of the shire for Dorset and Kent informed the commons *that they had in charge from their constituents* seven articles of grievances, which they accordingly laid before the House, where they were received and acted on. In the 33rd year of Charles II, the citizens of London instructed their members to insist on the bill for excluding the Duke of York (afterward King James II) from the succession to the throne; and their representative said "that his *duty* to his electors *obliged* him to vote the bill." At a subsequent election, in 1681, in many places, formal instructions were given to the members returned, to insist on the same exclusion bill; we know, from history, how uniformly and faithfully those instructions were obeyed. . . . In 1741, the citizens of London instructed their members to vote against standing armies, excise laws, the septennial bill, and a long train of evil measures, already felt, or anticipated; and expressly affirm their right of instruction—"We think it" (say they) "our *duty,* as it is *our undoubted right,* to acquaint you, with *what we desire and expect from you, in discharge of the great trust we repose in you,* and what we take to be *your duty as our*

From Commonwealth of Virginia, General Assembly, *Journal of the Senate,* 1812, pp. 82–89. In some instances, spelling and punctuation have been altered from the original in order to achieve greater clarity.

representative, etc." In the same year, instructions of a similar character were sent from all parts of England. In 1742, the cities of London, Bristol, Edinburgh, York, and many others, instructed their members in parliament to seek redress against certain individuals suspected to have betrayed and deserted the cause of the people. . . .

Instances also are on record of the deliberate formal knowledgement of the right of instruction by the House of Commons itself, especially in old times. Thus the commons hesitated to grant supplies to King Edward III *till they had the consent of their constituents*, and desired that a new parliament might be summoned, which might be *prepared with authority from their constituents*. . . .

"Instructions" (says a member of the House of Commons) "ought to be *followed implicitly*," after the member has *respectfully* given his constituents *his opinion* of them: *"Far be it from me to oppose my judgment to that of 6000 of my fellow citizens."* "The practice" (says another) "of consulting our constituents was good. I wish it was continued. *We can discharge our duty no better, than in the direction of those who sent us hither. What the people choose is right, because they choose it."* . . .

Without referring to the minor political authors . . . who have maintained these positions (quoted from one of them)—"that the people have a right to instruct their representatives; that no man ought to be chosen that will not receive instructions; that the people understand enough of the interests of the country to give general instructions; that it was the custom formerly to instruct all the members; and the nature of deputation shows that the custom was well grounded"—it is proper to mention that the great constitutional lawyer Coke . . . says, "It is the *custom of parliament*, when any new device is moved for on the king's behalf, for his aid and the like, that the commons may answer, *they dare not agree to it without conference with their counties."* And Sydney . . . maintains "that members derive their power from those that choose them; that those who give power do not give an unreserved power; that many members, in all ages, and sometimes the whole body of the commons have refused to vote until they consulted with those who sent them; that the houses have often adjourned to give them time to do so and if this were done more frequently, or if cities, towns and counties had on some occasions given instructions to their deputies, matters would probably have gone better in parliament than they have done." . . . The celebrated Edmund Burke, a man, it must be admitted, of profound knowledge, deep foresight, and transcendent abilities, disobeyed the instructions of his constituents; yet, by placing his excuse on the ground that the instructions were but the clamour of the day, he seems to admit the authority of instructions soberly and deliberately given; for he agrees, "he ought to look to their opinions" (which he explains to mean their permanent settled opinions) "but not the flash of the day"; and he says elsewhere, that he could not bear to show himself "a representative, whose face did not reflect the face of his constituents—a face that did not joy in their joys and sorrow in their sorrows." It is remarkable that, notwithstanding a most splendid display of warm and touching eloquence, the people of Bristol would not reelect Mr. Burke, for this very offense of disobeying instructions. . . .

It appears, therefore, that the right of the constituent to instruct the representative, is firmly established in England, on the broad basis of the nature of representation. The existence of that right, there, has been demonstrated by the only practicable evidence, by which the principles of an unwritten constitution can be ascertained—history and precedent.

To view the subject upon principle, the right of the constituent to instruct the representative, seems to result, clearly and conclusively, from the very nature of the representative system. Through means of that noble institution, the largest nation may, almost as conveniently as the smallest, enjoy all the advantages of a government by the people, without any of the evils of democracy—precipitation, confusion, turbulence, distraction from the ordinary and useful pursuits of industry. And it is only to avoid those and the like mischiefs, that representation is substituted for the direct suffrage of the people in the office of legislation. The representative, therefore, must in the nature of things, represent his own particular constituents only. He must, indeed, look to the general good of the nation, but he must look also, and especially to the interests of his particular constituents as concerned in the commonweal; because the general good is but the aggregate of individual happiness. He must legislate for the whole nation; but laws are expressions of the general will; and the general will is only the result of individual wills fairly collected and compared. In order . . . to express the general will . . . it is plain that the representative must express the will and speak the opinions of the constituents that depute him.

It cannot be pretended that a representative is to be the organ of his own will alone; for then, he would be so far despotic. *He must be the organ of others*— of whom? Not of the nation, for the nation deputes him not; but of his constituents, who alone know, alone have trusted, and can alone displace him. And if it be his province and his duty, in general, to express the will of his constituents, to the best of his knowledge, without being particularly informed thereof, it seems impossible to contend that he is not bound to do so when he is so especially informed and instructed.

The right of the constituent to instruct the representative, therefore, is an essential principle of the representative system. It may be remarked that wherever representation has been introduced, however unfavorable the circumstances under which it existed, however short its duration, however unimportant its functions, however dimly understood, the right of instruction has always been regarded as inseparably incidental to it. . . .

A representative has indeed a wide field of discretion left to him; and great is the confidence reposed in his integrity, fidelity, wisdom, zeal; but neither is the field of discretion boundless, nor the extent of confidence infinite; and the very discretion allowed him, and the very confidence he enjoys, is grounded on the supposition that he is charged with the will, acquainted with the opinions, and devoted to the interests of his constituents. . . .

Various objections have been urged to this claim of the constituent, of a right to instruct the representative, on which it may be proper to bestow some attention.

The first objection that comes to be considered . . . is grounded on the supposed impossibility of fairly ascertaining the sense of the constituent body. The *impossibility* is denied. It may often be a matter of great *difficulty;* but then the duty of obedience resolves itself into a question, not of principle, but of fact: whether the right of instruction has been exercised or not. The representative cannot be bound by an instruction that is not given; but that is no objection to the obligation of an instruction *actually given.* . . .

It has been urged that the representatives are not bound to obey the instructions of their constituents because the constituents do not hear the debates, and therefore, cannot be supposed judges of the matter to be voted. If this objection has force enough to defeat the right of instruction, it ought to take away, also, the right of rejecting the representative at the subsequent election. For it might be equally urged on that occasion, as against the right of instruction, that the people heard not the debate that enlightened the representative's mind— the reasons that convinced his judgment and governed his conduct. . . . In other words, the principle that mankind is competent to self-government should be renounced. The truth is, that our institutions suppose that although the representative ought to be, and generally will be, selected for superior virtue and intelligence, yet a greater mass of wisdom and virtue still reside in the constituent body than the utmost portion allotted to any individual. . . .

Finally, it has been objected, that the instructions of the constituent are not obligatory on the representative because the obligation insisted on is fortified with no sanction—the representative cannot be punished for his disobedience, and his vote is valid notwithstanding his disobedience. It is true that there is no mode of legal punishment provided for this . . . default of duty and that the act of disobedience will not invalidate the vote. It is true, too, that a representative may perversely advocate a measure which he knows to be ruinous to his country; and that neither his vote will be invalidated by his depravity, nor can he be punished by law for his crime, heinous as it surely is. But it does not follow that the one representative is *not bound to obey the instructions* of his constituents any more than that the other is not bound to obey the dictates of his conscience. Both duties stand upon the same foundation, with almost all the great political and moral obligations. The noblest duties of man are without any legal sanction: the great mass of social duties . . . , our duties to our parents, to our children, to our wives, to our families, to our neighbor, to our country, our duties to God, are, for the most part, without legal sanction, yet surely not without the strongest obligation. The duty of the *representative* to obey the instructions of the *constituent* body cannot be placed on higher ground.

Such are the opinions of the General Assembly of Virginia, on the subject of this great right of instruction, and such the general reasons on which those opinions are founded. . . .

The Legislator as Trustee
John F. Kennedy

The primary responsibility of a senator, most people assume, is to represent the views of his state. Ours is a federal system—a union of relatively sovereign states whose needs differ greatly—and my constitutional obligations as senator would thus appear to require me to represent the interests of my state. Who will speak for Massachusetts if her own senators do not? Her rights and even her identity become submerged. Her equal representation in Congress is lost. Her aspirations, however much they may from time to time be in the minority, are denied that equal opportunity to be heard to which all minority views are entitled.

Any senator need not look very long to realize that his colleagues are representing *their* local interests. And if such interests are ever to be abandoned in favor of the national good, let the constituents—not the senator—decide when and to what extent. For he is their agent in Washington, the protector of their rights, recognized by the vice president in the Senate Chamber as "the senator from Massachusetts" or "the senator from Texas."

But when all of this is said and admitted, we have not yet told the full story. For in Washington we are "United States senators" and members of the Senate of the United States as well as senators from Massachusetts and Texas. Our oath of office is administered by the vice president, not by the governors of our respective states; and we come to Washington, to paraphrase Edmund Burke, not as hostile ambassadors or special pleaders for our state or section, in opposition to advocates and agents of other areas, but as members of the deliberative assembly of one nation with one interest. Of course, we should not ignore the needs of our area—nor could we easily as products of that area—but none could be found to look out for the national interest if local interests wholly dominated the role of each of us.

There are other obligations in addition to those of state and region—the obligations of the party. . . . Even if I can disregard those pressures, do I not have an obligation to go along with the party that placed me in office? We

John F. Kennedy, 35th President of the United States, was Democratic member of the U.S. Senate from the state of Massachusetts from 1952 to 1960 and a member of the U.S. House of Representatives from 1947 to 1952. Selected excerpts from pp. 33–39 from *Profiles in Courage* by John F. Kennedy. Copyright © 1955, 1956, 1961 by John F. Kennedy. Copyright renewed © 1983, 1984, 1989 by Jacqueline Kennedy Onassis. Foreword copyright © 1964 by Robert F. Kennedy. Reprinted by permission of HarperCollins Publishers, Inc.

believe in this country in the principle of party responsibility, and we recognize
the necessity of adhering to party platforms—if the party label is to mean anything to the voters. Only in this way can our basically two-party nation avoid
the pitfalls of multiple splinter parties, whose purity and rigidity of principle, I
might add—if I may suggest a sort of Gresham's Law of politics—increase in-
versely with the size of their membership.

And yet we cannot permit the pressures of party responsibility to sub-
merge on every issue the call of personal responsibility. For the party which, in
its drive for unity, discipline and success, ever decides to exclude new ideas, independent conduct or insurgent members, is in danger. . . .

Of course, both major parties today seek to serve the national interest. They
would do so in order to obtain the broadest base of support, if for no nobler reason. But when party and officeholder differ as to how the national interest is to
be served, we must place first the responsibility we owe not to our party or
even to our constituents but to our individual consciences.

But it is a little easier to dismiss one's obligations to local interests and
party ties to face squarely the problem of one's responsibility to the will of his
constituents. A senator who avoids this responsibility would appear to be accountable to no one, and the basic safeguards of our democratic system would
thus have vanished. He is no longer representative in the true sense, he has violated his public trust, he has betrayed the confidence demonstrated by those
who voted for him to carry out their views. "Is the creature," as John Tyler
asked the House of Representatives in his maiden speech, "to set himself in opposition to his Creator? Is the servant to disobey the wishes of his master?"

> How can he be regarded as representing the people when he speaks, not their
> language, but his own? He ceases to be their representative when he does so,
> and represents himself alone.

In short, according to this school of thought, if I am to be properly responsive to the will of my constituents, it is my duty to place their principles, not
mine, above all else. This may not always be easy, but it nevertheless is the
essence of democracy, faith in the wisdom of the people and their views. To be
sure, the people will make mistakes—they will get no better government than
they deserve—but that is far better than the representative of the people arrogating for himself the right to say he knows better than they what is good for
them. Is he not chosen, the argument closes, to vote as they would vote were
they in his place?

It is difficult to accept such a narrow view of the role of a United States senator—a view that assumes the people of Massachusetts sent me to Washington
to serve merely as a seismograph to record shifts in popular opinion. I reject
this view not because I lack faith in the "wisdom of the people," but because
this concept of democracy actually puts too little faith in the people. Those who
would deny the obligation of the representative to be bound by every impulse
of the electorate—regardless of the conclusions his own deliberations direct—
do trust in the wisdom of the people. They have faith in their ultimate sense of
justice, faith in their ability to honor courage and respect judgment, and faith

that in the long run they will act unselfishly for the good of the nation. It is that kind of faith on which democracy is based, not simply the often frustrated hope that public opinion will at all times under all circumstances promptly identify itself with the public interest.

The voters selected us, in short, because they had confidence in our judgment and our ability to exercise that judgment from a position where we could determine what were their own best interests, as a part of the nation's interests. This may mean that we must on occasion lead, inform, correct and sometimes even ignore constituent opinion, if we are to exercise fully that judgment for which we were elected. But acting without selfish motive or private bias, those who follow the dictates of an intelligent conscience are not aristocrats, demagogues, eccentrics, or callous politicians insensitive to the feelings of the public. They expect—and not without considerable trepidation—their constituents to be the final judges of the wisdom of their course; but they have faith that those constituents—today, tomorrow, or even in another generation—will at least respect the principles that motivated their independent stand.

If their careers are temporarily or even permanently buried under an avalanche of abusive editorials, poison-pen letters, and opposition votes at the polls—as they sometimes are, for that is the risk they take—they await the future with hope and confidence, aware of the fact that the voting public frequently suffers from what ex-Congressman T. V. Smith called the lag "between our way of thought and our way of life." . . .

Moreover, I question whether any senator, before we vote on a measure, can state with certainty exactly how the majority of his constituents feel on the issue as it is presented to the Senate. All of us in the Senate live in an iron lung—the iron lung of politics, and it is no easy task to emerge from that rarefied atmosphere in order to breathe the same fresh air our constituents breathe. It is difficult, too, to see in person an appreciable number of voters besides those professional hangers-on and vocal elements who gather about the politician on a trip home. In Washington I frequently find myself believing that forty or fifty letters, six visits from professional politicians and lobbyists, and three editorials in Massachusetts newspapers constitute public opinion on a given issue. Yet in truth I rarely know how the great majority of the voters feel, or even how much they know of the issues that seem so burning in Washington.

Today the challenge of political courage looms larger than ever before. For our everyday life is becoming so saturated with the tremendous power of mass communications that any unpopular or unorthodox course arouses a storm of protests. . . . Our political life is becoming so expensive, so mechanized, and so dominated by professional politicians and public relations men that the idealist who dreams of independent statesmanship is rudely awakened by the necessities of election and accomplishment. . . .

And thus, in the days ahead, only the very courageous will be able to take the hard and unpopular decisions necessary for our survival. . . .

The Legislator as Politico
George B. Galloway

One question which the conscientious congressman must often ask himself, especially when conflicts arise between local or regional attitudes and interests and the national welfare, is this: "As a member of Congress, am I merely a delegate from my district or state, restricted to act and vote as the majority which elected me desire, bound by the instructions of my constituents and subservient to their will? Or am I, once elected, a representative of the people of the United States, free to act as I think best for the country generally?"

In a country as large as the United States, with such diverse interests and such a heterogeneous population, the economic interests and social prejudices of particular states and regions often clash with those of other sections and with conceptions of the general interest of the whole nation. The perennial demand of the silver-mining and wool interests in certain western states for purchase and protection, the struggle over slavery, and the . . . filibuster of southern senators against the attempt to outlaw racial discrimination in employment are familiar examples of recurring conflicts between local interests and prejudices and the common welfare. These political quarrels are rooted in the varying stages of cultural development attained by the different parts of the country. It is the peculiar task of the politician to compose these differences, to reconcile conflicting national and local attitudes, and to determine when public opinion is ripe for legislative action. Some conflicts will yield in time to political adjustment; others must wait for their legal sanction upon the gradual evolution of the conscience of society. No act of Congress can abolish unemployment or barking dogs or racial prejudices. . . .

TYPES OF PRESSURES ON CONGRESS

One can sympathize with the plight of the conscientious congressman who is the focal point of all these competing pressures. The district or state he represents may need and want certain roads, post offices, courthouses, or schools. Irrigation dams or projects may be needed for the development of the area's re-

George B. Galloway (1898–1967) formerly was senior specialist in American government with the Legislative Reference Service of the Library of Congress. Selected excerpts are from pp. 284–85, 301, and 319–22 from *Congress at the Crossroads* by George B. Galloway. Copyright 1946 by George B. Galloway. Reprinted by permission of HarperCollins Publishers, Inc.

sources. If the representative is to prove himself successful in the eyes of the people back home, he must be able to show, at least occasionally, some visible and concrete results of his congressional activity. Or else he must be able to give good reasons why he has not been able to carry out his pledges. The local residence rule for congressmen multiplies the pressures that impinge upon him. Faithful party workers who have helped elect him will expect the congressman to pay his political debts by getting them jobs in the federal service. Constituents affected by proposed legislation may send him an avalanche of letters, telegrams, and petitions which must be acknowledged and followed up. The region from which he comes will expect him to protect and advance its interests in Washington. All the various organized groups will press their claims upon him and threaten him if he does not jump when they crack the whip. Party leaders may urge a congressman to support or oppose the administration program or to "trade" votes for the sake of party harmony or various sectional interests. He is also under pressure from his own conscience as to what he should do both to help the people who have elected him and to advance the best interests of the nation. Besieged by all these competing pressures, a congressman is often faced with the choice of compromising between various pressures, of trading votes, of resisting special interests of one sort or another, of staying off the floor when a vote is taken on some measure he prefers not to take a stand on, of getting support here and at the same time running the risk of losing support there. Dealing with pressure blocs is a problem in political psychology which involves a careful calculation of the power of the blocs, the reaction of the voters on election day, and the long-haul interests of the district, state, and nation. . . .

SHOULD CONGRESS LEAD OR FOLLOW PUBLIC OPINION?

It is axiomatic to say that in a democracy public opinion is the source of law. Unless legislation is sanctioned by the sense of right of the people, it becomes a dead letter on the statute books, like Prohibition and the Hatch Act. But public opinion is a mercurial force; now quiescent, now vociferous, it has various moods and qualities. It reacts to events and is often vague and hard to weigh.

Nor is public opinion infallible. Most people are naturally preoccupied with their personal problems and daily affairs; national problems and legislative decisions seem complex and remote to them, despite press and radio and occasional Capitol tours. Comparatively few adults understand the technicalities of foreign loans or reciprocal trade treaties, although congressional action on these aspects of our foreign economic policy may have far-reaching effects upon our standard of living. . . .

In practice, a congressman both leads and follows public opinion. The desires of his constituents, of his party, and of this or that pressure group all enter into his decisions on matters of major importance. The influence of these factors varies from member to member and measure to measure. Some congressmen consider it their duty to follow closely what they think is the majority opinion of their constituents, especially just before an election. Others feel that they should make their decisions without regard to their constituents' wishes in the first place, and then try to educate and convert them afterward. Some members are strong party men and follow more or less blindly the program of the party leaders. Except when they are very powerful in the home district, the pressure groups are more of a nuisance than a deciding influence on the average member. When a legislator is caught between the conflicting pressures of his constituents and his colleagues, he perforce compromises between them and follows his own judgment.

The average legislator discovers early in his career that certain interests or prejudices of his constituents are dangerous to trifle with. Some of these prejudices may not be of fundamental importance to the welfare of the nation, in which case he is justified in humoring them, even though he may disapprove. The difficult case occurs where the prejudice concerns some fundamental policy affecting the national welfare. A sound sense of values, the ability to discriminate between that which is of fundamental importance and that which is only superficial, is an indispensable qualification of a good legislator.

Senator Fulbright* gives an interesting example of this distinction in his stand on the poll-tax issue and isolationism. "Regardless of how persuasive my colleagues or the national press may be about the evils of the poll tax, I do not see its fundamental importance, and I shall follow the views of the people of my state. Although it may be symbolic of conditions which many deplore, it is exceedingly doubtful that its abolition will cure any of our major problems. On the other hand, regardless of how strongly opposed my constituents may prove to be to the creation of, and participation in, an ever stronger United Nations Organization, I could not follow such a policy in that field unless it becomes clearly hopeless."[1]

A TWO-WAY JOB

As believers in democracy, probably most Americans would agree that it is the duty of congressmen to follow public opinion insofar as it expresses the desires, wants, needs, aspirations, and ideals of the people. Most Americans probably would also consider it essential for their representatives to make as careful an appraisal of these needs and desires as they can, and to consider, in connection with such an appraisal, the ways and means of accomplishing them. Legislators have at hand more information about legal structures, economic problems, productive capacities, manpower possibilities, and the like, than the average citizen they represent. They can draw upon that information to inform and lead the people—by showing the extent to which their desires can be realized.

In other words, a true representative of the people would follow the people's desires and at the same time lead the people in formulating ways of accomplishing those desires. He would lead the people in the sense of calling to

*At the time this article was written, J. William Fulbright was a U.S. senator from Arkansas—*Editors.*

their attention the difficulties of achieving those aims and the ways to over-come the difficulties. This means also that, where necessary, he would show special interest groups or even majorities how, according to his own interpretation and his own conscience, their desires need to be tempered in the common interest or for the future good of the nation.

Thus the job of a congressman is a two-way one. He represents his local area and interests in the national capital, and he also informs the people back home of the problems arising at the seat of government and how these problems affect them. It is in the nature of the congressman's job that he should determine, as far as he can, public opinion in his own constituency and in the whole nation, analyze it, measure it in terms of the practicability of turning it into public policy, and consider it in the light of his own knowledge, conscience, and convictions. Occasionally he may be obliged to go against public opinion, with the consequent task of educating or reeducating the people along lines that seem to him more sound. And finally, since he is a human being eager to succeed at his important job of statesmanship and politics, he is realistic enough to keep his eyes on the voters in terms of the next election. But he understands that a mere weather-vane following of majority public opinion is not always the path to reelection. . . .

NOTE

1. In an address on "The Legislator" delivered at the University of Chicago on February 19, 1946. *Vital Speeches,* May 15, 1946, pp. 468–72.

Legislative Process: The Filibuster *→ in senate   used by minority*

*T*he legislative process in Congress requires the building of coalitions among its members over and over again until all legislative hurdles have been overcome. Thus, successful legislators are those who are able to shepherd legislation through various committees in both houses, then to the floors of the House and Senate, then to the conference committees, and back to the floors. If the legislation requires an appropriation, then the whole process is repeated with different committees.

Although there is much that is the same legislatively in the House of Representatives and the Senate, there are some critical differences that, in the end, make the passage of legislation very difficult. One such difference is the filibuster in the Senate.

In the House of Representatives, the majority party leadership (i.e., the speaker of the house, the majority leader, and others) control the flow of legislation. In the Senate that control is ultimately in the hands of senators themselves. Typically, if the speaker of the house wants something, he or she can get it. In the Senate, however, a group of senators determined to block action can do so through the filibuster.

The filibuster is a legislative device to prevent action on a bill. It grows out of the necessity, under Senate custom and rules, for the Senate as a whole to determine when debate shall end on a bill. Under the current rule, a three-fifths vote is required to end debate. This "supermajority"—sixty senators—is extremely difficult to achieve.

For much of the twentieth century, the filibuster was used sparingly, and usually on the most critical of issues, such as civil rights bills. In recent years, however, the filibuster has been elevated to a new level, with senators from both parties either threatening or carrying out a filibuster almost as a matter of course on any manner of bills. Indeed, there have been more than thirty filibusters a year since 1993.

The central issue surrounding the filibuster is the extent to which a minority of senators should be able to block the will of the majority. Some argue, as does Senator Tom Harkin (D-Iowa) in the first selection, that whatever validity the filibuster had in history (and he thinks it was very little), it should not be allowed to continue unchanged today. The filibuster, he argues, only leads to gridlock in the legislative process, contributing to even greater cynicism and frustration among the American people.

In the second selection, a former member of the House of Representatives, Bill Frenzel (R-Minn.), makes the case for keeping the filibuster. Frenzel argues that the filibuster fits into the general scheme of limited government fashioned by the framers of the Constitution and should not be cast aside merely because it is viewed today as a major impediment to majority rule. According to Frenzel, if a majority of the people truly want the government to act, the Congress, including the Senate, will act. In the meantime, the filibuster is a useful device to filter out unneeded or unwise legislation.

It's Time to Change the Filibuster
Tom Harkin

Mr. HARKIN. Mr. President, for the benefit of the Senators who are here and watching on the monitors, we now have before us an amendment by myself, Senator LIEBERMAN, Senator PELL, and Senator ROBB that would amend rule XXII, the so-called filibuster rule of the U.S. Senate. . . .

This amendment would change the way this Senate operates more fundamentally than anything that has been proposed thus far this year. It would fundamentally change the way we do business by changing the filibuster rule as it currently stands.

Mr. President, the last Congress showed us the destructive impact filibusters can have on the legislative process, provoking gridlock after gridlock, frustration, anger, and despondency among the American people, wondering whether we can get anything done at all here in Washington. The pattern of filibusters and delays that we saw in the last Congress is part of the rising tide of filibusters that have overwhelmed our legislative process.

While some may gloat and glory in the frustration and anger that the American people felt toward our institution which resulted in the tidal wave of dissatisfaction that struck the majority in Congress, I believe in the long run that it will harm the Senate and our Nation for this pattern to continue. . . . Mr. President, there has . . . been a rising tide in the use of the filibuster. In the last two Congresses, in 1987 to 1990, and 1991 to 1994, there have been twice as many filibusters per year as there were the last time the Republicans controlled the Senate, from 1981 to 1986, and 10 times as many as occurred between 1917 and 1960. Between 1917 and 1960, there were an average of 1.3 per session. However, in the last Congress, there were 10 times that many. This is not healthy for our legislative process and it is not healthy for our country.

I have [also] compare[d] filibusters in the entire 19th century and in the last Congress. We had twice as many filibusters in the 103d Congress as we had in the entire 100 years of the 19th century.

Clearly, this is a process that is out of control. We need to change the rules. We need to change the rules, however, without harming the longstanding Senate tradition of extended debate and deliberation, and slowing things down.

Tom Harkin is a Democratic U.S. Senator from the state of Iowa. Excerpt from a speech delivered in the U.S. Senate, *Congressional Record,* Proceedings and Debates of the 104th Congress. First Session, Senate, January 4, 1995, vol. 141, No. 1, 530–33, and January 5, 1995, vol. 141, No. 2, 5431.

I have here [also] the issues that were subject to filibusters in the last Congress. Some of these were merely delayed by filibusters. Others were killed outright, despite having the majority of both bodies and the President in favor of them. That is right. Some of these measures had a majority of support in the Senate and in the House, and by the President. Yet, they never saw the light of day. Others simply were perfunctory housekeeping types of issues.

For example, one might understand why someone would filibuster the Brady Handgun Act. There were people that felt very strongly opposed to that. I can understand that being slowed down, and having extended debate on it. Can you say that about the J. Larry Lawrence nomination? I happen to be a personal friend of Mr. Lawrence. He is now our Ambassador to Switzerland, an important post. He was nominated to be Ambassador there, and he came through the committee fine. Yet, his nomination was the subject of a filibuster. Or there was the Edward P. Berry, Jr., nomination. There was the Claude Bolton nomination. You get my point.

We had nominations that were filibustered. This was almost unheard of in our past. We filibustered the nomination of a person that actually came through the committee process and was approved by the committee, and it was filibustered here on the Senate floor.

Actually, Senators use these nominations as a lever for power. If one Senator has an issue where he or she wants something done, it is very easy. All a Senator needs to do is filibuster a nomination. Then the majority leader or the minority leader has to come to the Senator and say, "Would you release your hold on that, give up your filibuster on that?"

"OK," the Senator will reply. "What do you want in return?"

Then the deals are struck.

It is used, Mr. President, as blackmail for one Senator to get his or her way on something that they could not rightfully win through the normal processes. I am not accusing any one party of this. It happens on both sides of the aisle.

Mr. President, I believe each Senator needs to give up a little of our pride, a little of our prerogatives, and a little of our power for the good of this Senate and for the good of this country. Let me repeat that:Each Senator, I believe, has to give up a little of our pride, a little of our prerogatives, and a little of our power for the better functioning of this body and for the good of our country.

I think the voters of this country were turned off by the constant bickering, the arguing back and forth that goes on in this Senate Chamber, the gridlock that ensued here, and the pointing of fingers of blame.

Sometimes, in the fog of debate, like the fog of war, it is hard to determine who is responsible for slowing something down. It is like the shifting sand. People hide behind the filibuster. I think it is time to let the voters know that we heard their message in the last election. They did not send us here to bicker and to argue, to point fingers. They want us to get things done to address the concerns facing this country. They want us to reform this place. They want this place to operate a little better, a little more openly, and a little more decisively.

Mr. President, I believe this Senate should embrace the vision of this body that our Founding Fathers had. There is a story—I am not certain whether it is true or not, but it is a nice story—that Thomas Jefferson returned from France, where he had learned that the Constitutional Convention had set up a separate body called the U.S. Senate, with its Members appointed by the legislatures and not subject to a popular vote. Jefferson was quite upset about this. He asked George Washington why this was done. Evidently, they were sitting at a breakfast table. Washington said to him, "Well, why did you pour your coffee in the saucer?" And Jefferson replied, "Why, to cool it, of course." Washington replied, "Just so: We created the Senate to cool down the legislation that may come from the House."

I think General Washington was very wise. I think our Founding Fathers were very wise to create this body.

They had seen what had happened in Europe—violent changes, rapid changes, mob rule—so they wanted the process to slow things down, to deliberate a little more, and that is why the Senate was set up.

But George Washington did not compare the Senate to throwing the coffee pot out the window. It is just to cool it down, and slow it down.

I think that is what the Founding Fathers envisioned, and I think that is what the American people expect. That is what we ought to and should provide. The Senate should carefully consider legislation, whether it originates here, or whether it streams in like water from a fire hose from the House of Representatives, we must provide ample time for Members to speak on issues. We should not move to the limited debate that characterizes the House of Representatives. I am not suggesting that we do that. But in the end, the people of our country are entitled to know where we stand and how we vote on the merits of a bill or an amendment.

Some argue that any supermajority requirement is unconstitutional, other than those specified in the Constitution itself. I find much in this theory to agree with—and I think we should treat all the rules that would limit the ability of a majority to rule with skepticism. I think that this theory is one that we ought to examine more fully, and that is the idea that the Constitution of the United States sets up certain specified instances in which a supermajority is needed to pass the bill, and in all other cases it is silent. In fact, the Constitution provides that the President of the Senate, the Vice President of the United States, can only vote to break a tie vote—by implication, meaning that the Senate should pass legislation by a majority vote, except in those instances in which the Constitution specifically says that we need a supermajority.

The distinguished constitutional expert, Lloyd Cutler, a distinguished lawyer, has been a leading proponent of this view. I have not made up my mind on this theory, but I do believe it is something we ought to further examine. I find a lot that I agree with in that theory.

But what we are getting at here is a different procedure and process, whereby we can have the Senate as the Founding Fathers envisioned—a place to cool down, slow down, deliberate and discuss, but not as a place where a handful—yes, maybe even one Senator—can totally stop legislation or a nomination.

Over the last couple of years, I have spent a great deal of time reading the history of this cloture process. Two years ago, about this time, I first proposed this to my fellow Democratic colleagues at a retreat we had in Williamsburg, VA. In May of that year, I proposed this to the Joint Committee on Congressional Reform. Some people said to me at that time: Senator HARKIN, of course you are proposing it, you are in the majority, you want to get rid of the filibuster. Well, now I am in the minority and I am still proposing it because I think it is the right thing to do.

Let me take some time to discuss the history of cloture and the limitations on debate in the Senate. Prior to 1917 there was no mechanism to shut off debate in the Senate. There was an early version in 1789 of what was called the "previous question." It was used more like a tabling motion than as a method to close debate.

In the 19th century, Mr. President, elections were held in November and Congress met in December. This Congress was always a lame duck session, which ended in March of the next year. The newly elected members did not take office until the following December, almost 13 months later. During the entire 19th century, there were filibusters. But most of these were aimed at delaying congressional action at the end of the short session that ended March 4. A filibuster during the 19th century was used at the end of a session when the majority would try to ram something through at the end, over the objections of the minority. Extended debate was used to extend debate to March 4, when under the law at that time, it automatically died.

If the majority tried to ram something through in the closing hours, the minority would discuss it and hold it up until March 4, and that was the end of it. That process was changed. Rather than going into an automatic lame-duck session in December, we now convene a new Congress in January with the new Members. I think this is illustrative that the filibuster used in the 19th century was entirely different in concept and in form than what we now experience here in the U.S. Senate.

So those who argue that the filibuster in the U.S. Senate today is a time-honored tradition of the U.S. Senate going clear back to 1789 are mistaken, because the use of the filibuster in the 19th century was entirely different than what it is being used for today, and it was used in a different set of laws and circumstances under which Congress met.

So that brings us up to the 20th century. In 1917, the first cloture rule was introduced in response to a filibuster, again, at the end of a session that triggered a special session. This cloture rule provided for two-thirds of Members present and voting to cut off debate. It was the first time since the first Congress met that the Senate adopted a cloture rule in 1917. However, this cloture rule was found to be ineffective and was rarely used. Why? Because rulings of the chair said that the cloture rule did not apply to procedural matters. So, if someone wanted to engage in a filibuster, they could simply bring up a procedural matter and filibuster that, and the two-thirds vote did not even apply to that. For a number of years, from 1917 until 1949, we had that situation.

In 1949 an attempt was made to make the cloture motion more effective. The 1949 rule applied the cloture rule to procedural matters. It closed that loophole but did not apply to rules changes. It also raised the needed vote from two-thirds present and voting to two-thirds of the whole Senate, which at that time meant 64 votes. That rule existed for 10 years.

In 1959, Lyndon Johnson pushed through a rules change to change the needed vote back to two-thirds of those present and voting, and which also applied cloture to rules changes.

There were many attempts after that to change the filibuster. In 1975, after several years of debate here in the Senate, the current rule was adopted, as a compromise proposed by Senator BYRD of West Virginia. The present cloture rule allows cloture to be invoked by three-fifths of Senators chosen and sworn, or 60 votes, except in the case of rules changes, which still require two-thirds of those present and voting.

This change in the rule reducing the proportion of votes needed for cloture for the first time since 1917, was the culmination of many years of efforts by reformers' numerous proposals between 1959 and 1975.

Two of the proposals that were made in those intervening years I found particularly interesting. One was by Senator Hubert Humphrey in 1963, which provided for majority cloture in two stages. The other proposal I found interesting was one by Senator DOLE in 1971 that moved from the then current two-thirds present and voting down to three-fifths present and voting, reducing the number of votes by one with each successive cloture vote.

We drew upon Senator DOLE's proposal in developing our own proposal. Our proposal would reduce the number of votes needed to invoke cloture gradually, allowing time for debate, allowing us to slow things down, but ultimately allowing the Senate to get to the merits of a vote.

Under our proposal, the amendment now before the Senate, Senators still have to get 16 signatures to offer a cloture motion. The motion would still have to lay over 2 days. The first vote to invoke cloture would require 60 votes. If that vote did not succeed, they could file another cloture motion needing 16 signatures. They would have to wait at least 2 further days. On the next vote, they would need 57 votes to invoke cloture. If you did not get that, well, you would have to get 16 signatures, file another cloture motion, wait another couple days, and then you would have to have 54 votes. Finally, the same procedure could be repeated, and move to a cloture vote of 51. Finally, a simple majority vote could close debate, to get to the merits of the issue.

By allowing this slow ratchet down, the minority would have the opportunity to debate, focus public attention on a bill, and communicate their case to the public. In the end, though, the majority could bring the measure to a final vote, as it generally should in a democracy.

Mr. President, in the 19th century as I mentioned before, filibusters were used to delay action on a measure until the automatic expiration of the session.

Senators would then leave to go back to their States, or Congressmen back to their districts, and tell people about the legislation the majority was trying to ram through. They could get the public aroused about it, to put pressure on Senators not to support that measure or legislation.

Keep in mind that in those days, there was no television, there was no radio, and scant few newspapers. Many people could not read or write and the

change in technology,
change filibuster?

best means of communication was when a Senator went out and spoke directly with his constituents. So it was necessary to have several months where a Senator could alert the public as to what the majority was trying to do, to protect the rights and interests of the minority.

That is not the case today. Every word we say here is instantaneously beamed out on C-SPAN, watched all over the United States, and picked up on news broadcasts. We have the print media sitting up in the gallery. So the public is well aware and well informed of what is happening here in the Senate on a daily basis. We do have a need to slow the process down, but we do not need the several months that was needed in the 19th century.

So as a Member of the new minority here in the Senate, I come to this issue as a clear matter of good public policy. I am pleased to say that it is a change that enjoys overwhelming support among the American people.

A recent poll conducted by Action Not Gridlock . . . found that 80 percent of Independents, 84 percent of Democrats, and 79 percent of Republicans believe that once all Senators have been able to express their views, the Senate should be permitted to vote for or against a bill. . . .

. . . [S]laying the filibuster dinosaur—and that is what I call it, a dinosaur, a relic of the ancient past—slaying the filibuster dinosaur has also been endorsed by papers around the country, including the *New York Times*, *USA Today*, and the *Washington Post*. . . .

* * *

But I will close my opening remarks, with this quote:

> It is one thing to provide protection against majoritarian absolutism; it is another thing again to enable a vexatious or unreasoning minority to paralyze the Senate and America's legislative process along with it.

I could not have said it better, and it was said by Senator ROBERT DOLE, February 10, 1971.

If Senator DOLE thought the filibuster was bad in 1971, certainly when we are down here, the filibuster has increased at least threefold on an annual basis since then. So it is time to get rid of this dinosaur. It is time to move ahead with the people's business in a productive manner.

Defending the Dinosaur
The Case for Not Fixing the Filibuster
Bill Frenzel

Defending the filibuster may not be quite as nasty as taking candy from a baby, but neither is it a good route to popular acclaim. Few kind words are ever spoken in defense of filibusters. Conventional wisdom and political correctness have pronounced them to be pernicious. The very word is pejorative, evoking ugly images of antidemocratic activities.

During the last biennium, filibusters became so unlovable that a group, including former senators, formed "Action, Not Gridlock!" to try to stamp them out. The public, which had tested both gridlock and action, seemed to prefer the former. The organization disappeared.

As that public reaction suggests, political correctness is a sometime thing and conventional wisdom oft goes astray. The American public may not be rushing to embrace the filibuster, but neither has it shown any inclination to root it out. The Senate's overwhelming vote . . . against changing the filibuster means that the practice won't go away soon, so it is worth examining. Despite its bad press, the story of the modern filibuster is not one-sided.

FILIBUSTERS, THE CONSTITUTION, AND THE FRAMERS

Filibuster haters claim they are contrary to the spirit of the Constitution because they require extraordinary majorities. The rationale is that the Framers, who created a majority system and rejected supermajorities, would be horrified by filibusters. Perhaps, but don't be too sure. Remember that no one has dug up a Framer lately to testify to the accuracy of this theory.

The Framers created our system based on their profound distrust of government. They loaded the system with checks and balances to make it work very slowly and with great difficulty. Their intention was to prevent swift enactment of laws and to avoid satisfying the popular whimsy of each willful majority. Maybe they would trade popular election for a filibuster rule.

Without any live Framers, we can only speculate about their feelings. However, it is hard to believe that, having designed an extremely balky system, they

Bill Frenzel is a former Republican U.S. Representative from the State of Minnesota (1971–1991). From Bill Frenzel, "Defending the Dinosaur: The Case for Not Fixing the Filibuster," *The Brookings Review* (Summer 1995): 47–49. Reprinted by permission.

would want to speed it up today. More likely, they would merely remind us that for more than 200 years major American policymaking has been based on "concurrent majorities" anyway.

PARLIAMENTARY COMPARISONS

Most of the parliaments of the world are copies, or variants, of Westminster [England]. With only one strong house and no separated executive branch, they can usually deliver laws swiftly. But when their actions affront public opinion, there is a political price to be paid, often very quickly. The government that offends the people soon becomes the opposition.

In our regional system, our majorities, assisted by a wide range of taxpayer-paid perks, do not usually pay any price. Our members of Congress are unbeatable (even in the earthquake of 1994, more than 90 percent of them who sought reelection were reelected). Our majorities are not eternal, but they are long-lived, unlike the Westminster forms.

It might make sense to consider trading the filibuster for congressional mortality (perhaps through term limits), but it is probably unwise to accept the blockbuster majority power of the Westminster system without accepting its balance of political turnover in return.

Actually, filibusters are not unique to the United States. Other parliaments are finding new opportunities for dilatory practices. The Japanese upper house recently presented its "ox-step," and an appointed majority in the Canadian Senate frustrated the intentions of the prime minister and his government on the ratification of the U.S.–Canada Free Trade Agreement. The strokes are different for different folks, but we are not alone. Delay is a time-honored political exercise that transcends political boundaries.

THE FILIBUSTER AND THE POPULAR WILL

The filibuster has been often indicted for denying the popular will, but over recent history, that point is hard to demonstrate. In the first place, it is not easy to get, and hold, 41 votes in the Senate under any circumstances. It is practically impossible to do so against a popular proposal. Filibusters simply do not succeed *unless* they have popular support or unless there is a lack of enthusiasm for the proposal being filibustered.

In 1993 Senator Bob Dole (R-KS) led a filibuster against the Clinton Emergency Spending Bill. It succeeded because the public liked the filibuster better than the spending. In the Bush years, Senator George Mitchell (D-ME) stopped a capital gains proposal by threat of filibuster. Senator Mitchell succeeded because the people saw no urgency in the proposal. In both cases, political reality prevailed.

If the public wants a vote, it tells its representatives. In 1994 Senate Republicans tried to filibuster the Crime Bill. Based on hot flashes from home, more than 60 senators perceived that the bill was popular, so the filibuster was broken quickly. The same thing happened to the Motor Voter Bill, the National Service Bill, and five out of six presidential appointments. If any proposal has substantial public support, a couple of cloture votes will kill the filibuster. The political reality is: frivolous filibusters do not succeed. The modern filibuster can gridlock ideas that are not popular, but it has not gridlocked the people.

THE BICAMERAL SYSTEM

In our unique system, the two houses of Congress have developed similar, but not identical, personalities and processes. The House of Representatives, with 440 orators, is harder to manage and has therefore created a set of rules to limit debate. In recent years, its majority has handled bills under rules that permitted few, if any, amendments and only an hour or two of debate.

The Senate, with only 100 orators, has stayed with free debate and an open amendment system. That is not a bad division of process. One house has been too closed, the other too open. The House operates with the relentlessness of Westminster majority, and the Senate has more time to examine, to delay, to amend, and, if necessary, to kill. All are vital functions of any legislature. . . .

There is still a relatively open pipeline for bills flowing from the House. . . . Following the Framers' wisdom, it is prudent to have a sieve in the Senate to compete with that open pipe in the House. At least some of the worst legislative lumps may be smoothed out in the finer mesh. . . .

KEY TO COMPROMISE

Many filibusters are not filibusters at all, but merely threats. Most are undertaken to notify the managers of the proposal that problems exist. They are a signal from a minority to a majority that negotiations are in order. Sometimes the majority tries a cloture vote or two before negotiating. Sometimes it negotiates. Sometimes it does not.

Most of these procedures end in a modified bill, not a dead bill. The Crime Bill noted above passed. The Dole filibuster of emergency spending did not prevent passage of many of its bits of pork in regular appropriations bills. . . .

The filibuster surely gives a minority a little more clout, but it does not prevent a majority from passing reasonably popular proposals. It gives a minority the opportunity to negotiate what it believes is an intolerable proposal into one it can live with. That compromise may serve the needs of the majority tolerably well too.

NO NEED FOR A HEAVY HAND

One political reality test for the filibuster is the congressional ingenuity in finding ways to avoid it when necessary. Trade and Reconciliation bills are considered under laws that obviate filibusters. When there is a good reason to finesse the filibuster, the Senate always seems to get the job done.

already rules /preventens for too long filibusters

Many other Senate rules, only dimly understood by common folks, reduce the legislative pace. I do not mean to bless multiple efforts to filibuster the same proposal. Once on the bill and once on the conference report is enough. Unlimited amendment after cloture is also too much opportunity for mischief.

Former Senate Majority Leader Mitchell has left constructive proposals to speed the work of the Senate without damaging the filibuster. They ought to be considered. The minority needs rights for protection. The majority needs the ability to move its program. Both needs can be well served by the modern 60-vote cloture rule. It should not be changed.

KEEP THE FILIBUSTER

The test of the filibuster ought to be whether it is fair, appropriate, and constructive. It may have been a killer in the old days, when it slew civil rights bills, but under the new 60-vote system, it is difficult to recall a filibustered proposition that stayed dead if it was popular.

Most antifilibuster noise comes from advocates of ideas that were going to fail anyway. It is not essential for every idea that comes bouncing up or down Pennsylvania Avenue to become law. The filibuster is a useful legislative tool, consistent with the goals of the Framers, that keeps whimsical, immature, and ultimately unpopular bills out of the statute books. . . .

Internet Resources

Visit our website at http://www.mhhe.com/diclerico for links and resources relating to Congress.

chapter 11

The Presidency

In 1973, the noted historian Arthur Schlesinger wrote a book titled The Imperial Presidency *in which he argued that the powers and prerogatives of the office had grown so extensive that our cherished principle of balanced government was being seriously threatened.*

The resignation of President Richard Nixon, along with the travails of those presidents who followed him, have caused many political observers to conclude that warnings of an imperial presidency are no longer applicable. In the first selection that follows, however, Michael Lind argues quite the contrary. He insists that, on the crucial questions of foreign policy, presidents can still do pretty much as they please; and, thanks to actions taken by Carter, Reagan, and Bush, future presidents will find their powers considerably greater in the domestic sphere as well. Meanwhile, according to Lind, the imperial character of the office continues to be reinforced by two other disturbing developments that have actually been in place for some time. One is the view of the presidency as the "tribune of the people"—a view first articulated by Andrew Jackson, later embellished by Woodrow Wilson, and now routinely embraced by our presidents; and the second is a White House bureaucracy that has been steadily expanding since the end of the Second World War. According to Lind, we urgently need to cut the presidency down to size, and he proposes a number of changes designed to do so.

The author of the second selection, the late R. Gordon Hoxie, rejected any notion of an imperial presidency, suggesting instead that "imperiled" would be a more apt description of the office. Where Lind saw power grabs by our recent presidents, Hoxie saw presidents conscientiously exercising their responsibilities under the Constitution; or making use of options and resources granted to the president by Congress; or bolstering the institutional presidency so that it can more effectively compete against both an overreaching Congress and hostile bureaucratic interests within the Executive branch. As Hoxie saw it, presidents, operating as they must in a separation-of-powers system, nearly always have to struggle for what they get. This constitutional fact of life, moreover, has become even more burdensome for presidents in light of the diminished importance of political parties in the American political process.

The Out-of-Control Presidency
Michael Lind

I.

The president is shrinking. The institution of the presidency, magnified by half a century of world war and cold war, is rapidly diminishing in terms of both power and respect. . . . Meanwhile, Congress has become bloated and arrogant, swelling the ranks of its own staff while encroaching on the constitutional prerogatives of the White House. Congressional supremacy would be a disaster, particularly in foreign affairs. We cannot have 535 commanders in chief.

This tale of the decline of the presidency and the rise of Congress is the emerging conventional wisdom in Washington. It is familiar, widely believed—and wrong. . . .

[The president elected in 2000] will be handed the Nixonian imperial presidency, with most of its powers intact and with a few new prerogatives added.

In foreign policy, the president [will] discover that, like every president since Truman, he can wage war at will, without consulting Congress. Though he might consent to a congressional vote as a matter of public relations (as Bush did before the Gulf war), he is more likely to invoke his supposed "inherent" authority as commander-in-chief. If necessary, his aides will concoct legalistic rationalizations, citing dangers to U.S. citizens (Grenada, Panama), authorization by the United Nations (Somalia, Haiti), NATO treaty obligations (Libya). Whether a liberal or a conservative, the president will dismiss the War Powers Resolution as unconstitutional.

Nor is de facto presidential supremacy in foreign affairs limited to warmaking, the president will discover. Bush and Clinton will have bequeathed an important technique for ramming economic treaties through Congress with little debate: fast-track legislation, which limits the time allowed for debate and forbids amendments. The Senate, which the Founders wanted to have weigh treaty commitments deliberately, was granted a mere 20 hours to consider the treaty that committed the United States to the jurisdiction of the World Trade Organization (WTO). Perhaps the president can insist that it be limited even further—to, say, half an hour or 15 minutes.

Michael Lind is an author and frequent contributor to national magazines and newspapers. He formerly served as assistant to the director of the Center for the Study of Foreign Affairs, the Foreign Service Institute, U.S. Department of State. From Michael Lind, "The Out-of-Control Presidency," *The New Republic* (August 14, 1995): 18–23. Reprinted by permission of *The New Republic*. © 1995, The New Republic, Inc.

In the domestic arena, the president will find even greater enhancements of his prerogatives. Thanks to Jimmy Carter, who reformed the Senior Executive Service to give the White House more control over career bureaucrats, and Ronald Reagan, who politicized the upper levels of the executive branch to an unprecedented degree, the president will find it easy to stack government with his spoilsmen or reward partisan bureaucrats. And he can thank George Bush for a technique that enhances presidential prerogative even further—signing laws while announcing he will not obey them.

Bush engaged in the greatest institutional power grab of any president since Nixon. In 1991 Bush, delivering a commencement address at Princeton, said: "[O]n many occasions during my presidency, I have stated that statutory provisions that violate the Constitution have no binding legal force." As Charles Tiefer points out in the *Semi-Sovereign Presidency*, Bush used "signing statements"—statements accompanying his signing of a bill, during which he announced he would not enforce this or that provision—to exercise an unconstitutional line-item veto (White House counsel C. Boyden Gray concocted the idea). In one such instance, when Congress amended the Clean Air Act in 1990 to permit lawsuits by citizen groups against companies that had violated the act, Bush used a signing statement to declare, on supposed "constitutional grounds," that the executive branch would continue to act as though such citizen lawsuits were prohibited—nullifying the intent of Congress. Ironically, the "take care" clause of the Constitution was intended to compel the president to enforce laws he disapproved of (often, Colonial governors had refused to enforce parts of legislation passed by Colonial legislatures). As Tiefer points out, Bush was asserting a sovereign power to ignore statutes that had been denied the English king in the Seven Bishops case of 1688.

Yet another new instrument of arbitrary presidential power is the "czar." The institution of presidential commissars with vague, sweeping charges that overlap with or supersede the powers of department heads is utterly alien to the American constitutional tradition. Most famous is the celebrated position of "drug czar," which William Bennett held under Bush, . . . which arrogates duties that were previously handled perfectly adequately by agencies of Justice and other departments. Similarly, Vice President Dan Quayle acted as a "czar" as the head of Bush's Council on Competitiveness, designed to circumvent Cabinet heads and Congress in regulatory matters.

The White House staff that has ballooned since World War II seems close to becoming an extra-constitutional "fourth branch" of government. For obvious reasons, presidents have preferred to govern through their staffers, most of whom need not be confirmed by the Senate and many of whom are young and pliant, rather than deal with the heads of Cabinet departments and independent agencies, experienced people who are less likely to be mere tools of the president's will. Nor is it any accident that the major presidential scandals of the past generation—Watergate and Iran-contra—have involved attempts by shadowy and scheming courtiers of law-breaking presidents to circumvent or suborn the older, established executive departments. Every time the high-handed actions of

White House courtiers drag a president into scandal, Congress, the press and the public denounce the courtiers—Nixon's plumbers, Ollie North—or the president and then, under a new president, sigh with relief: the system worked. That future presidents will almost certainly be tempted to use their White House staffers as Nixon and Reagan did is ignored.

The imperial presidency, then, is intact, merely waiting to be powered up and taken out of the hangar. . . .

II.

Madison and other Founders did not conceive of the president as a "representative" with a popular constituency at all. The president was to be a nonpartisan chief magistrate. The Founders designed the Electoral College with the expectation that presidents would frequently be chosen by the House, voting by states, from lists of candidates nominated by special state electors. The idea of the chief executive as chief representative is French, not American. As Louis Napoleon observed, his uncle Napoleon I "earnestly claimed the title of first Representative of the People, a title which seemed about to be given exclusively to members of the Legislative Body."

Andrew Jackson was the first president to claim, like the two Napoleons, to be a tribune of the masses: "The president is the direct representative of the American people." His attempt to act as a democratic monarch produced a backlash against such claims until the 20th century. Lincoln justified his sweeping war powers using legal arguments, not the claim that he was the sole legitimate representative of the nation; indeed, this former Whig opponent of "King Andrew" Jackson was hesitant about suggesting legislation to Congress, for fear of arousing suspicions of executive supremacy. "My political education," he declared, "strongly inclines me against a very free use of any of these means [recommending legislation and using the veto], by the Executive, to control the legislation of the country. As a rule, I think it better that Congress should originate, as well as perfect its measures, without external bias."

The modern conception of the president as an all-powerful tribune of the people comes from Woodrow Wilson. . . . Wilson argued for a different, Rousseauian conception of democracy, in which the president is the nation personified: "The nation as a whole has chosen him, and is conscious that it has no other political spokesman." Wilson was the first president since Washington to address Congress in person. He argued that the American constitutional tradition should never obstruct an activist president: "If he rightly interpret the national thought and boldly insist upon it, he is irresistible; and the country never feels the zest of action so much as when its president is of such insight and caliber. Its instinct is for unified action, and it craves a single leader."

The Great Leader is to lead not only the United States but the world: "Our president must always, henceforth, be one of the great powers of the world, whether he act wisely or not." Not the United States, but the presidency itself, is to be a great power! Wilson called for the president to ignore the prerogatives of the House and the Senate in foreign policy and to present the legislature with treaties as faits accomplis. "He need disclose no step of negotiation until it is complete." This strategy backfired when Wilson tried to impose the League of Nations treaty on the Senate, but later presidents have used it effectively. Bush's military buildup in the Gulf more or less forced Congress to ratify his planned war against Iraq, while the Clinton administration followed its Republican predecessors in ramming through GATT and NAFTA by means of fast-track legislation.

The plebiscitary theory of the presidency, the theory that the president, like Napoleon I, is First Representative of the Nation, is shared by all presidents to-day, Republican or Democratic. Though most presidents are elected with a plurality, not a majority—meaning most voters wanted someone else—every president today claims a "mandate" from the "majority" of "the people," considered as an undifferentiated mass with one General Will. The nomination of today's presidential candidates by primaries, rather than by congressional caucuses (the first system) or brokered party conventions (the system from the 1830s to the 1960s), has reinforced the illusion that the president represents the popular will, unmediated by either government structures or party organizations. The plebiscitary president is free to run against Washington, and even against political parties, in the manner of Ross Perot.

Running against Washington means running against Congress and "the bureaucracy," which are treated as villains in a morality play. The virtuous heroes are the president, and (for conservatives) state governments and an idealized free market. Presidentialists build up the legitimacy of the presidency by grossly exaggerating the faults of Congress and the parts of the executive branch that the White House does not directly control, such as the civil service and the independent agencies.

Consider the myth that the budgets and staffs of Congress and federal agencies have been escalating out of control. The money spent on the entire legislative branch is minuscule compared to that which goes to the executive. As James Glassman has pointed out, "You can eliminate all of Congress . . . just get rid of the whole darn thing, you'd save exactly as much as you would save if you cut the defense budget by less than 1 percent." What's more, during the 1980s, appropriations for Congress actually fell, in real terms. U.S. representatives are paid much less than their counterparts in many other democracies, such as Japan, and their salaries compare unfavorably with those of professionals and corporate executives, many of whom have less onerous responsibilities. Congressional staff, though it has grown along with government in general, actually declined in the 1980s, while the number of employees in the executive and judicial branches expanded. . . .

Nor has the other half of the hated "Washington establishment," the federal bureaucracy, been growing out of control. Most Americans would be surprised to learn that in terms of manpower—about 2 million—the federal government has hardly grown at all since World War II. State bureaucracies have grown faster, local bureaucracies even faster still. Federal funds, to be sure, have paid for much of the expansion of state and local bureaucracies, but conservatives have been concentrating their attacks not on federal funds, but on federal employees.

But, unlike Congress and the federal civil service, one federal institution does resemble the caricature of an ever-expanding, arrogant, corrupt bureaucracy. Since World War II, the White House staff and the Executive Office of the President have metastasized. Dwight Eisenhower made do with 29 key assistants as his White House staff in 1960; Bush needed 81 in 1992. The Executive Office of the President, created in 1939, has grown to include thousands of bureaucrats functioning in a presidential court, a miniature executive branch superimposed on the traditional departmental executive envisioned by the Constitution.

Meanwhile, the number of presidential appointees and senior executives has ballooned an astonishing 430 percent between 1960 and 1992, from 451 to 2,393. Most of this growth has not been in jobs for the hated career civil servants, but in positions for upper-middle-class political activists who donated money to, or worked in, presidential campaigns, or roomed with somebody in college, or whatever.

Presidents have consistently sought to expand the number of these political appointees. Mostly from elite law, lobbying, business, banking or academic backgrounds, these courtiers have ever more elaborate titles: principal deputy assistant secretary, assistant associate office director. As the titles grow, the average tenure shrinks (down to 18 months from three years during the Johnson years). The in-and-outers, once in, can't wait to get out and cash in their fancy titles for higher lobbyist fees or an endowed professorship of government. If conservatives are serious about cutting back government, why not abolish most of the post-'60s presidential branch? Where is the outcry against the expansion of the presidential bureaucracy? Why is a congressional barbershop a greater enormity than four White House staffers devoted to dealing with flowers? . . .

Ideologues of all persuasions have an interest in promoting presidential prerogative. Why battle over years to build a congressional majority, when you can persuade a president to enact your favored reform—gays in the military or gays out of the military—with a stroke of a pen? This accounts for the spitting fury with which op-ed pundits, think tankers and spin doctors pounce on any president who does not use "the power of his office" to enact their pet projects by ukase [i.e., direct order—*eds.*], preferably in the next few days or weeks.

Our press also helps the presidentialists of right and left by its obsessive focus on the person of the president at the expense of other executive branch officials, to say nothing of members of Congress and the judiciary. It makes for an easier story, of course, but laziness is no excuse for distorted coverage. Would the country crumble into anarchy if the major networks ignored the president for a week and followed the speaker, or the Senate majority leader, or the chief justice of the Supreme Court? Newspaper editors are just as bad. Several times, when I have written op-eds concerning government policy, I have been told by an editor, "You need to conclude by saying what the president should do."

Robert Nisbet has it right: "It is nearly instinctual in the political clerisy . . . to portray the president as one elected representative of the entire people . . .

with congressmen portrayed as like mayors and city councilmen, mere representatives of wards, sections and districts." When appeals to plebiscitary legitimacy are insufficient, presidentialists can turn to the "court party" of legal and constitutional scholars, who are always ready with a defense of this or that supposed presidential prerogative. Judge Robert Bork, for example, has argued "that the office of the president of the United States has been significantly weakened in recent years and that Congress is largely, but not entirely, responsible." If one were comparing Reagan, Bush or Clinton to FDR at the height of his power, this might seem plausible. In a 200-year perspective it is absurd. . . .

III.

Presidential democracy is not democracy. In theory a single politician could be answerable to a constituency of hundreds of millions—but only in theory. In practice, the more presidential the U.S. government becomes, the less responsive it is to most Americans. Stunts like Jimmy Carter's "Phone the President" notwithstanding, any president will necessarily be remote from most citizens and accessible chiefly to concentric tiers of CEOs, big-money contributors, big-labor leaders, network anchors and movie stars. Any reader who doubts this should try to get appointments with both his or her representative and the president.

Under the Constitution of 1787, representative democracy in the United States means congressional democracy. Restoring congressional democracy must begin with discrediting in the public mind the plebiscitary theory of democracy. Americans must conclude that democracy does not mean voting for this or that elective monarch every four years and then leaving government to the monarch's courtiers. Democracy means continuous negotiation among powerful and relatively autonomous legislators who represent diverse interests in society.

This battle on the level of theory should be accompanied by a campaign at the level of symbolism. Congress, as an institution, is slighted by our public iconography. "We celebrate Presidents' Day," Thomas Langston notes in his new book about the presidency, *With Reverence and Contempt*. "Why not celebrate Speakers' Day? How about a Speakers' Memorial in Washington, D.C., . . . [or] proposing that famous speakers of the House, or senators, also ennoble our currency[?]" The royalism symbolized by pharaonic presidential libraries should be combated by a law requiring that all presidential papers hereafter be deposited permanently in a single, modest presidential library in Washington.

Changes in government organization would need to accompany changes in perceptions of congressional legitimacy. An electoral reform such as proportional representation for the House might actually strengthen the separation of powers; it would encourage a multiparty system, but the same multiparty coalition would not likely hold the House, Senate and White House at once. In a multiparty system, the president might also be forced to appoint coalition Cabinets, as in parliamentary regimes. He would have less influence over a Cabinet secretary of another party than over some servile functionary from his own.

As for the executive branch, the slow seeping of authority from Cabinet secretaries to courtiers needs to be halted and reversed. Congress could drastically
cut the White House staff—if representatives aren't intimidated by the divinity
that hedges our elected king. The depths of the reverence surrounding the presidential court became clear on Thursday, June 25, 1995 when a House Appropriations subcommittee released a plan to abolish the Council of Economic Advisers. "Democrats," *The New York Times* reported, "said they were startled at
the lack of respect for a separate and equal branch of government displayed by
the gesture, and even the subcommittee chairman, [Republican] Representative
Jim Ross Lightfoot of Iowa, said he recognized that they could be accused of
'micromanagement' and lack of proper respect for the office of the president."
It is as though the British parliament had threatened to cancel the changing of
the guard at Buckingham Palace. The irony is particularly delicious since the
Council of Economic Advisers was imposed on the presidency as part of the
Employment Act of 1946 by conservatives in Congress hoping to check a free-
spending White House.

The evolution of the council is typical of the process by which every agu-
mentation of the executive branch in the interest of "efficiency" soon serves to
enhance the power and prestige of the presidency. An even better example is
the Office of Management and Budget, which was created after World War I as
an independent agency (the Bureau of the Budget), drifted under presidential
control during the administration of FDR and under Reagan became one of the
White House's chief instruments of partisan control of executive agencies. Like
a black hole, the presidency grows by absorbing ever more power and light.

Unlike a black hole, however, the presidency can be shrunk. Congress can not
only scale back the White House to bring it in line with the staffs of prime min-
isters, but it can also make the heads of executive departments more independent of the president. The Founders expected department heads to carry out
their duties more or less on their own (the Constitution gives the president the
modest power to request reports in writing from department heads). The idea
that department heads should be mere creatures of particular presidents is a
modern misconception. Their duty is to use their own judgment to implement
the laws passed by Congress, not to promote an imaginary "mandate" given
the president by 40 or 45 percent of the voters. The Constitution permits Congress to vest the appointment of "inferior officers" in the heads of departments.
Why not give it a try? It would strengthen their ties to their department head—
and make it more likely that they would hang up when a White House staffer
phoned to intervene, for the short-run political benefit of his boss, in the department's operations.

Reducing the president from a Latin American–style caudillo to something
like a 19th- or 18th-century U.S. chief magistrate can be done, then, without revising the Constitution, merely by passing a few laws. It is hard to see how else
the U.S. can avoid the completion of its slow evolution from a congressional republic into a full-fledged presidential state. The real trend in the world at the
end of the 20th century, it can be argued, is not so much from "dictatorship" to

"democracy" as from unelected dictatorship to elective dictatorship—from Gorbachev to Yeltsin. The executive rulers have to face election, but rule by decree still tends to supplant rule by laws passed by representative legislatures. It could happen here—as the Founding Fathers feared it would. Ben Franklin, among others, predicted, "The Executive will always be increasing here, as elsewhere, till it ends in a monarchy." The new Republican majority in Congress should ponder that warning. . . .

The Not-So-Imperial Presidency
R. Gordon Hoxie

In a recent essay entitled "The Out-of-Control Presidency," Michael Lind contends that recent portrayals "of the decline of the presidency and the rise of Congress" are "wrong." He concludes, "The imperial presidency . . . is intact, merely waiting to be powered up and taken out of the hangar."

This perception predated Lind's essay, or even Arthur Schlesinger's 1973 volume, *The Imperial Presidency.* At least one early and strong president, Andrew Jackson (1829–1837) was even termed "King Andrew I" by his political enemies. Many presidents since have enjoyed presidential pomp. However, the American constitutional system, together with the media and public opinion have generally held in check any tendencies toward presidential excesses. Each of the four 20th-century presidents who won the biggest victories, and thereafter engaged in excesses, were slapped down by a combination of Congress, the courts, the media, and public opinion: Franklin Roosevelt in 1937 with his scheme to pack the Supreme Court with additional judges; Lyndon Johnson after 1965 with his escalation of the Vietnam War; Richard Nixon in 1973 with his Watergate cover-up; and Ronald Reagan in 1985 with the Iran-Contra affair.

Michael Lind portrays the president as an all-powerful chief executive. To the contrary, among the leading industrial nations the American president is one of the weakest political leaders. The French president and the British prime minister have the fewest constraints on their power. In the *New York Times,* May 1, 1997, political scientist and pollster Stanley B. Greenberg, comparing British prime minister Tony Blair to the American president, asserted that the difference "could not be more stark. Mr. Clinton was unable to move his party in a new direction. Mr. Blair, however, was able to change his party before his campaign began." Despite our common language and political heritage, the British system of government, with its clear lines of accountability, could not be more different from the American system, with its system of checks and balances, which defies clear lines of accountability and imperialistic aspirations.

Far from being imperial and out of control, presidents are frustrated and unable to carry out the principal programs on their agenda. This frustration comes primarily from two sources: the framers of the Constitution, who distrusted centralization of powers and therefore created a separation-of-powers system; and the contemporary decline of the American political party system, which, in the past has been the engine of presidential strength.

R. Gordon Hoxie (1919–2002) was founder and former director of the Center for the Study of the Presidency, Washington, D.C. This essay was written especially for *Points of View* in 1997.

I.

With respect to the decline of political parties, it is not unreasonable to suggest that, except for Washington, whose presidency preceded parties, our strongest presidents—Jefferson, Jackson, Polk, Lincoln, Wilson, and the two Roosevelts— all led through effective *party support*. In the case of Wilson, that support was lost in his last two years in office when Republicans gained control of Congress.

Today party no longer strengthens the presidency. This can be seen in the decline of voting turnout, which, in part, is a reflection of the diminished importance that voters attach to parties; and secondly, the decline of elections of the same party in Congress and the presidency. These factors have weakened the presidency and caused it to seek the means of support that Lind criticizes.

The sharp decline in voting for candidates for the presidency means there is no strong popular mandate for the programs of the candidate who is elected president. By contrast, a high voter turnout coupled with a wide margin of victory sends a strong signal to Congress to support the winning presidential candidate's programs. This was clearly indicated in the record number of voters for the presidency and the landslide victories of Franklin Roosevelt in the 1932 and 1936 presidential elections and in the record number of voters for the presidency in 1964 and Lyndon Johnson's formidable margin of victory. In these instances, Congress responded with overwhelming support for the Roosevelt and Johnson programs, changing the social structure of the nation. By contrast, the low voter turnout in the 1996 election—a mere 49 percent and the lowest since 1924—is reflected in few presidential program initiatives pending or enacted by the current Congress.

In the election of 1900, only 3.4 percent of congressional districts recorded split results (i.e., voting for one party for Congress and another for presidential candidates) for presidential and congressional candidates. Partisanship binding the Congress and the presidency was alive and well. By 1948, however, 21.3 percent of congressional districts recorded split voting. In 1996, split results occurred in 25 percent of congressional districts. In brief, the "coattail" effect of presidential candidates influencing the election of congressional candidates of their own party has diminished considerably, thereby increasing the incidence of divided government in which one party controls the presidency and the other one or both houses of Congress.

II.

While party support may serve to mute the struggle between the legislative and executive branches, it cannot eliminate it altogether, for the separation-of-power system builds competition into the relationship. From the presidency of George Washington to the present there has been a struggle between the Congress and the president, a struggle that has manifested itself in both foreign and domestic arenas. In foreign policy, the framers of the Constitution made the president both the chief diplomat and the commander-in-chief. Although Jefferson was highly critical of the conduct of foreign policy by President Washington, and proposed roles for Congress in foreign policy, when he became president, he insisted that the conduct of foreign affairs is "executive altogether." The War Powers Resolution of 1973, an attempt to curb presidential war making, and forced upon a weakened President Nixon, has, as Lind acknowledges, been viewed as unconstitutional by Nixon and subsequent presidents. But Lind fails to note that the act gives Congress the authority to contravene the orders of the president as commander-in-chief by forcing the withdrawal of troops from combat at the end of 60 to 90 days. Nixon's successor, Gerald Ford, referring to the 535 members of Congress, where he had been a member, asserted, "Our forefathers knew you could not have 535 commanders-in-chief and secretaries of state."

As for the Gulf War, the congressional vote authorizing the use of force in this military engagement in spring 1991 was not "a matter of public relations," as Lind charges. Indeed, any assertion to that effect wholly misreads the seriousness of the entire war and the historic debate that transpired on the floors of Congress as it considered whether or not to authorize military action. The fact is President Bush sought, and by a narrow voting margin, got congressional support. Other presidents as early as John Adams and Jefferson engaged in undeclared wars *without* congressional authorization: In the case of Adams there was a naval war with France and in the case of Jefferson a punitive expedition led by the United States Navy and Marines against the Barbary pirates in the Tripolitan War. Adams and Jefferson acted in their capacity as commander-in-chief as many presidents have since. By contrast, Bush did earnestly seek congressional support, even while necessarily readying a force to repel Iraqi aggression.

There are, of course, times of grave emergency when the very security of the nation is so threatened that a president must in his position as commander-in-chief assume authority, even before turning to Congress for legislative authorization. Indeed, such was the action taken by President Lincoln in the Civil War and by President Roosevelt in aiding Great Britain in the desperate 1940–41 period before the United States, by congressional declaration, entered World War II.

In another area related to the separation-of-powers issue, Lind charges Bush with "the greatest institutional power grab of any president since Nixon." He portrays Bush's White House counsel, C. Boyden Gray, as having "concocted" the idea of using the "signing statements" that accompany the signing of a bill to declare invalid provisions of a law with which the president disagreed. President Bush's signing statement policy of ignoring what he views as unconstitutional provisions is nothing more than a reflection of his oath to see that the laws are faithfully executed, pursuant to which the Constitution always supersedes a statute—for all three branches of government. Prudentially, of course, the president has to have a high degree of certainty about constitutionality, higher than the other two branches, but this factor does not negate his oath to uphold the Constitution. And even in this context, the president can rarely act unilaterally in any event. Every president, while enforcing the law, has the right to inquire as to the wisdom of any legislation and seek revision or repeal of legislation deemed unwise. However, as for example, the War Powers Resolution, which presidents have deemed unconstitutional, remains on the statute books and presidents go through the motions of seeking to comply.

In the domestic arena, Lind charges that President Bush created "a new instrument of arbitrary presidential power" called the "czar," and calls this action "entirely alien to the American constitutional system." He also chastises Bush for making his vice-president, Dan Quayle, a czar in the Council on Competitiveness. It is perhaps a compliment that any vice-president—the occupant of the weakest political office in the American political system—could be considered a "czar" of anything.

Actually, the term "czar" was coined to emphasize the urgent need to combat the drug problem. Moreover, the drug czar is a statutory office set up by Congress itself to compensate for its own hopeless fragmentation of responsibility among 50 or more committees and subcommittees.

Lind charges that the Republicans' newly won control of Congress is contributing to a new imperial presidency. He asserts that "having captured Congress [in 1994] after a half century, the Republicans are hastening to give away the powers of the branch they control." He cites their advocacy of the line-item veto and term limits. These are not advocacies only of Republicans, however. True, the line-item veto was a favorite of Reagan, but it has also been advocated by Democrats, as have congressional term limits.

Mr. Lind laments the large executive branch staffs in the American system. These staffs, however, grow out of weakness rather than strength, as the president seeks to respond to the pressures of both the Congress and the courts as they relate to presidential proposals and programs. It is Congress that often creates executive agencies as it did the National Security Council, Council of Economic Advisers, and Bureau of the Budget, the latter restructured as the Office of Management and Budget. Nor should it be forgotten that the strength of the judicial system in our three-part government causes the executive departments as well as the president and vice-president to appoint large numbers of government counsels to see how far they can go in testing the limits of our checks-and-balances system. Finally, the enormous growth of entitlements since the beginning of the Social Security system in 1935, and the social sensitivity that is aroused whenever there are proposals for reductions, indicates that it is the public, not the presidents, which has demanded the growth in government. In this connection, let us not forget that President and Mrs. Clinton's efforts to revise the health care system were completely defeated when it became known that the public opposed the plan.

Lind laments, in particular, the growth of the White House staff, but much of that growth, it should be noted, was a reaction to the growth of the congressional staff. By creating its own budget office, the Congress challenged the White House Office of Management and Budget to further growth in order to address the questions posed to it by the Congressional Budget Office. Further, ever since the Senate Watergate Hearings in 1973–74, the Congress has continued to increase its oversight activity. In 1961, only 8.2 percent of congressional committee hearings and meetings related to oversight of the executive branch.

Between 1961 and 1983, however, oversight activity rose 207.3 percent. Currently, there is a record amount of congressional oversight in all areas of public policy. Congressional efforts to micromanage both foreign and domestic policy cause increase in all executive branch staffs as they constantly seek to respond to questions and defend executive positions.

III.

Lind concludes that "like a black hole, the presidency grows by absorbing ever more power and light." What this comparison overlooks, however, is that the policy-making machinery in our government has for a long time been characterized by "iron triangles" or, if you will, subgovernments consisting of three key actors that together comprise a powerful policy-making machine. One part of the triangle are the special interest lobbyists, the second are the members of Congress located in the congressional subcommittees, and the third are the federal bureaucrats working within the myriad administrative agencies in the executive branch of government. Whether it is in agriculture, defense policy, education, labor, veterans affairs, or whatever, as Hedrick Smith has written, "The object of the Iron Triangle is a closed power game," and such triangles are often arrayed against the president. Lind denies this, asserting that "Presidentialists build up the legitimacy of the presidency by grossly exaggerating the faults of Congress and the parts of the executive branch that the White House does not directly control, such as the civil service and the independent agencies." In point of fact, Lind makes no reference to the reality of these "iron triangles."

Lind perceives in any presidential reforms a scheme to grab power. He does so even with President Carter's proposal to enhance the civil service by the addition at the top of the Executive Service Corps. Lind finds in this a scheme to tie the civil service more closely to the presidency. Given the influence of the iron triangles, any president is to be applauded for his efforts to more effectively relate the civil service to the presidency.

In the final analysis, there is a need for a strong and vigorous presidency. This was so very well set forth by Alexander Hamilton on March 15, 1788, during the period when the ratification of the Constitution was being debated. In *Federalist 70* he wrote, "Energy in the executive is a leading character in the definition of good government. It is essential to the protection of the community against foreign attacks. It is not less essential to the steady administration of the laws. . . ." Hamilton concluded, "The ingredients, which constitute energy in the executive, are first unity, secondly duration, thirdly an adequate provision for this support, fourthly competent powers." In *Federalist 69,* in 1788, Hamilton made clear that there is nothing imperial in the presidency as created by the Constitution and in 70 he points to the fallacy that vigor in the executive "is inconsistent with the genius of republican government." To the contrary, Hamilton states "a feeble executive" is a source of "bad government." In *Federalist 71,* Hamilton goes further and warns of "the tendency of the legislative authority to absorb every other." He adds, "The representatives of the people, in a popular assembly seem sometimes to fancy that they are the people themselves." That is what Lind would invite with his call for congressional democracy.

True, strong presidents, including Jackson and the two Roosevelts, have viewed themselves as the tribune of the people—a formulation denounced by Lind as a "plebiscitary presidency" (i.e., representing the will of the whole people). But that is precisely what the two Roosevelts stated they were doing: Theodore representing the people against the powerful moneyed interests, the railroads, monopolies, the trusts; and Franklin in combating unemployment, lack of social security, and in defense of the nation. Quite unfairly, Lind describes presidents as elective monarchs, and presidential libraries as symbols of royalism. Quite the contrary, it is not a question of monarchy, but a matter of leadership. In a dangerous world, bold leadership is required, and that leadership, thrust upon the United States more than a half-century ago, must, of necessity, be exercised by the president. As for presidential libraries, they are not symbols of royalism, but rather valuable depositories of our historical heritage.

So far as the separation of powers is concerned, we would do well to recall Madison in *Federalist 47*. Therein he contended that the Constitution set forth not so much a *separation* as it did a *sharing* of powers, asserting that "the legislative, executive, judiciary departments are by no means totally separate and distinct from each other." He perceived not so much a struggle as, by necessity, a working together of Congress and the presidency. Former Senator Nancy Landon Kassebaum (R-Kansas) likened it to two people in a three-legged race: "If one balks the other trips." What is needed is more coming together of the Congress and the presidency, not a shutdown of government as the Congress caused in 1996 over the budget. Bipartisan consensus with the president peaked at nearly 70 percent during the two terms of Eisenhower, and unfortunately, steadily went down thereafter, reaching a low point in 1995–96. Far from Lind's contention that we have been moving into "a full-fledged presidential state," we have been moving into a congressional state. What we have seen from the Nixon presidency to the present is a constantly more constrained and impeded presidency. Contrary to Lind's view we are *not* witnessing an imperial presidency. Rather we are witnessing a presidency more and more in a state of siege, and a Congress more and more unwilling to work with the president. A balance must be restored. One can only hope that the budget agreement that, as of this writing (spring 1997), appears to have been reached between Congress and the Clinton administration, signals an effort to restore that balance.

Lind concludes with a quote from Benjamin Franklin about our executive becoming a monarch. There is another quote, however, that Lind might have recalled. When asked after the Constitutional Convention what kind of government had been created, Franklin replied, "a Republic if you can keep it." We have kept it, and will continue to do so.

Internet Resources

Visit our website at http://www.mhhe.com/diclerico for links and resources relating to the Presidency.

chapter 12

Bureaucracy

The Pendleton Act, a landmark piece of legislation passed in 1883, created a system whereby certain federal employees would be hired and rewarded on the basis of merit rather than political connections. Although the purpose behind this civil service system was a noble one—to protect us from unqualified political hacks placed in the permanent government by the old "spoils system"—Philip Howard, author of the first selection, maintains it has become overburdened with rules and regulations that protect the incompetent, demoralize the capable, frustrate accountability, and discourage change. Believing that these pathologies will paralyze the critical mission of the newly created Department of Homeland Security, Howard enthusiastically endorses the successful efforts of the Bush Administration to gain greater control over the career civil servants housed in that department.

In the accompanying selection, Gerald Pops, while readily acknowledging the faults of the merit system, also maintains that these faults are not principally rooted in a maze of deadening rules, as Howard claims, but rather lie elsewhere. Moreover, the "management flexibility" built into the new Department of Homeland Security, so earnestly sought by the president and strongly endorsed by Howard, may well, according to Pops, reintroduce the very problems the merit system was designed to correct. Pops also predicts that the ability of this new department to deliver security to the American people is destined to be compromised, not by anything having to do with the civil service system, but rather by its unwieldy size and decision-making structure.

Civil Service Rules: A Drag on Our National Security

Philip K. Howard

A Department of Homeland Security is essential, both political parties agree, to avoid a repeat of the failures of coordination and intelligence that allowed terrorists to slip into the country and clues to be dropped. But the new department was temporarily stalled over the application of civil service rules for its employees. The Democratic majority in the Senate said the proposal did not "protect the rights of federal workers." President Bush said he wouldn't sign a bill without "management flexibility."

On the surface, this looked like just a petty political dispute over obscure administrative details—bullying Republicans against bleeding-heart Democrats. In fact, the fight goes to the heart of why government is too often ineffective. Warren Rudman and Lee Hamilton, co-chairmen of the U.S. Commission on National Security/21st Century, could not be more blunt; they assert that "today's civil service has become a drag on our national security."

Jim King, head of the Office of Personnel Management under President Bill Clinton, once noted that the civil service system looks great in theory but trying to accomplish anything is "like swallowing a 64-pound pill." The layers in internal regulations would be unimaginable to most Americans. At the core of civil service is one assumption that paralyzes daily choices; public employees and their unions can demand a legal hearing whenever there is a disagreement.

For personnel decisions, the civil service rules operate as a kind of legal air bag, allowing a disgruntled worker to force the supervisor to prove the wisdom of an adverse decision, even a negative comment on an evaluation form. The process of dismissing a worker who is incompetent or worse can take years. (The minimum generally is 18 months.) Getting rid of someone who has bad judgment is basically impossible: How would a supervisor prove bad judgment? Last year, according to the Office of Personnel Management, out of an estimated 64,000 federal employees who were designated poor performers," only 434 were dismissed through the legal hearings. That's seven out of 1,000.

Assigning the best person to a new job is impossible unless you're prepared to prove in a hearing that more senior personnel aren't up to the task. After Sept. 11, 2001, the U.S. Customs Service immediately reassigned its best inspectors to

Philip K. Howard is a lawyer and author and chairman of Common Good, a legal reform coalition. From Philip K. Howard, "A Drag on Our National Security," as appeared in *The Washington Post*, (October 15, 2002): p. A19. Used by permission.

better secure our northern border. The union filed a legal proceeding claiming that the reassignments required a nationwide survey of interested civil servants, from which choices should be made on the basis of seniority.

No decision, no matter how important or how trivial, is immune from a legal proceeding alleging that it violates the rights of federal workers. In August, following a directive outlining standard protective measures under each of the homeland security threat levels, the union filed a proceeding to overturn it because it was issued "without first notifying and affording (the union) the opportunity to negotiate." Several years ago a decision that U.S. Border Patrol officers should carry a side-handled club was rejected as not being within their job description.

Imagine being a supervisor in this environment. Do you go through the day thinking about how to stop terrorists, or are you preoccupied with how to negotiate the legal minefield of civil service?

The bureaucratic mind-set may be tolerable in a department processing crop reports, but not where instinct and agility can make the difference between life and death. The public servants guarding our freedom must be alert to subtle clues and suspicions, and be willing to go the extra mile to figure out what's really going on. Some people will be good at it; others will not. Other than our military, which operates with similar flexibility, it's hard to imagine a greater or graver public responsibility.

Bureaucracy inevitably flows from the absence of personal accountability, because the only alternative is *rule* accountability. Having a rule for everything was an idea that fit neatly with early 20th century theories that government could be run like an assembly line, with each person doing his or her delineated task. But that's much like central planning, and it works just as badly, because it suppresses the human instincts needed for success.

What's amazing is that anything gets done. That's a tribute to the fact that most public employees are good and many superb. Instead of defending the system, Congress should take note of the one characteristic that all effective public institutions seem to have in common: an internal culture in which employees basically ignore the rules, focusing instead on getting the job done.

Public employees are the victims, not the villains of this system. Imagine being a dedicated public servant and having to work, day after day, with an incompetent colleague. The destructive effect on morale, as a personnel report to Clinton noted, is "far greater than the number of poor employees." Imagine what it's like to have your instincts of right and wrong suppressed by mind-numbing bureaucracy. Study after study has confirmed the debilitating effects of working in this kind of environment, including higher stress and cardiac disease and as an "institutional neurosis marked by apathy, withdrawal, lack of initiative and spontaneity."

Every administration in memory has tried to overhaul the civic service system. Al Gore's Reinventing Government initiative got beaten back almost at the gate. The Volcker Commission in 1989 concluded that civil service "is legally trammeled and intellectually confused" and "certainly not hiring the most meritorious candidates."

The Carter administration actually succeeded in increasing accountability, but only for the most senior civil servants. The most effective reformer in recent history is Sen. Zell Miller (D-Ga.), who in 1996, when he was governor of Georgia, abolished civil service for all new hires. Almost alone among active political leaders, Miller has been willing to say that this emperor has no clothes: "Despite its name, the merit system is not about merit. It offers no reward to good workers. It only provides cover for bad workers."

No one is advocating a return to the spoils system. Under the proposal supported by the administration, agencies would still be subject to general strictures against patronage hiring and arbitrary dismissals. Probably the one weakness of the proposal in this age of distrust is that it leaves to a later date how to accomplish non-litigation safeguards. But new safety nets are not hard to imagine—for example, a management-labor committee with power to guard against arbitrariness.

What's ultimately needed is a new deal for public servants. The civil service system is broken. The worst flaw—that it suppresses the human element needed to get the job done—is precisely what America cannot afford when ferreting out the terrorists trying to destroy the fabric of our free society.

A Strong Civil Service System
Is the Cure, Not the Problem
Gerald Pops

President Bush has gotten what he asked for—a Homeland Security Department with the executive branch authority to strip federal employees of their civil service protection. Comprised of twenty-six former agencies and approximately 170,000 employees, this mammoth new bureaucracy will constitute almost 10 percent of the total federal workforce. With this new department comes executive flexibility to hire, promote, transfer, discipline, fire, and otherwise treat employees without reference to the civil service rules that apply to the other 90 percent of federal workers hired under the civil service system. However, along with this "management flexibility" also comes a dangerous undermining of the system that has undergirded public service, at all levels of government, for more than a century. Furthermore, management flexibility is not likely to lead to greater homeland security.

In gaining his prize, the president argued strenuously that homeland security is too important a function to hamstring with restrictions on hiring, assignment, transfer, discipline, and promotion that characterize the system. Philip K. Howard's argument contains most of a familiar litany that goes like this: The civil service system is broken. American business has the answers to questions such as how to produce at higher levels and how to increase innovation and excellence. Civil servants are overprotected to the point that the "deadwood" are protected as well as the worthy. Civil service promotes more concern with compliance with the rules than it does performance. Efforts to discipline or fire poorly performing employees lead to frustration and failure because of the excessive legal protections associated with tenure. Civil service employees are over-concerned with job security and under-concerned about production. The fact that they are protected by unions makes matters much worse. It is interesting to note, moreover, that neither economic recession nor the shameful and destructive practices of Enron, WorldCom, Arthur Andersen, and their ilk, both signs that all is not well in American business practice, have cooled enthusiasm for the private sector model.

Gerald Pops is professor of public administration at West Virginia University. This article was written especially for *Points of View* in 2003.

THE MERIT OF THE MERIT SYSTEM

To be an informed critic, it is necessary to have a complete sense of the history of the civil service, why it came into existence, and what type of system or systems might possibly replace it, were it to vanish. Actually, its use has been decreasing and so we have some clear evidence of what is taking its place as well as the dangers of the substitution. As originally conceived in the Civil Service Act of 1883, the civil service was designed to (1) promote the competitive selection of employees; (2) allow employes who prove competent in their jobs to keep them (this was the intent of "tenure rights") in the face of removal for political or personal reasons by managers (most frequently managers who are politically appointed by new administrations); and (3) promote equality by assuring that no person would be turned away from applying for and being selected for a federal job except on the basis that he or she lacked the ability to do it. Non-political selection, continuity of a competent civil service that is able to survive elections, and equal access to public jobs on the basis of merit are the original and essential values of the civil service system. As augmented over the years, civil service jobs were "classified" (specifically described, to include duties, qualifications, and pay associated with each position), and the concept spread to virtually all state and local government employment in America. The system was to function so as to enshrine the basic principle of merit, which can be most simply defined as "the individual's ability to perform the job." Thus, the civil service system came to be known as "the merit system."

CRACKS IN THE MERIT SYSTEM IDEAL

It would be foolish to argue that the merit system always works in a way that promotes the merit principle. Pressures developed over the years that interfered with the merit ideal, a short list of which follows:

1. Public policies favoring the hiring and promotion of veterans (called "veteran preference laws") redirected hiring, promotion, and retention in the event of reduction of positions, on a basis not clearly related to merit.
2. Discrimination on the basis of race, ethnicity, religion, physical appearance, sex and sexual orientation, age, and disability often interfered with hiring, reward, and separation based on merit.
3. Centralization of testing and hiring procedures in the central "personnel agencies" of governments often worked against the interests of the hiring agencies who had a better idea of what kinds of skills and talents they needed.
4. The growing legalities surrounding the tenure/hearing process, although often increasing fairness to individual employees involved, also created obstacles in the firing of incompetent employees.
5. Most importantly, the position classification system became outdated and dysfunctional, causing rigidity and the underutilization of human talents.

Union-related problems, to the extent that they exist, are not a part of this list. Much of the protectionism (job security, keeping incompetent employees, resisting management decisions that may improve operations but reduce the number of employees) that the Bush administration objects to is largely the result of the unionization of the public service. But public unionization is a phenomenon that developed independently and came well after establishment of the civil service (about 80 years!). Unionization, as even its opponents acknowledge, results from bad management—worker resentment builds to the point that public employees do not feel their voice will be carried or understood by management. It is not the result of unhappiness over merit practices. Nor is unionization very far advanced in government—only 30 percent of government employees are unionized! A frequent tactic of civil service opponents is to confuse civil service with unionism, so as to use popular anti-union feeling to reduce support for the civil service. Whatever the arguments for and against unionization, and this is a complex debate that needs to be aired, this subject should be separated from the current discussion over the value of the civil service system.

In light of the problems that have developed over time, it is accurate to argue, as did President Carter when proposing broad reforms to civil service law in 1978, that the merit system does not always serve the merit principle. Unfortunately, Carter's attempts to reform the system did not go far enough to solve the problems. Position classification still dominates with the result that the development and flexible use of people is secondary. Cumbersome legal processes still control in the area of discipline and firing the incompetent. On the other hand, much decentralization has occurred, innovations have appeared, and the merit system is less impaired by racial and sexual discrimination than it once was.

CIVIL SERVICE REFORM?

With this mixed record of success, is it wise to give up on civil service reform and to sacrifice the effort to sustain and improve a professional and public-spirited workforce more dedicated to service than to making money? Or do we continue to have faith in the original wisdom of the merit concept, recognize that political and economic realities have changed, and try to make reasonable reforms to correct the problems that are clear to most student-scholars of the system? The more reasonable view is that the greatest "inefficiencies" of government employment are rooted in causes other than excessive legalism or failure to adopt the market-driven ideals of the business sector. These inefficiencies are, principally, (1) the conflict and competition among branches of government that are written into the American Constitution and (2) the nature of hierarchical decision making found in bureaucratic structure. As these sources of inefficiency in government service are examined, we will find that the Homeland Security "super-department" approach and greater executive branch control make things worse, not better.

The constitutional system that we have erected in this country intentionally creates conflict among branches of government so as to promote separation of powers with the aim of preventing tyranny. Many of the rules placed upon the operations of public agencies are put there by the Congress to prevent abuse of power by the executive branch. Typically, these constraints are lessened during periods of national emergency and reimposed during more normal times. The purposes of these constraints are many, but they include, importantly, ensuring administrative functioning in line with legislative budget and program authorization, prevention of waste and fraud by executive branch managers, and protection of civil servants from arbitrary and unfair actions of executive branch managers undertaken for political reasons. Thus, many of the rules imbedded in civil service are not "meaningless," as the critics allege.

CIVIL SERVICE AND HOMELAND SECURITY

What stands in the path of abuse of power by the executive branch if the civil service is destroyed? "No one is advocating a return to the spoils system," says Howard, but the growth of an executive-dominated, entrepreneurial system of human resources creates the conditions for just such a result. Without civil service guarantees that protect against political patronage, what obstacle is there to awarding government contracts on the basis of political favoritism or ideological purity? How will management-labor committees emerge during an administration that is admittedly hostile to labor? What will prevent the creation of a professional contract monitoring process in which those government monitors guarding the public interest, usually underpaid relative to their private sector counterparts, must excel in their jobs and themselves enter the kind of legal wars that are supposedly making the civil service system so impossible?

Will "Christian values" be allowed to dictate hiring decisions at the expense of a knowledge of Muslim and Arabic needs and dynamics (imagine the value of enlisting the help of the American-Arab community, stimulating their patriotism and tapping into their knowledge of Arab languages)? Will undue reliance be placed on European and Israeli intelligence to the exclusion of Iranian and Saudi and Turkish intelligence? Will certain response units in the nonprofit sector and state and local governments be underutilized because they bear Democratic Party associations or links to group causes like pro-choice or civil liberties? Are we to have homeland security provided by government contractors with Texas or with Massachusetts connections? Will contract recipients more likely be centered in important electoral states that the party in power hopes to influence? While executive leaders may not intend to weaken response networks, political agendas inevitably creep in and displace the original goals. "Government by contracting-out" is already attracting from its critics the label of "the new patronage" because of the tendency of contracts to flow in the direction of political friends and financial supporters.

Finally, the creation of a giant new department, with new levels of command authority and reporting, hugely increases the type of "big bureaucracy" that both parties have recognized as paralyzing to the type of inter-agency cooperation, flexibility, and quick decision making essential to linking information that the administration says it must have. House Democratic Whip Nancy Pelosi, the ranking Democrat on the Select Committee on Homeland Security, issued the following statement as debate ended on H.R. 5005, the Homeland Security Act:

> I had hoped that we could present to the American people a Department of Homeland Security that was lean and of the future, not a monstrous bureaucracy of the 1950s that would have been obsolete even then. I had hoped that this new lean department would, instead of size, have capitalized on the technological revolution in order to increase communication and coordination. I had hoped that the Secretary of Homeland Security could coordinate, rather than have to manage and administer staff.

Unfortunately, of course, Congress took a different course of action. Moreover, the General Accounting Office, which works for the Congress, declared it will take five to ten years for DHS to be up and running, after a startup cost of $4.5 billion dollars.

Briefly put, the major problem that can be foreseen in the managing of homeland security is bureaucracy and hierarchical decision making, *not* civil service. The meaningful interaction among different units of the federal government, state and local government units, and non-governmental organizations (NGOs) such as the American Red Cross and veterans' organizations will be stifled in favor of rigid bureaucratic reporting procedures that cause delays and exclude many of these groups from participating in decision making. The twenty-six old agencies that make up the new department will continue to fight for control and a piece of the decision-making action that will be concentrated at the higher echelons of the DHS hierarchy. Congressional funds will go to the most effective lobbyists, and these will be centered within the DHS and exclude the multitude of state and local police departments, local hospital and emergency response centers, state health units and volunteer units so vital to "first response" who will remain uncoordinated.

The new department, despite its size and resources, still lacks the two agencies critical to real security, the Central Intelligence Agency (CIA) and the Federal Bureau of Investigation (FBI). These two agencies are the key organizations for gathering foreign intelligence and maintaining surveillance of terrorist organizations within the country, respectively. How does the reorganization help to bring these vital functions within a "more rational decision process"?

Although it is true that both political parties cooperated in passing the act, the only debate that occurred centered on civil service protection and unionism, and virtually nothing was said about whether the creation of a huge new bureaucracy, lacking essential components (i.e., CIA, FBI), was a good approach to solving problems of homeland security. Those who make a profession of thinking about these matters favored a "networking" approach to homeland security information collection and decision making, not bureaucracy. Coordination of the activities of all state and local governments and NGOs and decision making through consultation were preferred to hierarchical review. Apparently, neither party was prone to listen to or consider these arguments.

The Department of Homeland Security is not an efficient way to handle the national need for homeland security. It is this mindless approach to organizing through bureaucratization, and not the civil service with its proud tradition of political neutrality and competence, that is at fault. The stakes are high, and the nation is moving in the wrong direction.

Internet Resources

Visit our website at http://www.mhhe.com/diclerico for links and resources relating to Bureaucracy.

chapter 13

Courts

The Supreme Court and Judicial Review

*W*hile *few would question the Supreme Court's authority to interpret the Constitution, there has long been disagreement over how the nine justices should approach this awesome responsibility. This debate grew in intensity during the Reagan era as the president and his attorney general inveighed against the Supreme Court, charging that justices had all too often substituted their own values and principles for those contained in the Constitution.*

In the first selection, Edwin Meese, U.S. attorney general during part of the Reagan administration, calls upon judges to interpret the Constitution in accordance with the intent of those who wrote and ratified it. Insisting that the Founding Fathers expected as much from the members of the Supreme Court, Meese goes on to suggest how the justices should approach this task. He remains convinced that the application of original intent—undistorted by the personal values of well-meaning judges—will best preserve the principles of democratic government.

The second selection offers a markedly different perspective from someone who has had the responsibility of interpreting our Constitution. Irving Kaufman, chief judge of the United States Court of Appeals for the Second Circuit, maintains that ascertaining the original intent of the Founding Fathers is decidedly more difficult than Edwin Meese would lead us to believe. Nor, for that matter, is the strict application of original intent necessarily desirable in every instance. This is not to say that judges are at liberty to read whatever they choose into the wording of our Constitution, and Kaufman points to several factors that serve to restrain judges from doing so.

A Jurisprudence of Original Intention

Edwin Meese III

... Today I would like to discuss further the meaning of constitutional fidelity. In particular, I would like to describe in more detail this administration's approach.

Before doing so, I would like to make a few commonplace observations about the original document itself. ...

The period surrounding the creation of the Constitution is not a dark and mythical realm. The young America of the 1780s and '90s was a vibrant place, alive with pamphlets, newspapers, and books chronicling and commenting upon the great issues of the day. We know how the Founding Fathers lived, and much of what they read, thought, and believed. The disputes and compromises of the Constitutional Convention were carefully recorded. The minutes of the convention are a matter of public record. Several of the most important participants—including James Madison, the "father" of the Constitution—wrote comprehensive accounts of the convention. Others, Federalists and Anti-Federalists alike, committed their arguments for and against ratification, as well as their understandings of the Constitution, to paper, so that their ideas and conclusions could be widely circulated, read, and understood.

In short, the Constitution is not buried in the mists of time. We know a tremendous amount of the history of its genesis. ...

With these thoughts in mind, I would like to discuss the administration's approach to constitutional interpretation. ...

Our approach . . . begins with the document itself. The plain fact is, it exists. It is something that has been written down. Walter Berns of the American Enterprise Institute has noted that the central object of American constitutionalism was "the effort" of the Founders "to express fundamental governmental arrangements in a legal document—to 'get it in writing.'"

Indeed, judicial review has been grounded in the fact that the Constitution is a written, as opposed to an unwritten, document. In *Marbury v. Madison* John Marshall rested his rationale for judicial review on the fact that we have a written constitution with meaning that is binding upon judges. "[I]t is apparent," he wrote, "that the framers of the Constitution contemplated that instrument as a rule for the government of *courts,* as well as of the legislature. Why otherwise does it direct the judges to take an oath to support it?"

Edwin Meese III served as U.S. Attorney General under President Ronald Reagan. Excerpted from a speech by Attorney General Meese before the Washington, D.C., chapter of the Federal Society, Lawyers Division, November 15, 1985, pp. 2–14.

The presumption of a written document is that it conveys meaning. As Thomas Grey of the Stanford Law School has said, it makes "relatively definite and explicit what otherwise would be relatively indefinite and tacit."

We know that those who framed the Constitution chose their words carefully. They debated at great length the most minute points. The language they chose meant something. They proposed, they substituted, they edited, and they carefully revised. Their words were studied with equal care by state ratifying conventions.

This is not to suggest that there was unanimity among the framers and ratifiers on all points. The Constitution and the Bill of Rights, and some of the subsequent amendments, emerged after protracted debate. Nobody got everything they wanted. What's more, the framers were not clairvoyants—they could not foresee every issue that would be submitted for judicial review. Nor could they predict how all foreseeable disputes would be resolved under the Constitution. But the point is, the meaning of the Constitution can be known.

What does this written Constitution mean? In places it is exactingly specific. Where it says that Presidents of the United States must be at least 35 years of age it means exactly that. (I have not heard of any claim that 35 means 30 or 25 or 20.) Where it specifies how the House and Senate are to be organized, it means what it says.

The Constitution also expresses particular principles. One is the right to be free of an unreasonable search or seizure. Another concerns religious liberty. Another is the right to equal protection of the laws.

Those who framed these principles meant something by them. And the meanings can be found. The Constitution itself is also an expression of certain general principles. These principles reflect the deepest purpose of the Constitution—that of establishing a political system through which Americans can best govern themselves consistent with the goal of securing liberty.

The text and structure of the Constitution is instructive. It contains very little in the way of specific political solutions. It speaks volumes on how problems should be approached, and by *whom*. For example, the first three articles set out clearly the scope and limits of three distinct branches of national government. The powers of each being carefully and specifically enumerated. In this scheme it is no accident to find the legislative branch described first, as the framers had fought and sacrificed to secure the right of democratic self-governance. Naturally, this faith in republicanism was not unbounded, as the next two articles make clear.

Yet the Constitution remains a document of powers and principles. And its undergirding premise remains that democratic self government is subject only to the limits of certain constitutional principles. This respect for the political process was made explicit early on. When John Marshall upheld the act of Congress chartering a national bank in *McCulloch v. Maryland* he wrote: "The Constitution [was] intended to endure for ages to come, and, consequently, to be adapted to the various crises of human affairs." But to use McCulloch, as some have tried, as support for the idea that the Constitution is a protean, changeable thing is to stand history on its head. Marshall was keeping faith with the original intention that Congress be free to elaborate and apply constitutional powers and principles. He was not saying that the Court must invent some new constitutional value in order to keep pace with the times. In Walter Berns's words: "Marshall's meaning is not that the Constitution may be adapted to the 'various crises of human affairs,' but that the legislative powers granted by the Constitution are adaptable to meet these crises."

The approach this administration advocates is rooted in the text of the Constitution as illuminated by those who drafted, proposed, and ratified it. In his famous Commentary on the Constitution of the United States Justice Joseph Story explained that:

> The first and fundamental rule in the interpretation of all instruments is, to construe them according to the sense of the terms, and the intention of the parties.

Our approach understands the significance of a written document and seeks to discern the particular and general principles it expresses. It recognizes that there may be debate at times over the application of these principles. But it does not mean these principles cannot be identified.

Constitutional adjudication is obviously not a mechanical process. It requires an appeal to reason and discretion. The text and intention of the Constitution must be understood to constitute the banks within which constitutional interpretation must flow. As James Madison said, if "the sense in which the Constitution was accepted and ratified by the nation . . . be not the guide in expounding it, there can be no security for a consistent and stable, more than for a faithful exercise of its powers."

Thomas Jefferson, so often cited incorrectly as a framer of the Constitution, in fact shared Madison's view: "Our peculiar security is in the possession of a written Constitution. Let us not make it a blank paper by construction."

Jefferson was even more explicit in his personal correspondence:

> On every question of construction [we should] carry ourselves back to the time, when the constitution was adopted; recollect the spirit manifested in the debates; and instead of trying [to find] what meaning may be squeezed out of the text, or invented against it, conform to the probable one, in which it was passed.

In the main a jurisprudence that seeks to be faithful to our Constitution—a jurisprudence of original intention, as I have called it—is not difficult to describe. Where the language of the Constitution is specific, it must be obeyed. Where there is a demonstrable consensus among the framers and ratifiers as to a principle stated or implied by the Constitution, it should be followed. Where there is ambiguity as to the precise meaning or reach of a constitutional provision, it should be interpreted and applied in a manner so as to at least not contradict the text of the Constitution itself.

Sadly, while almost everyone participating in the current constitutional debate would give assent to these propositions, the techniques and conclusions of some of the debaters do violence to them. What is the source of this violence? In large part I believe that it is the misuse of history stemming from the neglect of the idea of a written constitution.

There is a frank proclamation by some judges and commentators that what matters most about the Constitution is not its words but its so-called "spirit." These individuals focus less on the language of specific provisions than on what they describe as the "vision" or "concepts of human dignity" they find embodied in the Constitution. This approach to jurisprudence has led to some remarkable and tragic conclusions.

In the 1850s, the Supreme Court under Chief Justice Roger B. Taney read blacks out of the Constitution in order to invalidate Congress's attempt to limit the spread of slavery. The *Dred Scott* decision, famously described as a judicial "self-inflicted wound," helped bring on civil war.

There is a lesson in this history. There is danger in seeing the Constitution as an empty vessel into which each generation may pour its passion and prejudice.

Our own time has its own fashions and passions. In recent decades many have come to view the Constitution—more accurately, part of the Constitution, provisions of the Bill of Rights and the Fourteenth Amendment—as a charter for judicial activism on behalf of various constituencies. Those who hold this view often have lacked demonstrable textual or historical support for their conclusions. Instead they have "grounded" their rulings in appeals to social theories, to moral philosophies or personal notions of human dignity, or to "penumbras," somehow emanating ghostlike from various provisions—identified and not identified—in the Bill of Rights. The problem with this approach, as John Hart Ely, Dean of the Stanford Law School, has observed with respect to one such decision, is not that it is bad constitutional law, but that it is not constitutional law in any meaningful sense, at all.

Despite this fact, the perceived popularity of some results in particular cases has encouraged some observers to believe that any critique of the methodology of those decisions is an attack on the results. This perception is sufficiently widespread that it deserves an answer. My answer is to look at history.

When the Supreme Court, in *Brown v. Board of Education,* sounded the death knell for official segregation in the country, it earned all the plaudits it received. But the Supreme Court in that case was not giving new life to old words, or adapting a "living," "flexible" Constitution to new reality. It was restoring the original principle of the Constitution to constitutional law. The *Brown* Court was correcting the damage done 50 years earlier, when in *Plessy v. Ferguson* an earlier Supreme Court had disregarded the clear intent of the framers of the Civil War amendments to eliminate the legal degradation of blacks, and had contrived a theory of the Constitution to support the charade of "separate but equal" discrimination.

Similarly, the decisions of the New Deal and beyond that freed Congress to regulate commerce and enact a plethora of social legislation were not judicial adaptations of the Constitution to new realities. They were in fact removals of encrustations of earlier courts that had strayed from the original intent of the framers regarding the power of the legislature to make policy.

It is amazing how so much of what passes for social and political progress is really the undoing of old judicial mistakes.

Mistakes occur when the principles of specific constitutional provisions—such as those contained in the Bill of Rights—are taken by some as invitations to read into the Constitution values that contradict the clear language of other provisions.

Acceptances to this illusory invitation have proliferated in recent decades. One Supreme Court justice identified the proper judicial standard as asking "what's best for this country." Another said it is important to "keep the Court out in front" of the general society. Various academic commentators have poured rhetorical grease on this judicial fire, suggesting that constitutional interpretation appropriately be guided by such standards as whether a public policy "personifies justice" or "comports with the notion of moral evolution" or confers "an identity" upon our society or was consistent with "natural ethical law" or was consistent with some "right of equal citizenship."

Unfortunately, as I've noted, navigation by such lodestars has in the past given us questionable economics, governmental disorder, and racism—all in the guise of constitutional law. Recently one of the distinguished judges of one of our federal appeals courts got it about right when he wrote: "The truth is that the judge who looks outside the Constitution always looks inside himself and nowhere else." Or, as we recently put it before the Supreme Court in an important brief: "The further afield interpretation travels from its point of departure in the text, the greater the danger that constitutional adjudication will be like a picnic to which the framers bring the words and the judges the meaning."

In the *Osborne v. Bank of United States* decision 21 years after *Marbury*, Chief Justice Marshall further elaborated his view of the relationship between the judge and the law, be it statutory or constitutional:

> Judicial power, as contradistinguished from the power of the laws, has no existence. Courts are the mere instruments of the law, and can will nothing. When they are said to exercise a discretion, it is a mere legal discretion, a discretion to be exercised in discerning the course prescribed by law; and, when that is discerned, it is the duty of the Court to follow it.

Any true approach to constitutional interpretation must respect the document in all its parts and be faithful to the Constitution in its entirety.

What must be remembered in the current debate is that interpretation does not imply results. The framers were not trying to anticipate every answer. They were trying to create a tripartite national government, within a federal system, that would have the flexibility to adapt to face new exigencies—as it did, for example, in chartering a national bank. Their great interest was in the distribution of power and responsibility in order to secure the great goal of liberty for all.

A jurisprudence that seeks fidelity to the Constitution—a jurisprudence of original intention—is not a jurisprudence of political results. It is very much concerned with process, and it is a jurisprudence that in our day seeks to depoliticize the law. The great genius of the constitutional blueprint is found in its creation and respect for spheres of authority and the limits it places on governmental power. In this scheme the framers did not see the courts as the exclusive custodians of the Constitution. Indeed, because the document posits so few conclusions it leaves to the more political branches the matter of adapting and vivifying its principles in each generation. It also leaves to the people of the states, in the Tenth Amendment, those responsibilities and rights not committed to federal care. The power to declare acts of Congress and laws of the states null and void is truly awesome. This power must be used when the Constitution clearly speaks. It should not be used when the Constitution does not.

In *Marbury v. Madison,* at the same time he vindicated the concept of judicial review, Marshall wrote that the "principles" of the Constitution "are deemed fundamental and permanent," and except for formal amendment, "unchangeable." If we want a change in our Constitution or in our laws we must seek it through the formal mechanisms presented in that organizing document of our government.

In summary, I would emphasize that what is at issue here is not an agenda of issues or a menu of results. At issue is a way of government. A jurisprudence based on first principles is neither conservative nor liberal, neither right nor left. It is a jurisprudence that cares about committing and limiting to each organ of government the proper ambit of its responsibilities. It is a jurisprudence faithful to our Constitution.

By the same token, an activist jurisprudence, one which anchors the Constitution only in the consciences of jurists, is a chameleon jurisprudence, changing color and form in each era. The same activism hailed today may threaten the capacity for decision through democratic consensus tomorrow, as it has in many yesterdays. Ultimately, as the early democrats wrote into the Massachusetts state constitution, the best defense of our liberties is a government of laws and not men.

On this point it is helpful to recall the words of the late Justice Frankfurter. As he wrote:

> [T]here is not under our Constitution a judicial remedy for every political mischief, for every undesirable exercise of legislative power. The framers carefully and with deliberate forethought refused so to enthrone the judiciary. In this situation, as in others of like nature, appeal for relief does not belong here. Appeal must be to an informed, civically militant electorate. . . .

What Did the Founding Fathers Intend?

Irving R. Kaufman

. . . In the ongoing debate over original intent, almost all federal judges hold to the notion that judicial decisions should be based on the text of the Constitution or the structure it creates. Yet, in requiring judges to be guided solely by the expressed views of the framers, current advocates of original intent seem to call for a narrower concept. Jurists who disregard this interpretation, the argument runs, act lawlessly because they are imposing their own moral standards and political preferences on the community.

As a federal judge, I have found it often difficult to ascertain the "intent of the framers," and even more problematic to try to dispose of a constitutional question by giving great weight to the intent argument. Indeed, even if it were possible to decide hard cases on the basis of a strict interpretation of original intent, or originalism, that methodology would conflict with a judge's duty to apply the Constitution's underlying principles to changing circumstances. Furthermore, by attempting to erode the base for judicial affirmation of the freedoms guaranteed by the Bill of Rights and the 14th Amendment (no state shall "deprive any person of life, liberty, or property without due process of law; nor deny to any person . . . the equal protection of the laws"), the intent theory threatens some of the greatest achievements of the Federal judiciary.

Ultimately, the debate centers on the nature of judicial review, or the power of courts to act as the ultimate arbiters of constitutional meaning. This responsibility has been acknowledged ever since the celebrated 1803 case of *Marbury v. Madison,* in which Chief Justice John Marshall struck down a congressional grant of jurisdiction to the Supreme Court not authorized by Article III of the Constitution. But here again, originalists would accept judicial review only if it adhered to the allegedly neutral principles embalmed in historical intent.

In the course of 36 years on the federal bench, I have had to make many difficult constitutional interpretations. I have had to determine whether a teacher could wear a black armband as a protest against the Vietnam War; whether newspapers have a nonactionable right to report accusatory statements; and whether a school system might be guilty of de facto segregation. Unfortunately, the framers' intentions are not made sufficiently clear to provide easy answers. A judge must first determine what the intent was (or would have been)—a notoriously formidable task.

Irving R. Kaufman (1910–1992) was a judge of the 2d U.S. Circuit Court of Appeals. From Irving R. Kaufman, "What Did the Founding Fathers Intend?" as it appeared in *The New York Times Magazine,* February 23, 1986, 59–69.

An initial problem is the paucity of materials. Both the official minutes of the Philadelphia Convention of 1787 and James Madison's famous notes of the proceedings, published in 1840, tend toward the terse and cursory, especially in relation to the judiciary. The congressional debates over the proposed Bill of Rights, which became effective in 1791, are scarcely better. Even Justice William Rehnquist, one of the most articulate spokesmen for original intent, admitted in a recent dissent in a case concerning school prayer that the legislative history behind the provision against the establishment of an official religion "does not seem particularly illuminating."

One source deserves special mention. *The Federalist Papers*—the series of essays written by Alexander Hamilton, James Madison and John Jay in 1787 and 1788—have long been esteemed as the earliest constitutional commentary. In 1825, for example, Thomas Jefferson noted that *The Federalist* was regularly appealed to "as evidence of the general opinion of those who framed and of those who accepted the Constitution of the United States."

The Federalist, however, did not discuss the Bill of Rights or the Civil War amendments, which were yet to be written. Moreover, the essays were part of a political campaign—the authors wrote them in support of New York's ratification of the Constitution. The essays, therefore, tended to enunciate general democratic theory or rebut anti-Federalist arguments, neither of which offers much help to modern jurists. (In light of the following passage from *The Federalist*, No. 14, I believe Madison would be surprised to find his words of 200 years ago deciding today's cases: "Is it not the glory of the people of America that . . . they have not suffered a blind veneration for antiquity . . . to overrule the suggestions of their own good sense . . . ?")

Another problem with original intent is this: Who were the framers? Generally, they are taken to be the delegates to the Philadelphia Convention and the congressional sponsors of subsequent amendments. All constitutional provisions, however, have been ratified by state conventions or legislatures on behalf of the people they represented. Is the relevant intention, then, that of the drafters, the ratifiers or the general populace?

The elusiveness of the framers' intent leads to another, more telling problem. Originalist doctrine presumes that intent can be discovered by historical sleuthing or psychological rumination. In fact, this is not possible. Judges are constantly required to resolve questions that 18th-century statesmen, no matter how prescient, simply could not or did not foresee and resolve. On most issues, to look for a collective intention held by either drafters or ratifiers is to hunt for a chimera.

A reading of the Constitution highlights this problem. The principles of our great charter are cast in grand, yet cryptic, phrases. Accordingly, judges usually confront what Justice Robert Jackson in the 1940s termed the "majestic generalities" of the Bill of Rights, or the terse commands of "due process of law," or "equal protection" contained in the 14th Amendment. The use of such open-ended provisions would indicate that the framers did not want the Constitution to become a straitjacket on all events for all times. In contrast, when the framers held a clear intention, they did not mince words. Article II, for example, specifies a minimum Presidential age of 35 years instead of merely requiring "maturity" or "adequate age."

The First Amendment is a good example of a vaguer provision. In guaranteeing freedom of the press, some of our forefathers perhaps had specific thoughts on what publications fell within its purview. Some historians believe, in light of Colonial debates, that the main concern of the framers was to prevent governmental licensing of newspapers. If that were all the First Amendment meant today, then many important decisions protecting the press would have to be overruled. One of them would be the landmark *New York Times v. Sullivan* ruling of 1964, giving the press added protection in libel cases brought by public figures. Another would be *Near v. Minnesota,* a case involving Jay Near, a newspaper publisher who had run afoul of a Minnesota statute outlawing "malicious, scandalous and defamatory" publications. The Supreme Court struck down the statute in 1931, forbidding governmental prior restraints on publication; this ruling was the precursor of the 1971 Pentagon Papers decision.

The Founding Fathers focused not on particularities but on principles, such as the need in a democracy for people to engage in free and robust discourse. James Madison considered a popular government without popular information a "Prologue to a Farce or a Tragedy." Judges, then, must focus on underlying principles when going about their delicate duty of applying the First Amendment's precepts to today's world.

In fact, our nation's first debate over constitutional interpretation centered on grand principles. Angered at John Adams's Federalist Administration, advocates of states' rights in the late 18th century argued that original intent meant that the Constitution, like the Articles of Confederation, should be construed narrowly—as a compact among separate sovereigns. The 1798 Virginia and Kentucky Resolutions, which sought to reserve to the states the power of ultimate constitutional interpretation, were the most extreme expressions of this view. In rejecting this outlook, a nationalistic Supreme Court construed the Constitution more broadly.

The important point here is that neither side of this debate looked to the stated views of the framers to resolve the issue. Because of his leading role at the Philadelphia Convention, Madison's position is especially illuminating. "Whatever veneration might be entertained for the body of men who formed our Constitution," he declaimed on the floor of Congress in 1796, "the sense of that body could never be regarded as the oracular guide in expounding the Constitution."

Yet, I doubt if strict proponents of original intent will be deterred by such considerations. Their goal is not to venerate dead framers but to restrain living judges from imposing their own values. This restraint is most troublesome when it threatens the protection of individual rights against governmental encroachment.

According to current constitutional doctrine, the due process clause of the 14th Amendment incorporates key provisions of the Bill of Rights, which keeps in check only the Federal Government. Unless the due process clause is construed to include the most important parts of the first eight amendments in the

Bill of Rights, then the states would be free, in theory, to establish an official church or inflict cruel and unusual punishments. This doctrine is called incorporation.

Aside from the late Justice Hugo Black, few have believed that history alone is a sufficient basis for applying the Bill of Rights to the states. In his Georgetown University address, Justice Brennan noted that the crucial liberties embodied in the Bill of Rights are so central to our national identity that we cannot imagine any definition of "liberty" without them.

In fact, a cramped reading of the Bill of Rights jeopardizes what I regard as the true original intent—the rationale for having a written Constitution at all. The principal reason for a charter was to restrain government. In 1787, the idea of a fundamental law set down in black and white was revolutionary. Hanoverian England in the 18th century did not have a fully written, unified constitution, having long believed in a partially written one, based on ancient custom and grants from the Crown like the Magna Carta. To this day, the British have kept their democracy alive without one. In theory, the "King-in-Parliament" was and is unlimited in sovereign might, and leading political theorists, such as Thomas Hobbes and John Locke, agreed that governments, once established by a social contract, could not then be fettered.

Although not a Bill of Rights, the Magna Carta—King John's concessions to his barons in 1215—was symbolic of the notion that even the Crown was not all-powerful. Moreover, certain judges believed that Parliament, like the king, had to respect the traditions of the common law. This staunch belief in perpetual rights, in turn, was an important spark for the Revolutionary conflagration of 1776.

In gaining independence, Americans formed the bold concept that sovereignty continually resided with the people, who cede power to governments only to achieve certain specific ends. This view dominated the Philadelphia Convention. Instead of merely improving on the Articles of Confederation, as they had been directed to do, the framers devised a government where certain powers—defined and thereby limited—flowed from the people to the Congress, the President and the Federal judiciary.

Alexander Hamilton recognized that the basic tenets of this scheme mandated judicial review. Individual rights, he observed in *The Federalist*, No. 78, "can be preserved in practice no other way than through the medium of courts of justice, whose duty it must be to declare all acts contrary to the manifest tenor of the Constitution void." Through a written constitution and judicial enforcement, the framers intended to preserve the inchoate rights they had lost as Englishmen.

The narrow interpretation of original intent is especially unfortunate because I doubt that many of its proponents are in favor of freeing the states from the constraints of the Bill of Rights. In fact, I believe the concern of many modern "intentionalists" is quite specific: outrage over the right-of-privacy cases, especially *Roe v. Wade*, the 1973 Supreme Court decision recognizing a woman's right to an abortion. (The right of privacy, of course, is not mentioned in the Constitution.) Whether one agrees with this controversial decision or not, I would submit that concern over the outcome of one difficult case is not sufficient cause to embrace a theory that calls for so many changes in existing law. . . .

. . . [I]f original intent is an uncertain guide, does some other, more functional approach to interpreting the Constitution exist?

One suggestion is to emphasize the importance of democratic "process." As John Hart Ely, dean of the Stanford Law School forcefully advocates, this approach would direct the courts to make a distinction between "process" (the rules of the game, so to speak) and "substance" (the results of the game). Laws dealing with process include those affecting voting rights or participation in society; the Supreme Court correctly prohibited segregation, for example, because it imposed on blacks the continuing stigma of slavery. Judges, however, would not have the power to review the substantive decisions of elected officials, such as the distribution of welfare benefits.

Basically, such an approach makes courts the guardians of democracy, but a focus on process affords little help when judges decide between difficult and competing values. Judicial formulation of a democratic vision, for example, requires substantive decision-making. The dignities of human liberty enshrined in the Bill of Rights are not merely a means to an end, even so noble an end as democratic governance. For example, we cherish freedom of speech not only because it is necessary for meaningful elections, but also for its own sake.

The truth is that no litmus test exists by which judges can confidently and consistently measure the constitutionality of their decisions. Notwithstanding the clear need for judicial restraint, judges do not constitute what Prof. Raoul Berger, a retired Harvard Law School fellow, has termed an "imperial judiciary." I would argue that the judicial process itself limits the reach of a jurist's arm.

First, judges do not and cannot deliberately contravene specific constitutional rules or clear indications of original intent. No one would seriously argue or expect, for instance, that the Supreme Court could or would twist the Presidential minimum-age provision into a call for "sufficient maturity," so as to forbid the seating of a 36-year-old.

I doubt, in any event, that federal judges would ever hear such a question. The Constitution limits our power to traditional "cases" and "controversies" capable of judicial resolution. In cases like the hypothetical one regarding the presidential age, the High Court employs doctrines of standing (proving injury) and "political question" to keep citizens from suing merely out of a desire to have the government run a certain way.

Moreover, the issues properly before a judge are not presented on a *tabula rasa*. Even the vaguest constitutional provisions have received the judicial gloss of prior decisions. Precedent alone, of course, should not preserve clearly erroneous decisions; the abhorrent "separate but equal" doctrine survived for more than 50 years before the Warren Court struck it down in 1954.

The conventions of our judicial system also limit a jurist's ability to impose his or her own will. One important restraint, often overlooked, is the tradition that appellate judges issue written opinions. That is, we must support our decisions with reasons instead of whims and indicate how our constitutional rulings relate to the document. A written statement is open to the dissent of colleagues, possible review by a higher court and the judgment, sometimes scathing, of legal scholars.

In addition, the facts of a given case play a pivotal role. Facts delineate the reach of a legal decision and remind us of the "cases and controversies" requirement. Our respect for such ground rules reassures the public that, even in the most controversial case, the outcome is not just a political ruling.

Judges are also mindful that the ultimate justification for their power is public acceptance—acceptance not of every decision, but of the role they play. Without popular support, the power of judicial review would have been eviscerated by political forces long ago.

Lacking the power of the purse or the sword, the courts must rely on the elected branches to enforce their decisions. The school desegregation cases would have been a dead letter unless President Eisenhower had been willing to order out the National Guard—in support of a decision authored by a Chief Justice, Earl Warren, whose appointment the President had called "the biggest damned-fool mistake I ever made."

Instead of achieving the purple of philosopher-kings, an unprincipled judiciary would risk becoming modern King Canutes, with the cold tide of political reality and popular opprobrium lapping at their robes.

My revered predecessor on the Court of Appeals, Judge Learned Hand, remarked in a lecture at Harvard in the late 1950s that he would not want to be ruled by "a bevy of Platonic Guardians." The Constitution balances the danger of judicial abuse against the threat of a temporary majority trampling individual rights. The current debate is a continuation of an age-old, and perhaps endless, struggle to reach a balance between our commitments to democracy and to the rule of law. . . .

Judicial Selection

The U.S. Constitution empowers presidents of the United States to appoint individuals to serve on the federal courts, provided they secure the consent of the Senate. It should occasion no surprise that this division of power creates the potential for conflict between the two branches. Over the course of our history presidents have in fact had some of their most bitter fights with the Senate over who should serve on the highest court in the land. Witness, for example, Ronald Reagan's failed attempt to appoint Robert Bork to the U.S. Supreme Court in 1987—a confrontation that left a residue of ill will between the two parties—and George Bush's successful but similarly bruising battle to place Clarence Thomas there four years later.

With the atmosphere in Washington having grown decidedly more partisan in recent years, some have voiced concern that senators' votes on federal court nominees are being determined more and more by political considerations, and less and less by qualifications for the office. In the first article, John Eastman and Timothy Sandefur give voice to this concern, charging that liberal senators are employing an ideological litmus test for prospective court nominees, viewing favorably those who share their expansive view of the Constitution, while declining to support those espousing a more conservative and restrictive judicial philosophy. By doing so, Eastman and Sandefur maintain, these senators are not only violating the expressed intent of the Founding Fathers, but also seriously compromising the principle of separation of powers.

Erwin Chemerinsky, author of the second selection, totally disagrees. He insists that presidents and senators have always factored ideology into their decisions on nominees for the courts, and offers a number of reasons why it is wholly appropriate for them to do so.

The Senate Is Supposed to Advise and Consent, Not Obstruct and Delay

John C. Eastman and Timothy Sandefur

I. THE FRAMERS OF THE CONSTITUTION ASSIGNED TO THE PRESIDENT THE PRE-EMINENT ROLE IN APPOINTING JUDGES

Article II of the Constitution provides that the President "shall nominate, and by and with the Advice and Consent of the Senate, shall appoint . . . Judges of the supreme Court [and such inferior courts as the Congress may from time to time ordain and establish]."[1] As the text of the provision makes explicitly clear, the power to choose nominees—to "nominate"—is vested solely in the President,[2] and the President also has the primary role to "appoint," albeit with the advice and consent of the Senate. The text of the clause itself thus demonstrates that the role envisioned for the Senate was a much more limited one than is currently being claimed.

The lengthy debates over the clause in the Constitutional Convention support this reading. According to Madison's notes, an initial proposal on July 18, 1787, to place the appointment power in the Senate was opposed because, as Massachusetts delegate Nathaniel Ghorum noted, "even that branch [was] too numerous, and too little personally responsible, to ensure a good choice."[3] Ghorum suggested instead that Judges be appointed by the President with the advice and consent of the Senate, as had long been the method successfully followed in his home state. James Wilson and Governeur Morris of Pennsylvania, two of the Convention's leading figures, agreed with Ghorum and moved that judges be appointed by the President.

In contrast, Luther Martin of Maryland and Roger Sherman of Connecticut argued in favor of the initial proposal, contending that the Senate should have the power because, "[b]eing taken fro[m] all the States it [would] be best informed of the characters & most capable of making a fit choice."[4] And Vir-

John C. Eastman is an associate professor, Chapman University School of Law, and Director, The Claremont Institute Center for Constitutional Jurisprudence. He formerly served as a law clerk to the Honorable Clarence Thomas, Associate Justice, Supreme Court of the United States. Timothy Sandefur is a contributing editor of *Liberty* magazine and articles editor of NEXUS. This article is from John C. Eastman and Timothy Sandefur, "The Senate Is Supposed to Advise and Consent, Not Obstruct and Delay," *NEXUS: A Journal of Opinion,* 7 (2002), pp. 11–25. Notes have been renumbered to correspond to edited text. Reprinted by permission.

ginia's George Mason argued that the President should not have the power to appoint judges because (among other reasons) the President "would insensibly form local & personal attachments . . . that would deprive equal merit elsewhere, of an equal chance of promotion."[5]

Ghorum replied to Mason's objection by noting that the senators were at least equally likely to "form their attachments."[6] Giving the power to the President would at least mean that he "will be responsible in point of character at least" for his choices, and would therefore "be careful to look through all the States for proper characters." For him, the problem with placing the appointment power in the Senate was that "Public bodies feel no personal responsibility, and give full play to intrigue & cabal,"[7] while if the appointment power were given to the President alone, "the Executive would certainly be more answerable for a good appointment, as the whole blame of a bad one would fall on him alone."[8]

Seeking a compromise, James Madison suggested that the power of appointment be given to the President with the Senate able to veto that choice by a 2/3 vote.[9] Another compromise was suggested by Edmund Randolph, who "thought the advantage of personal responsibility might be gained in the Senate by requiring the respective votes of the members to be entered on the Journal."[10] These compromises were defeated, however, and the vote on Ghorum's motion—that the President nominate and with the advice and consent of the Senate, should appoint—resulted in a 4–4 tie.[11] The discussion was then postponed.

When the appointment power was taken up again on July 21, the delegates returned to their previous arguments. One side argued that the President should be solely responsible for the appointments, because he would be less likely to be swayed by "partisanship"—what Madison's generation called "faction"[12]—than the Senate. The other side opposed vesting the appointment power in the President for a similar reason: he would not know as many qualified candidates as the Senate would, and might still be swayed by personal considerations or nepotism. . . .

In the end, the Convention agreed that the President would make the nominations, and the Senate would have a limited power to withhold confirmation as a check against political patronage or nepotism. Governeur Morris put the decision succinctly: "as the President was to nominate, there would be responsibility, and as the Senate was to concur, there would be security."[13] As the Supreme Court subsequently recognized, "the Framers anticipated that the President would be less vulnerable to interest-group pressure and personal favoritism than would a collective body."[14] No one argued that the Senate's participation in the process should include second-guessing the judicial philosophy of the President's nominees or attempting to mold that philosophy itself. Indeed, such a suggestion was routinely rejected as presenting a dangerous violation of the separation of powers, by allowing the Senate to control the President's choices and, ultimately, intrude upon the judiciary. . . .

In short, by assigning the sole power to nominate (and the primary power to appoint) judges to the President, the Convention specifically rejected a more expansive Senate role; such would undermine the President's responsibility, and far from providing security against improper appointments, would actually lead to the very kind of cabal-like behavior that the Convention delegates feared. . . .

II. THE CURRENT STATE OF THE CONFIRMATION POWER

Despite the original understanding of the Senate's limited role in the confirmation process . . . the Senate today appears bent on using its limited confirmation power to impose ideological litmus on presidential nominees and even to force the President to nominate judges preferred by individual senators, thus arrogating to itself the nomination as well as the confirmation power.

The Senate's expanded use of its confirmation power should perhaps come as no surprise. As a result of the growing role of the judiciary—and of government in general—in the lives of Americans today, the Senate's part in the nomination process has become a powerful political tool, and, like all powerful political tools, it is the subject of a strenuous competition among interest groups every time the President seeks to fill a judicial vacancy. Moreover, it is a tool that poses grave dangers to our constitutional system of government. In its current manifestation, the Senate's ideological use of the confirmation power threatens the separation of powers by undermining the responsibility for appointments given to the President, by demanding of judicial nominees a commitment to a role not appropriate to the courts, and, perhaps most importantly, by threatening the independence of the judiciary.

The reason that some senators are so intent on delving into the judicial philosophy of nominees is deeply connected to their view of the proper role of the judiciary in American government. Viewing the Constitution as a "living document," modern-day liberals see the Court as a place where the Constitution is stretched, shaped, cut, and rewritten in order to put in place so-called "progressive" policies that could never emerge from the legislative process. . . .

Judicial ideology is therefore critically important to modern-day liberals because an honest reading of the Constitution reveals that it is incompatible with their scheme of government. Senator Charles Schumer of New York, for example, has been quite candid in acknowledging that his opposition to President Bush's judicial nominees is based on the fact that they respect and will enforce the Constitution's limitations on the power of Congress. "Elected officials," Sen. Schumer told the press on May 9, 2002,

> should get the benefit of the doubt with respect to policy judgments and courts should not reach out to impose their will over that of elected legislatures. . . . Many of us on our side of the aisle are acutely concerned with the new limits that are now developing on our power to address the problems of those who elect us to serve—these decisions affect, in a fundamental way, our ability to address major national issues like discrimination against the disabled and the aged, protecting the environment, and combating gun violence.[15]

This is not to say that ideology should never play a role in the confirmation process. Some ideologically-based views render it impossible for a nominee who holds them to fulfill his oath of office. Consider, for instance, Judge Harry

Pregerson, who, when he was nominated to the Court of Appeals for the Ninth Circuit by President Carter, was asked whether he would follow his conscience or the law, if the two came into conflict. "I would follow my conscience," he replied.[16] That statement, grounded in Pregerson's own ideology, should easily have been grounds for disqualification, yet Pregerson was not only confirmed to the bench, but roundly praised for this statement, despite the fact that it threatens to undermine the very essence of constitutionalism and the rule of law.[17]

Contrast this with Justice Antonin Scalia, who in a recent speech said that he was glad the Pope had not declared the Catholic Church's opposition to the death penalty a matter of infallible Church doctrine, because if the Pope had done so, Justice Scalia would, as a practicing and committed Catholic, feel compelled to resign, unable to abide by his oath to enforce the law. In his view,

> the choice for the judge who believes the death penalty to be immoral is resignation, rather than simply ignoring duly enacted constitutional laws and sabotaging death penalty cases. He has, after all, taken an oath to apply the laws and has been given no power to supplant them with rules of his own. . . . This dilemma, of course, need not be confronted by a proponent of the "living Constitution," who believes that it means what it ought to mean. If the death penalty is (in his view) immoral, then it is (hey, presto!) automatically unconstitutional, and he can continue to sit while nullifying a sanction that has been imposed, with no suggestion of its unconstitutionality, since the beginning of the Republic. (You can see why the "living Constitution" has such attraction for us judges.)[18]

Ideology understood in this light is of course relevant in selecting a judicial nominee. Broadly understood, "ideology" would encompass a nominee's honor and character, which are necessary to fulfill the oath of office.[19] A nominee who for ideological reasons cannot "support and defend the Constitution of the United States"—say, an agent working for the Taliban—would be unfit for office because he would lack the *qualifications* necessary for the position. In fact, although we tend to take the concept of an oath lightly today, James Madison wrote that under the Constitution, *"the concurrence of the Senate* chosen by the State Legislatures, in appointing the Judges, *and the oaths* and official tenures of these, with the surveillance of public Opinion, [would be] relied on as *guarantying their impartiality. . . ."*[20] This is very different than demanding of a nominee that he toe the line of leftist jurisprudence.

Today, senators inquire into a nominee's ideology for precisely the opposite reason: to ensure that the nominee will *not* abide by the Constitution—to ensure that he will stretch and bend the Constitution in the directions that the senator prefers.

On top of the danger that this presents to the fair resolution of controversies in Constitutional law, it presents a great danger to another vital principle of American government: separation of powers. In *Federalist* 78, Alexander Hamilton declared the judiciary the "least dangerous branch" of the new federal government. "[T]he general liberty of the people can never be endangered" by the judiciary, he wrote, "so long as the judiciary remains truly distinct from both the legislature and the Executive. . . . [L]iberty can have nothing to fear from the judiciary alone, but would have every thing to fear from its union with either of the other departments," and "all the effects of such a union must ensue from a dependence of the former on the latter, notwithstanding a nominal and apparent separation."[21] The enforcement of political orthodoxy on the bench is creating precisely this dependence, strengthened even more by judicial "deference" to Congressional acts that exceed the limited scope of the federal government's Constitutional powers.

"The complete independence of the courts of justice is peculiarly essential in a limited Constitution," wrote Hamilton. The courts alone could "declare all acts contrary to the manifest tenor of the Constitution void."[22] But the current attempt to block judges who believe in limited government is not motivated by a desire to maintain inviolate the "exceptions to the legislative authority." It is motivated by a desire to ensure that the judiciary will interpret the Constitution in a way most suited to *extend* that legislative authority as far as possible.

What that essentially means is that the current attempt to use the Senate's confirmation power to regulate the ideology of judges is part of an overall trend which is turning the *judiciary* into a second *legislative* branch. The fundamental differences between the legislative and the judicial branch is that in the former, parties lobby, contend, vote, and decide on procedures that may infringe on the private rights of individuals. The courts are supposed to act as a "countermajoritarian" mechanism to ensure that the legislature does not engage in "the invasion of private rights . . . from acts in which the Government is the mere instrument of the major number of the constituents."[23] The very existence of the judiciary is premised on the fact that the majority is not always right. Allowing the Senate—elected by the majority—too great a hand in regulating the federal bench risks eroding the judiciary's power to perform this most crucial task. . . .

CONCLUSION

In June of 2001, President Clinton's White House Counsel, Lloyd Cutler, told the Senate Judiciary Committee that "it would be a tragic development if ideology became an increasingly important consideration in the future. To make ideology an issue in the confirmation process is to suggest that the legal process is and should be a political one. That is not only wrong as a matter of political science; it also serves to weaken public confidence in the courts."[24]

Today the Senate is doing precisely what one delegate to the North Carolina ratification convention warned against: it is taking over the nomination power which the Constitution vested in the President alone. "[T]he President may nominate, but they have a negative upon his nomination, till he has exhausted the number of those he wishes to be appointed: He will be obliged finally to acquiesce in the appointment of those which the Senate shall nominate, or else no appointment will take place."[25] The dangers posed by such a system are as real today as they were to the founding generation. It is time to rid ourselves of all ideological litmus tests save one: "Mr. Nominee, are you prepared to honor your oath to support the Constitution as written and not as you would like it to be, if we confirm you to this important office?"[26] Any nominee who answers that question in the negative deserves to be rejected. Unfortunately, the Senate is today refusing a hearing to several nominees precisely because the current leadership knows that those nominees would honestly answer that question in the affirmative.

NOTES

1. U.S. Const. art. II § 2 cl. 2; art. III § 1.
2. See also *Weiss v. United States,* 510 U.S. 163, 185 n. 1 (1994) (Souter, J., concurring) ("the President was . . . rightly given the sole power to nominate").
3. 2 M. Farrand, Records of the Federal Convention 41 (1911).
4. *Id.*
5. *Id.* at 42. Mason's objections were actually more complicated. He argued that the President should not appoint judges because the judges might try impeachments of the President. This problem was later avoided by having the Senate try impeachments with the Chief Justice of the Supreme Court merely presiding. *See* U.S. Const. art. I § 3 cl. 6. Governeur Morris, in replying to Mason, argued that impeachments should not be "tried before the Judges." Farrand, *supra* note 6 at 41–42. Mason also worried that "the Seat of Govt must be in some state," and the President would form personal attachments to people in that state, which might exclude citizens of other states from the federal bench—an understandable objection from an antifederalist like Mason. This problem was at least partly obviated by placing the capital in a federal district which would not be subject to the jurisdiction of any state. *See* U.S. Const. art. I § 8 cl. 17.
6. Farrand, supra note 6 at 42.
7. *Id.*
8. *Id.* at 43.
9. *Id.* at 42.
10. *Id.* at 43.
11. The Convention voted by state. Georgia abstained from this vote, and Rhode Island never sent a delegate. Other states' delegates were sometimes absent for various reasons—for instance, although the Convention had been under way for more than a month, New Hampshire's delegates had still not arrived. In addition, this debate came during one of the lowest points of the Convention, when the differences between the delegates was at its severest. New York delegates, Robert Yates and John Lansing, had left the Convention on July 10, opposed to all its proceedings. New York's third delegate, Alexander Hamilton, had left ten days earlier. *See* Catherine Drinker Bowen, *Miracle at Philadelphia* 140 (Book of the Month Club, 1986) (1966). The day Lansing and Yates left the Convention, Washington wrote to Hamilton that he "almost despaired" of the Convention's success. *id.* at 185–186. (Hamilton returned to the Convention in September and was New

York's only signer). Thus the vote on July 18 was Massachusetts, Pennsylvania, Maryland and Virginia in favor of Ghorum's motion, and Connecticut, Delaware, North Carolina and South Carolina against.

12. See *The Federalist* Nos. 10 & 51 (C. Rossiter ed. 1961).
13. Farrand, *supra* note 6 at 539.
14. *Edmond v. United States,* 520 U.S. 651, 659 (1997).
15. Statement at Courts Subcommittee hearing, May 9, 2002 (visited May 26, 2002) <http://schumer.senate.gov/SchumerWebsite/pressroom/pressreleases/PR00978.html>.
16. John Johnson, "Judge Harry Pregerson, Choosing between Law and His Conscience," *Los Angeles Times,* May 3, 1992 at B5.
17. In 1992, Judge Pregerson ordered a stay to the execution of the serial killer Robert Alton Harris, the *fourth* such stay that was issued on the night of Harris' scheduled execution. The result was an unprecedented decision from the Supreme Court of the United States, ordering that "no further stays of Robert Alton Harris' execution shall be entered by the federal courts except upon order of this Court." *Vasquez v. Harris,* 503 U.S. 1000 (1992). See further Charles Fried, *Impudence,* 1992 Sup. Ct. Rev. 155, 188–92.
18. Antonin Scalia, "God's Justice and Ours," *First Things,* May 1, 2002 at 17.
19. The oath of office is prescribed in U.S. Const. art. VI § 3.
20. Letter to Thomas Jefferson (June 27, 1798), *in* Rakove, *supra* note 3 at 801 (emphasis added).
21. *The Federalist* No. 78 at 466 (C. Rossiter ed. 1961).
22. *Id.*
23. Letter from James Madison to Thomas Jefferson (Oct. 17, 1788) *in* Madison: *Writings* (J. Rakove ed. 1999) at 418, 421.
24. Statement to Administrative Oversight And The Courts Subcommittee (June 26, 2001) 2001 WL 21756493.
25. Samuel Spencer, *Speech at the North Carolina Ratification Convention,* July 28, 1788, *reprinted* in 2 Bailyn, DEBATE ON THE CONSTITUTION, at 879.
26. In this view, the qualifications of judges are similar to the qualifications of jurors as explained in *Wainwright v. Witt,* 469 U.S. 412 (1985). There the Court held that "the proper standard for determining when a prospective juror may be excluded for cause because of his or her views on capital punishment. That standard is whether the juror's views would 'prevent or substantially impair the performance of his duties as a juror in accordance with his instructions and his oath.'" *Id.* at 424 (*quoting Adams v. Texas,* 448 U.S. 38, 45 (1980)).

Of Course Ideology Should Matter in Judicial Selection

Erwin Chemerinsky

I. IDEOLOGY ALWAYS HAS MATTERED IN JUDICIAL SELECTION

The debate over the place of ideology in the judicial selection process has so far been framed in terms of whether it is appropriate for the United States Senate to consider the views of the prospective judge during the confirmation process. No one seems to deny that it is completely appropriate for the President to consider ideology when making appointments. In fact, they always have done so. Every President has appointed primarily, if not almost exclusively, individuals from the President's political party. Ever since George Washington, Presidents have looked to ideology when making judicial picks. Some Presidents are more ideological than others; not surprisingly, these Presidents focus more on ideology in their judicial nominations. President Franklin Roosevelt, for example, wanted judges who would uphold his "New Deal" programs and President Ronald Reagan emphasized selecting conservative jurists.

Senates always have done the same, using ideology as a basis for evaluating presidential nominees for the federal bench. Early in American history, President George Washington appointed John Rutledge to be the second Chief Justice of the United States.[1] Rutledge was impeccably qualified; he already had been confirmed by the Senate as an Associate Justice (although he never actually sat in that capacity) and had even been a delegate to the Constitutional Convention. But the Senate rejected Rutledge for the position as Chief Justice, because of its disagreement with Rutledge's views on a United States treaty with Great Britain.

During the nineteenth century, the Senate rejected twenty-one presidential nominations for the United States Supreme Court.[2] The vast majority of these individuals were defeated because of Senate disagreement with their ideology.[3] Professor Grover Rees explains that "during the nineteenth century only four Supreme Court Justices were rejected on the ground that they lacked the requisite credentials, whereas seventeen were rejected for political or philosophical reasons."[4]

Erwin Chemerinsky is Sydney M. Irmas Professor of Public Interest Law, Legal Ethics, and Political Science, University of Southern California Law School. This article is from Erwin Chemerinsky, "Of Course Ideology Should Matter in Judicial Selection," *NEXUS: A Journal of Opinion*, 7 (2002), pp. 3–10. Notes have been re-numbered to correspond to edited text. Reprinted by permission.

During the twentieth century, too, nominees for the Supreme Court were rejected solely because of their ideology. In 1930, a federal court of appeals judge, John Parker, was denied a seat on the high Court because of his anti-labor, anti-civil rights views.[5] In 1969, the Senate rejected United States Court of Appeals judge Clement Haynsworth largely because of his anti-union views.[6] The Senate then rejected President Nixon's next pick for the Supreme Court, Federal Court of Appeals Judge Harold Carswell.[7]

In 1987, the Senate rejected Robert Bork, even though he had impeccable professional qualifications and unquestioned ability. Bork was rejected because of his unduly restrictive views of Constitutional law, for instance, he rejected constitutional protection for a right to privacy,[8] believed freedom of speech was limited only to political expression,[9] and denied protection for women under the Equal Protection Clause. The defeat of Robert Bork was in line with a tradition as old as the republic itself.[10]

Those who contend that ideology should play no role in judicial selection are arguing for a radical change from how the process has worked from the earliest days of the nation. Never has the selection or confirmation process focused solely on whether the candidate has sufficient professional credentials.

There is a widespread sense that the focus on ideology has increased in recent years. . . . There are several explanations for why there is such intense focus on ideology at this point in American history. First, the demise of the general public's belief in formalism encourages a focus on ideology. People have come to recognize that law is not mechanical, that judges often have great discretion in deciding cases. They realize that how judges rule on questions like abortion, affirmative action, the death penalty, and countless other issues is a reflection of the individual jurist's views. *Bush v. Gore*[11] simply reinforced the widespread belief that judges' political views often determine how they vote in important cases. Thus, Democratic voters want Democratic Senators to block conservative nominees and Republican voters want Republican Senators to block liberal nominees. This creates a political incentive for Senators to do so, and means that they will certainly not risk alienating their core constituency by using ideology in evaluating nominees.

Second, the lack of "party government" in recent years explains the increased focus on ideology. During the last six years of the Clinton presidency, the Senate was controlled by Republicans. During at least the first two years of the current Bush presidency, the Senate has been controlled by Democrats. If the Senate is of the same political party as the President, there will obviously be far fewer fights over judicial nominations. Certainly, confirmation battles are still possible, for instance through filibusters, or if the President lacks support from a faction of his own party. But in general confirmation fights are a product of the Senate and the President being from different political parties.

Finally, confirmation fights occur when there is the perception of deep ideological divisions over issues likely to be decided by the courts. Now, for example, conservatives and liberals deeply disagree over countless issues: the appropriate method of constitutional interpretation; the desirable scope of Congress's power and the judicial role in limiting it; the content of individual rights, such as privacy. It is widely recognized that the outcome of cases concerning these questions will be determined by who is on the bench. Therefore, Senators know, and voters recognize, that the confirmation process is enormously important in deciding the content of the law. Interest groups on both sides of the ideological divide have strong reasons for making judicial confirmation a high priority, because they know what is at stake in who occupies the federal bench.

II. IDEOLOGY SHOULD BE CONSIDERED IN THE JUDICIAL SELECTION AND CONFIRMATION PROCESS

There are many reasons why ideology should be considered in the judicial selection process.

First, most simply and most importantly, ideology should be considered because ideology matters. Judges are not fungible; a person's ideology influences how he or she will vote on important issues. It is appropriate for an evaluator—be it the President, the Senate, or the voters in states with judicial elections[12]—to pay careful attention to the likely consequences of an individual's presence on the court.

This seems so obvious as to hardly require elaboration. Imagine that the President appoints someone who turns out to be an active member of the Ku Klux Klan or the American Nazi Party and repeatedly has expressed racist or anti-semitic views.[13] Assume that the individual has impeccable professional qualifications: a degree from a prestigious university, years of experience in high level legal practice, and a strong record of bar service. Notwithstanding these credentials, I think virtually everyone would agree that the nominee should be rejected. If I am correct in this assumption, then everyone agrees that ideology *should* matter and the only issue is *what* views should be a basis for excluding a person from holding judicial office.

On the Supreme Court, the decisions in a large proportion of cases are a product of the judges' views. The federalism decisions of recent years—limiting the scope of Congress's power under the commerce clause and section five of the Fourteenth Amendment, reviving the Tenth Amendment as a limit on federal power, and the expansion of sovereign immunity—have almost all been 5-4 rulings reflecting the ideology of the Justices.[14] Beyond the obviously controversial issues like abortion, affirmative action, and the death penalty, virtually all cases about individual liberties and civil rights are a product of who sits on the bench. Criminal procedure cases often require balancing the government's interests in law enforcement against the rights of individuals; this balancing will reflect the individual Justice's views. Decisions in statutory cases, too, are a result of the ideology of the Justices. Frequently in statutory civil rights cases, the Court is split exactly along ideological lines.[15]

Obviously this is not limited to the Supreme Court. Every case before the Supreme Court was first decided by the lower federal courts, and ideology matters there just as much. There may be more cases in the lower courts where ideology does not matter in determining outcomes—that is, where regardless of ideology any judge would come to the same conclusion—but that does not deny the large number of cases in which the judge's views matter greatly. When I talk to a lawyer who is about to have an argument before a federal court of appeals, the first question I always ask is: *who is your panel?* That is because ideology matters so much in determining the result in so many cases.

Second, the Senate should use ideology precisely because the President uses it. Republicans who today are arguing for the Senate to approve nominations without regard to their views are being disingenuous when the President—from their party—is basing his picks so much on ideology. Under the Constitution, the Senate should not be a rubber-stamp and should not treat judicial selection as a presidential prerogative. The Senate owes no duty of deference to the President and, as explained above, never has shown such deference through American history.

Finally, ideology should be considered because the judicial selection process is the key majoritarian check on an anti-majoritarian institution. Once confirmed, federal judges have life tenure. A crucial democratic check is the process of determining who will hold these appointments. A great deal of constitutional scholarship in the last quarter-century has focused on what Professor Alexander Bickel termed the "counter-majoritarian difficulty"—the exercise of substantial power by unelected judges who can invalidate the decisions of elected officials.[16] The most significant majoritarian check is at the nomination and confirmation stage. Selection by the President and confirmation by the Senate is a legitimate mechanism of majoritarian control over the composition of the federal courts.

Those who oppose the use of ideology in the judicial selection process must sustain one of two arguments: either that an individual's ideology is unlikely to affect his or her decisions on the bench, or that, even if ideology will influence decisions, it should not be examined because the disadvantages to such consideration will outweigh the benefits.

The former argument—that a person's ideology is unlikely to affect performance in office—is impossible to sustain. Unless one believes in truly mechanistic judging,[17] it is clear that judges possess discretion and that the exercise of discretion is strongly influenced by that judge's preexisting ideological beliefs. In cases involving questions of constitutional or statutory interpretation, the language of the document and the intent of the drafters often will be unclear. Judges will have to decide the meaning, and this is going to be a product of their views. Many cases, especially in Constitutional law, require a balancing of interests. The relative weight assigned to the respective claims often turns on the judge's own values. Given the reality of judicial decision-making, it is impossible to claim that a judge's ideology will not affect his or her decisions.

So opposition to considering ideology must be based on the latter argument: that even though ideology matters, it is undesirable for the Senate to consider it. One argument is that considering ideology will undermine judicial independence. Professor Stephen Carter makes this argument: "if a nominee's ideas fall within the very broad range of judicial views that are not radical in any non-trivial sense—and Robert Bork has as much right to that middle ground as any other nominee in recent decades—the Senate enacts a terrible threat to the independence of the judiciary if a substantive review of the nominee's legal theories brings about a rejection."[18]

But Professor Carter never explains why judicial independence requires blindness to ideology during the confirmation or selection of a federal judge. Judicial independence means that a judge should feel free to decide cases according to his or her view of the law and not in response to popular pressure. This is why Article III's assurance of life tenure, and its protection against a reduction in salaries, provide independence.[19] Judges are free to decide each case according to their consciences and best judgment; they need not worry that their rulings will cause them to be ousted from office. Professor Carter never justifies why this is insufficient to protect judicial independence. He subtly shifts the definition of independence from autonomy while in office to autonomy from scrutiny before taking office. But he does not explain why the latter, freedom from evaluation before ascending to the bench, is a prerequisite for judicial independence in the former, far more meaningful sense. In fact, the opposite order makes more sense. It is precisely because the framers of the Constitution's protections for judicial independence *understood* that judges would be subject to great ideological pressures, that they saw fit to insulate them from expressions of popular resentment. Judicial independence was therefore created by people who understood that judicial ideology matters.[20]

Another argument against considering ideology is that it will deadlock the selection process, with liberals blocking conservatives and vice versa. The reality is that this is a risk only when the Senate and the President are from different political parties. Even then, every Senate—including the Republican Senate during the Clinton years and the Democratic Senate today—has approved a large number of presidential nominations for the federal bench. There have been times when a number of nominations have been rejected—for instance, the Senate refused to confirm *any* of President John Tyler's picks for the Supreme Court,[21] and rejected two nominations in a row by President Nixon.[22] But in over 200 years of history, deadlocks have been rare.

Most importantly . . . the solution to deadlocks is in the President's hands: nominate individuals who are acceptable to the Senate. Presidents will have to select more moderate individuals than if the Senate was controlled by their political party. President Clinton undoubtedly was forced to select more moderate judges because the Senate was controlled by Republicans for the last six years of his presidency. President Bush would be far more successful in getting his nominations through the Senate if he chose less conservative individuals. The President has the prerogative to pick conservatives like Pickering, McConnell, Kuhl, or Estrada, but he should expect resistance in a Democratic Senate that would not be there if Bush selected more moderate nominees.

Finally, some suggest that using ideology is undesirable because it will encourage judges to base their rulings on ideology. The argument is that ideology must be hidden from the process so as to limit the likelihood that once on the bench judges will base their decisions on ideology. This argument is based on numerous unsupportable assumptions: it assumes that it is possible for judges to decide cases apart from their views and ideology; that judges don't already often decide cases because of their views and ideology; that considering ideology in the selection process will somehow increase this tendency. All of these are simply false. Long ago, the Legal Realists exploded the myth of formalistic value-neutral judging.[23] Having the judicial confirmation process recognize the demise of formalism won't change a thing in how judges behave on the bench.

The argument for considering ideology in judicial selection is simple: people should care about the decisions of the Supreme Court and other federal courts; they affect millions of people's lives in subtle but profound ways. The ideological composition of the court will determine those decisions, and the appropriate place for majoritarian influences in the judicial process is at the selection stage.

CONCLUSION

I bring some personal experience to this topic. Twice during the Clinton years, I was under serious consideration for a federal judgeship. Once, the press reported that I was on a list of three names being considered to fill two vacancies on the federal bench.[24] The other two individuals were picked. Another time, I received a call from the White House Counsel's office that I was being considered for the Ninth Circuit.

In each instance, I was told that I was not selected because the Republican-controlled Senate would find me too liberal and not confirm me. In the latter instance, I was informed that my opposition to Proposition 209, which eliminated affirmative action in California, would likely prevent Republicans from confirming me.

I confess to being disappointed, but not at all surprised; I knew from the outset that ideology always has been a key part of the confirmation process. But now I feel outrage when I hear Republicans say that it is wrong for a Democratic-controlled Senate to look at ideology, when that is exactly what Republicans did for the last six years of the Clinton presidency. . . .

Ultimately, disputes over confirmations are battles over the proper content of the law. This is as it should be, and attention should not be diverted by claims that it is improper to consider a nominee's ideological orientation. Of course, ideology should and must be considered in the judicial selection process.

NOTES

1. Laurence Tribe, *God Save This Honorable Court* 87, 90–91 (1985).
2. Grover Rees, *Questions for Supreme Court Nominees at Confirmation Hearings: Excluding the Constitution,* 17 Ga. L. Rev. 913, 944 (1983).
3. *See also* Jeffrey K. Tulis, *Constitutional Abdication: The Senate, The President, and Appointments to the Supreme Court,* 47 Case W. Res. 1331 (Summer 1997).

4. Rees, *supra* note 2.
5. *See* Gail Fruchtman, *et al.*, *Questions and Answers*, 84 Law Libr. J. 627, 637 (Summer, 1992); "Background Paper," in *Twentieth Century Fund, Judicial Roulette: Report of the Task Force on Judicial Selection* 77 (1988).
6. *Id.* at 77. See also Bob Woodward & Scott Armstrong, *The Brethren* 56–57 (1979).
7. *See id.* at 74–75.
8. See Robert Bork, *The Tempting of America: The Political Seduction of the Law* (1990) 95–100.
9. *See* Robert Bork, *Neutral Principles and Some First Amendment Problems*, 47 Ind. L.J. 1 (1971).
10. *See further* Mark Gitenstein, *Matters of Principle: An Insider's Account of America's Rejection of Robert Bork's Nomination to the Supreme Court* (1992).
11. 121 S.Ct. 545 (2000).
12. It is ironic that those opposed to the use of ideology in the judicial nomination process rarely comment on the fact that *state* judges are elected in almost all the states of the union.
13. This is not so ridiculous a proposition. Justice Hugo Black was a member of the KKK. *See* Gerald T. Dunne, *Hugo Black and the Judicial Revolution* 71–75 (1977).
14. *See, e.g., United States v. Lopez*, 514 U.S. 549 (1995); *United States v. Morrison*, 529 U.S. 598 (2000); *University of Alabama v. Garrett*, 531 U.S. 356 (2001).
15. *See, e.g., Alexander v. Sandoval*, 532 U.S. 275 (2001) (5-4 decision finding no private cause of action under Title VI of 1964 Civil Rights Act against recipients of federal funds for practices that have discriminatory impact in violation of regulations promulgated under that provision); *Circuit City v. Adams*, 532 U.S. 105 (2001) (5-4 decision that Federal Arbitration Act requires arbitration of state law employment discrimination claims); *Buckhannon Board v. West Virginia Department of Health and Human Services*, 532 U.S. 598 (2001) (5-4 decision holding that to be "prevailing party" under attorney fees statute, it is insufficient that plaintiff is catalyst for legislative action).
16. Alexander Bickel, *The Least Dangerous Branch* 16 (1962).
17. This is a difficult proposition to swallow. If judicial decisions could be made so algorithmically, there would be little reason to have a court, let alone any nomination and confirmation process, to begin with! The decision could be made merely according to a set of written equations, or even by a computer. Moreover, if a judge's own values did not affect his or her decisions, there would be no reason for judges to recuse themselves from cases giving rise to conflicts of interest.
18. Stephen Carter, *The Confirmation Mess*, 101 Harv. L. Rev. 1185, 1198 (1988).
19. U.S. Const. art. III § 1 ("The Judges, both of the supreme and inferior Courts, shall hold their Offices during good Behaviour, and shall, at stated Times, receive for their Services, a Compensation, which shall not be diminished during their Continuance in Office").
20. This is a very old principle. Lord Edward Coke, for instance, one of the most important figures in English legal history, wrote, "Honorable and reverend

judges and justices, that do or shall sit in high tribunals and courts or seats of justice . . . fear not to do right to all, and to deliver your opinions justly according to the laws; for feare is nothing but a betraying of the succors that reason should afford. And if you shall sincerely execute justice, be assured . . . that though thereby you may offend a great many favourites, yet you shall have the favourable kindnesse of the Almighty. . . ." Quoted in Catherine Drinker Bowen, *The Lion and The Throne: The Life of Edward Coke* 523 (Atlantic Monthly 1957) (1956). King James I fired Coke as Chief Justice of King's Bench because of Coke's rulings in cases like Dr. Bonham's Case, 8 Co. Rep 113b, 77 Eng. Rep 646 (K.B. 1610), which famously declared that the Court had the power to strike down laws which violated the common law. See Bowen at 314–317, 384–388.

21. Tulis, *supra* note 3 at 1350.
22. *Id.* at 1336; Woodward & Armstrong, *supra* note 14 at 15–16.
23. "Legal realism" refers to a school of thought which sees law as developing not by the discovery of internally operating logical or natural laws, but according to political pressures, experiences, and experiments which result in social structures designed to perpetuate (or to alter) existing sociological or class lines. *See* Karl N. Llewellyn, *A Realistic Jurisprudence—The Next Step*, 30 Harv. L. Rev. 431 (1930). *See further* N.E.H. Hull, *Reconstructing The Origins of Realistic Jurisprudence: A Prequel to The Llewellyn-Pound Exchange over Legal Realism*, 1989 Duke L.J. 1302.
24. Henry Weinstein, "Boxer Recommends L.A. Jurist to Be Nominated for Federal Judgeship," *Los Angeles Times,* Jan. 28, 1995 at B1.

Internet Resources

Visit our website at http://www.mhhe.com/diclerico for links and resources relating to Bureaucracy.

chapter 14

Civil Liberties

Free Speech

Freedom of speech is one of the most important freedoms accorded citizens of the United States. Nowhere is that freedom more highly prized than in its universities, whose central mission—the generation and transmission of knowledge—is predicated upon the free expression of ideas. Thus, it should occasion no surprise that considerable debate erupts on campuses from time to time over the extent to which universities are fostering an environment conducive to free expression.

The most recent debate on this question centers around the matter of student fees—a practice whereby the university imposes mandatory fees on students for the purpose of supporting various student organizations and activities on campus. More specifically, five students at the University of Wisconsin took strong exception to the fact that their student fees were going to support certain campus organizations whose views and purposes they did not share. Indeed, they were so offended by it that they decided to challenge this practice in court.

The first selection consists of portions of an amicus curiae *brief submitted to the U.S. Supreme Court by the American Council on Education on behalf of the University of Wisconsin. It insists that universities have a responsibility to create an environment that fosters a free marketplace of ideas. One of the ways to do so is to support with student fees a host of different campus organizations. Such support, in the view of the American Council on Education, in no way diminishes the free speech of students paying those fees.*

The second selection also contains portions of an amicus curiae *brief submitted to the U.S. Supreme Court—this one by the Pacific Legal Foundation on behalf of the five students. It argues that by requiring students to support, through their fees, organizations with which they disagree, the University of Wisconsin is in fact abridging their right to freedom of speech.*

Mandatory Student Fees Do Not Abridge Freedom of Speech

American Council on Education

I. A UNIVERSITY'S USE OF COMPULSORY FEES TO CREATE A STUDENT ACTIVITY FUND SHOULD BE ANALYZED AS THE CREATION OF A FORUM, RATHER THAN AS COMPELLED SPEECH AND ASSOCIATION

A. A University, as a Marketplace of Ideas, Has a Compelling Interest in Promoting the Presence of a Diversity of Viewpoints

"It is the business of a university to provide that atmosphere which is most conducive to speculation, experiment and creation."[1] A university can provide this atmosphere only by offering an environment in which a rich diversity of ideas, values, and perspectives is championed and challenged. In this sense, "[t]he college classroom with its surrounding environs is peculiarly the 'marketplace of ideas.'"[2]

This marketplace trains future citizens and leaders by providing "wide exposure to that robust exchange of ideas which discovers truth 'out of a multitude of tongues.'"[3] If a university is to provide such training, some members of the academic community will inevitably encounter speech that they find unfamiliar, even abhorrent. Furthermore, learning to tolerate and respond to such speech is an important part of the educational process. "To endure the speech of false ideas or offensive content and then to counter it is part of learning how to live in a pluralistic society, a society which insists upon open discourse towards the end of a tolerant citizenry."[4]

The marketplace extends beyond the classroom to extracurricular activities, which are "a critical aspect of campus life."[5] Education involves more than tests, textbooks, lectures, and libraries. Fundamentally, it is about the development of character.[6] Consequently, education does not end at the classroom door, but permeates campus and university life. As this Court recognizes, a "great deal of learning occurs informally."[7] Indeed, since the nineteenth century, extracurricular activities have played an increasingly significant role in advancing the core mission of universities:

From the *amicus curiae* brief filed by the American Council on Education in support of the University of Wisconsin in the U.S. Supreme Court case of *Board of Regents, University of Wisconsin v. Scott Southworth* (1999), 5–21.

240

> Over time . . . extracurricular programs have come to be seen not merely as use-
> ful services but as an integral part of the educational process itself. Educators
> point to the dangers of a college that stresses only learning and cognitive skills
> while ignoring opportunities for students to engage in cooperative activities in
> which each relies on the efforts of others and is relied upon by others in return.
> . . . More and more, [extracurricular activities] are regarded not only as a source
> of enjoyment but as ideal experiences for learning to cooperate and take re-
> sponsibility for the welfare of one's peers.
>   . . . The contemporary college or university does not concentrate only on
> formal education; it assumes the larger responsibility of promoting human de-
> velopment in all its forms.[8]

    . . . In sum, colleges and universities hold a unique position in our society
and pursue a correspondingly unique mission. Their business is to provide
"that atmosphere which is most conducive to speculation, experiment and creation."[9] This mission can be achieved only by fostering a marketplace of ideas
on campus and by ensuring that the resultant diversity of thoughts and perspectives informs the full range of experiences—from course selections to lecture series to student organizations. If a university is barred from this essential
business, it cannot prepare its students "to live in a pluralistic society, a society
which insists upon open discourse towards the end of a tolerant citizenry."[10]

B. Consistent with the First Amendment, a University Can Use Mandatory Fees to Fund a Neutral Forum That Helps Support a Diverse Variety of Organizations

. . . [T]he University of Wisconsin (and many other colleges and universities)
pay fees not to particular groups but to the student government, which then
uses the money to fund a wide array of organizations in a viewpoint-neutral
manner.[11] "The speech of the offending groups can hardly be attributed to the
student government, which funds groups of radically different views."[12] . . .

    The University of Wisconsin simply requires its students to support a neutral
forum, just as if it "built a large auditorium and held it open for everyone."[13] The
fact that this case concerns a fund, rather than a physical space like an auditorium
or an amphitheater, does not mean that forum analysis does not apply. . . .

    Application of these principles makes clear that a critical difference exists
between (a) supporting a forum and (b) supporting the speakers that ultimately
use that forum. Thus, in *Widmar v. Vincent*,[14] this Court rejected a university's
argument that if it were to allow religious groups to use its buildings it would
create an impression that it endorsed religion in violation of the Establishment
Clause:"[B]y creating a forum the University does not thereby endorse or promote any of the particular ideas aired there."[15] A student compelled to pay a
restoration fee for a university amphitheater can hardly complain that her First
Amendment rights are violated because she disagrees with some of the speakers who appear there. She has no greater constitutional cause to complain of a
content-neutral student activity fund because she disagrees with some of the
organizations it ultimately supports.

If a forum supports organizations in a truly neutral fashion, as is stipulated here, . . . and thereby funds groups that take radically differing positions on the same issues, it cannot be said to endorse or promote any particular group or any specific position.[16] . . .

II. EVEN IF A UNIVERSITY'S USE OF MANDATORY FEES TO FUND STUDENT GOVERNMENT AND ORGANIZATIONS IS ANALYZED UNDER ABOOD-KELLER AS COMPELLED SPEECH AND ASSOCIATION, RATHER THAN AS THE CREATION OF A NEUTRAL FORUM, SUCH A USE OF FEES DOES NOT VIOLATE THE FIRST AMENDMENT

A. The Challenged Use of Mandatory Fees Is Germane to a University's Broad Educational Mission, Including Its Interests in Promoting Diverse Expression and in Providing a Marketplace of Ideas

Abood and *Keller* involve contexts very different from colleges and universities. *Keller* holds that compulsory state bar dues cannot be used to finance ideological activities unrelated to the purposes of the compelled association—regulation of the legal profession and improvement of legal services. Similarly, *Abood* holds that a union may not use a dissenting individual's dues to fund ideological activities not germane to collective bargaining. The purposes of the State Bar in *Keller,* to supervise attorney conduct, and of the union shop in *Abood,* to negotiate contracts, are relatively narrow and definable. The educational mission of a university is substantially broader.[17] ("The goals of the university are much broader than the goals of a labor union or a state bar, and they are inextricably connected with the underlying policies of the First Amendment."[18])

It is the business of a university to create a marketplace of ideas, exposing its students to a broad range of viewpoints on many issues, including the political and the ideological. This happens in classrooms—in courses in history, literature, political science, sociology, philosophy, and many other disciplines. It happens in auditoriums—when guest lecturers speak on ethics, contemporary problems, civil rights, and the like. And it happens in extracurricular activities—in connection with student government, student newspapers, and student organizations identical to those at issue here. Neither state bars nor unions—nor perhaps any institutions other than American colleges and universities—have this broad mission and mandate.

As a result, numerous courts recognize that a university's mission unquestionably reaches the funding of student organizations. Thus, the Second Circuit holds that a university may allocate student activity fees to a group with whose speech some students disagree.[19] *Carroll* recognizes three distinct university interests served by the compulsory fee:"the promotion of extracurricular life, the transmission of skills and civic duty, and the stimulation of energetic campus debate."[20] . . .

B. Courts Should Afford Universities Wide Latitude to Determine Whether the Use of Student Fees Is Germane to Their Educational Mission

Amici respectfully submit that the court below failed to give proper deference to the University of Wisconsin's decision that the use of mandatory fees advances its educational mission. Universities have interests in academic freedom that are a special concern of the First Amendment. This freedom is lost if courts do not afford universities discretion to define the contours of their educational mission and to determine the most effective means of achieving it. Judicial intervention in academic decision-making affects not only the academic freedom of the university, but it results as well in a loss of the freedom of the students, faculty, and other members of the academic community, all of whom participate in and help to create the marketplace of ideas.

For these reasons, this Court has recognized that government intervention in the intellectual life of a university is to be avoided.[21] Universities are "characterized by the spirit of free inquiry," and academic freedom gives the university the ability "to determine for itself on academic grounds who may teach, what may be taught, how it shall be taught, and who may be admitted to study."[22] . . .

In this case, the University of Wisconsin—a campus with a rich history of the "robust exchange of ideas"[23]—made a judgment that funding a forum that supports a wide variety of student groups, including some engaged in political and ideological activities, plays an important role in its educational mission. This decision deserves respect, "breathing room," and some significant measure of deference. . . .

III. FORCING THE UNIVERSITY TO DISTINGUISH BETWEEN "EDUCATIONAL" ORGANIZATIONS AND "POLITICAL" OR "IDEOLOGICAL" ORGANIZATIONS RISKS VIOLATING STUDENTS' FIRST AMENDMENT RIGHTS

The court below effectively requires universities to distinguish political from non-political, and ideological from non-ideological organizations, and then to grant or withhold funding based upon these distinctions. Such distinctions may be constitutionally workable in the context of the activities of a union or a state bar, where the government has a narrower interest and where that interest does not include exposure to a diverse marketplace of ideas. Such distinctions emphatically do not work in the context of a university, however, where the government has a broad interest, and where that interest includes exposure to various political and ideological perspectives. Further, in the context of a university campus activities, such distinctions not only fail to work, but they actually create significant constitutional mischief.

Consider a student debate club that sponsors a public forum on presidential impeachment; or a student economic society that hosts a series of speakers on tax reform; or a student group that distributes leaflets asserting that a university discriminates because it hires too few minority professors; or a film society that sponsors a film concerning the events at Tiananmen Square; or an environmental organization that presents a series of lectures on the impact of logging; or a literary studies club that funds a panel discussion of alternative theories of literary criticism, including Marxist, feminist, deconstructionist, and Freudian approaches. At some point it simply becomes impossible to separate the ideological and political from the educational and informative.[24]

Furthermore, a university that attempts to make such distinctions, and then to make funding decisions based upon them, may run afoul of First Amendment prohibitions against content- and viewpoint-based discrimination. In other words, forcing universities to draw these lines does not avoid constitutional difficulties; it compounds them. The University of Wisconsin uses the mandatory activity fee to create a public forum that distributes fees on a content-neutral basis. . . . By supporting groups without regard to the content or viewpoint of their speech, the forum detaches funding decisions from endorsement or condemnation of the political or ideological positions of the different organizations. In contrast, the holding of the *Southworth I* court, which would require the University to refuse funding for groups that are too ideological or political, violates the rule against content and viewpoint discrimination in a public forum. . . .

Faced with a project that calls upon them to do the impossible, with the knowledge that in the effort they might also do the unconstitutional, many universities will respond by funding no student organizations at all or only those that seem to pose no risk whatsoever.[25] As the dissenting judges in *Southworth II* cautioned, such a requirement may "spell the end, as a practical matter, to the long tradition of student-managed activities on these campuses."[26] As funding fails, and as organizations disband, some voices—including, in all likelihood, the most provocative and stimulating, if also the least popular voices—will no longer be heard at our universities. The marketplace of ideas on our campuses will suffer immeasurably.

NOTES

1. *Sweezy v. New Hampshire*, 354 U.S. 234, 263 (1957) (Frankfurter, J., concurring).
2. *Healy v. James*, 408 U.S. 169, 180 (1972) (quoting *Keyishian v. Board of Regents of Univ. of N.Y.*, 385 U.S. 589, 603 (1967)).
3. Keyishian, 385 U.S. at 603 (quoting *United States v. Associated Press*, 52 F. Supp. 362, 372 (D.N.Y., 1943)).
4. *Lee v. Weisman*, 505 U.S. 577, 590 (1992).
5. *Widmar v. Vincent*, 454 U.S. 263, 279 n. 2 (1981) (Stevens, J., concurring).
6. See Higher Education Amendments of 1998, Pub. L. No. 105-244, §863, 112 Stat. 1581, 1826 (Congress recognizes that "the development of virtue and moral character, those habits of mind, heart, and spirit that help young people to know, desire, and do what is right, has historically been a primary mission of colleges and universities. . . .").

7. *Regents of the Univ. of Cal. v. Bakke*, 438 U.S. 265, 313 n. 48 (1978) (opinion of Powell, J.) (quoting William J. Bowen, "Admissions and the Relevance of Race," *Princeton Alumni Weekly 7*, 9 (Sept. 26, 1977)).

8. Derek C. Bok, *Higher Learning* 51–52 (1986). . . .

9. *Sweezy*, 354 U.S. at 263 (Frankfurter, J., concurring).

10. *Lee*, 505 U.S. at 590.

11. The only exception to this procedure may be Wisconsin PIRG, for which funding is authorized by direct student referendum. This brief does not address the separate and different issue raised by this direct funding, although the "germaneness" analysis discussed below would apply to this funding as well.

12. *Southworth II*, 157 F. 3d at 1125.

13. Id. at 1129 (Wood, J., dissenting).

14. 454 U.S. 263 (1981).

15. See also Carolyn Wiggin, Note, *A Funny Thing Happens When You Pay for a Forum: Mandatory Student Fees to Support Political Speech at Public Universities*, 103 Yale L.J. 2009, 2017 (1994) ("[T]he lack of content-based standards . . . enables the system to support a legitimate campus forum, and this in turn creates a distance between those who fund the forum and any particular view expressed within it, thus avoiding unconstitutional forced speech").

16. See Robert M. O'Neil, "Student Fees and Student Rights: Evolving Constitutional Principles," 15 J.C. & U.L. 569, 574 (1999). . . .

17. See *Rounds*, 166 F. 3d at 1039.

18. See also William Walsh, Comment, *Smith v. Regents of the University of California: The Marketplace Is Closed*, 21 J.C. & U.L. 405, 423 (1994) ("[T]he organizations' purposes in *Keller* and *Abood* were much narrower than the university's purpose. It is much easier to see something as 'political or ideological,' and therefore ineligible for funding, because it is unrelated to collective bargaining than it is to distinguish the same from and 'educational mission'").

19. See *Carroll v. Blinken*, 957 F. 2d 991, 992 (2d Cir. 1992).

20. Id. at 1001. . . .

21. See, e.g., *Sweezy*, 354 U.S. at 262 (Frankfurter, J. concurring).

22. Id. at 262–63.

23. *Keyishian*, 385 U.S. at 603.

24. See Smith, 844 P. 2d at 524–25 (Arabian, J., dissenting).

25. An "opt-out refund" procedure might address certain constitutional concerns, see O'Neil, supra, 575, 578, and use of such a procedure certainly should not be foreclosed by this Court. For the reasons set forth in this brief, however, such a procedure should not be required to save the constitutionality of mandatory fees.

26. 157 F. 3d at 1127 (Wood, J., dissenting).

Mandatory Student Fees Violate Students' Right to Free Speech

Pacific Legal Foundation

THE UNIVERSITY HAS NO CONSTITUTIONAL JUSTIFICATION TO COMPEL PAYMENT OF FEES TO PROMOTE STUDENT EXPRESSIVE ACTIVITIES

A. The University Has No Compelling Interest in Coercing Students to Subsidize Voluntary Organizations' Political and Ideological Activities

While a university may well have a compelling interest in *exposing* students to various conflicting viewpoints, it does not have a compelling interest in coercing *support* for those viewpoints.

> [T]he freedom to keep silent as well as to speak is grounded in something broader than a national fear of the state. It is equally the product of our view of personhood, which encompasses what the Supreme Court later referred to as "freedom of thought," "freedom of mind" and a "sphere of intellect and spirit." Were there no state at all, or were it inalterably benign, our conception of what it means to be human would still lead us to respect the individual autonomy of intellect and will enshrined in the First Amendment.[1]

By coercing support for political groups, the university sends a troubling message to students: If students want to advance a political position for which they cannot find support, the government will give them money to propagate their unpopular views. This is an illegitimate lesson for a public university to teach its students. The defendants in *Abood* and *Keller* understood that mandating support for an organization smothers, rather than stokes, contrary speech.[*2] Moreover, the university, let alone the political groups themselves, does not create a free marketplace or forum for the expression of ideas. Rather it requires students to be the financial sponsors of someone else's speech. Indeed, the notion that a free marketplace of ideas can be created and encouraged by involuntary contributions is an oxymoron. The strength of an idea (*i.e.,* its acceptance

*Two previous cases in which the Supreme Court ruled that non-union teachers and members of a bar association did not have to support the political activities of their groups—*Editors.*

From the *amicus curiae* brief filed by the Pacific Legal Foundation in support of the plaintiff, Scott Southworth, in the U.S. Supreme Court case of *Board of Regents, University of Wisconsin v. Scott Southworth* (1999), 24–27.

in the marketplace) is best measured by how many people will volunteer to spread the idea or to help finance its propagation.

The university's position also implies that the First Amendment has only limited application within the confines of a public university campus. As the court below noted,

> far from *serving* the school's interest in education, forcing objecting students to fund objectionable organizations undermines that interest. In some courses students are likely taught the values of individualism and dissent. Yet despite the objecting students' dissent they must fund organizations promoting opposing views or they don't graduate.[3]

If the university really wants students to learn practical civics lessons, it should encourage politically active groups to learn the art of fund-raising. In real political campaigns, opponents of the message do not give money to the cause.

B. A State University May Permit Voluntary Funding of Student Groups as a Less Intrusive Method of Promoting Such Groups on Campus

Universities are free to adopt any system of funding student activities that avoids constitutional defects. The best system, however, is the "positive check-off" voluntary system. Such a check-off could be designed in a number of ways. For example, it could list each recognized student group eligible for funding and permit students to choose which particular groups they wish to subsidize. Alternatively, it could simply provide a single box which, if checked, would mean that the student assents to funding all eligible student groups. By requiring students to designate affirmatively that they wish to fund particular groups, either individually or as a whole, the university advances several compelling goals. First, it requires thought on the part of the student, rather than mindless contributions to groups the student may not even be able to identify. Second, it encourages student groups to organize and articulate their messages clearly so as to attract as much financial support as possible.[4] Third, and most importantly, it sends a strong message to the entire student body that the university respects the constitutional rights of *all* students and has taken the strongest measures possible to protect those rights.[5]

Supporters of compelled funding have derided such a method, complaining that

> funding will soon devolve into a political *popularity* contest. Thus, in a setting where provocative ideas should receive the most support and encouragement, precisely the opposite will occur; student groups will be subject to an ideological referendum, and the most marginal groups will receive the least financial assistance. This is truly Orwellian.[6]

Justice Arabian's reasoning is backwards. What is Orwellian is a situation in which marginal groups are presented to the community as having support where there is none and presented as mainstream rather than extreme. Giving these ideas the cover of legitimacy and acceptability because of coerced subsidization from students who oppose the message perpetrates a great disservice. Students who wish to attract adherents to unconventional ideas must do so by convincing others of the soundness of their theories. Giving these unconventional thinkers the unwilling financial support of their dissenters grants them the means to speak more loudly than their actual support would permit.

CONCLUSION

The students in *West Virginia State Board of Education v. Barnette,* by being forced to salute the flag, were more than exposed to patriotism; they were forced to support it with a raised hand. Like them, the students at UW–Madison were not simply exposed to divergent views, they were forced to reach into their pockets to finance their opponents' views. Ideas that could not win adherence through persuasion and reason were thus kept alive by the state by imposing fees on those who do not support the idea in question. The First Amendment was designed to prevent just such an exercise of state power.

Attempts by the government, whether through a public agency, a legislature, or a court, to force individuals to financially support political and ideological activities with which they disagree have been rejected from the time of Thomas Jefferson to the present. This Court has on numerous occasions protected the rights of teachers, attorneys, and nonunion agency shop fee payers to refrain from supporting speech which they oppose. Students are entitled to no less protection.

NOTES

1. *Carroll v. Blinken,* 957 F. 2d 991, 996 (2d Cir.) cert. denied, 506 U.S. 906 (1992).
2. *Abood v. Detroit Board of Education* 431 U.S. 209 (1977) and *Keller v. State Bar of California* 496 U.S. 1 (1990).
3. *Southworth v. Grebe* 151 F. 3d 728 (1998).
4. The groups benefit in another way: if they suffer a funding shortfall when their opponents are no longer forced to subsidize their activities, the groups will likely turn to their own members to make up the difference. A person who pays a membership fee to belong to one of these groups will have a more personal stake in the group's successful attainment of its objectives. Bevilacqua, *Public Universities, Mandatory Student Activity Fees, and the First Amendment,* 24 J.L. & Educ. 1, 29–30 (1995).
5. La Fetra, "Recent Developments in Mandatory Student Fee Cases," 10 J.L. & Pol. 579, 612–13 (1994).
6. *Smith v. Regents of the University of California,* 4 Cal. 4th 843, 881 (1993) (Arabian, J., dissenting).

Pornography

*T*he two previous selections highlighted the difference of opinion over what we should be free to say. Similar disagreement exists over what we should be free to see, read, and hear, when the subject matter in question is "obscene" or "pornographic" in character.

In the first of the following essays, Ernest van den Haag is concerned with two basic questions: First, is pornographic material clearly definable so that it can be distinguished from other kinds of expression we would not want to suppress? Second, even if we can define it, is there any public interest to be served by prohibiting our citizens from having access to it? Van den Haag answers both questions in the affirmative.

Geoffrey Stone does not object to laws against child pornography nor to age and zoning restrictions limiting access to pornography in general. In contrast to van den Haag, however, he wholly opposes any attempt to limit the distribution of obscene material to consenting adults. In his judgment, a careful weighing of the costs and benefits associated with censorship clearly reveals that the individual incurs very great costs, while the society derives very little benefit.

Pornography and Censorship
Ernest van den Haag

Ultramoralists want to prohibit any display of nudity while ultralibertarians feel that even the most scabrously prurient display must be tolerated. However, most people are not that extreme. They are uneasy about obscene incitements to lechery; but uncertain about what to do about them. They wonder whether distaste, even when shared by a majority, is reason enough to prohibit what a minority evidently wants. Beyond distaste, is there enough actual harm in pornography? Where will suppression end, and how harmful might it be? Can we legally distinguish the valuable from the pornographic, the erotic from the obscene? Would courts have to act as art critics? Not least, we wonder about our own disapproval of obscenity. We are aware, however dimly, of some part of us which is attracted to it. We disapprove of our own attraction—but also worry whether we may be afraid or hypocritical when we suppress what attracts us as well as many others.

Still, most people want something done about pornography. As so often in our public life, we turn to the Constitution for a rule. "Congress" it tells us "shall make no law . . . abridging the freedom of speech or of the press." Although addressed to the federal government only, the First Amendment has been echoed in many state constitutions and applied to all states by the courts. Further, its scope has been broadened, perhaps unduly so, by court decisions which hold that all expressions rather than just words are protected by the First Amendment. Yet speech—words, spoken, or printed, or otherwise reproduced—is a narrow subclass of expression and the only one protected by the First Amendment. Music, painting, dance, uniforms, or flags—expressions but not words—are not.[1] The framers wanted to protect political and intellectual discourse—they thought free verbal interchange of ideas indispensable to consensual government. But obscenity hardly qualifies as an interchange of ideas, and is no more protected than music is. Whatever their merits, neither addresses the intellect, nor is indispensable to free government. For that matter words without cognitive content, words not used as vehicles for ideas—e.g., "dirty words" or expletives—may not be constitutionally protected. And even the constitutional right to unfettered verbal communication of ideas is limited

Ernest van den Haag (1914–2002) was John M. Olin Professor of Jurisprudence and Public Policy at Fordham University before joining the Heritage Foundation as distinguished scholar in 1981. From Ernest van den Haag, "Pornography and Censorship," *Policy Review,* 13 (Summer 1980): 73–81. Reprinted with permission of *Policy Review.* Published by the Heritage Foundation.

by other rights and by the rights of others. Else there could be no libel or copy-right laws and no restrictions on incitements to illicit or harmful action.

The Constitution, then, gives us the right to outlaw pornography. Should we exercise it? Is there a sufficient social interest in suppression? And how can we separate pornography from things we constitutionally cannot or do not want to suppress?

Some people feel that there can be no objective standard of obscenity: "Beauty is in the eye of the beholder—and so is obscenity," they argue. This notion is popular among pseudo-sophisticates; but it seems wildly exaggerated. Is the difference between your mother-in-law and the current Miss America merely in the eye of the beholder (yours)? How come everyone sees the difference you see? Is the distinction between pictures which focus on exposed human genitals or on sexual intercourse, and other pictures only in the eye of the beholder? To be sure, judgments of beauty, or of obscenity, do have subjective components—as most judgments do. But they are not altogether subjective. Why else do even my best friends not rate me a competitor to Apollo? For that matter judgments of art are not altogether subjective either. Museums persistently prefer Rembrandt's paintings to mine. Do they all have a subjective bias against me?

Pornography seems a reasonably objective matter which can be separated from other things. Laws, if drawn sensibly, might effectively prohibit its display or sale. An in-between zone between the obscene and the nonobscene may well remain, just as there is such a twilight zone between brightly lit and dark areas. But we still can tell which is which; and where necessary we can draw an arbitrary, but consistent (i.e., non-capricious), line. The law often draws such a line: to enable the courts to deal with them the law treats as discontinuous things that in nature may be continuous. The law quite often leaves things to the judgment of the courts: just how much spanking is cruelty to children? Just when does behavior become reckless?—courts always have to decide cases near the dividing line. But courts would have to decide only the few cases near the line which divides obscene from nonobscene matters. Most of the obscene stuff now displayed is not even near that line. With sensible laws it will no longer be displayed or offered for sale. The doubtful cases will be decided by juries applying prevailing standards. Such standards vary greatly over time and space, but at any given time, in any place, they are fairly definite and knowable. Lawyers who argue otherwise never appear in court, or for that matter in public places, without pants (or skirts, as the case may be). They seem to know what is contrary to the standards prevailing in the community in which they practice—however much they pretend otherwise.

A word on the current legal situation may not be amiss. The courts have not covered themselves with glory in clarifying the notion of obscenity. At present they regard the portrayal of sex acts, or of genitalia, or of excretion, as obscene if (a) patently offensive by contemporary community standards and if (b) taken as a whole[2] it appeals dominantly to a prurient (morbid or shameful) interest in sex and if (c) it lacks serious scientific, literary or artistic merit. The courts imply that not all appeals to sexual interest are wrong—only prurient ones are.

They have not said directly which appeals are prurient. The courts might have been more explicit but they are not unintelligible.

An appeal to sexual interest need not be obscene per se; only attempts to arouse sexual interest by patently offensive, morbid, shameful means are. By contemporary standards a nude is not obscene. But an appeal to sexual interest is, when carried out by focusing on exposed genitalia, or on the explicit, detailed portrayal of sex acts. Detailed portrayals of excretion may be patently offensive too, but since they scarcely appeal to the sexual interest of most people they may pass under present law unless specifically listed as unlawful; so may portrayals of sexual relations with animals for the same reason—if the jury is as confused as the law is. The courts never quite made up their minds on the relative weight to be given to "offensive," to "prurient," and to "sexual." Thus intercourse with animals may be offensive to most people and prurient, i.e., morbid and shameful, but not necessarily sexual in its appeal to the average person. Therefore some exhibitors of such spectacles have been let off. But should the fact that some sexual acts are so disgusting to the majority as to extinguish any sexual appeal they might otherwise have legitimize these acts? Offensiveness, since in effect it is also a criterion for the prurience of a sexual appeal, is a decisive element of obscenity; yet the other two elements must be present.

If more clearly drawn laws would leave few doubtful cases for juries to decide, why do many literary, sociological, or psychological experts find it so hard to determine what is obscene? Why do they deny that such laws can be fashioned? Most people who protest that they cannot draw the line dividing the pornographic from the nonpornographic are deliberately unhelpful. "None so blind as they that won't see." They don't want to see because they oppose any pornography laws. They certainly have a right to oppose them. But this right does not entitle anyone to pretend that he cannot see what he does see. Critics who testify in court that they cannot distinguish pornography from literature, or that merely pornographic stuff has great literary or educational merit, usually know better. If they didn't they would have no business being critics or experts. To oppose pornography laws is one thing. It is quite another thing to attempt to sabotage them by testifying that hardcore stuff cannot be separated from literature or art, pornographic from aesthetic experience. Such testimony is either muddleheaded beyond belief or dishonest.

Once we have decided that the obscene is not inseparable from the nonobscene, we can address the real issue: are there compelling grounds for legally restraining public obscenity?

Some argue that pornography has no actual influence. This seems unpersuasive. Even before print had been invented Francesca blamed a book for her sin: "Galeotto fu il libro" (the book was the panderer) she told Dante in the *Divine Comedy*. Did she imagine the book's influence? Literature—from the Bible to Karl Marx or to Hitler's *Mein Kampf*—does influence people's attitudes and actions, as do all communications, words or pictures. That is why people write, or, for that matter, advertise. The influence of communications varies, depending on their own character, the character of the person exposed to them, and on many other circumstances. Some persons are much influenced by the Bible—or by pornography—others not. Nor is the direction of the influence, and the action to which it may lead altogether predictable in each case. But there is little doubt that for the average person the Bible fosters a religious disposition in some degree and pornography a lecherous one.

Granted that it has some influence, does pornography harm nonconsenting persons? Does it lead to crime? Almost anything—beer, books, poverty, wealth, or existentialism—can "lead" to crime in some cases. So can pornography. We cannot remove all possible causes of crime—even though we might remove those that can be removed without much difficulty or loss. But crime scarcely seems the major issue. We legally prohibit many things that do not lead to crime, such as polygamy, cocaine, or dueling. Many of these things can easily be avoided by those who do not wish to participate; others cannot be shown to be actually harmful to anyone. We prohibit whatever is *perceived* as socially harmful, even if merely contrary to our customs, as polygamy is.

When we prohibit cartels, or the sale of marijuana, when we impose specific taxes, or prohibit unlicensed taxis from taking fares, we believe our laws to be useful, or to prevent harm. That belief may be wrong. Perhaps the tax is actually harmful or unjust, perhaps we would all be better off without licensing any taxis, perhaps cartels are economically useful, perhaps marijuana smoking is harmless or beneficial. All that is needed to justify legislation is a rational social interest in accomplishing the goals of the legislation. Thus, an activity (such as marijuana smoking) can be prohibited because it is *perceived* to be socially harmful, or even merely distasteful. Pornography is. The harm it actually may do cannot be shown the way a man can be shown to be guilty of a crime. But such a demonstration of harm or guilt is not required for making laws—it is required only if someone is to be convicted of breaking them.

Still, unless we are convinced that pornography is harmful the whole exercise makes little sense. Wherein then is pornography harmful? The basic aim of pornographic communication is to arouse impersonal lust, by, in the words of Susan Sontag (incidentally a defender of pornography), driving "a wedge between one's existence as a full human being and one's sexual being . . . a healthy person prevents such a gap from opening up. . . ." A healthy society too must help "prevent such gaps from opening up," for, to be healthy, a society needs "full human beings," "healthy persons" who integrate their libidinal impulses with the rest of their personality, with love and with personal relationships.

We all have had pre-adolescent fantasies which ignore the burdens of reality, of commitment, concern, conflict, thought, consideration and love as they become heavier. In these fantasies others are mere objects, puppets for our pleasure, means to our gratification, not ends in themselves. The Marquis de Sade explored such fantasies most radically; but all pornographers cater to them: they invite us to treat others merely as means to our gratification. Sometimes they suggest that these others enjoy being so treated; sometimes they suggest, as the Marquis de Sade did, that pleasure lies in compelling unwilling others to suffer. Either way pornography invites us to reduce fellow humans to mere means. The cravings pornography appeals to—the craving for contextless, impersonal, anonymous, totally deindividualized, as it were abstract, sex—are not easy to control and are, therefore, felt as threats by many persons, threats to their own impulse-control and integration. The fear is real and enough sex crimes certainly occur . . . to give plausibility to it. People wish to suppress pornography, as they suppress within themselves impulses that they feel threaten them. Suppression may not be an ideal solution to the problem of anxiety arousing stimuli, external or internal. Ideally we should get rid of anxiety, and of unwelcome stimuli, by confrontation and sublimation. But we are not ideal and we do not live in an ideal world. Real as distinguished from ideal persons must avoid what threatens and upsets them. And real as distinguished from utopian societies must help them to do so.

However, there are stronger grounds for suppressing pornography. Unlike the 18th-century rationalists from whom the ultralibertarians descend, I do not believe that society is but an aggregation of individuals banded together for their mutual convenience. Although society does have utilitarian functions, it is held together by emotional bonds, prior to any rational calculations. Societies survive by feelings of identification and solidarity among the members, which lead them to make sacrifices for one another, to be considerate and to observe rules, even when they individually would gain by not doing so. In animal societies (e.g., among social insects) the members identify one another instinctively, for example, by smell. The identification leads them not to attack or eat one another and it makes possible many manifestations of solidarity. It makes the insect society possible. Human societies, too, would be impossible without such identification and solidarity among the members. Else we would treat one another as we now treat insects or chickens—or as the Nazis treated Jews. It is to preserve and strengthen traditional emotional bonds, and the symbols that stand for them, that the government of Israel prohibits the raising of pigs, that of India the slaughtering of cows.

Solidarity is as indispensable to the United States as it is to Israel. It is cultivated by institutions which help each of us to think of others not merely as means to his own gratification, but as ends in themselves. These institutions cultivate shared customs, expectations, traditions, values, ideals and symbols. The values we cultivate differ from those of an aboriginal tribe; and the range left to individual choice is broader. Social solidarity is less stringent than it is in most primitive tribes. But neither our society nor an aboriginal tribe could survive without shared values which make it possible for us to identify with one another.

One of our shared values is the linkage of sexual to individual affectional relations—to love and stability. As our society has developed, the affectional bonds associated with sexual love have become one of its main values. Indeed with the weakening of religious institutions these bonds have acquired steadily more importance. Love is worshiped in numerous forms. There is, to be sure, a gap between the reality and the ideal, just as there is a gap between the reality of patriotism—or nationalism—and the ideal. But it would be silly to deny that patriotism plays an important role in our society—or that love, affection, and compassion do.

Pornography tends to erode these bonds, indeed, all bonds. By inviting us to reduce others and ourselves to purely physical beings, by inviting each of us to regard the other only as a means to physical gratification, with sensations, but without emotions, with contacts but without relations, pornography not only degrades us (and incidentally reduces sex to a valueless mechanical exercise),[3] but also erodes all human solidarity and tends to destroy all affectional bonds. This is a good enough reason to outlaw it.

There are additional reasons. One is very simply that the majority has a right to protect its tradition. The minority is entitled to argue for change. But not to impose it. Our tradition has been that sexual acts, sexual organs, and excretion are private rather than public. The majority is entitled to preserve this tradition by law where necessary just as the majority in India, offended by the slaughtering of cows which is contrary to Hindu tradition, can (and does) prohibit it.

Nobody is forced to see the dirty movie or to buy the pornographic magazine. Why then should the minority not be allowed to have them? But a public matter—anything for sale—can never be a wholly private matter. And once it is around legally one cannot really avoid the impact of pornography. One cannot avoid the display and the advertising which affect and pollute the atmosphere even if one does not enter or buy. Nor is it enough to prohibit the movie marquee or the display of the magazine. Anything legally for sale is the more profitable the more customers it attracts. Hence the purveyors of pornography have a strong interest in advertising and in spreading it, in persuading and in tempting the public. Prohibitions of advertising will be circumvented as long as the sale of pornography is lawful. Moreover, if the viewer of the pornographic movie is not warned by the marquee that he is about to see a dirty movie, he might very likely complain that he has been trapped into something that upsets him without being warned.

I should not prohibit anyone from reading or seeing whatever he wishes in his own home. He may be ill advised. But interfering with his home habits surely would be more ill advised. Of course if the stuff is not legally available the pornography fan will have difficulty getting it. But society has no obligation to make it easy. On the contrary, we can and should prohibit the marketing, the public sale of what we perceive as harmful to society even if we do not wish to invade homes to punish those who consume it.

NOTES

1. The First Amendment right to peacefully assemble may protect whatever is part of, or required for, peaceful assembly. It is hard to see that either nudity or swastikas are needed for that purpose.
2. Thus a prurient passage does not make a magazine or a book offensive unless, taken as a whole, the magazine or book dominantly appeals to the prurient interest.
3. As feminists have pointed out, pornography often degrades females more directly than males. But, in reducing themselves to a mere craving for physical gratification males degrade themselves as well.

Repeating Past Mistakes

The Commission on Obscenity and Pornography

Geoffrey R. Stone

[In 1986] the Attorney General's Commission on Pornography had a unique opportunity to redirect society's regulation of obscene expression. The current state of the law is marred by overly broad, ineffective, and wasteful regulation. This was an appropriate opportunity to take a fresh look at the problem and to strike a new balance—a balance that more precisely accommodates society's interests in regulation with the individual's often competing interests in privacy, autonomy, and free expression. The commission squandered this opportunity. Instead of taking a fresh look, it blindly performed its appointed task of renewing and reaffirming past mistakes.

The United States Supreme Court has held that federal, state, and local government officials have the power, consonant with the First Amendment, to prohibit all distribution of obscene expression. The mere existence of power, however, does not mean that its exercise is sound. The commission should have recommended that government officials exercise restraint. Specifically, the commission should have recommended the repeal of laws that criminalize the distribution of obscene expression to consenting adults.

The Supreme Court itself is sharply divided over the constitutional power of government officials to prohibit the distribution of obscene expression to consenting adults. In its 1973 decisions in *Miller v. California* and *Paris Adult Theatre v. Slaton*, the Court divided five-to-four on this issue. Justices Douglas, Brennan, Stewart, and Marshall concluded that the First Amendment strips government officials of any power to deny consenting adults the right to obtain obscene expression.

Even apart from the division of opinion in these cases, the Court's analysis of obscene expression is anomalous in terms of its overall First Amendment jurisprudence. At one time, obscene expression was merely one of several categories of expression held by the Supreme Court to be "of such slight social value as a step to truth that any benefit that may be derived from them is clearly outweighed by the social interest in order and morality." In the past quarter-century, the Court has increasingly recognized that such previously un-

Geoffrey R. Stone is Harry Kalven Jr. Professor of Law and former Provost, University of Chicago. Reprinted by permission of Transaction Publishers. "Repeating Past Mistakes," by Geoffrey R. Stone, *Society*, 24, July/August 1987, pp. 30–32. Copyright © 1987 by Transaction Publishers.

protected categories of expression as profanity, commercial advertising, incitement, and libel can no longer be regarded as wholly unprotected by the First Amendment. The Court has held that, although such categories of expression have only a "subordinate position in the scale of First Amendment values," they can nonetheless be restricted only if government has at least a substantial justification for the restriction. The Court has thus recognized that even low-value expression may have some First Amendment value, that government efforts to restrict low-value expression will often chill more valuable expression, and that the constitutional and institutional risks of restricting low-value expression are worth taking only if the restriction furthers at least a substantial governmental interest.

Obscene expression now stands alone. No other category of expression is currently regarded as wholly outside the protection of the First Amendment. No other category of expression may be suppressed merely because it has only "slight social value." No other category of expression may be censored without a showing that the restriction serves at least a substantial governmental interest. The current analysis of obscene expression is thus the sole remaining artifact of a now discarded jurisprudence.

The current analysis of obscenity is not necessarily wrong as a matter of constitutional law. Nevertheless, the constitutional authority to act in this context hangs by the slender thread of a single vote and is very much in doubt as a matter of constitutional principle. In such circumstances, government must exercise special care in deciding whether and how to exercise its power. We should not simply assume that because it is constitutional to act it is wise to do so. The very closeness of the constitutional question is itself a compelling reason for caution.

In deciding on the appropriate regulation of obscene expression, we must consider both the costs and benefits of regulation. Laws prohibiting the distribution of obscene expression to consenting adults impose at least three types of costs. First, although the Court has held that such expression has only low First Amendment value, it may nonetheless serve a useful function both for society and the individual. That the demand for sexually explicit expression is as great as it is, suggests that such expression serves an important psychological or emotional function for many individuals. It may satisfy a need for fantasy, escape, entertainment, stimulation, or whatever. Thus, whether or not obscene expression has significant First Amendment value, it may have important value to the individual. Laws prohibiting its distribution to consenting adults may frustrate significant interests in individual privacy, dignity, autonomy, and self-fulfillment.

The suppression of obscene expression may also have a severe chilling effect on more valuable expression. The legal concept of obscenity is vague in the extreme. As a consequence, individuals who wish to purchase or distribute sexually explicit expression will invariably censor themselves in order to avoid being ensnared in the ill-defined net of our obscenity laws. Laws prohibiting the distribution of obscene expression spill over and significantly limit the distribution of constitutionally protected expression as well.

Any serious effort to enforce laws prohibiting the distribution of obscene expression to consenting adults necessarily draws valuable police and prosecutorial

resources away from other areas of law enforcement. In a world of limited resources, we must recognize that the decision to criminalize one form of behavior
renders more difficult and less effective the enforcement of laws directed at other
forms of behavior. It is necessary to set priorities, for the failure to enforce our laws
vigorously can serve only to generate disrespect for law enforcement and bring
the legal system into disrepute.

Two interests are most commonly asserted in support of laws prohibiting
the distribution of obscene expression to consenting adults. First, it is said that
government must suppress the distribution of such expression to consenting
adults in order to prevent the erosion of moral standards. The moral fabric of a
society undoubtedly affects the tone and quality of life. It is thus a legitimate
subject of government concern; but as Justice Brennan recognized in his opinion in *Paris Adult Theatre,* "the State's interest in regulating morality by suppressing obscenity, while often asserted, remains essentially ill-focused and ill-
defined." It rests ultimately on "unprovable . . . assumptions about human
behavior, morality, sex, and religion." Perhaps more importantly, the notion
that government may censor expression because it may alter accepted moral
standards flies in the face of the guarantee of free expression. A democratic society must be free to determine its own moral standards through robust and
wide-open debate and expression. Although government may legitimately in-
culcate moral values through education and related activities, it may not suppress expression that reflects or encourages an opposing morality. Such pater-
nalism is incompatible with the most basic premises of the First Amendment.

Second, it is said that government must suppress the distribution of obscene
expression to consenting adults because exposure to such expression may
"cause" individuals to engage in unlawful conduct. The prevention of unlawful
conduct is a legitimate governmental interest, but the correlation between exposure to obscene expression and unlawful conduct is doubtful, at best. As the President's Commission on Obscenity and Pornography found in 1970, there is "no
evidence to date that exposure to explicit sexual materials plays a significant role
in the causation of delinquent or criminal behavior." The Attorney General's
Commission's contrary conclusion in 1986 is based more on preconception than
on evidence. An issue that has long divided social scientists and other experts in
the field can hardly be definitively resolved by a commission of nonexperts, most
of whom were appointed because of their preexisting commitment to the suppression of obscene expression. In any event, even those who claim a connection
between exposure to obscene expression and unlawful conduct claim no more
than an indirect and attenuated "bad tendency." Thus, although some individuals may on some occasions commit some unlawful acts "because of" their exposure to obscene expression, the connection is indirect, speculative, and unpre-
dictable. It is not even remotely comparable to the much more direct harm caused
by such products as firearms, alcohol, and automobiles. The suppression of obscene expression is also a stunningly inefficient and overly broad way to deal
with this problem, for even a modest change in law enforcement or sentencing
practices would have a much more direct and substantial impact on the rate of
unlawful conduct than the legalization or criminalization of obscene expression.

Laws prohibiting the distribution of obscene expression to consenting adults impose significant costs on society and frustrate potentially important privacy and autonomy interests of the individual for only marginal benefits. It is time to bring our regulation of such expression into line with our constitutional traditions, our law enforcement priorities, and our own self-interest and common sense.

The course I propose, and which the commission emphatically rejected, would leave government free to direct its enforcement energies at the more important concerns generated by obscene expression. These fall into three related categories: the protection of juveniles, the protection of captive viewers, and the regulation of the secondary effects of obscene expression. The Court has long recognized government's interest in sheltering children from exposure to obscene expression. What I propose does not undermine this interest. Nor does it interfere with society's substantial interest in restricting child pornography, which poses significantly different issues. My proposal would not in any way prevent government from protecting individuals against the shock effect of unwanted exposure to obscene expression. Government would remain free to prohibit children from viewing movies or buying books found "obscene," and it would remain free to prohibit or otherwise regulate the exhibition of obscene expression over the airwaves. Sensible accommodations can also be devised for other media, such as cable television. Also, my proposal would not prevent government from using zoning and other regulatory devices to control the distribution of obscene expression in order to prevent the decay of neighborhoods or other secondary effects associated with the availability of obscene expression.

By leaving consenting adults free to obtain obscene expression at their discretion, and by protecting our important interests through narrowly defined regulations, we can strike a sensible balance, protecting important societal interests while at the same time preserving our traditional respect for free expression and for the privacy and autonomy of the individual.

The commission has opted to do otherwise and repeat past mistakes—with a vengeance. It has recommended, among other things, significant changes in state and federal legislation to enable more vigorous enforcement of antiobscenity laws; creation of a special Obscenity Task Force in the office of the attorney general to coordinate the prosecution of obscenity cases at the national level; allocation of additional resources at the federal, state, and local levels for the prosecution of obscenity cases; "aggressive" Internal Revenue Service investigation of the "producers and distributors of obscene materials"; and imposition of "substantial periods of incarceration" for violators of anti-obscenity laws. This draconian approach is wasteful, misguided, and inconsistent with the real concerns of most of our citizens.

Internet Resources
Visit our website at http://www.mhhe.com/diclerico for links and resources relating to Civil Liberties.

Criminal Rights

Courts have a special role to play in our society. Unlike the two political branches of our government—Congress and the Executive—which are most sensitive to majority public opinion, courts must protect and defend minorities. Indeed, courts most often are called upon to ensure that the government acts in a fair and reasonable manner and to make certain that individual rights are protected.

Courts have a particularly important role to play in the protection of criminal rights, for in this area they must see that no injustice is done to the person accused of a crime. In the last thirty years, the U.S. Supreme Court has taken great care in enforcing the constitutional rights of persons accused of a crime. These include such protections as the right to remain silent and the right to counsel. Some of these criminal procedural safeguards have evoked considerable controversy among law-enforcement officials, political leaders, commentators, and the general public. Typically, critics of the criminal justice system point to its failures—failures that either put criminals back on the streets or penalize innocent and unsuspecting people.

The two articles that follow examine the role of the courts in the criminal justice system. In the first article, journalist Bernard Gavzer reports on the views of New York State judge Harold Rothwax, an outspoken critic of today's criminal justice system and author of Guilty: The Collapse of Criminal Justice. According to Judge Rothwax, the criminal justice system, with all its procedural guarantees, is tilted too much in favor of criminal suspects, so much so that he believes "We're in the fight of our lives" to preserve a law-abiding society.

In the second article John Kilwein, a professor of political science at West Virginia University, challenges the views of Judge Rothwax. While conceding that crime continues to be a major problem in the United States, Professor Kilwein argues that it would be unwise to adopt Judge Rothwax's "reforms" of the criminal justice system. Kilwein contends that the real issue in the criminal justice system is whether all citizens are fully protected from the possible abuses and excesses of law-enforcement officials. The many procedural guarantees of the Constitution and the courts, he argues, are merely the means to assure a "fair fight" between a criminal defendant and a criminal justice system that is stacked heavily in favor of the government. Without these guarantees, he contends, there exists the very real possibility that innocent persons might be accused, tried, convicted, and punished without adequate protection of the law.

"We're in the Fight of Our Lives"
Bernard Gavzer

At 2 A.M. on November 20, 1990, Leonardo Turriago was pulled over for speeding by two state troopers. They asked if they could look into his van, and Turriago said they could. Inside, the troopers saw a trunk and asked Turriago about it. He sprang open its lock, then ran away. Opening the trunk, the troopers found the body of a man shot five times.

Turriago was quickly caught. In his apartment, police found 11 pounds of cocaine and guns. The suspect told them where to look for the murder weapon, and it was recovered. Turriago was convicted of second-degree murder and sentenced to 45 years to life.

The defense appealed, saying the troopers had no right to search the van. On June 6, 1996, Turriago's conviction was overturned. A New York appellate court ruled that the police search was not justified and had been coerced.

"Criminal justice in America is in a state of collapse," says Judge Harold J. Rothwax, who has spent 25 years presiding over criminal cases in New York City. "We have formalism and technicalities but little common sense. It's about time America wakes up to the fact that we're in the fight of our lives."

Rothwax believes cases such as Turriago's illustrate that the procedural dotting of every "i" and crossing of every "t" has become more important than the crime's substance. "The bottom line is that criminals are going free," he says. "There is no respect for the truth, and without truth, there can be no justice."

While the search for truth should be the guiding principle of our courts, instead, the judge says, "our system is a carefully crafted maze, constructed of elaborate and impenetrable barriers to the truth." . . .

Practices we have taken for granted—such as the *Miranda* warning, the right to counsel, even unanimous jury verdicts—need to be reconsidered, says the judge. "You know," Rothwax confides, "more than 80 percent of the people who appear before me are probably guilty of some crime."

Rothwax insists there is a fundamental difference between the investigative and the trial stages of a case. The investigative stage is marked by the notion of probable guilt, he asserts, not the presumption of innocence. "Until a defendant goes on trial, he is probably guilty," the judge says, noting that by the time a person reaches trial he has been deemed "probably guilty" several times. "When a person is arrested, indicted by a grand jury, held in detention or released on bail, it is all based on probable guilt." Rothwax adds, "Once *on trial*, he is presumed innocent." . . .

The positions the judge has staked out in what he regards as his crusade to bring sense to the criminal justice system have shocked those who long associated him with strong liberal causes. A lifelong Democrat, Rothwax was a senior defense trial attorney for the Legal Aid Society in New York and a stalwart of the New York Civil Liberties Union early in his career.

"I represented Lenny Bruce and Abbie Hoffman, the Black Panthers and the Vietnam war protesters," he says, "I am today as much a civil libertarian as ever. But that does not mean I must close my eyes to the devastation that has occurred in criminal justice. We have the crime, but where is the justice? It is all tilted in favor of the criminal, and it is time to bring this into balance."

The interests of the victim weigh solidly in Rothwax's courtroom in the Criminal Court Building in Manhattan. However, he is troubled by some decisions of the U.S. Supreme Court, saying: "Its rulings over the last 35 years have made the criminal justice system incomprehensible and unworkable."

Although neither the Supreme Court nor the Courts of Appeals decide the guilt or innocence of a defendant, they do make rulings on the constitutionality of acts by the police and lower courts and thus have a significant impact on our justice system. Key practices of our current system—which have come about as a result of Supreme Court rulings in recent decades—need to be changed, Rothwax believes. Among them are:

The Miranda Warning.   In New York, Alfio Ferro was arrested in 1975 in connection with a fur robbery that turned into a murder. In the lockup, a detective—without saying a word—dropped some of the stolen furs in front of Ferro's cell. Ferro then made incriminating statements that led to his conviction for second-degree murder.

In 1984, an appellate court overturned the conviction, saying that the detective's action amounted to interrogation and violated Ferro's *Miranda* rights. The *Miranda* warning requires that the suspect be told he has a right to remain silent, that any statement he makes might be used against him and that he has the right to have a lawyer present.

"*Miranda* came about because of abuses such as prolonged custodial interrogation, beatings and starving in order to get a confession," says Rothwax. "I think those abuses have been largely dealt with. Now the police officer is put in the position of telling a suspect in a murder or rape, 'Look, you don't have to tell us anything, and that may be the best thing for you.' And it produces a situation in which a proper confession is thrown out because of the way in which it was read or that it wasn't read at the right time."

Rothwax believes *Miranda* can be replaced by the recording of an arrest and interrogation through videotapes, tape recorders and other technology. This would probably show whether a confession or statement was coerced.

The Exclusionary Rule.   [In the winter of 1996] Federal Judge Harold Baer Jr. refused to admit as evidence 80 pounds of cocaine and heroin obtained in the arrest of a drug courier in the Washington Heights neighborhood of New York City. The evidence was excluded because, said Baer, the police had violated the Fourth Amendment protection against unreasonable search and seizure when they searched the car in which the drugs were found.

The police said their search was proper in view of the fact that they saw men hastily loading bags into an out-of-state car in a high drug area in the middle of the night, and the men ran away when the police approached. Judge Baer, however, said just because the men ran off was no reason to suspect them of a crime. In Washington Heights, the judge said, it was not unusual for even innocent people to flee, because police there were regarded as "corrupt, violent and abusive."

Under a growing chorus of criticism, Judge Baer first reversed himself and then asked that the case be assigned to another judge. It was. Rothwax says this is the sort of muddled episode which arises from the exclusionary rule, producing "truth and justice denied on a technicality."

"The Supreme Court has consistently ruled that evidence seized in violation of the Fourth Amendment *should* be excluded from a criminal trial. But if you read the Fourth Amendment, nowhere does it say that *illegally* obtained evidence *must* be excluded," says Rothwax. "In my view, when you exclude or suppress evidence, you suppress the truth."

Judge Rothwax has a remedy: "Make the exclusionary rule *discretionary* instead of mandatory. If it was at the discretion of the judge, there could be a test of reasonableness. A judge could consider factors such as whether a police officer acted with objective reasonableness and subjective good faith. As it is now, the exclusionary rule is irrational, arbitrary and lacks proportion. No wonder that in 90 percent of exclusionary cases, the police don't know what the law is."

The Right to Counsel.   In 1982, Kenneth West of New York, an alleged drug dealer, was suspected of being involved in killing a man who had taken his parking place. His lawyer, at a police lineup, told the police not to question West in his absence. Nothing came of the case for three years. Then police arrested a former cohort of West who said West had been one of the shooters. The informer secretly taped West talking about the killing. West was convicted, but in 1993 the New York Court of Appeals reversed the conviction, saying the secret taping amounted to questioning him without the presence of counsel.

The right to counsel is provided by the Sixth Amendment. "It is essential there be a right to counsel," Judge Rothwax says. "But the amendment doesn't say it has to be during police questioning and investigation. As a result of technicalities over this issue of counsel, I have seen murderers go free. Make it clear that the right to a lawyer shouldn't be a factor in the *investigative* stage but only in pre-trial and trial stages."

Instructions to the Jury.   After closing arguments in the O. J. Simpson murder trial, Judge Ito took great care in telling jurors that Simpson's failure to take the stand in his own defense should in no way be taken to mean anything negative or to draw any other adverse conclusion.

This instruction to the jury occurs in all cases in which the defense asks for it, because of a Supreme Court ruling in 1981 that said not to do so amounted to a violation of the Fifth Amendment. [The Fifth Amendment states that no person shall be forced to testify against himself.] "The Fifth Amendment does *not* say that one might not draw reasonable inferences from the silence of a defendant," Judge Rothwax says. "I think we must find a way to return to the standard that existed before, that the judge could tell the jury that the failure to explain could amount to an inability to explain."

The judge would like to see other changes made to the jury system. Among them:

1. *Unanimous jury verdicts should no longer be required.* Why? Rothwax cites a murder case he presided over. "It was an overwhelming case of clear guilt. Yet there was a hung jury. One juror was convinced the defendant was not guilty. How did she know? Well, as she explained it, 'Someone that good-looking could not commit such a crime.' We had to retry the case, and the man was quickly found guilty."

   By allowing verdicts to be decided by a vote of 11–1 or 10–2, Rothwax says, there could be a reduced risk that a single juror could cause a retrial or force a compromise in the face of overwhelming evidence of guilt.

2. *Peremptory challenges to prospective jurors should be strictly limited or abolished.* Peremptory challenges allow lawyers to knock someone off the jury without giving any reason. "As we saw in the Simpson case," Rothwax says, "it makes it possible to stack a jury so that the most educated juror is excused, and you end up with a jury that can be manipulated to accept innuendo as evidence."

Judge Rothwax regards the entire conduct of the Simpson trial as an unspeakable insult to the American people, one that left them "feeling wounded and deeply distrustful of the system." He adds: "There was an opportunity to show a vast audience the potential vitality of justice at work. Instead we are assaulted by an obscene circus. We saw proof that the American courtroom is dangerously out of order." . . .

To sit with Rothwax in court, as this writer did, is to get a sense of his urgency for reform. In three hours, there was a procession of men and women charged with felonies from murder to drug dealing. Rothwax was all business, and he was tough with everyone. After 47 cases had been considered and dealt with, the judge turned to me and asked, with irony, about the defendants we had seen: "Did you notice the huge display of remorse?" There hadn't been any. "That's why" he said, "we are in the fight of our lives."

Just Make It a Fair Fight

John C. Kilwein

Crime is a significant problem in this country. In 2000, 15,517 Americans became victims of homicide.[1] Property loss and medical expenses related to crime approach $20 billion per year. Responding to these and other troubling statistics, Congress has "federalized" dozens of crimes that were formerly only state offenses, and state legislatures have passed mandatory-minimum sentence laws that require convicted criminals to spend more time in prison. The U.S. Bureau of Justice Statistics reports that as a result of these changes the number of people incarcerated in federal and state prisons more than quadrupled, increasing from 319,600 in 1980 to 1,406,031 in 2001. In addition, Congress has made it much more difficult for prisoners to use the federal courts, the Constitution, and writ of *habeas corpus* to appeal their convictions. All of this is evidence of a concerted national effort, some might argue excessive effort, to deal with the crime problem.

But efforts such as these are not enough for New York Judge Harold Rothwax. He wants to shock us into taking action in the criminal courts, and in so doing he uses arguments that are based on fear.[2] Judge Rothwax warns Americans, as they read their Sunday papers, of the ominous threats of such dark predators as Leonardo Turriago, who cart murder victims around in the trunks of their automobiles, and who walk the streets thanks to legal "technicalities." But as Judge Rothwax spins his frightening yarn, he fails to tell the reader that the crime rate is actually dropping, in spite of the alleged flaws of the criminal justice system. Violent crime, for example, dropped 10 percent in 2000–2001. Why the paradox?: A *reduction* in crime, while Judge Rothwax thinks we are in "the fight of our lives!"

Judge Rothwax offers us a new system of criminal justice that assumes that all police officers and prosecutors do their jobs in a fair and objective manner, free of any systematic bias against groups or individuals in society. The Rothwax system assumes that prosecutors will base their prosecutorial decisions strictly on legal grounds, ignoring other factors such as political gain or racial animus. Judge Rothwax believes that as a society we have largely solved the problem of police brutality; that American law enforcement officials no longer use uncomfortable detention, physical violence, or psychological coercion to secure convictions. The Rothwax system assumes that criminal defendants in

John C. Kilwein is a professor of political science at West Virginia University. He wrote this article especially for *Points of View* in 1997 and revised it in 2000 and again in 2003.

the United States have more legal representation than they deserve, and that the system would benefit from reducing the formal rules that lawyers bring to the pre-trial process. Unfortunately, the real world of American criminal justice is far more complex than the "good vs. evil" morality play suggested by Judge Rothwax.

THE GOVERNMENT VS. THE CRIMINAL DEFENDANT: A FAIR FIGHT?

The legal system in the United States is based on the belief that the best way for a court to discover the truth in a legal dispute is to allow the parties to battle it out in the courtroom before a jury or judge. The judge acts as an independent and objective arbiter or referee who makes sure that the disputants battle fairly by following the rules of law. The disputants are responsible for developing the case they will bring into the courtroom, and they understandably have a strong incentive to seek out any evidence or witnesses that might assist them. The disputants also have the right to challenge the veracity of their opponents' presentations. The confrontation in court between these two competing sides, each presenting a very different version of a contested dispute, will, in theory, maximize the likelihood that the truth will come out.[3] Of course, the difficult job for the judge or the jury is sifting through the two accounts to arrive at a sense of what actually took place and what justice should be.

When applied to disputes involving a crime, the disputants in the adversarial system are the defendant, or the person charged with committing the crime, and the state. The state, rather than the victim, is the litigant in criminal cases because, by definition, crimes not only harm victims, they also harm and threaten society as a whole. In a criminal case, therefore, the battle to be played out in the courtroom is between a person charged with a crime and a prosecutor who represents the interests of society—a battle that strains the notion of a fair fight. The government clearly has a lot more advantages than the criminal defendant. The extent of this mismatch is underscored by the fact that prosecutors have available to them the machinery of government, including the vast investigative powers of law enforcement, whereas defendants must do it on their own.

The American justice system takes into account this disparity, however, by providing the defendant with certain procedural rights and advantages that are intended to equalize the courtroom battle in criminal cases. This system assumes that when a powerful litigant, the state, faces a weaker litigant, the defendant, there is a high probability of a wrongful conviction of an innocent person unless the state follows procedures designed to make it a fair fight. And in our criminal legal tradition, there is no greater miscarriage of justice than sending innocent individuals to prison or to their death. Modern-day criminal procedure protections seek to prevent such an outcome.

Among the equalizers built into the American legal system are the presumption of innocence, the beyond-a-reasonable-doubt standard of proof; the prohibitions against unreasonable search and seizure, forced self-incrimination, excessive bail, excessive fines, double jeopardy, and cruel and unusual punishment; and the right to counsel, to a trial by jury, to a public and speedy trial, to speak at trial, to confront and cross-examine hostile witnesses, to present favorable witnesses, and to access the writ of *habeas corpus*. Some of these "equalizers" have been incorporated into our system as part of formal documents, or constitutions, that act as the blueprints for our American governments, while others were added as our criminal justice system evolved and became part of our legal tradition.

For Judge Rothwax the balance between the state and the criminally accused is fundamentally flawed. Criminal defendants are not the "weak sisters" in a criminal trial; the state is. For Judge Rothwax, a "liberal" judiciary led by the U.S. Supreme Court has conspired to create new and extreme rights for the defendant. These extravagant rights, moreover, make it extremely difficult for the prosecutor and the police to do their jobs. Seemingly guilty defendants are released from custody because their defense lawyers exploited some constitutional technicality. The murder trial of O. J. Simpson is given as a case in point. Overworked, underpaid, and inept prosecutors fumbled before a group of highly paid "dream team" defense lawyers, who exploited every procedural technicality to achieve a verdict of innocence.

Judge Rothwax offers up an alternative system of criminal justice that tips the balance in the courtroom battle toward the side of the prosecution by limiting a defendant's right to counsel, altering the presumption of innocence, increasing the power of police to search for proof of criminality and to interrogate defendants, allowing more evidence favoring the prosecution's case to be admitted in court, and altering the nature of jury deliberations in criminal trials. In short, the Rothwax system makes it easier for the prosecution to prove to a jury that a criminal defendant is guilty as charged and deserving of punishment.

THE "SUSPECT RIGHTS" OF SUSPECTS

The Presumption of Innocence

Our legal system recognizes that a criminal dispute is more serious than a civil dispute. In criminal law, society has the capacity to publicly punish the convicted criminal, using several forms of punishment. First, the defendant faces the shame and consequences associated with being declared a convicted criminal, including the loss of certain freedoms and rights, as for example, access to a variety of licenses or the freedom to perform certain jobs. Second, criminal conviction can bring with it the possibility of substantial monetary fines, often in the thousands of dollars. Third, criminal conviction can result in a complete loss of freedom through incarceration, with all the unintended consequences of life behind bars, a violent world often filled with physical assault, rape, and other indignities. Finally, in thirty-eight states and at the federal level, defendants charged with capital crimes face the ultimate punishment of being put to death by the state.

Given the seriousness of being charged with a crime, the American legal system confers on the defendant an important protection: the presumption of innocence. The primary purpose of this rule is to prevent a wrongful conviction that sends an innocent person to prison or to death. There is a simple, yet profound logic behind this rule. When a criminal victimizes an individual, society intervenes to find, try, and punish the criminal. The harm suffered by the victim can never be undone, but some solace comes from the fact that the state takes a direct interest in resolving the criminal dispute. On the other hand, when the state wrongfully punishes an innocent defendant, the victimization is absolute. There is no solace available to the innocent person since the perpetrator is the state. This perspective gives rise to the old saw that it is better to let ten guilty persons go free, than to send one innocent individual to prison or death. For Judge Rothwax, however, that old saw is apparently a bit rusty and should be replaced by a new motto: The criminal justice system almost never convicts the wrong person; and those guilty individuals who are set free are threatening us all.

Judge Rothwax makes a distinction between the investigative (pre-trial) and trial stages of the criminal process. Rothwax argues that, during the investigative stage, defendants are assumed to be guilty by the police and the prosecutor or they would not have been arrested and indicted in the first place. He concludes that when defendants appear before his bench, they are probably guilty of the charges or their cases would never have reached his court. In short, Judge Rothwax gives the state the benefit of the doubt that it only prosecutes clearly guilty people. This perspective is troubling because it ignores the basic idea behind adversarial justice: Legal conflicts are not pre-judged but decided through the courtroom battle.

While it is true that the great majority of police officers and prosecutors are honest people who play by the rules and who have no desire to harm innocent people, Rothwax's position ignores a number of very real problems. The most obvious problem of the proposed system is that it fails to take into account that justice officials can and do make mistakes, and the importance of the trial process in detecting these honest errors. Second, Judge Rothwax ignores the fact that a minority of justice officials, however small, are lazy, dishonest, corrupt, racist, or some combination of these. Examples of these troubling behaviors abound in our criminal justice system. In 2003, the Republican governor of Illinois, George Ryan, took the unprecedented action of commuting the death sentences of all men and women on death row, 167 prisoners, to life imprisonment. Governor Ryan based his decision on his research into the machinery of Illinois' capital justice system, which left him with serious questions about its inherent fairness.[4] Ryan cited misconduct by prosecutors and police officers as factors that can lead to unjust capital sentences. A year earlier in Los Angeles, police officers admitted to systematically committing crimes to convict innocent individuals.[5] The Los Angeles District Attorney's Office took the unprecedented action of seeking the reversal of forty felony convictions, because it had clear evidence that those convictions were based on the false testimony of the errant officers.

In 1997, an internal U.S. Department of Justice investigation revealed that agents of the highly respected F.B.I. crime laboratory altered evidence and skewed testimony to assist prosecutors.[6] In Texas and West Virginia false testimony given by an incompetent and dishonest medical examiner sent at least six innocent men to prison.[7] To avoid the embarrassment and political fallout of being unable to convict the perpetrators of an arson fire with multiple deaths in New York[8] and the killing of a police officer in Houston,[9] prosecutors in both cities tenaciously pursued capital murder charges against apparently innocent individuals, while ignoring or concealing exculpatory evidence in the prosecution's possession. And evidence that some police officers and prosecutors target young black and Hispanic men for questionable arrest and prosecution comes to light with alarming clarity, as in the case of Carlton Brown.[10]

The case of Carlton Brown is particularly enlightening. Mr. Brown, who is black, is paralyzed from the chest down following injuries he sustained while under arrest in New York City's 63rd Precinct. Charged with driving with a suspended license, Mr. Brown contended that the arresting officers, after becoming irritated with his demands for information on his arrest, smashed his head, while he was handcuffed, into a bulletproof, double-plate glass window and severely injured his spine. The two police officers involved with his arrest countered that Mr. Brown had hurt himself falling down in the police station. The police officers were charged, tried before a judge, and acquitted. In a subsequent civil proceeding, however, the city of New York agreed to pay Mr. Brown $4.5 million in civil damages, a record-setting pre-trial settlement. Needless to say, such a settlement calls into question Judge Rothwax's confidence in the criminal justice system's ability to function in an unbiased manner. Our system of justice assumes that people, including law enforcement officials, are not angels[11] or saints; nor are they infallible; and it builds in protections, like the presumption of innocence, accordingly. The Rothwax system depends on an angelic conversion among these officials, an unlikely occurrence now or ever.

Miranda, the Right to Remain Silent and the Right to Counsel

Judge Rothwax reserves some of his harshest criticism for the U.S. Supreme Court's 1966 decision in *Miranda v. Arizona*.[12] In that decision the Court ruled that a confession made by Ernest Miranda, who was charged with kidnapping and raping an eighteen-year-old woman, was unconstitutionally obtained by police interrogators.[13] Extending its ruling beyond the immediate circumstances of the arrest and interrogation of Miranda, the Court required that henceforth all police officers and prosecutors must inform defendants of their rights to remain silent and to have counsel.[14] Commenting on state law enforcement officials, the Court observed,

> The use of physical brutality and violence is not, unfortunately, relegated to the past or to any part of the country. Only recently in Kings County [Brooklyn Borough], New York, the police brutally beat, kicked and placed lighted cigarette butts on the back of a potential witness under interrogation for the purpose of securing a statement incriminating a third party.[15]

The Court added that, although not using physical violence, other police interrogators use psychological abuse and lies to trick defendants into confessing to crimes.

Seen as an indictment against all police officers and prosecutors, the decision in *Miranda* was, and, as highlighted by Judge Rothwax, still is very unpopular within the law enforcement community.[16] This is unfortunate because, as Chief Justice Warren argued in the opinion, the *Miranda* requirements do not prevent good law enforcement officers from doing their job. Indeed, as pointed out by Warren, agents of the F.B.I. had already been using the warnings and were still able to investigate and assist in the conviction of federal defendants. What the warnings were designed to do was prevent an innocent defendant from confessing in order to bring an end to an abusive interrogation. The fact of the matter is that police officers who do not abuse defendants have nothing to fear from the *Miranda* requirements.

The *Miranda* decision also sought to make effective two important equalizers in the Bill of Rights: the prohibition against self-incrimination and the right to counsel. The right against self-incrimination, or the right to remain silent, is based on an old common law principle that the state cannot force defendants to testify against themselves. Rather, the state makes the charges and must prove its case. Although the right to counsel came later in the Anglo-American legal tradition, it is based on the belief that it is unreasonable to expect ordinary persons to understand the legal implications of statements they might make or actions they might take in the pre-trial stage, actions that might again lead to their wrongful conviction. The *Miranda* requirement was based on the reasonable assumption that illiterate or uninformed defendants probably are not aware of these protections and therefore the state has a responsibility to inform them.

Judge Rothwax argues against this necessity, contending that, because defense attorneys step in and convince their clients to do otherwise, *Miranda* prevents the police from securing confessions from cooperative defendants. Apparently Judge Rothwax is opposed to the general principle of informed consent; that is, that defendants should know what they are doing before they say anything or confess. Judge Rothwax also seems to believe that the abuse of defendants while in police custody, cited by Chief Justice Warren in *Miranda*, is no longer a problem. Unfortunately, evidence suggests that, in his zeal to get tougher on crime and criminals, Judge Rothwax is ignoring the fact that abuses continue in the interrogation stage of the pre-trial process. An example from Rothwax's own hometown underscores this conclusion.[17] Police officers in New York's 24th Precinct arrested a seventeen-year-old white male for a misdemeanor. He refused to confess. The defendant was held in a jail cell for two nights. At one point, he was placed in a van and chained in the sweltering heat. At another point a police officer waved his gun in front of the defendant and threatened to "shoot his dick off." One wonders if the cameras in the precinct, called for by Judge Rothwax to protect against such abuse, would have captured this particular "Kodak moment"! The evidence suggests that this incident is not a random occurrence, in New York or nationally. Amnesty International has cited ninety cases of police brutality allegedly perpetrated by officers of the New York Police Department alone. Similar charges by other watchdog groups have been leveled at other departments around the country.[18]

Sometimes law enforcement officers use less violent forms of coercion in the interrogation room. For example, in 1999, F.B.I. agents lied to Wen Ho Lee, a Department of Energy employee suspected of spying for China, by informing him that he had failed a lie detector test, when, in fact, he had registered a score indicating he was telling the truth.[19] Building on this lie, the agents then told Mr. Lee that if he did not provide them with a confession, he would likely die in the electric chair.

For most first-time defendants the pre-trial process can be a very frightening experience. Defendants, innocent or guilty, who cannot post bail are held in jail until their trial. The pace of some criminal justice systems can be glacial, taking up to two years for a case to make it to trial. This delay, moreover, can be used to entice or coerce a defendant into making a confession, even a false one. For example, a prosecutor can offer defendants awaiting trial a plea bargain that gives them credit for time served while awaiting trial in exchange for a guilty plea. Given this offer, an innocent defendant might make a false confession, assuming that the conviction is a small price to pay for immediate release from prison.[20] The deal may be especially appealing if the defendant considers that a guilty verdict by jury at trial could yield an even stiffer sentence. Interrogations are also daunting for a defendant unfamiliar with the law. And although the great majority of questionings are conducted by professional officers observing all relevant constitutional requirements, the fact remains that police officers have substantially more experience in the process than do defendants, thereby increasing the probability that defendants will unwittingly damage their own case. In these and every other pre-trial situation, defendants would be at a severe disadvantage without legal representation.

In the end, the Rothwax system would punish the ignorant, the weak, and the poor. Wealthy or more highly educated defendants, who have a basic understanding of the legal system, are more likely to know they have the right to remain silent and to make informed choices about its use. Likewise, sophisticated defendants who are not intimidated by pre-trial detention and rough treatment are also more likely to refuse to assist the police in developing the state's case against them. Moreover, defendants with long-standing criminal records are also likely to be especially cognizant of their right to remain silent. In addition, multiple offenders who have experienced the daily violence of the corrections system are probably less likely to be frightened into confessing as the result of a difficult interrogation.

The most troubling aspect of Rothwax's system, however, from the point of view of equal justice for all, is that it rewards wealthier criminal defendants. Individuals who can afford to hire a lawyer and post bail are able to avoid the various forms of pre-trial pressure since they can await trial in the comfort of their own homes; and, with the advice of counsel, they are more likely to remain silent, thereby putting the government to its full task of convicting them without their assistance. It is quite possible, therefore, that the system proposed by Judge Rothwax will have the unintended consequence of convicting more innocent, first-time criminal defendants, while releasing those defendants with experience and/or money. These potential biases do not seem to concern Judge Rothwax. Like some American generals in Vietnam, Judge Rothwax seems to be singularly concerned only with body counts: So what if these new convictions are gained at the expense of fairness? They're convictions; and that's what counts! A justice system that operates in this manner has abandoned any pretense of being blind to a defendant's wealth or social status. It is a justice system more likely to convict an innocent defendant whose real crime is that he or she lives in the South Bronx rather than on Long Island.

The Exclusionary Rule

The exclusionary rule is an American invention, created by the U.S. Supreme Court in 1914.[21] It was designed to resolve the question of what should be done when a police officer or prosecutor violates the constitutional protections of defendants who have been the targets of illegal searches or interrogations. By making this ruling, the Supreme Court, using a classic American "free-market" approach, has ruled that such evidence is tainted and must therefore be excluded from trial. The exclusionary rule, the Court has argued, removes any incentive for law enforcement officials to engage in unconstitutional and illegal activities, since ill-gotten gains cannot be used in court.

Since the Bill of Rights makes no mention of this rule in the Fourth Amendment's prohibition against unreasonable searches and seizures, Judge Rothwax contends that the rule is an illegitimate hindrance to the criminal justice system's operation. He argues that excluded evidence prevents the court from getting the total truth surrounding a case. To accept this logic, however, one must, again, accept, as Rothwax clearly does, that in the rule's absence, police officers or prosecutors are unlikely to violate the Fourth or Fifth Amendments in their search for evidence or confessions. Given the examples of illegal police conduct cited, it is difficult to share Justice Rothwax's views of the motives and actions of the police.

Judge Rothwax is also upset because the exclusionary rule has, in his view, been used by judges in an overly technical and picky manner, with good cases being thrown out because investigating officers forgot to "dot the i's and cross the t's." He blames the "liberal" U.S. Supreme Court for decisions that favor criminal defendants. The Supreme Court of 2003, however, is, in fact, a very conservative one, particularly in its decisions dealing with the rights of criminal defendants. Since the mid-1970s, the U.S. Supreme Court has consistently shifted the constitutional advantage in criminal matters away from criminal defendants toward the police and prosecution. Specifically, in terms of the exclusionary rule, the Court has ruled in ways that enable prosecutors to use more questionable evidence and confessions against criminal defendants. Two examples highlight this shift. In *U.S. v. Havens*,[22] the Court allowed illegally obtained evidence to be used in trial to discredit testimony during cross-examination. And in *Nix v. Williams*,[23] the Court ruled that tainted evidence can be used against the defendant if the trial court judge concludes that evidence would inevitably have been discovered. Still, this very pro-police U.S. Supreme Court drew the line by refusing to overturn Miranda when given the opportunity in *Dickerson v. U.S.*[24]

Peremptory Challenges and Unanimous Jury Verdicts

Judge Rothwax's remaining indictments of the present criminal justice system deal with criminal juries. Responding to the controversy surrounding the O. J. Simpson murder trial, he criticizes the defense team's use of peremptory challenges to eliminate prospective jurors.[25] He argues that the Simpson defense team used such challenges to seat a jury that could easily be fooled by courtroom pyrotechnics. Whether this is true or not is a matter of conjecture, but it should be noted that Judge Rothwax ignores the fact that the prosecution had the same opportunity to affect the makeup of the jury. In reality, peremptory challenges help both sides in the courtroom battle, and thus we can assume that their removal would potentially hurt both sides as well. In 1997, for example, a videotape surfaced that was used as a training device for assistant prosecutors in Philadelphia.[26] The tape shows a senior prosecutor counseling his trainees to exclude black citizens from serving on criminal juries because they are distrustful of the police and therefore less likely to convict. The tape tells the trainees they should especially avoid placing young black women on their juries, because they are very bad for the prosecution's case. Although this episode remains to be investigated, and the attorney featured in the video vehemently denies having done anything illegal or morally wrong, the advice presented on this tape would appear to violate a Supreme Court ruling prohibiting race from being used as a factor in selecting jurors. More fundamentally, this example calls into question Judge Rothwax's contention that the justice system has solved the problem of systemic racism.

Judge Rothwax also opposes the requirement that a criminal jury reach a verdict of guilt unanimously, suggesting instead that we should allow a jury to convict a defendant with a substantial majority, such as a vote of 11–1 or 10–2. In fact, the practice of jury unanimity[27] is merely a legal custom and not an explicit constitutional right, and the U.S. Supreme Court has established that, if states choose, they can allow juries to reach their decision with a clear, nonunanimous verdict.[28] Given the Supreme Court's view on this issue, Judge Rothwax's gripe, then, is with the legal system of the state of New York, which apparently has decided to continue the practice of jury unanimity, and not with the rulings of the so-called "liberal" U.S. Supreme Court in Washington.

WE FACE THE CHOICE OF OUR LIVES

The late Senator Sam Ervin once said, "In a free society you have to take some risks. If you lock everybody up, or even if you lock up everybody you think might commit a crime, you'll be pretty safe, but you won't be free."[29] To this one might add, "And you might end up getting locked up yourself!"

This country was shaped in part by a healthy concern for the potential abuses of governments. The U.S. Bill of Rights and the civil liberty protections of the state constitutions were created to ensure certain fundamental protections for all citizens. These guarantees were designed to withstand the shifting winds created by agitated majorities. Judge Rothwax is not the first American, nor will he likely be the last, to tell his fellow citizens that we live in a particularly dangerous time and that to survive we must forgo the "luxury" of our civil liberties.

Judge Rothwax is wrong. The guarantees created by James Madison and the Constitution are not luxuries. Rather, they make up a very battered constitutional firewall that barely protects us from the police state that he, cynical politicians, and a very conservative U.S. Supreme Court seem to be inching toward. These civil liberties are not excessive; if anything, they provide too little protection for the realities of daily life in an increasingly urban, multicultural society facing the twenty-first century.

Of course, many Americans share Judge Rothwax's concern over criminal predators like Leonardo Turriago who prey on their fellow citizens. These violent criminals should be punished severely. But the same level of concern ought to be expressed in regard to how today's criminal justice system treats black, Hispanic, American Indian, poor, and uneducated Americans. Americans ought to be concerned about the rights of innocent, hardworking Americans who are harassed, injured, maimed, or killed every day by abusive police officers for being in the "wrong" neighborhood or driving too "nice" a car. Judge Rothwax's system will not win the war against the Leonardo Turriagos of the world; it will likely create more Carlton Browns.

NOTES

1. Federal Bureau of Investigation, *Uniform Crime Report*, 2000.
2. Bernard Gavzer, "We're in the Fight of Our Lives." *Parade* (July 28, 1996): 4–6.
3. In other countries, such as most of the nations of continental Europe, an inquisitorial system of justice is used. In this system, it is the judge who determines the direction of the trial by calling witnesses, examining evidence and drawing final conclusions of fact. When compared to an adversarial justice system, inquisitorial disputants and, more importantly, their lawyers play a much less active role in affecting the composition of the case. Instead of a courtroom battle, the inquisitorial trial might be likened to a trip to the principal's office to determine who did what to whom and what should be done about it.
4. Jodi Wilgoren, "Citing Issue of Fairness, Gov. Clears out Death Row in Ill." *The New York Times* (January 12, 2003).
5. James Sterngold, "Los Angeles Police's Report Cites Vast Command Lapses." *The New York Times* (March 2, 2000): A14.
6. David Johnston, "Report Criticizes Scientific Testing at FBI Crime Lab." *The New York Times* (April 16, 1997): A1.

7. Mark S. Warnick, "A Matter of Conviction." *Pittsburgh Post-Gazette* (September 24, 1995): A1.

8. Bob Herbert, "Brooklyn's Obsessive Pursuit." *The New York Times* (August 21, 1994): E15.

9. "Mexican Once Nearly Executed Wins Freedom in Texas." *The New York Times* (April 17, 1997): A8.

10. Bob Herbert, "Savagery Beyond Sense." *The New York Times* (October 18, 1996): A12.

11. James Madison, the leading figure in the development of the U.S. Constitution and Bill of Rights, commented on the need for checks on human behavior associated with the affairs of the state in *Federalist* No. 51: "If men were angels, no government would be necessary. If angels were to govern men, neither external nor internal controls on government would be necessary."

12. 384 U.S. 436.

13. Both sides conceded that, during the interrogation, the police did not use any force, threats, or promises of leniency if Miranda would confess. Both sides also conceded that at no point did the police inform Miranda that he had a constitutional right to refuse to talk to the police and that he could have counsel if he so desired.

14. Thus yielding the famous *Miranda* warnings:
    - You have the right to remain silent.
    - Anything you say can and will be used against you in a court of law.
    - You have a right to a lawyer.
    - If you can't afford a lawyer one will be provided to you.
    - If you say at any point that you do not want to talk to the police the interrogation must cease.

15. 384 U.S. 446.

16. It is worth noting that critics of the Miranda decision often ignore the fact that Ernesto Miranda did not go unpunished as a result of the Court's action. Instead, he was prosecuted by the State of Arizona in a second trial, without the use of his confession, and was convicted and sentenced to prison.

17. *Economist* (July 13, 1996): 29.

18. Ibid.

19. David Ignatius, "Tricks, Lies and Criminal Confessions." *The Washington Post National Weekly Edition* (January 24, 2000): 26.

20. It is important to note that only about 10 percent of criminal cases are resolved through the formal trial process. Most criminal convictions in this country are the result of plea bargaining between the defendant and the prosecutor.

21. *Weeks v. U.S.*, 232 U.S. 383 (1914).

22. 446 U.S. 620 (1980).

23. 467 U.S. 431 (1984).

24. 530 U.S. 428 (2000).

25. When a jury is used as the fact finder in a criminal case, the defense and prosecution have a significant role in determining who will sit on the jury. In the jury selection process both sides can challenge a prospective juror in

two ways. A challenge for cause is used when an attorney can show the court that there are tangible characteristics of the prospective jurors that make them biased and warrant their removal from consideration; lawyers have an unlimited ability to challenge for cause. A peremptory challenge allows a lawyer to remove a potential juror without giving a reason; each lawyer in a case gets a limited number of these. But peremptory challenges are not as peremptory as their name implies. The Supreme Court has ruled that lawyers cannot use them to systematically exclude all blacks or women from consideration for jury service.

26. Michael Janofsky, "Under Siege, Philadelphia's Criminal Justice System Suffers Another Blow." *The New York Times* (April 10, 1997): A9.

27. Jury unanimity is another balancer. It is based on the notion that the prosecutor should be required to present a case that convinces all jurors that the defendant is guilty beyond a reasonable doubt.

28. *Johnson v. Louisiana,* 406 U.S. 356 (1972), and *Apodaco v. Oregon,* 406 U.S. 404 (1972).

29. Quoted in Richard Harris, *Justice.* New York: Avon, 1969, p. 162.

Internet Resources

Visit our website at http://www.mhhe.com/diclerico for links and resources relating to the Courts.

chapter 15

Civil Rights

Affirmative Action

*F*or more than three decades, the federal government and many state governments have pursued a policy of "affirmative action," which requires government agencies and many public and private groups to take positive steps to guarantee nondiscrimination and a fair share of jobs, contracts, and college admissions for racial minorities and women. The underlying assumption of these requirements has been that because racial minorities, particularly African Americans, have been historically discriminated against, special efforts must be made to correct past discriminatory policies and practices and to assure greater opportunities in the future.

In recent years, "affirmative action" has become a "hot-button" issue, often generating heated debate between proponents and opponents. The debate revolves around these fundamental questions: Should minorities and women, because of past discrimination, be given special consideration in employment, admission to colleges and universities, government contracts, and the like; or should race and gender be totally ignored, even if the result leads to a lack of diversity and opportunity in many fields?

The two selections in this chapter speak to these and other questions in the affirmative action debate. In the first article, Terry Eastland presents the case for ending affirmative action, arguing that government should never use race either "to confer or deny a benefit" in society. To do otherwise is to act at odds with the "best principles" of our nation, including the principle of equal protection of the law without regard to race, color, or gender. The response to Eastland is provided by Barbara R. Bergmann, who argues that the abandonment of affirmative action is neither warranted by present-day conditions nor contrary to historic principles, including principles of racial and cultural diversity and a fair and just society.

Ending Affirmative Action
The Case for Colorblind Justice
Terry Eastland

BY ANY OTHER NAME

When he joined the police department in Memphis, Tennessee, in 1975, Danny O'Connor wanted someday to make sergeant. In 1988, he took a shot at it. Like the other 209 officers competing for 75 promotions, O'Connor completed the written exam and sat for his interview. When his scores on both parts were added to points awarded for seniority and on-the-job performance over the past year, he placed fifty-sixth on the Composite Scores List. The department had indicated that the 75 top-ranked officers on this list would be the ones promoted. O'Connor knew his ranking and thought he had realized his dream. But then affirmative action struck.

When the candidates took the written exam, they were required on the answer sheets to indicate their race and sex. On the basis of this information, the department created a second set of rankings—the Promotional Eligibility List. This new list, created to satisfy the department's affirmative action plan, modified the Composite Scores List by bumping blacks up into every third position. Necessarily, whoever had been there originally was bumped down. Some 26 blacks were on the eligibility list; 7 had been on the composite list. So 19 blacks (originally ranked between 76 and 132) had been bumped up the list—in some cases way up—and were promoted. Whites were bumped down, and those who had been ranked in the lower regions of the composite list were bumped below the 75th spot—and thus out of a promotion, Danny O'Connor, who is white, was one of these.

Undaunted, O'Connor tried again the next year. The department proceeded much as it had in 1988, using the same four-part process (though it changed the basis for awarding seniority points). Of 177 candidates, 94 would be promoted. They received their composite scores and on the basis of those scores were ranked. Affirmative action stepped in again, however, as the department used race to rerank the candidates. Where 15 blacks had made the top 94 on the composite list, 33 blacks were among the top 94 on the new list. Eigh-

Terry Eastland is former Director of Public Affairs in the U.S. Department of Justice (1985–1988) and currently publisher of *The Weekly Standard* magazine. Excerpted from Terry Eastland, *Ending Affirmative Action: The Case of Colorblind Justice*, pp. 1–20, 219–220. Copyright © 1996 by Terry Eastland. Reprinted by permission of Basic Books, a member of Perseus Books, L.L.C. Notes have been renumbered to correspond to edited text.

teen blacks had been bumped up into the top 94 and 18 whites previously in the top 94 had been bumped down. One of these was O'Connor, 75th on the original list.

Over the two years, while Danny O'Connor remained a patrol officer, 43 candidates with lower composite scores were bumped ahead of him and promoted to sergeant in the name of affirmative action.

Affirmative action was begun in the late 1960s to benefit blacks and over time has come to embrace certain other minority groups, as well as women (in the areas of employment and public contracting). There are, of course, forms of affirmative action that do not bump people out of an opportunity on account of race or sex. In employment, these forms of affirmative action can include outreach, recruitment, and training programs that are open to all, regardless of race or sex. But the affirmative action Danny O'Connor experienced is the kind that for years has been unsettling America. While it takes different guises and has different justifications, this type of affirmative action makes a virtue of race, ethnicity, and sex in order to determine who gets an opportunity and who does not. To call it by its proper name, it is discrimination.

Cheryl Hopwood had an experience like Danny O'Connor's. In 1992 she applied for admission to the University of Texas School of Law. She had earned a degree in accounting from California State University in 1988, achieving a 3.8 grade point average and scoring 39 (the highest score being 48) on the Law School Admissions Test (LSAT). She was, in addition, a certified public accountant. In the four years since finishing at Cal State, Hopwood had married and moved close to San Antonio, where her husband, an air force captain, was stationed. A Texas resident, she had just given birth to her first child when she applied for admission to the prestigious University of Texas law school.

Hopwood thought her credentials were excellent, but the law school turned her down. "The only thing I could think of," she says of her initial response to the news, "was that the class the school admitted must have been very, very good." Wanting to find out just how good, she discovered instead that because she is white she had not been able to compete with all other applicants for admission. Under the school's affirmative action plan, 15 percent of the approximately 500 seats in the class had been set aside for blacks and Mexican Americans, who were admitted under academic standards different from—in fact, lower than—those for all other students. Hopwood's admissions score—a composite number based on her undergraduate grade point average and her LSAT score—was 199. Eleven resident Mexican-American applicants had scores this high or higher, and only one resident black had a score of 199. The school admitted all 12 of these applicants but not Hopwood, and then, in pursuit of its 15 percent affirmative action goal, admitted 84 additional resident Mexican-American and black applicants. Their scores were lower—in some cases substantially lower—than Hopwood's. Indeed, the school admitted every resident black with a score of 185 or higher. If Hopwood were black or Mexican American, she would have been admitted.

Hopwood's experience differs from O'Connor's only in terms of the opportunity she sought, an educational one. Like O'Connor, she was bumped down and out by affirmative action that bumped others below her up and in. "I can't change my race," she says.

Neither can Randy Pech. The owner of Adarand Constructors, Inc., in Colorado Springs, Colorado, Pech, who is white, submitted the low bid for the guardrail portion on a federal highway construction project. But the business went to Gonzales Construction Company, which submitted a higher bid but is Hispanic-owned. That happens to be a virtue in the eyes of the U.S. Department of Transportation, which enforces a law that "sets aside" a portion of federal construction funds for businesses owned by minorities and women. Pech says he competes with four other companies in Colorado that build guardrails. Two are owned by Hispanics. Two are owned by women. Set-aside laws, he says, work solely against him. "If I weren't here, they'd have no impact.". . .

Danny O'Connor, Cheryl Hopwood, [and] Randy Pech, decided to challenge in court the discrimination that goes by the name of affirmative action.[1] They are gallant foot soldiers in the fight against a policy that by allocating opportunity on the basis of race and sex is dividing and damaging the nation. The time has come for us to end it.

A BARGAIN WITH THE DEVIL

. . . The original purpose of affirmative action was to remedy the ill effects of past discrimination against blacks. "To get beyond racism," as Justice Harry Blackmun famously put it in his opinion in the 1978 case *Regents of the University of California v. Bakke*, "we must first take account of race."[2] "Taking account of race" meant distinguishing on the basis of race and treating blacks differently. In the old days, this would have looked like racial discrimination. But the first advocates of affirmative action assured us that affirmative action was well intentioned. Race could be regulated to good effect, we were told, and affirmative action would end soon enough, with the nation the better for it. As one of the early architects of affirmative action put it, "We are in control of our own history."[3]

By the early 1970s, affirmative action was extended to cover additional minority groups and in some contexts women, and over the years its backers have offered additional justifications, such as overcoming "underrepresentation" and achieving "diversity." But the nation has paid a steep price for departing from colorblind principle, for affirmative action has turned out to be a bargain with the devil. Not only has the policy worked discrimination against those it does not favor—a Danny O'Connor or a Cheryl Hopwood, for example—but it also has guaranteed the salience of race and ethnicity in the life of the nation, thus making it harder to overcome the very tendency the civil rights movement once condemned; that of regarding and judging people in terms of their racial and ethnic groups. . . .

By formally drawing racial and ethnic lines, affirmative action invites judgments about the abilities and achievements of those who are members of the targeted groups. One persistent judgment is that those who received a benefit through affirmative action could not have secured it on their own. In many cases, this happens to be true. Indeed, the whole point of many affirmative action programs is to help those who otherwise could not have landed the opportunity in open competition. The program Cheryl Hopwood encountered at the Texas law school lowered the school's academic standards in order to admit blacks and Mexican Americans. The school also segregated the applications of blacks and Mexican Americans, assigning them to a separate admissions committee while a different committee reviewed the merits of the "white and other" applicants. Thus treated differently, the members of the two minority groups competed only among themselves. Had they competed among all applicants under the same standards, many fewer blacks and Mexican Americans would have gained admission to the Texas law school.

This is not, however, the whole story. The black and Mexican-American applicants admitted under affirmative action were not *un*qualified to study law; their academic qualifications were good enough to win admission under non-affirmative action standards at fully two-thirds of the nation's law schools.[4] Affirmative action thus stigmatizes beneficiaries who could succeed—and be seen to succeed—without it. At the same time, it stigmatizes those eligible for it who are not its beneficiaries. At the Texas law school, one Hispanic student who had a composite score good enough to warrant admission under the standards applicable to "whites and others" said that he felt he needed a shirt indicating he got in on his own, just to let people know the genuine nature of his accomplishment.[5] It is sadly ironic that affirmative action can put a non–affirmative action minority student in this situation, but the student's response is hardly irrational. He knows that the mere existence of the law school's program invites people to think, in his case: "You're Hispanic, so you got in through affirmative action."

An abiding truth about much affirmative action is that those who are its ostensible beneficiaries are burdened with the task of overcoming it—if, that is, they wish to be treated as individuals, without regard to race. It is possible, of course, for someone extended an opportunity through affirmative action to overcome it by doing extraordinarily well, meeting the highest standards. But some minorities have concluded that the best way to escape the public implications of affirmative action is to say "no" when they know it is being offered. In 1983, Freddie Hernandez, a Hispanic who serves in the Miami fire department, rejected an affirmative action promotion to lieutenant. Instead, he waited three years until he had the necessary seniority and had scored high enough to qualify for the promotion under procedures that applied to nonminorities. This decision cost Hernandez $4,500 a year in extra pay and forced him to study 900 additional hours to attain the required test results. But, as he proudly told the *Wall Street Journal*, "I knew I could make it on my own."[6]

Hernandez rejected the affirmative action bargain. He wanted to be judged as an individual, on his own merits, without regard to his ethnic background—just the way the old civil rights pioneers said he had a right to be judged.

THE LANGUAGE OF AFFIRMATIVE ACTION

Affirmative action has taken a toll on public discourse. Through the years its supporters have said, for example, that they do not support quotas. But . . . there was a reason police officer Danny O'Connor was bumped down and out of a promotion. There was a reason black officers were bumped up into every third position. The Memphis police department was trying to fill a quota that reserved one-third of the promotions for blacks. Bumping blacks up into every third position on the list of 75 may have been a crude way of making the quota, but it got the job done. Faced with evidence of a quota, supporters of affirmative action backtrack, saying that they are against "hard and fast" or "rigid" quotas and for "flexible" goals. The distinction in practice may mean that a slightly lesser number of the preferred minority group or women is hired or admitted. This happened at the University of Texas School of Law, which in 1992 fell a bit short of its 15 percent goal for black and Mexican-American admittees. But whatever term is used to describe what the law school was doing, race was determining the bulk of these admissions decisions.

Affirmative action supporters may concede that race is the determining factor but insist that the practice benefits only qualified people. Yet what matters to those competing for a limited number of openings or opportunities is not whether they are qualified in the abstract, but whether they are *more* qualified than the others seeking that position. The rankings Danny O'Connor earned showed that he was more qualified than officers bumped above him and promoted to sergeant on account of race. And Cheryl Hopwood's composite score showed she was more qualified than many of those with lower scores who were admitted under the Texas law school's affirmative action plan. Some supporters of affirmative action respond by claiming that differences in qualifications—above a certain minimum—are negligible. They will not say, however, that differences in qualifications are unimportant in the case of those who are *not* eligible for affirmative action. And judgments about who is better are routinely made by all of us when we seek the services of, say, a doctor or lawyer. Not surprisingly, though most unfortunately, some affirmative action programs have dispensed with even minimal qualifications. In 1993, in an effort to increase the "diversity" of its workforce, the U.S. Forest Service's Pacific Southwest Region established "upward mobility positions" that it set aside for applicants who do not meet the service's usual employment requirements. The dictionary of affirmative action does not appear to include words like "excellence" and "outstanding" and "best." . . .

THE MYTH OF "TEMPORARY" AFFIRMATIVE ACTION

In the late 1960s and during the 1970s, advocates of affirmative action often said that it was only a temporary measure whose success would render it unnecessary in the future. But these temporary measures often seem to go on and on and on—well beyond the point at which they were supposed to end.

Let us return to Danny O'Connor's story. It actually began back in 1974, when the Justice Department sued the city of Memphis under Title VII of the Civil Rights Act of 1964, alleging that it had engaged in unlawful employment discrimination against blacks and women. Quickly, the city and the federal government settled the suit through a consent decree that won federal court approval. Other lawsuits followed: black police officers sued the city in 1975, charging racially discriminatory promotion practices, and a black firefighter filed a similar suit in 1977. Judicially approved consent decrees also concluded these cases. And then, in 1981, the city and the federal government amended their 1974 agreement. Though the city never admitted to past discrimination, it did agree to hire and promote blacks and females in proportions, as the 1981 decree put it, "approximating their respective proportions in the relevant Shelby County civilian labor force."

Now, we may regard the lawsuits of the 1970s as necessary in forcing change upon an Old South city. And for the sake of argument, let us concede that proportional hiring and promoting were needed to effect change in the 1970s and early 1980s. But having achieved proportional representation in the fire and police workforces by the mid-1980s, the city did not end its attachment to proportionalism, as Danny O'Connor's case shows. City officials claim that the 1981 decree tied their hands, but it did not *require* race-based employment decisions. In fact, the decree provided that the city was not obligated to hire or promote a less-qualified person over a better-qualified person. The inconvenient truth appears to be that proportional hiring and promoting proved administratively a lot easier for the city than trying to treat applicants and employees fairly without regard to race. In 1994, a federal appeals court rejected the city's motion to dismiss the complaint brought by Danny O'Connor and other white employees. In its opinion the court expressed concern that the city "has made no effort to limit the duration of the [race-based promotional] remedies."[7]

The federal executive branch has made no effort in this regard, either. The 1981 consent decree governing the city of Memphis could have been dissolved by agreement of the parties as early as March 1984, but the Justice Department under Ronald Reagan did not ask the city to end its hiring and promotional remedies. Nor, for that matter, did the Justice Department under George Bush. And when the city found itself in 1994 in the court of appeals trying to fend off Danny O'Connor's lawsuit, the Justice Department under Bill Clinton filed a brief in support of the city's never-ending affirmative action. . . .

THE CHOICE

Failing to make good on its promise to be only temporary, affirmative action has entrenched itself more deeply in our institutions, attracting political constituencies that demand its retention. Surveys of public opinion show, however, that preferences have never enjoyed the majority support of the American people. Moreover, the substantial immigration the nation has experienced since, coincidentally, the advent of affirmative action is rendering the policy increasingly incoherent.

Roughly three-quarters of those who come to the United States each year are of a race or ethnic background that makes them eligible for affirmative action, and most affirmative action programs are indifferent as to whether their beneficiaries are U.S. citizens or not, or whether, if they are U.S. citizens, they recently arrived here or not. We thus have a policy originally designed to remedy the ill effects of past discrimination that is open to immigrants with no past in the United States during which they could have experienced discrimination. . . .

. . . [I]mmigration since the late 1960s has swollen the ranks of Hispanics and Asians, making them, combined, more numerous than blacks. As a result, we now face the prospect (especially in our largest cities, where the Hispanic and Asian populations are most concentrated) of increasing conflict among affirmative action groups.

Los Angeles, a city being dramatically reshaped by Hispanic immigration, is a case in point. In 1988 the Los Angeles County Office of Affirmative Action Compliance issued a report showing that while Hispanics made up 27.6 percent of the county population and held 18.3 percent of county jobs, blacks constituted 12.6 percent of the population and 30 percent of the workforce. The county board of supervisors accepted the affirmative action office's recommendation to hire minorities in accordance with a scheme of "population parity."[8] This meant members of the "underrepresented" group, that is, Hispanics—would be preferred over those belonging to the "overrepresented" group—blacks. Black county employees quickly protested, declaring their opposition to preferential treatment based on race and ethnicity. Over the years the struggle has continued, and now the county is thinking about dropping population parity in favor of an affirmative action approach that would result in fewer preferences for Hispanics, whose portion of the county population has risen to 38 percent. To prevent this change, Hispanic county employees have filed a lawsuit.[9]

The impact of immigration is another reason to reevaluate affirmative action. We can choose to stick with the status quo, perhaps mending it a bit here and there, or we can end affirmative action once and for all. The choice was clarified politically in the months following the 1994 midterm elections in which the Republicans, for the first time in 40 years, captured both houses of Congress. Though the campaign was not explicitly about affirmative action, the election results necessarily altered the nation's political agenda, pushing it in a more conservative direction. . . . [T]he new Congress voted to terminate a 17-year-old program under which corporations selling their broadcast outlets at a discounted price to minorities may defer sales taxes indefinitely. President Clinton, sensing the shift in political sentiment, signed the bill into law. Senator Robert Dole, preparing to draft legislation on affirmative action, asked the Congressional Research Service (CRS) to supply him with a list of programs containing preferences for minorities or women, whereupon President Clinton ordered his own review of government programs. Both branches of government had a lot to digest—the CRS reported to Dole more than 160 federal programs that might be construed as requiring or authorizing or encouraging preferences.

And then on June 12, 1995, the Supreme Court handed down its decision in the case involving Randy Pech. In *Adarand Constructors v. Pena,* the Court held that federal affirmative action programs must be held to a standard of "strict scrutiny," the most demanding level of justification, whose application routinely has led to the invalidation of governmental measures that classify on the basis of race and ethnicity.[10] Sending Randy Pech's case back to the lower courts for review under the tougher standard, the Court signaled that preferential treatment deserves not only strict judicial scrutiny but also strict political scrutiny, since the very idea that government should distinguish on the basis of race to confer or deny a benefit is at odds with our best principles as a nation. No fewer than four times did Justice Sandra Day O'Connor, who wrote the Court's opinion, refer to the luminous passage in the 1943 *Hirabayashi* decision: "Distinctions between citizens solely because of their ancestry are by their very nature odious to a free people whose institutions are founded upon the doctrine of equality." O'Connor emphasized that the Constitution protects *"persons,* not *groups,"* and that "all governmental action based on race" is a *"group* classification" that should be examined to make sure that "personal" rights have been protected.

Affirmative action broke with the colorblind tradition, one acknowledged in the Japanese Relocation Cases. Indeed, this tradition stretches back to the American founding. In making the choice before us about the future of affirmative action, it is imperative that we as a nation return to the place from which we began, and understand afresh the compelling and true case for colorblind justice.

NOTES

Note: Quotes besides those cited in the text itself or in the following endnotes are from interviews with the author.

1. In December 1995, all . . . cases were still in litigation.
2. 438 U.S. 265 (1978).
3. Alfred W. Blumrosen, *Black Employment and the Law* (New Brunswick, N.J.: Rutgers University Press, 1971), p. viii.
4. Lino A. Graglia, "*Hopwood v. Texas:* Racial Preferences in Higher Education Upheld and Endorsed," *Journal of Legal Education* 45, no. 1 (March 1995): 82.
5. "Suit Against U. of Texas Challenges Law School's Affirmative-Action Effort." *Chronicle of Higher Education,* February 9, 1994. Hopwood and three other applicants rejected by the law school filed the lawsuit. . . .
6. Sonia L. Nazario, "Many Minorities Feel Torn by Experience of Affirmative Action," *Wall Street Journal,* June 27, 1989.
7. *Aiken v. City of Memphis,* 37 F. 3d. 1155 (6th Cir. 1994).
8. Peter Skerry, "Borders and Quotas: Immigration and the Affirmative-Action State," *The Public Interest,* no. 96 (summer 1989): 93.
9. Jonathan Tilove, "Affirmative Action Has Drawbacks for Blacks," *Cleveland Plain Dealer;* July 20, 1995.
10. 115 S. Ct. 2097 (1995). . . .

In Defense of Affirmative Action
Barbara R. Bergmann

IS DISCRIMINATION A THING OF THE PAST?

Pollsters surveying people about their attitudes toward affirmative action frequently ask, "Do you think blacks or women should receive preference in hiring and promotion to make up for past discrimination?" This wording encourages respondents to assume that discrimination has ended and is no longer an important problem. Respondents to one such poll, when asked to comment on their answers, spoke of discrimination that had occurred "100 years ago" and said that such ancient history did not justify "preferences" in the present.[1]

As we shall see . . . there are good reasons to believe that discrimination by race and sex is not a thing of the past. Those under the impression that discrimination ended a long time ago are simply mistaken. However, they are right about one thing: our need for affirmative action depends not on what happened 100 years ago but on the situation in the labor market today. . . .

THE EVIDENCE ON WAGES

In judging the conflicting claims about the state of the labor market, it is useful to start by looking at how much change has actually occurred. Chart 1 and the note (p. 287) show the weekly wages of those who worked full-time in the years 1967–2000, corrected to eliminate the effect of inflation.[2] The inflation-corrected wages of white men have been on a downtrend since the mid-1970s. However, white men have not lost their superior position in the labor market: a substantial gap remains between their wages and those of white women and black men and women. Given the slowness of change in the labor market, as shown in Chart 1, that gap will not close anytime soon.

Modest reductions have been made in that gap since 1967. Black men's wages were 69 percent of white men's in 1967. By 1976 their wages had risen to 79 percent of white men's. Since then, they have been losing rather than gaining ground on white men. The loss of manufacturing jobs, some of them unionized and thus relatively well-paying, has hit both white and black men, but the

Barbara R. Bergmann is Professor Emerita of Economics at the University of Maryland and American University. This excerpt is from Barbara R. Bergmann, *In Defense of Affirmative Action* (New York: Basic Books, 1996), pp. 32–33, 36–38, 48–52, 78–81, 84–85, 94–96, 102–105, 126–130, 183–184, 186–187, and 190–191. Notes have been renumbered to correspond to edited text.

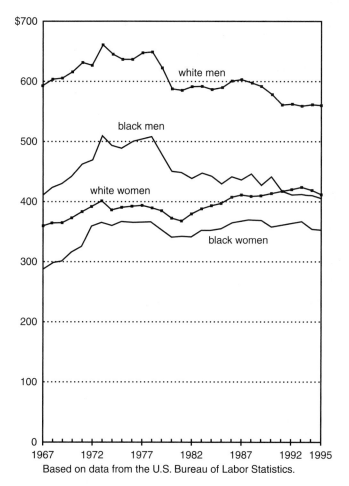

Based on data from the U.S. Bureau of Labor Statistics.

Chart 1 Weekly Wages by Sex and Race in 1995 Dollars

latter have been particularly hard hit.[3] White women gained no ground on white men until the early 1980s; they have been gaining in the years since. In 1995 their wages were 73 percent of white men's, compared with 61 percent in 1967. Black women have made gains throughout the period, but recently their gains have not matched those of white women. In 1995, black women's wages were 63 percent of white men's.*

The fall in black men's wages relative to white men's over the last twenty years suggests that whatever help they have received from affirmative action has been modest at best, and has not been enough to counterbalance the effects of their buffeting from market forces. The globalization of the labor market has reduced the demand by U.S. employers for the labor of the less skilled—both black and white—and black men have suffered disproportionately. While affirmative

*In 2000, the dollar figures (in 1995 constant dollars) were black women—$382, white women—$445, black men—$448, and white men—$596 (*editors.*)

action has allowed some college-educated black men to enter the middle class, the deterioration of the labor market for non–college-educated black men has been disastrous. It has made their lives increasingly precarious; their decreased chances for decently paid work have contributed to the fall in the black marriage rate, the increase in single parenthood, and the recruitment of black men into crime and the drug trade in the inner city. . . .

THE EVIDENCE FROM LAWSUITS

Lucky Stores, Inc., a West Coast grocery chain, agreed in 1993 to pay nearly $75 million in damages to women who had been denied promotion opportunities and another $20 million to set up and run affirmative action programs.[4] The women had been denied full-time slots, and the relatively small group of women in management jobs had been segregated into certain departments (bakery and delicatessen) marked off as dead end. The managers of these departments received lower pay than other managers. One of the women whose complaint sparked the suit had worked at the cash register for 21 years. When her teenage son came to Lucky and worked beside her, he was offered training opportunities that had been denied to her. Suits alleging similar employment practices have been filed against Safeway Stores and several other grocery chains.

The facts of the Lucky Stores case were strikingly similar to the facts in a 1972 suit against Giant Foods, a Washington, D.C.–area grocery chain. That suit was settled, with the company under order until the late 1980s to remedy the problems. However, a 1994 telephone survey to ascertain the sex of managers by department revealed that in the 20 years since the suit, very little integration of managerial positions had been accomplished.[5] Meat cutting, a skilled trade requiring apprenticeship, had been maintained as an all-male specialty. Bakery managers, still overwhelmingly female, continued to receive lower salaries than other department managers, almost all male. The cost of remedying the bakery managers' relatively low pay would have amounted to a few dollars an hour per store; the fact that their pay had not been increased raises questions about the symbolic significance of low pay to those in control. Giant's history illustrates the stubbornness of discrimination problems and the difficulty of fixing them when management is indifferent or opposed to change. A successful lawsuit may give the particular complainants some recompense but leave the underlying situation unchanged. The supermarket cases also show the complicity of some unions in maintaining segregation by sex and women's lower pay.

A recent claim of racial discrimination against the Shoney restaurant chain listed 211 Shoney officials against whom there was direct evidence of discriminatory behavior. Employment applications were color-coded by race, Blacks were tracked to kitchen jobs so that all employees in the dining area would be white. The case began when two white managers complained that they had been pressured by their supervisors to limit the number of black employees, and that they had been terminated when they resisted the pressure. The case was settled out of court for $65 million. Kerry Scanlon, an attorney for the black plaintiffs, said, "This was going on while the Bush Administration and others were telling the country that in the area of civil rights, the major problem was quotas and unfair protection for blacks. The quota that African Americans are most familiar with in employment is zero."[6]

EVIDENCE BASED ON "TESTING" THE JOB MARKET

So far, in reviewing the labor market situation for women and blacks, we have been looking at their treatment on the job, that is, where they are placed and what they are paid. We need also to look at their ability to land jobs. An important aspect of the labor market disadvantage suffered by African Americans is their high unemployment rate. People are counted as "unemployed" in government statistics only if they are actively looking for work. In good times and bad, unemployment rates for African Americans are twice as high as those for whites. The problem is particularly acute for 18- to 19-year-old black people, who suffer unemployment rates above 30 percent.[7] When they leave school, it is very hard for them to find jobs, and when they lose a job, they are typically in for a long spell of unemployment before landing the next one.

The results of a recent research project reveal the extent of discrimination against young black men in hiring and give an insight into the connection between that discrimination and their high rate of unemployment.[8] The Urban Institute assembled pairs of young men to serve as "testers." In each pair, one tester was black, the other white. Entry-level job openings were chosen at random from the newspaper, and a pair of testers was assigned to apply for each opening.

The researchers made the pairs of testers as similar as possible, except with regard to race. Testers were matched in physical size and in the education and experience they claimed to have. An attempt was also made to match each pair in openness, energy level, and articulateness. The testers were actually college students, but most of them posed as recent high school graduates and were supplied with fictional biographies that gave them similar job experience. They were put through mock interviews and coached to act like the person they were paired with to the greatest possible extent. The testers were then sent to apply for low-skill, entry-level jobs usually filled by young high-school graduates in manufacturing, hotels, restaurants, retail sales, and office work. The job titles ranged from general laborer to management trainee. The testers were instructed to refuse any job offered them so that the other member of the pair could have a chance at it.

The black testers posing as job seekers were carefully coached to present qualifications apparently equal to those of their white counterparts. In reality they were all, black and white, excellently qualified for the jobs they applied for. The Urban Institute researchers found that the young white men were offered jobs 45 percent more than the young black men. This result clearly reveals that some employers were not treating male minority job seekers equally with white males of similar qualifications.

The same researchers paired white Anglo testers and Hispanic testers who were fluent in English.⁹ Again, the pairs of young men were matched to minimize the differences between them; the only apparent differences were the slight accents, somewhat darker complexions, and Spanish names of the Hispanic testers. The Anglos received 52 percent more job offers than the Hispanics.

THE DIFFICULTY OF CHANGING HIRING HABITS

Patterns of occupational segregation by race and sex tend to persist in part because people have good reason to be cautious in making hiring and promotion decisions. These decisions are the most crucial to any organization's success. A bad mistake in hiring or promotion can result in large monetary losses and a lot of misery. When an unsuitable person has been chosen for a job, there may be painful weeks or months during which work is botched, tempers flare, feelings are bruised, and customers are alienated. Employers have an understandable tendency to move cautiously and to continue doing what has worked well previously. Hiring candidates of a different race or sex is likely to be seen as risky, as asking for trouble. . . .

If the people involved in the selection process want to do nothing more than select the candidate who will perform the best, regardless of sex, race, or ethnicity, they are not likely to select a candidate of a nontraditional race or gender, even if very promising candidates of this kind are available. People use minimal clues of manner and appearance and way of talking to make snap judgments about candidates of a familiar type. A white person who has little experience with the performance of blacks on the job may not feel capable of making good judgments about their abilities based on such clues, and he or she may find it safer to stick with candidates of a familiar kind.

One way employers stick with the kinds of workers they are used to is by filling their vacancies with people recommended by those already working there in the kind of job they are filling. There is a considerable incentive for employers to fill jobs this way, and the practice is apparently widespread.¹⁰ It saves recruiting expenses and may make for congenial work groups. A worker who recommends someone vouches for that person as someone likely to do well. Unfortunately, this seemingly innocent recruiting practice makes it particularly hard for African Americans to improve their status. Relying on employee recommendations effectively excludes from good jobs those who do not have relatives and friends with good jobs.

Women candidates may be particularly disadvantaged by sexual conventions. A woman who wears a standard amount of makeup and jewelry may be judged to be unbusinesslike, since the standard businessperson—a man—wears none. On the other hand, a woman who wears less than the standard amount of makeup and jewelry risks being considered not feminine enough to be a normal woman and is therefore judged to be peculiar. People making hiring decisions tend to shy away from people who seem peculiar.

PROBLEMS OF ACCEPTANCE BY COWORKERS

Production on the job has its social aspects. Each worker has to learn from and teach others, engage in cooperative endeavors, transmit and receive information, help provide a friendly environment, cover occasionally for another's mistakes, and at least appear to be amused by the jokes that go around. The people doing the hiring customarily consider not only a candidate's technical abilities and general pleasantness but also the chances of the candidate being accepted by coworkers so that they will interact well. . . .

Some of the hostility to the worker of untraditional race or sex may be motivated by self-defense. Men know that jobs in which white males predominate tend to be compensated with high status and pay; feeling those benefits threatened, they may not welcome a coworker who dilutes the maleness or whiteness of their job. They may fear that future vacancies will be filled with lower-status people or that they will have to leave the occupation or risk being trapped in a devalued job. As a result of such worries, there may be difficulties in convincing the old hands to introduce the newcomer of untraditional race or gender to the tricks of the trade.

Donald Tomaskovic-Devey reports an instance of this problem:

> A pilot told me a story about the first woman pilot at the busy corporate airport where he worked. The other pilots knew from the start that she would not be able to cut it. To give her a "fair" chance to prove herself, they had decided not to show her the ropes, to allow her to figure out on her own the controls on planes she had not flown before, and not to introduce her to the control tower and maintenance staffs, although this information was routinely shared with new male pilots. After all, they knew from the start that a woman could not be a pilot. Of course, what they knew did not matter; it was what they did that was decisive. By refusing to share their knowledge, they insured her failure. . . .[11]

GOALS AS ENERGIZING DEVICES

When critics of affirmative action say that goals are the same as quotas, and that quotas are bad, they presumably are saying, "Get rid of discrimination if there is any; give everyone a fair chance. But make sure you don't measure success or failure in numbers. If you do, you may be tempted to do some unfair and stupid things to make the numbers look good." The problem is that the directive "Be fair from now on" is far less energizing, and far more easily evaded, than "There are some good black people out there. Have one of them aboard by a month from next Thursday, or at least show that you've tried." Recruitment methods are highly resistant to change. And as our review of labor market realities has shown, there are many workplaces where these methods need changing if we are to make significant progress toward fairness.

The use of numerical goals to spur managers into action and to direct their behavior has been useful in all aspects of modern management; indeed, its use in affirmative action follows from its success in other areas. Modern businesses use numerical goals to manage production, productivity, sales, investments, and costs. The announcement of goals helps to specify explicit standards for performance of managers. In the absence of numerical goals and timetables for meeting them, it is difficult to determine whether managers have done a good job or to hold anyone responsible for failures. When people know they will not be held responsible, they are less likely to make significant efforts. . . .

If we were to establish goals for both sexes and for each of the ethnic groups represented in the United States, the labor market would become a balkanized nightmare: each slot would be earmarked for a person of a particular extraction and gender. Moreover, an expansion of the share of the population for whom goals are set might have an adverse impact on groups for which no goals are set, groups that contain relatively large numbers of high achievers—Jews and Asians, for example. A severe shrinking of the proportion of the population not included in affirmative action goals might reduce tolerance of the high success rates of such groups. In short, there are good reasons to have fewer goals rather than more. Establishing goals for a particular group should not be done without substantial reason. There is no sign that we are tending in the direction of an overproliferation of groups covered by affirmative action goals.

Common sense suggests that employment goals should be set for a group only if all of the following conditions are met:

1. The group is seriously underrepresented in an occupation or at a hierarchical level in the workplace.
2. The underrepresentation continues because of present discrimination, or because of current employer practices or habits that effectively exclude members of the group.
3. The pattern of exclusion is unlikely to change in the absence of special efforts.

For jobs in which discriminated-against groups are overrepresented, goals should be set for integrating whites and males into them. This effort will fail if the salaries for such jobs are significantly lower than what white males with the required skills can earn in other jobs. Nor will it be possible to recruit white males into jobs that have obviously been set up as dead ends, jobs whose duties are overly repetitive, or jobs over which the supervision is more rigid than white males of that skill level are used to. Integrating the all-female jobs with males, or the all-black jobs with whites, will force employers to rethink wage levels and working conditions—to the benefit of those members of disadvantaged groups who stay in traditionally sex- or race-specific occupations.

Different areas of the country, occupations, industries, and hierarchical levels call for different sets of goals. The evidence suggests that goals are needed almost everywhere for black men and women and white women, and in many places for Hispanics of both sexes. The Civil Rights Act would forbid discrimination against people of Hungarian extraction on account of their origin. However, if there is no reason to think that Hungarians are being excluded, we should not have goals for them.

Consider, however, the situation of a New England law firm that employs 40 lawyers and has no partners or associates of Irish or Jewish extraction. There are many people of Irish extraction in New England, and a considerable number of Jews as well. In the past these groups were commonly denied access to jobs reserved for upper-crust males of British extraction. Many lawyers of Irish and Jewish extraction now have elite legal credentials, and if a firm of that size has no such lawyers on its staff, it is likely that some aspects of the recruitment process are keeping them from being hired. Our guidelines suggest that having a goal for hiring lawyers of Irish and Jewish ancestry would be desirable for this firm. On the other hand, in other parts of the country, and in some occupations in which being of Irish or Jewish ancestry has not recently been a substantial disadvantage, goals for such people, even when they are underrepresented, would be unnecessary and undesirable. . . .

THE FUZZINESS OF MERIT

We frequently think and act as though there were only one correct way to define merit, one right and infallibly accurate way to measure it, and one right way to use measurements of merit in making hiring or school admission decisions. We also tend to assume that these obviously right ways are everywhere in current use. They are not, of course.

The rankings of candidates as to merit will depend on which of the candidates' characteristics are taken into consideration, how much weight is given to each characteristic, and how the judging is done—formally, objectively, and consistently for all candidates, or informally and inconsistently. Faye Crosby's research . . . shows that people do unconsciously give more weight to the good points of the person they consider appropriate for the job (for instance, a white man for a management job) and tend to ignore the good points of a person they think is less appropriate.

In thinking about affirmative action erroneous assumptions are frequently made:

1. That for each job opening there is one person who is unambiguously the best among the candidates.
2. That the identity of that candidate is unerringly revealed by the employer's selection process.
3. That the evaluation process is uninfluenced by the sex, race, ethnicity, age, or disability status of the candidates.
4. That the "best" candidate is head and shoulders above all the others, so that the substitution of the one judged third- or fourth-best instead of the one judged best would make a great difference to productivity.

These assumptions are unrealistic in many, even most cases. The American Society for Personnel Administration, in a brief supporting affirmative action in a case before the Supreme Court, said:

It is a standard tenet of personnel administration that there is rarely a single, "best qualified" person for a job. An effective personnel system will bring before the selecting official several fully-qualified candidates who each may possess different attributes which recommend them for selection. Especially where the job is an unexceptional, middle-level craft position, without the need for unique work experience or educational attainment and for which several well-qualified candidates are available, final determinations as to which candidate is "best qualified" are at best subjective.[12] . . .

Measurements of merit for a job or for school admission, then, are dependent on the methods used and subject to error and subversion; moreover, they may not differentiate among candidates with any great accuracy. A process of assessing merit that cuts out all but white males may mask purposeful discrimination or set up hurdles that female and black candidates, for no job-related reason, have particular difficulty in getting over. An interviewer whose method of measuring congeniality is to chat with candidates about golf is not going to be giving very many black or female candidates high grades for that quality. . . .

THE ILLUSION THAT BLACKS ALWAYS WIN

In their talk of fairness, the foes of affirmative action focus on two individuals—a black person and a white person—competing for a job. The black person in their story is poorly qualified for the job. The white person is highly qualified, has worked very hard to get himself qualified, and is innocent of any wrongdoing toward this black person or any other. Most likely, the white person is from a poor family and the black person grew up in comfortable circumstances. Affirmative action, its foes would have you believe, has turned the labor market into a succession of contests between pairs of individuals like these. In each contest, the undeserving black person is declared the winner and gets 100 percent of the prize, while the deserving white person is left with nothing. With this perennial outcome, the situation has become pretty hopeless if you are a white man. With white males depicted as losing in each of these matchups, one may get the impression that the white male group has suffered severely from affirmative action.

The evidence of how the labor market "contests" actually come out—who is getting seats on the "good jobs bus"—shows, of course, a quite different picture. There has been some desegregation since the 1960s, but as we have seen, many jobs in many workplaces remain segregated. In the wages they earn, black people and white women are still far behind white males of similar education and experience. Members of the white male group continue to win almost all of the contests for the best jobs in each of the major occupational groups in most workplaces.

Affirmative action's removal of white men's privilege of exclusive access to high-paying jobs does inflict losses on white men. The foes of affirmative action fixate on those losses and ignore the reasons they are necessary, desirable, and fair. Foes pay no attention to the losses of those individuals who, in the absence of affirmative action, have been excluded because they are black or female.

The press has spotlighted the loss of privilege of certain white men and rendered invisible those black individuals who are cut out when white privilege is allowed to persist. One suburban county adopted an affirmative action program to desegregate its fire department, which had a history of total segregation by race. Some of the rejected white applicants organized a demonstration and invited the press. The local newspaper ran a photograph of the group of rejected white candidates across the street from the headquarters of the fire department, gazing at it mournfully and reproachfully. No pictures ever appeared in that newspaper showing the far larger group of blacks who for years had been rejected from firefighter jobs by a selection system rigged to exclude them. Able blacks had been excluded in favor of less qualified or equally qualified whites. The invisibility of the blacks who have been excluded by discrimination promotes the topsy-turvy view that whites are victims and blacks are in a privileged position in our society—that blacks have been "given too much."

IS AFFIRMATIVE ACTION A ZERO-SUM GAME?

Would every gain for blacks and other minorities under affirmative action spell an equal loss for whites? Will men lose to the extent that women gain? If there were a rigidly fixed number of "good" jobs and "bad" jobs, then every time a "good" job was assigned through affirmative action to a black or a woman, a white man would be forced into a "bad" job. . . .

Affirmative action, which breaks up the labor market monopolies that have been held by favored groups and makes blacks and women eligible for a greater variety of jobs, should have the effect of reducing the gap in pay and conditions between jobs that whites and blacks with a given education typically get. If affirmative action is successful, some whites will find themselves applying for jobs that hitherto only blacks have applied for, and some men will be applying for jobs that only women have previously held. But these jobs are likely to be better jobs than they would have been in the absence of affirmative action.

Finally, if we can reduce discrimination and segregation in the labor market, there will be gains outside of the labor market as well. All of us will benefit from revitalized central cities, lower crime rates, and fewer panhandlers, fewer homeless. It will be easier, more pleasurable, less guilt-inducing, and safer to live in a more just society.

NOTES

1. Richard Morin and Sharon Warden, "Americans Vent Anger at Affirmative Action," *Washington Post*, March 24, 1995, pp. 1, 4.
2. Weekly wages of full-time workers by race and sex are published by the U.S. Bureau of Labor Statistics in the periodical *Employment and Earnings*.

3. See Francine D. Blau and Lawrence M. Kahn, "Gender and Pay Differentials," in *Research Frontiers in Industrial Relations and Human Resources*, ed. David Lewin, Olivia S. Mitchell, and Peter D. Sherer (Madison, Wisc.: IRRA, 1992), p. 389.
4. Jane Gross, "Big Grocery Chain Reaches Landmark Sex-Bias Accord," *New York Times*, December 17, 1993, pp. A1, B10.
5. Unpublished papers by Akiko Naono (1993) and Jacqueline Chu (1994), Economics Department, American University, Washington, D.C.
6. Lynne Duke, "Shoney's Bias Settlement Sends $105 Million Signal," *Washington Post*, February 5, 1993, pp. A1, A20.
7. *Employment and Earnings* (January 1995): table A-13.
8. Michael Fix and Raymond J. Struyk, eds., *Clear and Convincing Evidence: Measurement of Discrimination in America* (Washington, D.C.: Urban Institute Press, 1993).
9. Ibid.
10. Arthur Stinchcombe, *Information and Organizations* (Berkeley: University of California Press, 1990), pp. 243–44.
11. Donald Tomaskovic-Devey, *Gender and Racial Inequality at Work: The Sources and Consequences of Job Segregation* (Ithaca, N.Y.: ILR Press, 1993), pp. 161–62.
12. American Society for Personnel Administration, amicus curiae brief submitted to the Supreme Court, quoted in Justice William J. Brennan's majority opinion in *Johnson v. Transportation Agency of Santa Clara County, Calif.*, 107 Sup. Ct. 1442 (1987), p. 1457.

Gender Equity

*T*he modern era in civil rights has been unprecedented in the advancement of rights for minorities and women: elimination of racial segregation; removal of racial, gender, and disability discrimination in employment, school admissions, and other areas; and the extension of the vote to millions of Americans. Yet, in the face of much progress, there are areas in civil rights policy where opinion is strongly divided. One such area is gender equity in sports.

In 1972, Congress passed the Education Act Amendment. Title IX of this act prohibits discrimination against women on college campuses in housing, financial assistance, faculty and staff hiring and pay, and, most contentious of all, athletics. It is the latter area—gender equity in sports—that is the subject of the two essays in this section.

The main issue in regard to Title IX is the requirement that women be given athletic opportunities in proportion to their numbers at particular colleges and universities. Thus, if a college campus is 50 percent male, 50 percent female, then according to current interpretations of Title IX, the male-female ratio in sponsored sports must also be 50–50. This proportionality requirement has led some schools to eliminate athletic opportunities for men, as in the case of men's wrestling, in order to make room for more women.

In the essays that follow, the authors discuss the merits of eliminating or changing Title IX rules. The first author, John Irving, a prominent writer and a part-time wrestling coach, while conceding the value of Title IX, argues that it is simply unfair in application. According to Irving, men's teams should not have to suffer in order to meet a proportionality test that is, at best, unreasonable. The second author, law professor Joanna Grossman, disagrees, insisting that not only has Title IX permitted women to make unprecedented gains in sports—gains that they would likely not have obtained without it—but also that the current array of critics of Title IX are setting up a smoke screen to hide the real problem in providing equity for both men and women in sports—the favored position of college football.

Wrestling with Title IX

John Irving

Title IX, the federal law that prohibits sex discrimination in educational programs receiving federal assistance, may be in for an overhaul. This week [January 27, 2003] a committee appointed by the Bush administration will hold its final meetings before submitting its recommendations for changing the law to Secretary of Education Rod Paige. Since Title IX was enacted in 1972, it has been the subject of debate—much of it misguided—about its application to college athletics. At issue now is how to alter the law—or not—so that, as Secretary Paige has put it, we can find ways of "expanding opportunities to ensure fairness for all college athletes."

I hope the commission will realize that what's wrong with Title IX isn't Title IX. What's wrong is that, in practice, there are two Title IX's. The first Title IX was the one passed by Congress in 1972 to put an end to sex discrimination in schools—good for the original Title IX! The second Title IX, the one currently enforced, is the product of a policy interpretation in 1979 by the Department of Education's Office for Civil Rights (but never debated or approved by Congress)—and which is functioning as a gender quota law.

In its prohibition against sex discrimination, the 1972 law expressly states as "exceptions" any "preferential or disparate treatment because of imbalance in participation" or any "statistical evidence of imbalance." In English, this means that Congress recognized that the intent of Title IX was not to establish gender quotas or require preferential treatment as reparation for past discrimination. Smart thinking—after all, the legislation was intended to prohibit discrimination against either sex.

But what happened in 1979—and in subsequent re-evaluations of the law—has invited discrimination against male athletes. The 1979 interpretation required colleges to meet at least one of the following three criteria: that the number of athletes from each sex be roughly equivalent to the number of students enrolled; that colleges demonstrate a commitment to adding women's sports; and that they prove that the athletic interests of female students are effectively accommodated. The problems lie in complying with the first criterion. In order to achieve gender proportionality, men's collegiate sports are being undermined and eliminated. This was never the intention of Title IX.

The proportionality rule stipulates that the ratio of male to female athletes be proportionate to the ratio of male to female students at a particular college. On average, females make up about 56 percent of college enrollment, males 44 percent; for most colleges to be in compliance with proportionality, more than half the athletes on team rosters must be women. Can you imagine this rule being applied to all educational programs—classes in science, engineering, accounting, medicine or law? What about dance, drama or music—not to mention women's studies?

In 1996, the Department of Education further bolstered the proportionality zealots by requiring colleges to count every name on a team's roster—scholarship and nonscholarship athletes, starters and nonstarters. It is this ruling that has prompted a lawsuit by the National Wrestling Coaches Association, the Committee to Save Bucknell Wrestling, the Marquette Wrestling Club, the Yale Wrestling Association, and the National Coalition for Athletics Equity, all of whom argue that the 1996 rules exceed the Department of Education's statutory authority "by effectively mandating the very discrimination that Title IX prohibits."

Why are wrestlers so upset about this? The number of collegiate wrestling programs lost to Title IX compliance is staggering; this is especially alarming because, since 1993, wrestling has been a rapidly growing sport at the high-school level. Data compiled by Gary Abbott, director of special projects at USA Wrestling, indicates that in 2001, there were 244,984 athletes wrestling in high school; only 5,966 got to wrestle in the National Collegiate Athletic Association. Not to put too fine a point on it: there is only one N.C.A.A. spot for every 41 high-school wrestlers. The numbers have been going downhill for a while. In 1982, there were 363 N.C.A.A. wrestling teams with 7,914 wrestlers competing; in 2001, there were only 229 teams with fewer than 6,000 wrestlers. Yet, in that same period, the number of N.C.A.A. institutions has increased from 787 to 1,049. No wonder wrestlers are unhappy.

As for the virtual elimination of walk-ons (nonscholarship athletes) in many men's sports, and the unrealistic capping of male team rosters—again, to make the number of male athletes proportional to the number of females—the problem is that athletic programs are going to absurd lengths to fill the unfilled rosters for women's teams. But women, statistically, aren't interested in participating in intercollegiate athletics to the degree that men are. J. Robinson, wrestling coach at the University of Minnesota, cites intramural sports, which are wholly interest driven, as an example. In a column about Title IX published in the Chronicle of Higher Education, Robinson wrote that "men outnumber women 3-1 or 4-1 on the intramural field."

Don't we need to know the exact numbers for how many women are interested in playing college sports now? But the Women's Sports Foundation, an advocacy group that favors maintaining proportionality, opposes conducting surveys of incoming students—that is, expressly to gauge interest in athletics. These surveys, they say, would force "female athletes to prove their interest in sports in order to obtain the right to participate and be treated fairly." But men would fill out the same surveys.

One suggestion that the presidential commission is considering is counting the available spots on teams, rather than the actual participants. The Women's Sports Foundation rejects this idea, arguing that it counts "ghost female participants." However, the foundation has no objection to counting interest that isn't there.

In fact, those women's groups opposed to tampering with either the 1979 interpretation or the 1996 ruling, which endorses the proportionality arm of Title IX, often argue that there are three ways (at least on paper) for an institution to comply with Title IX—not just proportionality. But only proportionality can be measured concretely. A 1996 clarification letter from the Department of Education refers to the proportionality test as a "safe harbor"—meaning that this simple-to-apply numerical formula can assure an athletic director and a university president that their institution is in compliance and not subject to legal action. In other words, proportionality is not only wrong—it's lazy.

Some women's advocates argue that it is not proportionality that forces athletic directors to cut men's teams; they blame the budget excesses of Division I football and men's basketball. But there are countless examples where money was not the issue in the case of the sport that was dropped. Marquette University had a wrestling team that was completely financed by alumni and supporters; yet the sport was dropped in 2001, to comply with gender equity. (Marquette has no football team.)

Boston College dropped three sports that had only part-time coaches and offered no scholarships; these sports could easily have been sponsored by fundraising. Keep in mind, too, that the majority of male college teams dropped in the 1990s were from Division II and Division III programs, which don't have big-time football or men's basketball.

Furthermore, many Division I football and basketball programs earn millions of dollars a year, enough to support all the other sports programs—men's and women's. Moreover, most schools with high-profile football programs are schools where women's teams have thrived. (Witness the Big 10, the S.E.C., the Big 12 and other Division I athletic conferences, which have produced both winning football teams as well as great women's teams in other sports.)

While eliminating men's sports like wrestling, where the interest in participation is increasing, athletic programs go begging to find women athletes to fill the vacancies on an ever-expanding number of women's teams.

One of the most ludicrous examples of this was the attempt by Arizona State University in Tempe—a cactus-studded campus in the middle of the Sonoran Desert—to add a competitive women's rowing team. There's not a lot of water in Arizona. But the school asked the city to create a body of water (by flooding a dry gulch) on which the team could practice. Because of a lack of funds, the school had to drop the plan. This is probably just as well; taxpayer dollars would have financed scholarships either to rowers from out of state or to teach Arizona women (most of whom have never held an oar) how to row. But Arizona State is to be commended. It not only worked to meet the numerical demands of proportionality, it tried to adhere to the original spirit of Title IX by adding opportunities for women, not by cutting opportunities for men.

To apply the rule of proportionality to men's and women's collegiate athletics amounts to a feminist form of sex discrimination. And I won't be dismissed by that other argument I've heard (ad nauseam) from those women's advocates unwilling to let proportionality go—namely, that to oppose proportionality, or even the crudest enforcement of Title IX to eliminate men's sports programs, is tantamount to being antifeminist and hostile to women in sports. Don't try to lay that on me.

I *am* a women's advocate. I have long been active in the pro-choice movement; my principal political commitment is my longstanding and continuing role as an abortion-rights advocate. But I'm also an advocate of fairness. What is unfair is not Title IX—it is Title IX's enforcement of proportionality, which discriminates against men.

In 1992, Brian Picklo, a walk-on, asked the Michigan State Wrestling coach, Tom Minkel, if he could try out for the team. Picklo had wrestled for only two years in high school and never qualified for state tournaments. Minkel thought Picklo's chances of wrestling in the Big 10 were "slim to none." But Picklo became a two-time Division I All-American, and he won the Big 10 title at 190 pounds. In most wrestling programs across the country today, Brian Picklo wouldn't be allowed to be a walk-on.

Title IX, the original legislation, was conceived as a fairness-for-all law; it has been reinvented as a tool to treat men unfairly. Advocates of proportionality claim that universities that are not "proportional" are breaking the law, but they're not breaking the original law.

The Women's Sports Foundation has accused the presidential commission of politicizing Title IX. But Title IX was politicized by the Department of Education in 1979 and 1996—during Democratic administrations. Is it only now political because a Republican administration is taking a closer look at the way Title IX is applied? (I make this criticism, by the way, as a Democrat. I'd have a hard time being an abortion rights advocate in the Bush administration, wouldn't I?)

Based on 2001 membership data—raw data from the National Federation of State High Schools, and from the N.C.A.A.—for every single N.C.A.A. sports opportunity for a woman, there are 17 high school athletes available to fill the spot; for a man, there are 18. Isn't that equal enough? In fact, women have more opportunity to compete in college than men do. Yet the attitude represented by the Women's Sports Foundation, and other women's groups, is that women are far from achieving gender equity; by their continuing endorsement of proportionality in collegiate athletics, these women's advocates are being purely vindictive.

Years ago, I was playing in a Little League baseball game when an umpire made what I thought was a memorable mistake. Later, in another game, he made it again. I realized it was no mistake at all—he meant to say it. Instead of hollering "Play ball!" at the start of the game, this umpire shouted "Play fair!"

Keep Title IX; eliminate proportionality. Play fair.

Preserve, Not Reverse, Equity for Women in College Athletics

Joanna Grossman

The year 2003 marked the thirtieth anniversary of the passage of Title IX of the Education Amendments of 1972. . . . Title IX is a federal statute banning sex discrimination in educational programs receiving federal financial assistance. . . .

Title IX has been used to challenge gender inequity in a variety of contexts: sexual harassment; pregnancy; school admissions, testing, and scholarships; and, most controversially, school athletics. It is the statute's impact on collegiate athletics that has garnered it its highest praise, as well as its harshest criticism.

Critics have called for amendments of Title IX and its regulations that would make its demand for gender equity—particularly in the realm of college athletics—less strict. Among those critics is the Bush Administration, whose lackluster defense of the statute in a recent lawsuit reveals its utter lack of commitment to gender equity in athletics. (On this issue, the President is perhaps continuing the legacy of his father—who made headlines as vice-president for suggesting in a 1981 speech that Title IX had simply gone too far in the field of athletics.)

The Administration and other critics of Title IX, however, are wrong, and should be opposed. Title IX has turned out to be one of the most important pieces of protection for women against sex discrimination—and in particular, a crucial way to ensure women's equality in college athletics. Rather than going too far, it has held an important line—a line that should not now be moved backwards.

THE HISTORY OF TITLE IX AND ITS REGULATIONS RELEVANT TO COLLEGE ATHLETICS

In 1975, it was made clear that Title IX applied to athletics, as well as to other aspects of education—and the controversy that has plagued this application of the statute began.

That year, the Department of Health, Education, and Welfare (the predecessor to today's Department of Education) issued regulations to implement Title IX. The regulations required institutions to provide "equal athletic opportunity for members of both sexes."

Joanna Grossman is associate professor of law at Hofstra University. From Joanna Grossman, "On the Thirtieth Anniversary of Title IX, We Need to Preserve, Not Reverse, Its Guarantee of Equity for Women in College Athletics," www.FindLaw.com on June 18, 2002, pp. 1–6.

This general standard was supplemented by ten factors to be considered in determining whether equal opportunity was in fact being provided. The first of these factors—and the one most frequently at issue in litigation—asks "whether the selection of sports and levels of competition effectively accommodate the interests and abilities of both sexes."

In a 1979 Policy Interpretation, HEW broke down this factor further, into a three-prong test. Under that test, an institution can show effective accommodation by proving one of three things: First, it can show that it provides athletic opportunities to men and women substantially proportionate to their overall enrollment. Second, it can show that it is engaged in a continuing practice of program expansion with respect to the underrepresented sex (almost always women). Third, it can show that it has fully and effectively accommodated the interests and abilities of the members of the underrepresented sex.

In 1995, the Department of Education sent a "clarification" of the Policy Interpretation to thousands of interested parties. The clarification explained, among other things, that although proportionality alone can provide a "safe harbor" for institutions able to demonstrate it, they are also free to comply with the other prongs of the test instead.

The new clarification also said that institutions were authorized, though not required to eliminate teams, or cap team size, as a way of achieving gender proportionality. (For example, eliminating the men's lacrosse team could be a way to address the fact that there was no women's lacrosse team.)

Finally, the clarification said that participation opportunities should be measured based on actual athletes rather than "slots"—a healthy dose of realism that meant schools had to focus on women athletes, not theoretical possibilities that there could be women athletes.

TITLE IX'S IMPACT ON WOMEN'S SPORTS: OVERWHELMINGLY POSITIVE

There has been a dramatic increase in athletic participation of girls and women since Title IX was enacted. Every available statistic bears this out.

For instance, participation by high school girls in varsity sports has risen from one in twenty-seven to one in two-and-a-half. Meanwhile, participation by college female athletes has risen from under 30,000 to more than 150,000. Interestingly, during the same thirty years, participation by male athletes, at both the high school and college levels, has risen as well, though not nearly as dramatically.

While cause and effect are hard to pinpoint, Title IX litigation and administrative enforcement have clearly been important to these developments. However, there are still important areas of inequity.

For instance, an estimated 80 percent of high schools and colleges run athletic programs that do not comply with Title IX. And, of course, men's athletic programs continue to receive much more money for athletic scholarships, recruiting, coaching, and general operations than women's athletic programs do.

In addition, female coaches get paid a fraction of what male coaches earn, and only two percent of the head coaching jobs for men's teams. . . .

MORE THAN PROPORTIONALITY ALONE:
OTHER WAYS TO SATISFY TITLE IX

In the popular media, the three-prong test of the Title IX regulations has been reduced to a single idea—a requirement of proportionality. The media also suggests that the only way schools achieve proportionality is by cutting men's "minor" sports—like wrestling, swimming, and gymnastics—in order to bring the overall opportunities for men down to the level of women's.

As noted above, the "clarification" does allow men's programs to be cut in order to achieve equality. But in fact, the reality is quite different—as the fact that male athletes have prospered, rather than being harmed, over the last thirty years can attest.

As the clarification also notes, proportionality is only one way to comply with Title IX. Schools can also comply by showing a good-faith effort to expand opportunities for women. Alternatively, they can show that women's interests and abilities are fully accommodated, even though that means they have significantly fewer actual roster spots or teams. More than two-thirds of the schools involved in Title IX cases before the Department of Education during a recent five-year period chose to comply with one of these alternative prongs, rather than by instituting gender proportionality.

Moreover, for schools who do try to achieve proportionality, only some of them accomplish it by cutting men's teams or capping team size. Two-thirds of colleges and universities have not cut any men's teams at all in their efforts to achieve gender equity. (And many schools have cut both women's and men's teams in certain sports, like gymnastics, wrestling, and field hockey, and replaced them with more popular sports like soccer and track.)

But where schools have cut men's teams purportedly to comply with Title IX, those decisions have often been the target of litigation. Male athletes on teams that have been cut have alleged reverse discrimination, claiming that the decision to eliminate their particular team was made solely on the basis of sex.

However, every case bringing a reverse discrimination claim has ultimately been unsuccessful. As the relevant courts have often noted, when a school reallocates resources to remedy past inequity against women, it does not commit a new act of reverse discrimination. Thus, the school does not violate either Title IX or the Equal Protection Clause.

After all, if the remedy for discrimination were called "reverse discrimination" and forbidden, Title IX would be effectively unenforceable. If cutting men's teams were not sometimes an option, then it would be impossible for schools to cure past discrimination without dramatically expanding their budget for athletics, an option not available to most schools.

This conclusion may sound harsh, but consider the situation. A school has a men's lacrosse team and a men's hockey team, and no women's teams in either sport. It can't afford new teams, so it cuts men's lacrosse and creates women's hockey. Although the male lacrosse players will be understandably aggrieved (and so will would-be women's lacrosse players, who never had and never will have a team), the outcome is more fair than the status quo—and that is because of Title IX.

THE CURRENT ASSAULT ON TITLE IX, AND THE ADMINISTRATION'S FAILURE TO DEFEND IT

In February 2002, the National Wrestling Coaches' Association filed a lawsuit against the Department of Education. The Association alleges that the interpretation of Title IX embodied in the Policy Guidance and its subsequent clarification—and still currently in use—is unlawful.

More specifically, the Association argues that this interpretation of the statute authorizes intentional discrimination against male athletes. (Thus, the Association is making the same "reverse discrimination" argument that has failed every time it has been raised before.) Based on this argument, the Association is seeking an order declaring that the Policy Interpretation—and the three-part test it propounded—is invalid and unenforceable.

The Bush Administration had the opportunity in this lawsuit to mount a strong defense of Title IX and its regulations regarding athletics. The argument could have been based on law—consider the many suits dismissing similar "reverse discrimination" claims—not just on policy preferences. Yet instead, the Administration filed a motion to dismiss that cited only narrow technical defects in the lawsuit as a basis for throwing it out of court.

The government's brief is carefully worded to avoid any defense of Title IX on the merits. In fact, the implicit message is to the contrary—that the plaintiffs are wrong only in their choice of defendant (they have sued the government, not the schools), rather than on the merits.

That this Administration will not fight to protect Title IX is clear. So those who support the statute—and more generally, who support equality in women's high school and college athletics—will have to fight for it instead, and fight against the Administration if necessary.

THE RHETORICAL BATTLE OVER TITLE IX

Title IX's critics have tried to score rhetorical points by convincing the public, first, that Title IX's insistence on gender equity is misplaced. They make several arguments, but none are convincing.

First, they claim that women are naturally less interested in sports than men. But in fact, the evidence shows that women's interest in sport is not innately fixed, but dynamic and affected by tangible factors such as playing opportunities and available resources—as well as intangible factors like public opinion and culture.

Watching senior women soccer stars triumph, for example, can motivate a freshman high school girl to follow up on her athletic ambitions. If all the seniors had been cheerleaders and homecoming queens, she might have sacrificed the same ambitions to the ever-present urge to fit in. Are women "naturally" less interested in sports, or "socially" less interested? If the phenomenon is social, it can change.

And it has. Consider the eight-fold rise in female athletic participation at the high school level and the five-fold increase at the college level over the last 30 years—the lifetime of Title IX. It is pretty good—indeed, overwhelming—evidence that opportunities create athletes as much as biology does.

Second, critics often claim that greedy female athletes are responsible for the downfall of men's minor sports. (In our previous scenario, for instance, the men's lacrosse team has been sacrificed so the women's hockey team could be created.)

This argument, too, is unfair and inaccurate. It is unfair for the equality reason given above; women's hockey and lacrosse players should not both have to suffer so men's lacrosse players can prosper. It is inaccurate because of, in a word, football.

The greed and excess, both in terms of participation opportunities and resource allocation, endemic to men's collegiate football programs is by far the greatest reason that other men's sports get the sack. Football, with its unnecessarily large number of players and scholarships (an average of 94 per NCAA Division I team, compared with only 53 per NFL team), eats up the lion's share of athletic resources, which adversely impacts both men's minor sports and women's sports.

And when football is the culprit, there is no equality justification for the loss. The men's lacrosse team loses out simply because the brawnier sport wins out. A man who loses his lacrosse team due to emphasis on football should be upset about the gender-policing of his institution, which prefers more "masculine" sports. In contrast, a man who loses his lacrosse team due to Title IX can at least see that it was unfair that women never had such a team in the first place. But schools themselves feed these misperceptions, often expressly citing Title IX as the reason for cutting a particular men's team.

The reason men's teams must sometimes be cut is because for decades they have received more resources than they should have. Men had almost unlimited opportunities to participate in sports *because* women were denied them, and this denial freed up money the men's teams could use. This artificially inflated allocation of resources—due in large part to stereotypes about women and their lack of interest and ability in sports—does not create an entitlement to have such resources continue.

Ideally, men and women should both have a team in every sport and if the behemoth of football did not consume such huge resources, that might be possible. But if a new women's team must be created at the expense of an old male team, that is only fair. Women are not saying that years of men-only sports should be compensated with the same number of years of women-only sports. Rather, they are only asking for equality today.

Passage of the Nineteenth Amendment (granting women the right to vote) diluted the male vote by half, but nonetheless did not constitute an act of "reverse discrimination." Neither does a reallocation of resources for collegiate sports away from the sex that has historically had plentiful opportunities, and toward the sex that has had few.

Abortion

*P*robably *no domestic issue has polarized the nation more during the last thirty years than abortion. It has proved to be a hotly contested subject in state and national elections and has been the occasion for repeated mass demonstrations in our nation's capital. That abortion has aroused such strong feelings is not surprising, for some see the right to privacy at stake even as others insist that the real issue is the taking of human life.*

In the first selection, Susan Estrich and Kathleen Sullivan argue that, if the decision on abortion is taken out of the hands of the mother, then she will necessarily be forced to surrender autonomy over both her body and family decisions. Government intrusion into these spheres would constitute an intolerable infringement on the fundamental right to privacy—a view shared by the Supreme Court when it upheld a woman's right to an abortion in Roe v. Wade *(1973).*

In the second essay, James Bopp and Richard Coleson contend that the Roe v. Wade *decision was a glaring example of judicial power gone wild, with the justices manufacturing a right to privacy in the Constitution where it was nowhere to be found. In doing so, the Court not only violated its own stated criteria for determining what qualifies as a fundamental right, but also arrogated to itself a power which the people alone may exercise. Bopp and Coleson further argue that the right to abortion should be rejected on moral as well as legal grounds, and they also challenge pro-choice claims that the outlawing of abortions would have harmful social consequences for women.*

Abortion Politics
The Case for the Right to Privacy
Susan R. Estrich and Kathleen M. Sullivan

I. THE EXISTENCE OF A LIBERTY INTEREST

A. Reproductive Choice Is Essential to a Woman's Control of Her Destiny and Family Life

Notwithstanding the abortion controversy, the Supreme Court has long acknowledged an unenumerated right to privacy as a species of "liberty" that the due process clauses protect.[1] The principle is as ancient as *Meyer v. Nebraska*[2] and *Pierce v. Society of Sisters*,[3] which protected parents' freedom to educate their children free of the state's controlling hand. In its modern elaboration, this right continues to protect child rearing and family life from the overly intrusive reach of government.[4] The modern privacy cases have also plainly established that decisions whether to bear children are no less fundamental than decisions about how to raise them. The Court has consistently held since *Griswold v. Connecticut*[5] that the Constitution accords special protection to "matters so fundamentally affecting a person as the decision whether to bear or beget a child," and has therefore strictly scrutinized laws restricting contraception.[6] Roe held that these principles extend no less to abortion than to contraception.

The privacy cases rest, as Justice Stevens recognized in *Thornburgh*, centrally on "'the moral fact that a person belongs to himself [or herself] and not others nor to society as a whole.'"[7] Extending this principle to the abortion decision follows from the fact that "[f]ew decisions are . . . more basic to individual dignity and autonomy" or more appropriate to the "private sphere of individual liberty" than the uniquely personal, intimate, and self-defining decision whether or not to continue a pregnancy.[8]

In two senses, abortion restrictions keep a woman from "belonging to herself." First and most obviously, they deprive her of bodily self-possession. As Chief Justice Rehnquist observed in another context, pregnancy entails

Susan R. Estrich is Robert Kingsley Professor of Law at the University of Southern California, and Kathleen M. Sullivan is Richard E. Lang Professor of Law and Dean of Stanford University Law School. This selection is from Susan R. Estrich and Kathleen M. Sullivan, "Abortion Politics: Writing for an Audience of One," *University of Pennsylvania Law Review*, 138:125–32, pp. 150–55 (1989). Copyright © 1989 by the University of Pennsylvania. Reprinted by permission. Notes have been renumbered to correspond with edited text.

"profound physical, emotional, and psychological consequences."[9] To name a few, pregnancy increases a woman's uterine size 500–1,000 times, her pulse rate by 10 to 15 beats a minute, and her body weight by 25 pounds or more.[10] Even the healthiest pregnancy can entail nausea, vomiting, more frequent urination, fatigue, back pain, labored breathing, or water retention.[11] There are also numerous medical risks involved in carrying pregnancy to term: of every 10 women who experience pregnancy and childbirth, 6 need treatment for some medical complication, and 3 need treatment for major complications.[12] In addition, labor and delivery impose extraordinary physical demands, whether over the 6-to-12 hour or longer course of vaginal delivery, or during the highly invasive surgery involved in a cesarean section, which accounts for one out of four deliveries.[13]

By compelling pregnancy to term and delivery even where they are unwanted, abortion restrictions thus exert far more profound intrusions into bodily integrity than the stomach-pumping the Court invalidated in *Rochin v. California*,[14] or the surgical removal of a bullet from a shoulder that the Court invalidated in *Winston v. Lee*.[15] "The integrity of an individual's person is a cherished value of our society"[16] because it is so essential to identity: as former Solicitor General Charles Fried, who argued for the United States in *Webster*, recognized in another context: "[to say] that my body can be used is [to say] that I can be used."[17]

These points would be too obvious to require restatement if the state attempted to compel abortions rather than to restrict them. Indeed, in colloquy with Justice O'Connor during the *Webster* oral argument, former Solicitor General Fried conceded that in such a case, liberty principles, although unenumerated, would compel the strictest view. To be sure, as Mr. Fried suggested, restrictive abortion laws do not literally involve "laying hands on a woman."[18] But this distinction should make no difference: the state would plainly infringe its citizens' bodily integrity whether its agents inflicted knife wounds or its laws forbade surgery or restricted blood transfusions in cases of private knifings.[19]

Apart from this impact on bodily integrity, abortion restrictions infringe a woman's autonomy in a second sense as well; they invade the autonomy in family affairs that the Supreme Court has long deemed central to the right of privacy. Liberty requires independence in making the most important decisions in life.[20] "The decision whether or not to beget or bear a child" lies at "the very heart of this cluster of constitutionally protected choices,"[21] because few decisions can more importantly alter the course of one's life than the decision to bring a child into the world. Bearing a child dramatically affects "'what a person is, what [s]he wants, the determination of [her] life plan, of [her] concept of the good'" and every other aspect of the "'self-determination . . . [that] give[s] substance to the concept of liberty.'"[22] Becoming a parent dramatically alters a woman's educational prospects,[23] employment opportunities,[24] and sense of self.[25] In light of these elemental facts, it is no surprise that the freedom to choose one's own family formation is "deeply rooted in this Nation's history and tradition."[26]

Today, virtually no one disputes that these principles require heightened scrutiny of laws restricting access to contraception.[27] But critics of *Roe* sometimes argue that abortion is "different in kind from the decision not to conceive in the first place."[28] Justice White, for example, has asserted that, while the liberty interest is fundamental in the contraception context,[29] that interest falls to minimal after conception.[30]

Such a distinction cannot stand, however, because no bright line can be drawn between contraception and abortion in light of modern scientific and medical advances. Contraception and abortion are points on a continuum. Even "conception" itself is a complex process of which fertilization is simply the first stage. According to contemporary medical authorities, conception begins not with fertilization, but rather six to seven days later when the fertilized egg becomes implanted in the uterine wall, itself a complex process.[31] Many medically accepted contraceptives operate after fertilization. For example, both oral contraceptives and the intra-uterine device (IUD) not only prevent fertilization but in some instances prevent implantation.[32] Moreover, the most significant new developments in contraceptive technology, such as RU486, act by foiling implantation.[33] All such contraceptives blur the line between contraception and abortion.

In the absence of a bright physiological line, there can be no bright constitutional line between the moments before and after conception. A woman's fundamental liberty does not simply evaporate when sperm meets ovum. Indeed, as Justice Stevens has recognized, "if one decision is more 'fundamental' to the individual's freedom than the other, surely it is the postconception decision that is the more serious."[34] Saying this much does not deny that profound evolutionary changes occur between fertilization and birth. Clearly, there is some difference between "the freshly fertilized egg and . . . the 9-month-gestated . . . fetus on the eve of birth."[35] But as *Roe v. Wade* fully recognized, such differences go at most to the weight of the state's justification for interfering with a pregnancy; they do not extinguish the underlying fundamental liberty.

Thus *Roe* is not a mere "thread" that the Court could pull without "unravel[ing]" the now elaborately woven "fabric" of the privacy decisions.[36] Rather, *Roe* is integral to the principle that childbearing decisions come to "th[e] Court with a momentum for respect that is lacking when appeal is made to liberties which derive merely from shifting economic arrangements."[37] The decision to become a mother is too fundamental to be equated with the decision to buy a car, choose optometry over ophthalmology, take early retirement, or any other merely economic decision that the government may regulate by showing only a minimally rational basis.

B. Keeping Reproductive Choice in Private Hands Is Essential to a Free Society

Even if there were any disagreement about the degree of bodily or decisional autonomy that is essential to personhood, there is a separate, alternative rationale for the privacy cases: keeping the state out of the business of reproductive decision-making. Regimentation of reproduction is a hallmark of the totalitarian state, from Plato's Republic to Hitler's Germany, from Huxley's *Brave New World* to Atwood's *A Handmaid's Tale*. Whether the state compels reproduction or prevents it, "totalitarian limitation of family size . . . is at complete variance with our constitutional concepts."[38] The state's monopoly of force cautions against *any* official reproductive orthodoxy.

For these reasons, the Supreme Court has long recognized that the privacy right protects not only the individual but also our society. As early as *Meyer*[39] and *Pierce*,[40] the Court acknowledged that "[t]he fundamental theory of liberty" on which a free society rests "excludes any general power of the State to standardize" its citizens.[41] As Justice Powell likewise recognized for the Moore plurality, "a free society" is one that avoids the homogenization of family life.[42]

The right of privacy, like freedoms of speech and religion, protects conscience and spirit from the encroachment of overbearing government. "Struggles to coerce uniformity of sentiment," Justice Jackson recognized in *West Virginia State Board of Education v. Barnett*,[43] are the inevitably futile province of "our totalitarian enemies."[44] Preserving a private sphere for childbearing and childrearing decisions not only liberates the individual; it desirably constrains the state.[45]

Those who would relegate all control over abortion to the state legislatures ignore these fundamental, systematic values. It is a red herring to focus on the question of judicial versus legislative control of reproductive decisions, as so many of *Roe*'s critics do. The real distinction is that between private and public control of the decision: the private control that the courts protect through *Griswold* and *Roe*, and the public control that the popular branches could well usurp in a world without those decisions.

Precisely because of the importance of a private sphere for family, spirit, and conscience, the framers never intended to commit all moral disagreements to the political arena. Quite the contrary:

> The very purpose of a Bill of Rights was to withdraw certain subjects from the vicissitudes of political controversy, to place them beyond the reach of majorities and officials and to establish them as legal principles to be applied by the courts. One's right to life, liberty, and property, to free speech, a free press, freedom of worship and assembly, and other fundamental rights may not be submitted to vote; they depend on the outcome of no elections.[46]

Such "withdrawal" of fundamental liberties from the political arena is basic to constitutional democracy as opposed to rank majoritarianism, and nowhere is such "withdrawal" more important than in controversies where moral convictions and passions run deepest. The inclusion of the free exercise clause attests to this point.[47]

The framers also never intended that toleration on matters of family, conscience, and spirit would vary from state to state. The value of the states and localities as "laborator[ies for] . . . social and economic experiments"[48] has never extended to "'experiments at the expense of the dignity and personality of the individual.'"[49] Rather as Madison once warned, "'it is proper to take alarm at the first experiment on our liberties. We hold this prudent jealousy to be the first duty of citizens, and one of [the] noblest characteristics of the late Revolution.'"[50]

Roe v. Wade thus properly withdrew the abortion decision, like other decisions on matters of conscience, "from the vicissitudes of political controversy." It did not withdraw that decision from the vicissitudes of moral argument or social suasion by persuasive rather than coercive means.[51] In withdrawing the abortion decision from the hot lights of politics, *Roe* protected not only persons but the processes of constitutional democracy. . . .

II. THE POLITICAL PROCESS: NOT TO BE TRUSTED

On October 13, 1989, the *New York Times* declared that the tide had turned in the political process on abortion.[52] The Florida legislature, in special session, rejected a series of proposals to restrict abortion, and Congress voted to expand abortion funding for poor women to cases of rape and incest. And most stunningly of all, the Attorney General of Illinois on November 2, 1989, settled a pending challenge to Illinois' abortion clinic regulation rather than risk winning his case in the United States Supreme Court. These events have triggered the assessment that the post-*Webster* pro-choice mobilization has succeeded. Which raises the question: why not leave these matters to the political process?

The short answer, of course, is that we don't leave freedom of speech or religion or association to the political process, even on good days when the polls suggest they might stand a chance, at least in some states. The very essence of a fundamental right is that it "depend[s] on the outcome of no elections."[53]

The long answer is, as always, that fundamental liberties are not occasions for the experimentation that federalism invites. The right to abortion should not depend on where you live and how much money you have for travel.[54] And, regardless of our recent, at long-last successes, the reality remains that the political process is to be trusted the least where, as here, it imposes burdens unequally.

The direct impact of abortion restrictions falls exclusively on a class of people that consists entirely of women. Only women get pregnant. Only women have abortions. Only women will endure unwanted pregnancies and adverse health consequences if states restrict abortions. Only women will suffer dangerous, illegal abortions where legal ones are unavailable. And only women will bear children if they cannot obtain abortions.[55] Yet every restrictive abortion law has been passed by a legislature in which men constitute a numerical majority. And every restrictive abortion law, by definition, contains an unwritten clause exempting all men from its strictures.

As Justice Jackson wrote, legislators threaten liberty when they pass laws that exempt themselves or people like them: "The framers of the Constitution knew, and we should not forget today, that there is no more effective practical guaranty against arbitrary and unreasonable government than to require that the principles of law which officials would impose upon a minority must be imposed generally."[56] The Supreme Court has long interpreted the equal protection clause to require even-handedness in legislation, lest the powerful few too casually trade away for others key liberties that they are careful to reserve for themselves.

For example, in striking down a law permitting castration of recidivist chicken thieves but sparing white collar embezzlers the knife, the Court implied that, put to an all-or-nothing choice, legislators would rather sterilize no one than jeopardize a politically potent class.[57] In the words of Justice Jackson: "There are limits to the extent to which a legislatively represented majority may conduct biological experiments at the expense of the dignity and personality and natural powers of a minority—even those who are guilty of what the majority defines as crimes."[58]

At least there should be. Relying on state legislatures, as Chief Justice Rehnquist would, to protect women against "abortion regulation reminiscent of the dark ages,"[59] ignores the fact that the overwhelming majority of "those who serve in such bodies"[60] are biologically exempt from the penalties they are imposing.

The danger is greater still when the subject is abortion. The lessons of history are disquieting. Abortion restrictions, like the most classic restrictions on women seeking to participate in the worlds of work and ideas, have historically rested on archaic stereotypes portraying women as persons whose "paramount destiny and mission . . . [is] to fulfill the noble and benign office of wife and mother."[61] Legislation prohibiting abortion, largely a product of the years between 1860 and 1880, reflected *precisely* the same ideas about women's natural and proper roles as other legislation from the same period, long since discredited, that prohibited women from serving on juries or participating in the professions, including the practice of law.[62] And modern studies have found that support for laws banning abortion continues to be an outgrowth of the same stereotypical notions that women's only appropriate roles are those of mother and housewife. In many cases, abortion laws are a direct reaction to the increasing number of women who work outside of the home.[63] Those involved in anti-abortion activities tend to echo the well-known views of Justice Bradley in *Bradwell:*

> Men and women, as a result of . . . intrinsic differences, have different roles to play. Men are best suited to the public world of work, whereas women are best suited to rearing children, managing homes, and loving and caring for husbands. . . . Mothering, in their view, is itself a full-time job, and any woman who cannot commit herself fully to mothering should eschew it entirely.[64]

But the lessons of history are not limited to the powers of enduring stereotypes. History also makes clear that a world without *Roe* will not be a world without abortion but a world in which abortion is accessible according to one's constitutional case. While affluent women will travel to jurisdictions where safe and legal abortions are available, paying whatever is necessary, restrictive abortion laws and with them, the life-threatening prospect of back-alley abortion, will disproportionately descend upon "those without . . . adequate resources"[65] to avoid them. Those for whom the burdens of an unwanted pregnancy may be the most crushing—the young, the poor, women whose color already renders them victims of discrimination—will be the ones least able to secure a safe abortion.

In the years before *Roe*, "[p]oor and minority women were virtually pre-cluded from obtaining safe, legal procedures, the overwhelming majority of which were obtained by white women in the private hospital services on psychiatric indications."[66] Women without access to safe and legal abortions often had dangerous and illegal ones. According to one study, mishandled criminal abortions were the leading cause of maternal deaths in the 1960s,[67] and mortality rates for African-American women were as much as nine times the rate for white women.[68] To trust the political process to protect these women is to ignore the lessons of history and the realities of power and powerlessness in America today.

In the face of such lessons, those who would have us put our faith in the political process might first want to look a little more closely at the victories which are said to support such a choice. The Florida legislature's rejection of proposed abortion restrictions came days *after* the state's highest court held that the State Constitution protects the right to choose abortion, rendering the entire session, by the press's verdict before it began, symbolic at best. The session was still a triumph, but hardly one in which the courts were beside the point. And while extending funding to cases of rape and incest would have been a step forward, the narrowness of the victory and the veto of the resulting legislation should give pause, at least.[69]

We believe that energizing and mobilizing pro-choice voters, and women in particular, is vitally important on its own terms. We hope, frankly, that with apportionment approaching in 2000, that mobilization will affect issues well beyond abortion. We hope more women will find themselves running for office and winning. We hope pro-choice voters and the legislators they elect will attack a range of issues of particular importance to women, including the attention that children receive after they are born.

But we have no illusions. We will lose some along the way. Young and poor and minority women will pay most dearly when we do. That's the way it is in politics. That's why politics should not dictate constitutional rights. . . .

NOTES

1. The right of privacy is only one among many instances in which the Court has recognized rights that are not expressly named in the Constitution's text. To name just a few other examples, the Court has recognized unenumerated rights to freedom of association, see *National Association for the Advancement of Colored People v. Alabama*, 357 U.S. 449, 466 (1958); to equal protection under the Fifth Amendment due process clause, see *Bolling v. Sharpe*, 347 U.S. 497, 500 (1954); to travel between the states, see *Shapiro v. Thompson*, 394 U.S. 618, 638 (1966); to vote, see *Harper v. Virginia Bd. of Elections*, 383 U.S. 663, 665–66 (1966); *Reynolds v. Sims*, 377 U.S. 533, 554 (1964); and to attend criminal trials, see *Richmond Newspapers Inc. v. Virginia*, 448 U.S. 555, 579–80 (1980).
2. 262 U.S. 390 (1923).

3. 268 U.S. 510 (1925).

4. See, e.g., *Moore v. City of East Cleveland*, 431 U.S. 494, 503–06 (1977) (plurality opinion) (noting a constitutional right to live with one's grandchildren); *Loving v. Virginia*, 388 U.S. 1, 12 (1967) (affirming a right to interracial marriage).

5. 381 U.S. 479 (1965).

6. *Eisenstadt v. Baird*, 405 U.S. 438, 453 (1972).

7. *Thornburgh v. American College of Obstetricians & Gynecologists*, 476 U.S. 747, 777 n.5 (1985) (Stevens, J., concurring) (quoting former Solicitor General Fried, "Correspondence," 6 *Phil. & Pub. Aff.* 288–89 (1977)).

8. *Thornburgh*, 476 U.S. at 772.

9. *Michael M. v. Sonoma County Superior Court*, 480 U.S. 464, 471 (1981).

10. See J. Pritchard, P. McDonald & N. Gant, *Williams Obstetrics*, 181–210, 260–63 (17th ed. 1985) [hereinafter *Williams Obstetrics*].

11. See *Id.*

12. See R. Gold, A. Kenney & S. Singh, *Blessed Events and the Bottom Line: Financing Maternity Care in the United States*, 10 (1987).

13. See D. Danforth, M. Hughey & A. Wagner, *The Complete Guide to Pregnancy*, 228–31 (1983); S. Romney, M. J. Gray, A. B. Little, J. Merrill, E. J. Quilligan & R. Stander, *Gynecology and Obstetrics: The Health Care of Women*, 626–37 (2d ed. 1981).

14. 342 U.S. 165 (1952).

15. 470 U.S. 753 (1985).

16. *Id.* at 760.

17. C. Fried, *Right and Wrong*, 121 n.* (1978).

18. "Transcript of Oral Argument in Abortion Case," *N.Y. Times*, Apr. 27, 1989, at B12, col. 5.

19. Likewise, a state would surely infringe reproductive freedom by compelling abortions even if it became technologically possible to do so without "laying hands on a woman."

20. See *Whalen v. Roe*, 429 U.S. 589, 599–600 (1977).

21. *Carey v. Population Serv. Int'l*, 431 U.S. 678, 685 (1977).

22. *Thornburgh v. American College of Obstetricians & Gynecologists*, 476 U.S. 747, 777 n.5 (1985) (Stevens, J., concurring) (quoting C. Fried, *Right and Wrong*, 146–47 (1978)).

23. Teenage mothers have high dropout rates: 8 out of 10 who become mothers at age 17 or younger do not finish high school. See Fielding, *Adolescent Pregnancy Revisited*, 299 Mass. Dep't Pub. Health, 893, 894 (1978).

24. Control over the rate of childbirth is a key factor in explaining recent gains in women's wages relative to men's. See Fuchs, "Women's Quest for Economic Equality," 3 *J. Econ. Persp.* 25, 33–37 (1989).

25. This fact is evident even if the biological mother does not raise her child. Relinquishing a child for adoption may alleviate material hardship, but it is psychologically traumatic. See Winkler & VanKeppel, *Relinquishing Mothers in Adoption: Their Long-Term Adjustment*, Monograph No. 3, Institute of Family Studies (1984).

26. *Moore v. City of East Cleveland,* 431 U.S. 494, 503 (1977) (plurality opinion).

27. The United States has conceded before the Supreme Court that the *Griswold* line of cases was correctly decided. See *Brief for the United States as Amicus Curiae Supporting Appellants,* 11–13; *Webster v. Reproductive Health Serv.,* 1109 S.Ct. 3040 (1989) (No. 88-605); "Transcript of Oral Argument in Abortion Case," *N.Y. Times,* Apr. 27, 1989, at B13, col. 1 (Argument of former Solicitor General Fried on behalf of the United States).

28. *Thornburgh,* 476 U.S. at 792 n.2 (White, J., dissenting).

29. See *Eisenstadt v. Baird,* 405 U.S. 438, 463–64 (1972) (White, J., concurring in result); *Griswold v. Connecticut,* 381 U.S. 479, 502–03 (1965) (White, J., concurring in judgment).

30. See *Thornburgh,* 476 U.S. at 792 n.2 (White, J., dissenting) (arguing that the fetus's presence after conception changes not merely the state justification but "the characterization of the liberty interest itself").

31. See *Williams Obstetrics,* supra note 10, at 88–91; Milby, "The New Biology and the Question of Personhood: Implications for Abortion," 9 *Am. J.L. & Med.* 31, 39–41 (1983). Indeed, the American College of Obstetricians & Gynecologists, the preeminent authority on such matters, has adopted the following official definition of conception: conception consists of "the implantation of the blastocyst [fertilized ovum]" in the uterus, and thus is "not synonymous with fertilization." *Obstetric-Gynecologic Terminology* 229, 327 (E. Hughes ed. 1972). Such a definition is not surprising in view of the fact that less than half of fertilized ova ever successfully become implanted. See "Post-Coital Contraception," 1 *The Lancet* 855, 856 (1983).

32. See R. Hatcher, E. Guest, F. Stewart, G. Stewart, J. Trussell, S. Bowen & W. Gates, *Contraceptive Technology,* 252–53, 377 (14th rev. ed. 1988) [hereinafter *Contraceptive Technology*]; *United States Department of Health and Human Services, IUDs: Guidelines for Informed Decision-Making and Use* (1987).

33. See *Contraceptive Technology,* supra note 32, at 378; Nieman, Choate, Chrousas, Healy, Morin, Renquist, Merriam, Spitz, Bardin, Balieu & Loriaux, "The Progesterone Antagonist RU486: A Potential New Contraceptive Agent," 316 *N. Eng. J. Med.* 187 (1987). RU486 is approved for use in France but not in the United States.

34. *Thornburgh,* 476 U.S. at 776 (Stevens, J., concurring).

35. *Id.* at 779.

36. "Transcript of Oral Argument in Abortion Case," *N.Y. Times,* April 27, 1989, at B12, col. 5 (former Solicitor General Fried, arguing on behalf of the United States). Counsel for Appellees gave the following complete reply: "It has always been my personal experience that when I pull a thread, my sleeve falls off." *Id.* at B13, col. 1 (argument of Mr. Susman).

37. *Thornburgh,* 476 U.S. at 775 (Stevens, J., concurring) (citing *Griswold v. Connecticut,* 381 U.S. 479, 502–03 (1965) (White, J., dissenting)).

38. *Griswold,* 381 U.S. at 497 (Goldberg, J., concurring).

39. *Meyer v. Nebraska,* 262 U.S. 390 (1923).

40. *Pierce v. Society of Sisters,* 268 U.S. 510 (1925).

41. *Id.* at 535.

42. See *Moore v. City of East Cleveland*, 431 U.S. 494, 503 n.11 (1977) (quoting from a discussion of *Griswold* in Pollak, "Thomas I. Emerson, Lawyer and Scholar: *Ipse Custodiet Custodes*," 84 Yale L.J. 638, 653 (1975)).

43. 319 U.S. 624 (1943).

44. *Id.* at 640–41.

45. See generally Rubenfeld, "The Right of Privacy," 102 *Harv. L. Rev.* 737, 804–07 (1989) (arguing that the constitutional right of privacy protects individuals from being turned into instrumentalities of the regimenting state, or being forced into a state-chosen identity).

46. *Barnette*, 319 U.S. at 638.

47. Justice Douglas wrote:

> The Fathers of the Constitution were not unaware of the varied and extreme views of religious sects, of the violence of disagreement among them, and of the lack of any one religious creed on which all men would agree. They fashioned a charter of government which envisaged the widest possible toleration of conflicting views.

    United States v. Ballard, 322 U.S. 78, 87 (1944). See also *Webster*, 109 S. Ct. at 3085 & n.16 (Stevens, J., concurring in part and dissenting in part) (noting that "the intensely divisive character of much of the national debate over the abortion issue reflects the deeply held religious convictions of many participants in the debate").

48. *New State Ice Co. v. Liebmann*, 285 U.S. 262, 311 (1932) (Brandeis, J., dissenting).

49. *Poe v. Ullman*, 367 U.S. 497, 555 (1961) (Harlan, J., dissenting) (quoting *Skinner v. Oklahoma*, 316 U.S. 535, 546 (1942) (Jackson, J., concurring)).

50. *Everson v. Board of Educ.*, 330 U.S. 1, 65 (1947) (Appendix, Rutledge, J., dissenting) (quoting Madison, *Memorial and Remonstrance Against Religious Assessments*).

51. Nor, of course, did it bar political efforts to reduce the abortion rate through noncoercive means, such as funding sex education and contraception, or providing economic security to indigent mothers.

52. See Apple, "An Altered Political Climate Suddenly Surrounds Abortion," *N.Y. Times*, Oct. 13, 1989, at A1, col. 4; see also Berke, "The Abortion-Rights Movement Has Its Day," *N.Y. Times*, Oct. 15, 1989, § 4 at 1, col. 1.

53. *West Virginia Bd. of Educ. v. Barnette*, 319 U.S. 624, 638 (1943).

54. Even if only 10 or 11 states were to preclude abortion within their borders, many women would be held hostage there by the combination of geography, poverty, and youth. This situation would be no more tolerable than the enforcement of racial segregation in a "mere" ten or eleven states in the 1950s.

55. See *Michael M. v. Sonoma County Superior Court*, 450 U.S. 464, 473 (1981) ("[V]irtually all of the significant harmful and inescapably identifiable consequences of teenage pregnancy fall on the young female").

56. *Railway Express Agency v. New York*, 336 U.S. 106, 112 (1949) (Jackson, J., concurring).

57. See *Skinner v. Oklahoma*, 316 U.S. 535 (1942). Cf. Epstein, "The Supreme Court, 1987 Term: Foreword: Unconstitutional Conditions, State Power,

and the Limits of Consent," 102 *Harv. L. Rev.* 4 (1988) (arguing that enforcement of unconstitutional conditions doctrine similarly functions to
put legislatures to an all-or-nothing choice).

58. *Skinner,* 316 U.S. at 546 (Jackson, J., concurring).

59. *Webster,* 109 S. Ct. at 3045.

60. *Id.*

61. *Bradwell v. Illinois,* 83 U.S. (16 Wall.) 130, 142 (1873) (Bradley, J., concurring).

62. See J. Mohr, *Abortion in America: The Origins and Evolution of National Policy.
    1800–1900,* at 168–72 (1978). To many of the doctors who were largely respon-
    sible for abortion restrictions, "the chief purpose of women was to produce
    children; anything that interfered with that purpose, or allowed women to 'in-
    dulge' themselves in less important activities, threatened . . . the future of soci-
    ety itself." Id. at 169. The view of one such 19th-century doctor drew the par-
    allel even more explicitly: he complained that "the tendency to force women
    into men's places" was creating the insidious new idea that a woman's "min-
    istrations . . . as a mother should be abandoned for the sterner rights of voting
    and law making." Id. at 105; see also L. Gordon, *Woman's Body, Woman's Right:
    A Social History of Birth Control in America* (1976) (chronicling the social and po-
    litical history of reproductive rights in the United States).

63. See generally K. Luker, *Abortion and the Politics of Motherhood,* 192–215
    (1984) (describing how the abortion debate, among women, represents a
    "war" between the feminist vision of women in society and the home-
    maker's world view); Luker, "Abortion and the Meaning of Life," in *Abor-
    tion: Understanding Differences* 25, 31–33 (S. Callahan & D. Callahan eds.
    1984) (concluding that "[b]ecause many prolife people see sex as literally
    sacred, *and because, for women, procreative sex is a fundamental part of their "ca-
    reer* . . . abortion is, from their [the prolife] point of view, to turn the world
    upside down").

64. Luker, *supra* note 63, at 31. It is, of course, precisely such stereotypes, as
    they are reflected in legislation, which have over and over again been the
    focus of this Court's modern equal protection cases. See, e.g., *Califano v.
    Goldfarb,* 430 U.S. 199, 206–07 (1977) ("Gender-based differentiation . . . is
    forbidden by the Constitution, at least when supported by no more sub-
    stantial justification than 'archaic and overbroad' generalizations."); *Wein-
    berger v. Wiesenfeld,* 420 U.S. 636, 645 (1975) ("Gender-based generaliza-
    tions" that men are more likely than women to support their families
    "cannot suffice to justify the denigration of the effects of women who do
    work. . . ."); *Stanton v. Stanton,* 421 U.S. 7, 14 (1975) ("A child, male or fe-
    male, is still a child. No longer is the female destined solely for the home
    and the rearing of the family, and only the male for the marketplace and the
    world of ideas."); *Frontiero v. Richardson,* 441 U.S. 677, 684 (1973) ("[O]ur
    Nation has had a long and unfortunate history of sex discrimination . . .
    which in practical effect put women, not on a pedestal, but in a cage.").

65. *Griswold v. Connecticut,* 318 U.S. 479, 503 (1965) (White, J., concurring).

66. *Polgar & Fried,* "The Bad Old Days: Clandestine Abortions Among the Poor
    in New York City Before Liberalization of the Abortion Law," 8 *Fam. Plan.*

Persp. 125 (1976); see also Gold, "Therapeutic Abortions in New York: A 20-Year Review," 55 Am J. Pub. Health 964, 66 (1965) (noting that the ratio of legal hospital abortions per live birth was 5 times more for white women than for women of color, and 26 times more for white women than for Puerto Rican women in New York City from 1951–62); Pilpel, "The Abortion Crisis," in *The Case for Legalized Abortion Now* 97, 101 (Guttmacher ed. 1967) (noting that 93% of in-hospital abortions in New York State were performed on white women who were able to afford private rooms).

67. See Niswander, "Medical Abortion Practice in the United States," in *Abortion and the Law,* 37, 37 (D. Smith ed. 1967).

68. See Gold, *supra* note 66, at 964–65.

69. Requiring prompt reporting of cases of rape and incest to criminal authorities, measured in terms of days if not hours, as the White House has suggested, is to ignore study after study that has found precisely such cases among the least often reported to the police. Yet late reporting, which should be encouraged, becomes grounds to deny funding, and excludes altogether those who fear, often with reasons, to report at all. The pain and suffering of brutal victimization and of an unwanted pregnancy are in no way affected by the speed of the initial criminal report. A small victory, indeed.

President Bush vetoed the legislation on October 21, 1989. The House vote to override was 231–191, short of the necessary two-thirds majority. See 135 *Cong. Rec.* H7482-95 (daily ed. Oct. 25, 1989).

Abortion on Demand Has No Constitutional or Moral Justification

James Bopp Jr. and Richard E. Coleson

I. THE ABSENCE OF A CONSTITUTIONAL RIGHT TO ABORTION

Abortion is not mentioned in the United States Constitution. Yet, in *Roe v. Wade*,[1] the United States Supreme Court held that there is a constitutional right to abortion.

How could the Court justify such a decision? Actually, it never did. The Court simply *asserted* that the "right of privacy . . . is broad enough to encompass a woman's decision whether or not to terminate her pregnancy."[2] Leading constitutional scholars were outraged at the Court's action in *Roe* and vigorously argued that the Court had no constitutional power to create new constitutional rights in this fashion.[3] And, of course, many people were incensed that a whole class of innocent human beings—those awaiting birth—was stripped of all rights, including the right to life itself.

Why does it matter whether abortion is found in the Constitution? Why shouldn't the United States Supreme Court be free to create new constitutional rights whenever it chooses? The answers lie in the carefully designed structure of our democracy, whose blueprints were drawn over two centuries ago by the framers of the Constitution and ratified by the People. This design is explained below as the foundation for rejecting abortion on demand on a constitutional basis.

But what of abortion on demand as a legislative issue? Even if there is no constitutional right to abortion, how much should state legislatures restrict abortion? The answer lies in the states' compelling interest in protecting innocent human life, born or preborn. This interest is given scant attention by abortion rights advocates. Rather, they envision an extreme abortion-on-demand regime; but their societal vision is overwhelmingly rejected by public opinion. As shown below, the states constitutionally may and morally should limit abortion on demand.

James Bopp Jr. is an attorney in the law firm of Bopp, Coleson, & Bostrom, Terre Haute, Indiana, and general counsel to the National Right to Life Committee, Inc. Richard E. Coleson is an associate with Bopp, Coleson, & Bostrom and general counsel, Indiana Citizens for Life, Inc. This article was written especially for *Points of View* in 1992.

A. The People Have Created a Constitutional Democracy with Certain Matters Reserved to Democratic Control and Other Matters Constitutionally Protected

The United States Constitution begins with the words "We the People of the United States . . . do ordain and establish this Constitution for the United States of America."[4] Thus, our Republic is founded on the cornerstone of democratic self-governance—all authority to govern is granted by the People.[5] The only legitimate form of government is that authorized by the People; the only rightful authority is that which the People have granted to the institutions of government.[6]

The People have chosen to authorize a regime governed by the rule of law, rather than rule by persons.[7] The supreme law of the land is the Constitution,[8] the charter by which the People conferred authority to govern and created the governing institutions. Thus, the only legitimate form and authority for governance are found in the Constitution.

The constitutional grant of governing authority was not a general grant but one carefully measured, balanced, and limited. Three fundamental principles underlie the Constitution: (1) the People have removed certain matters from simple majority rule by making them constitutional rights but have retained other matters to be democratically controlled through their elected representatives[9]; (2) the People have distributed governmental powers among three branches of government, with each limited to its own sphere of power[10]; and (3) the People have established a federal system in which the power to regulate certain matters is granted to the national government and all remaining power is retained by the states or by the People themselves.[11]

Because these fundamental principles were violated by the Supreme Court in *Roe v. Wade*,[12] leading constitutional scholars condemned the decision. Law professors and dissenting Supreme Court Justices declared that the Court had seized power not granted to it in the Constitution, because (1) it had created new constitutional rights, which power only the People have,[13] (2) it had acted as a legislature rather than as a court,[14] and (3) it had trespassed into an area governed by the states for over two centuries.[15] The scholarly rejection of *Roe v. Wade* continues to the present.[16]

Although the Court's power grab in *Roe* was a seizure less obvious to the public than tanks in the street, it has nevertheless been rightly characterized as a "limited *coup d'état*."[17] The Court seized from the People a matter they had left to their own democratic governance by declaring a constitutional right to abortion without establishing any connection between the Constitution and a right to abortion. Richard Epstein attacked the Court's *Roe* decision thus, "*Roe* . . . is symptomatic of the analytical poverty possible in constitutional litigation."[18] He concluded: "[W]e must criticize both Mr. Justice Blackmun in *Roe v. Wade* . . . and the entire method of constitutional interpretation that allows the Supreme Court . . . both to 'define' and to 'balance' interests on the major social and political issues of our time."[19]

B. To Determine Which Matters Are Constitutionally Removed from Democratic Control, the Supreme Court Has Developed Tests to Determine Fundamental Rights

The Court did not violate the Constitution in *Roe* simply because there is no *express* mention of abortion in the Constitution. There are matters which the Constitution does not *expressly* mention which the Supreme Court has legitimately found to be within some express constitutional protection. But where the Court employs such constitutional analysis, it must clearly demonstrate that the newly recognized constitutional right properly falls within the scope of an express right. This requires a careful examination and explanation of what the People intended when they ratified the particular constitutional provision in question. It was the Roe Court's failure to provide this logical connection between the Constitution and a claimed right to abortion which elicited scholarly outrage.

Under the Supreme Court's own tests, the Court had to find that the claimed right to abortion was a "fundamental" right in order to extend constitutional protection to it under the Fourteenth Amendment, the constitutional provision in which the Court claimed to have found a right to abortion.[20] The Fourteenth Amendment guarantees that no "State [shall] deprive any person of life, liberty, or property, without due process of law."[21] While the provision on its face seems to guarantee only proper legal proceedings before a state may impose capital punishment, imprisonment, or a fine, the Court has assumed the authority to examine activities asserted as constitutional rights to determine whether—in the Court's opinion—they fall within the concept of "liberty."[22] The notion that the Court may create new constitutional rights at will by reading them into the "liberty" clause of the Fourteenth Amendment could readily lead to a rejection of the foundational constitutional premise of the rule of law, not of persons. If a handful of Justices can place whatever matters they wish under the umbrella of the Constitution—totally bypassing the People and their elected representatives—then these Justices have constituted themselves as Platonic guardians,[23] thereby rejecting the rule of law for the rule of persons. What would prevent a majority of the Supreme Court from declaring that there is a constitutional right to practice, e.g., infanticide or polygamy (matters which the states have historically governed)?

This danger has caused many scholars to reject the sort of analysis which allows five Justices (a majority of the Court) to read new constitutional rights into the "liberty" clause.[24] It led the Court in earlier years to forcefully repudiate the sort of analysis the Court used in *Roe v. Wade*.[25] This danger has caused the current Court to establish more rigorous tests for what constitutes a constitutional right to prevent the Supreme Court from "roaming at large in the constitutional field."[26] These tests had been established at the time of *Roe*, but were ignored in that case.[27]

The Court has developed two tests for determining whether a new constitutional right should be recognized. The first test asks whether an asserted fundamental right is "implicit in the concept of ordered liberty."[28] The second test—a historical test—is whether the right asserted as "fundamental" is "so rooted in the traditions and conscience of our people as to be ranked as fundamental."[29] The historical test is the one now primarily relied upon by the Court.

C. Applying the Proper Test for Determining Constitutional Rights Reveals That Abortion Is Not a Constitutional Right

In *Roe,* the Court should have determined whether or not there is a constitutional right to abortion by asking whether it has historically been treated as "implicit in the concept of ordered liberty" in this nation or whether it has been "deeply rooted [as a right] in this Nation's history and tradition."

The *Roe* opinion itself recounted how abortion had been regulated by the states by statutory law for over a century and before that it had been regulated by the judge-made common law inherited from England.[30] In fact, the period from 1860 to 1880—the Fourteenth Amendment was ratified in 1868[31]—saw "the most important burst of anti-abortion legislation in the nation's history."[32] Therefore, the framers of the Fourteenth Amendment and the People who ratified it clearly did not intend for the Amendment to protect the right to abortion, which was considered a crime at the time.

Now Chief Justice Rehnquist stated well the case against *Roe's* right to abortion in his 1973 dissent to that decision:

> To reach its result, the Court necessarily has had to find within the scope of the Fourteenth Amendment a right that was apparently completely unknown to the drafters of the Amendment. As early as 1821, the first state law dealing directly with abortion was enacted by the Connecticut Legislature. By the time of the adoption of the Fourteenth Amendment in 1868, there were at least 36 laws enacted by state or territorial legislatures limiting abortion. While many states have amended or updated their laws, 21 of the laws on the books in 1968 remain in effect today. Indeed, the Texas statute struck down today was, as the majority notes, first enacted in 1857 and has remained substantially unchanged to the present time.
>
> There apparently was no question concerning the validity of this provision or of any of the other state statutes when the Fourteenth Amendment was adopted. The only conclusion possible from this history is that the drafters did not intend to have the Fourteenth Amendment withdraw from the states the power to legislate with respect to this matter.[33]

Thus, applying the Court's own tests, it is clear that there is no constitutional right to abortion. As a result, the Supreme Court has simply arbitrarily declared one by saying that the right of privacy—previously found by the Court in the "liberty" clause—"is broad enough to encompass a woman's decision whether or not to terminate her pregnancy."[34] In so doing, the Court brushed aside the restraints placed on it by the Constitution, seized power from the People, and placed within the protections of the Constitution an abortion right that does not properly belong there.

One thing is clear from this nation's abortion debate: abortion advocates do not trust the People to decide how abortion should be regulated.[35] However, in rejecting the voice of the People, abortion partisans also reject the very foundation of our democratic Republic and seek to install an oligarchy—with the Court governing the nation—a system of government rejected by our Constitution.

II. THE INTEREST IN PROTECTING INNOCENT HUMAN LIFE

Abortion rights advocates generally ignore one key fact about abortion: abortion requires the willful taking of innocent human life. Abortion involves not merely the issue of what a woman may do with her body. Rather, abortion also involves the question of what may the woman do with the body of another, the unborn child.

A. The People Have an Interest in Protecting Preborn Human Life

The fact that human life begins at conception was well-known at the time the Fourteenth Amendment was ratified in 1868. In fact it was precisely during the time when this Amendment was adopted that the medical profession was carrying the news of the discovery of cell biology and its implications into the legislatures of the states and territories. Prior to that time, science had followed the view of Aristotle that the unborn child became a human being (i.e., received a human soul) at some point after conception (40 days for males and 80–90 days for females).[36] This flawed scientific view became the basis for the "quickening" (greater legal protection was provided to the unborn from abortion after the mother felt movement in the womb than before) distinction in the common law received from England, which imposed lesser penalties for abortions performed prior to "quickening." With the scientific discovery of cell biology, however, the legislatures acted promptly to alter abortion laws to reflect the newly established scientific fact that individual human life begins at conception.

Victor Rosenblum summarized the history well:

> Only in the second quarter of the nineteenth century did biological research advance to the extent of understanding the actual mechanism of human reproduction and of what truly comprised the onset of gestational development. The nineteenth century saw a gradual but profoundly influential revolution in the scientific understanding of the beginning of individual mammalian life. Although sperm had been discovered in 1677, the mammalian egg was not identified until 1827. The cell was first recognized as the structural unit of organisms in 1839, and the egg and sperm were recognized as cells in the next two decades. These developments were brought to the attention of the American state legislatures and public by those professionals most familiar with their unfolding import—physicians. It was the new research findings which persuaded doctors that the old "quickening" distinction embodied in the common and some statutory law was unscientific and indefensible.[37]

About 1857, the American Medical Association led the "physicians' crusade," a successful campaign to push the legal protection provided for the unborn by abortion laws from quickening to conception.[38]

What science discovered over a century before *Roe v. Wade* was true in 1973 (when *Roe* was decided) and still holds true today. For example, a recent textbook on human embryology declared:

> It is the penetration of the ovum by a spermatozoon and the resultant mingling of the nuclear material each brings to the union that constitutes the culmination of the process of *fertilization* and *marks the initiation of the life of a new individual.*[39]

However, abortion rights advocates attempt to obscure the scientific evidence that individual human life begins at conception by the claiming that conception is a "complex" process and by confusing contraception with abortion.[40]

The complexity of the process of conception does not change the fact that it marks the certain beginning of individual human life.[41] Moreover, the complex process of conception occurs in a very brief time at the beginning of pregnancy.[42]

Furthermore, the fact that some so-called "contraceptives" actually act after conception and would be more correctly termed "abortifacients" (substances or devices causing abortion, i.e., acting to abort a pregnancy already begun at conception) does nothing to blur the line at which individual human life begins. It only indicates that some so-called "contraceptives" have been mislabelled.[43] Such mislabelling misleads women, who have a right to know whether they are receiving a contraceptive or are having an abortion.

The "spin"[44] which abortion advocates place on the redefinition of "contraception" is deceptive in two respects. First, there is a clear distinction between devices and substances which act before conception and those which act after conception. This was admitted by Planned Parenthood itself (before it became involved in advocating, referring for, and performing abortions) in a 1963 pamphlet entitled *Plan Your Children:* "An abortion kills the life of a baby after it has begun. . . . Birth control merely postpones the beginning of life."[45]

Second, even if there were no "bright physiological line . . . between the moments before and after conception"[46] this does not mean there can be no constitutional line.[47] At *some point* early in pregnancy, scientific truth compels the conclusion that individual human life has begun. If the indistinction is the real problem, then abortion advocates should be joining prolife supporters in protecting unborn life from a time when there is certitude.[48] However, abortion partisans are not really interested in protecting unborn human life from the time when it may be certain that it exists. They are seeking to justify absolute, on-demand abortion throughout pregnancy.

B. Abortion Rights Advocates Envision an Abortion-on-Demand Regime Unsupported by the People

Abortion rights proponents often argue that our democratic Republic must sanction abortion on demand lest women resort to dangerous "back-alley" abortions. The claims of abortion advocates that thousands of women died each year when abortion was illegal are groundless fabrications created for polemical purposes.[49] In reality, the Surgeon General of the United States has estimated that only a handful of deaths occurred each year in the United States due to illegal abortions.[50] Even since *Roe,* there are still maternal deaths from legal abortions.[51] As tragic as the death of any person is, it must be acknowledged that women who obtain illegal abortions do so by choice and most women will choose to abide by the law. In contrast, preborn human beings are destroyed—without having a choice—at the rate of about 1.5 million per year in the United States alone.[52]

Abortion supporters also resort to the practice of personally attacking prolifers and making false charges about them.[53] A founding member of what is now called the National Abortion Rights Action League (NARAL) chronicles how prolifers were purposely portrayed as Catholics whenever possible, in an attempt to appeal to latent (and sometimes overt) anti-Catholic sentiment in certain communities.[54] It is also routinely claimed that opposition to abortion is really an attempt to "keep women in their place"[55]—to subjugate them—as if requiring fathers to support their children subjugates them. And prolifers are depicted as forcing what are merely their religious views upon society,[56] despite the fact that the United States Supreme Court has held that opposition to abortion "is as much a reflection of 'traditionalist' values towards abortion, as it is an embodiment of the views of any particular religion."[57] Those attempting so to "poison the well," by attacking prolife supporters with untruthful allegations, ignore the fact that polls consistently show that abortion opinion is rather evenly divided in our country within all major demographic groups. For example, women are roughly equally divided on the subject, as are whites, non-whites, Republicans and Democrats.[58] Abortion advocates also ignore the fact that most prolifers simply are opposed to the taking of what they consider (and science demonstrates) to be innocent human life.

Of even greater risk than the risk to a few women who might choose to obtain illegal abortions is the effect of abortion on demand—for any or no reason—on society. Abortion cheapens the value of human life, promotes the idea that it is permissible to solve one's problems at the expense of another, even to the taking of the other's life, legitimizes violence (which abortion is against the unborn) as an appropriate solution for problems, and exposes a whole class of human beings (those preborn) to discrimination on the basis of their age or place of residence (or sometimes their race, gender, or disability).

The regime which abortion-on-demand advocates envision for our society is a radical one. Their ideal society is one where abortions may be obtained for any reason, including simply because the child is the wrong sex; where a husband need not be given any consideration in (or even notice of) an abortion decision involving a child which he fathered; where fathers are shut out even when the child to be aborted might be the only one a man could ever have; where parents could remain ignorant of their daughter's abortion, even when she is persuaded to abort by counselors at an abortion mill whose practitioners care only about financial gain, practice their trade dangerously, and never bother to follow up with their patients; where abortion may be used as a means of birth control; where abortionists do not offer neutral, scientific information about fetal development (and about resources for choosing alternatives to abortion) to women considering abortion; where women are not given adequate time to consider whether they really want an abortion; where abortion is available right up to the time of birth; and where our taxes are used to pay for abortion on demand.[59]

The American People reject such a regime. In fact, polls show that an overwhelming majority would ban well over 90 percent of all abortions that are performed.[60] For example a *Boston Globe* national poll . . . revealed that:

> Most Americans would ban the vast majority of abortions performed in this country. . . .
>
> While 78 percent of the nation would keep abortion legal in limited circumstances, according to the poll, those circumstances account for a tiny percentage of the reasons cited by women having abortions.
>
> When pregnancy results from rape or incest, when the mother's physical health is endangered and when there is likely to be a genetic deformity in the fetus, those queried strongly approve of legal abortion.
>
> But when pregnancy poses financial or emotional strain, or when the woman is alone or a teen-ager—the reasons given by most women seeking abortions—an overwhelming majority of Americans believes abortion should be illegal, the poll shows.[61]

Yet *Family Planning Perspectives,* a publication of the Alan Guttmacher Institute, which is a research arm of the Planned Parenthood Federation, reveals that these are precisely the reasons why over 90 percent of abortions are performed.[62]

Thus, it is little wonder that the Supreme Court's effort to settle the abortion question with its decision in *Roe v. Wade* has utterly failed. That there is not an even greater groundswell of public opposition to abortion must be attributed to the fact that many Americans are not aware that *Roe* requires virtual abortion on demand for the full nine months of pregnancy.[63] Many people still believe that abortion is only available in the earliest weeks of pregnancy and that abortions are usually obtained for grave reasons, such as rape and incest, which abortion rights advocates always talk about in abortion debates. Of course, such "hard" cases make up only a tiny fraction of all abortions, and many state abortion laws, even before *Roe,* allowed abortions for such grave reasons. It is clear, therefore, that the People reject the radical abortion-on-demand regime promoted by abortion rights advocates.

III. CONCLUSION: STATES CONSTITUTIONALLY MAY AND MORALLY SHOULD LIMIT ABORTION ON DEMAND

One of the principles underlying our liberal democratic Republic is that we as a People choose to give the maximum freedom possible to members of our society. John Stuart Mill's essay *On Liberty,*[64] a ubiquitous source on the subject, is often cited for the principle that people ought to be granted maximum liberty—

almost to the degree of license. Yet, Mill himself set limits on liberty relevant to the abortion debate. Mill wrote his essay *On Liberty* to assert "one very simple principle," namely, "[t]hat the only purpose for which power can be rightfully exercised over any member of a civilized community, against his will, is to prevent harm to others."[65] Thus, under Mill's principles, abortion should go unrestricted only if it does no harm to another. But that, of course, is precisely the core of the abortion debate. If a fetus is not really an individual human being until he or she is born, then the moral issue is reduced to what duty is owed to potential life (which is still a significant moral issue). If however, a fetus is an individual human being from the moment of conception (or at least some time shortly thereafter), then the unborn are entitled to legal protection. Ironically, the United States Supreme Court neglected this key determination—when human life begins—in its *Roe* decision.[66]

Science, of course, has provided the answer to us for well over a hundred years. Indeed, modern science and technological advances have impressed upon us more fully the humanity and individuality of each unborn person. As Dr. Liley has said:

> Another fallacy that modern obstetrics discards is the idea that the pregnant woman can be treated as a patient alone. No problem in fetal health or disease can any longer be considered in isolation. At the very least two people are involved, the mother and her child.[67]

In fact, since *Roe,* the technology for improving fetal therapy is advancing exponentially.[68] In sum, modern science has shown us that:

> The fetus as patient is becoming more of a reality each year. New medical therapies and surgical technology increasingly offer parents a new choice when a fetus has a particular disorder. Recently, the only choices were abortion, early delivery, vaginal versus a cesarean delivery, or no intervention. We are now able to offer medical and/or surgical intervention as a viable alternative to a number of infants. With advancing technologies, it is clearly evident that many new and exciting therapies lie just ahead for the fetus.[69]

Because all civilized moral codes limit the liberty of individuals where the exercise of liberty would result in the taking of innocent human life, arguments that abortion is necessary to prevent the subjugation of women must also be rejected.[70] It cannot logically be considered the subjugation of anyone to prevent him or her from taking innocent human life; otherwise, society could not prevent infanticide, homicide, or involuntary euthanasia. No civilized society could exist if the unjustified killing of one citizen by another could not be prosecuted.

Nor do abortion restrictions deny women equality by denying them the same freedom which men have. Men do not have the right to kill their children, nor may they force women to do so. Thus, abortion rights advocates are really arguing for a right that men don't have, and, indeed, no one should have—the right to take innocent human life.

Society has recognized that in some situations men and women should be treated differently, because they are biologically different and are, therefore, not similarly situated for constitutional purposes. For example, the Supreme Court decided in 1981 that a statute that permitted only men to be drafted was not un-constitutional because "[m]en and women . . . are simply not similarly situated for purposes of a draft or registration for a draft."[71] The same principle, how-ever, made constitutional a Navy policy which allowed women a longer period of time for promotion prior to mandatory discharge than was allowed for men.[72] The Supreme Court in this case found that "the different treatment of men and women naval officers . . . reflects, not archaic and overbroad general-izations, but, instead, the demonstrable fact that male and female line officers . . . are not similarly situated."[73] Because men and women are not similarly sit-uated—by the dictates of nature rather than by society or the law—with respect to pregnancy, it is neither a denial of equality to women nor the subjugation of women to provide legal protection for unborn human beings.[74]

It is essential to a civilized society to limit liberties where reasonably nec-essary to protect others. Thus, government has required involuntary vaccina-tion to prevent a plague from decimating the community,[75] military conscrip-tion to prevent annihilation of the populace by enemies,[76] and the imposition of child support—for 18 years—upon fathers unwilling to support their chil-dren.[77] These and other limits on freedom are not the subjugation of citizens, but are the essence of life in a community.

In sum, the states constitutionally may and morally should limit abortion on demand.

NOTES

1. 410 U.S. 113 (1973).
2. *Id.* at 153.
3. See *infra*, notes 13–19 and accompanying text.
4. U.S. Const., preamble.
5. In the landmark case of *Marbury v. Madison*, 1 Cranch 137, 176 (1803), the United States Supreme Court explained, "That the people have an original right to establish, for their future government, such principles, as, in their own opinion, shall most conduce to their own happiness is the basis on which the whole American fabric has been erected. See also The Declara-tion of Independence, para. 2 (U.S. 1776); *The Federalist*, No. 49 (J. Madison).
6. *Marbury*, 1 Cranch at 176 ("The original and supreme will [of the People] organizes the government, and assigns to different departments their re-spective powers. It may either stop here, or establish certain limits not to be transcended by those departments. The government of the United States is of the latter description.").
7. See, e.g., *id.* at 163 ("The government of the United States has been em-phatically termed a government of laws, and not of men."); *Akron v. Akron Center for Reproductive Health*, 462 U.S. 416, 419–20 (1983) (We are a "society governed by the rule of law.").
8. *Marbury*, 1 Cranch at 177 ("Certainly all those who have framed written constitutions contemplate them as forming the fundamental and para-

mount law of the nation. . . ."); *id.* at 179 ("[T]he constitution of the United States confirms and strengthens the principle, supposed to be essential to all written constitutions, that a law repugnant to the constitution is void; and that courts, as well as other departments, are bound by that instrument.").

9. The Constitution enumerates certain rights; the creation of additional constitutionally protected rights is through amending the Constitution, which depends upon establishing public support for such a right by a supermajority of the People acting through their elected representatives. U.S. Const., art. V. Cf. Bork, "Neutral Principles and Some First Amendment Problems," 47 *Ind. L.J.* 1, 3 (1971).

10. U.S. Const., art. I, § 1, art. II, § 1, art. III, § 1.

11. U.S. Const., amend. IX ("The enumeration in the Constitution, of certain rights, shall not be construed to deny or disparage others retained by the people."), amend. X ("The powers not delegated to the United States by the Constitution, nor prohibited by it to the States, are reserved to the States respectively, or to the people.").

12. 410 U.S. 113.

13. Ely, "The Wages of Crying Wolf: A Comment on *Roe v. Wade,*" 82 Yale L.J. 920, 947 (1973) (*Roe* was "a very bad decision. Not because it [would] perceptibly weaken the Court . . . and not because it conflict[ed] with [his] idea of progress. . . . It [was] bad because it [was] bad constitutional law, or rather because it [was] not constitutional law and [gave] almost no sense of an obligation to try to be.") (emphasis in the original). *Doe v. Bolton,* 410 U.S. 179, 222 (1973) (White, J., dissenting in this companion case to *Roe*) (The Court's action is "an exercise of raw judicial power. . . . This issue, for the most part, should be left with the people and to the political processes the people have devised to govern their affairs.").

14. The *Michigan Law Review,* in an edition devoted to abortion jurisprudence, contained two passages which summarize the scholarly critiques well. In the first, Richard Morgan wrote:

> Rarely does the Supreme Court invite critical outrage as it did in *Roe* by offering so little explanation for a decision that requires so much. The stark inadequacy of the Court's attempt to justify its conclusions . . . suggests to some scholars that the Court, finding no justification at all in the Constitution, unabashedly usurped the legislative function.

Morgan, "*Roe v. Wade* and the Lesson of the Pre-*Roe* Case Law," 77 *Mich. L. Rev.* 1724, 1724 (1979). The editors of the journal concluded from their survey of the literature on *Roe*, "[T]he consensus among legal academics seems to be that, whatever one thinks of the holding, the opinion is unsatisfying." "Editor's Preface," 77 *Mich. L. Rev.* (no number) (1979).

15. *Roe,* 400 U.S. at 174–77 (Rehnquist, J., dissenting).

16. See, e.g., Wardle, " 'Time Enough': *Webster v. Reproductive Health Services* and the Prudent Pace of Justice," 41 *Fla. L. Rev.* 881, 927–49 (1989); Bopp & Coleson, "The Right to Abortion: Anomalous, Absolute, and Ripe for Reversal,"

3 *B.Y.U. J. Pub. L.* 181, 185–92 (1989) (cataloging critiques of *Roe* in yet another critique of *Roe*).

17. Bork, *supra* note 9, at 6.
18. Epstein, "Substantive Due Process by Any Other Name: The Abortion Cases," 1973 *Sup. Ct. Rv.* 159, 184.
19. *Id.* at 185.
20. The Court acknowledged this duty in Roe itself, but failed to apply the usual tests for determining what rights are rightfully deemed "fundamental." *Roe,* 410 U.S. at 152.
21. U.S. Const., amend. XIV, § 1, cl. 3.
22. *Roe v. Wade,* 410 U.S. 113, revived this sort of "substantive due process" analysis in recent years.
23. The Greek philosopher Plato advocated rule by a class of philosopher-guardians as the ideal form of government. A. Bloom, *The Republic of Plato,* 376c, lines 4–5, 412b–427d (1968).
24. See, e.g., Ely, *supra* note 13; Bork, *supra* note 9.
25. In repudiating an earlier line of "substantive due process" (i.e., finding new rights in the "liberty" clause of the Fourteenth Amendment) cases symbolized by *Lochner v. New York,* 198 U.S. 45 (1905), the Supreme Court declared that the doctrine "that due process authorizes courts to hold laws unconstitutional when they believe the legislature has acted unwisely, has been discarded." *Ferguson v. Skrupa,* 372 U.S. 726, 730 (1963). The Court concluded in *Ferguson,* "We have returned to the original constitutional proposition that courts do not substitute their social and economic beliefs for the judgment of legislative bodies, who are elected to pass laws." Id.
26. *Griswold v. Connecticut,* 381 U.S. 479, 502 (1965) (Harlan, J., concurring.)
27. Cf. *Duncan v. Louisiana,* 391 U.S. 145, 149–50 n.14 (1968), with *Roe v. Wade,* 410 U.S. at 152, and *Moore v. City of East Cleveland,* 431 U.S. 494, 503–04 n.12 (1977). See also Ely, *supra* note 13, at 931 n.79 (The *Palko* test was of "questionable contemporary vitality" when *Roe* was decided).
28. *Roe,* 410 U.S. at 152 (quoting *Palko v. Connecticut,* 302 U.S. 319, 325 (1937)) (quotation marks omitted).
29. *Palko,* 302 U.S., at 325 (quoting *Snyder v. Massachusetts,* 291 U.S. 97, 105 (1934)) (quotation marks omitted).
30. *Roe,* 410 U.S. at 139.
31. *Black's Law Dictionary,* 1500 (5th ed. 1979).
32. J. Mohr, *Abortion in America: The Origins and Evolution of National Policy 1800–1900,* 200 (1978). These laws were clearly aimed at protecting preborn human beings and not just maternal health, *id.* at 35–36, so that medical improvements bringing more maternal safety to abortions do not undercut the foundations of these laws, as *Roe* alleged. *Roe,* 410 U.S. at 151–52.
33. *Roe,* 410 U.S. at 174–77 (Rehnquist, J., dissenting) (citations and quotation marks omitted).
34. *Id.* at 153.
35. *Cf.* Estrich & Sullivan, "Abortion Politics: Writing for an Audience of One," 138 *U. Pa. L. Rev.* 119, 150–55 (1989), with *Webster v. Reproductive Health Ser-*

vices, 109 S. Ct. 3040, 3058 (1989) (plurality opinion). In *Webster*, the plurality opinion declared:

> The goal of constitutional adjudication is to hold true the balance between that which the Constitution puts beyond the reach of the democratic process and that which it does not. We think we have done that today. The dissent's suggestion that legislative bodies, in a Nation where more than half of our population is women, will treat our decision today as an invitation to enact abortion regulation reminiscent of the dark ages not only misreads our views but does scant justice to those who serve in such bodies and the people who elect them.

Id. (citation omitted).

36. *Roe*, 410 U.S. at 133 n.22.
37. *The Human Life Bill: Hearings on S. 158 Before the Subcomm. on Separation of Powers of the Senate Comm. on the Judiciary*, 97th Cong., 1st Sess. 474 (statement of Victor Rosenblum). See also Dellapenna, "The History of Abortion: Technology, Morality, and Law," 40 *U. Pitt. L. Rev.* 359, 402–04 (1979).
38. J. Mohr, *supra* note 32, at 147–70. This 19th-century legislation was designed to protect the unborn as stated explicitly by 11 state court decisions interpreting these statutes and implicitly by 9 others. Gorby, "The 'Right' to an Abortion, the Scope of Fourteenth Amendment 'Personhood,' and the Supreme Court's Birth Requirement," 1979 *S. Ill, U.L.J.* 1, 16–17. Twenty-six of the 36 states had laws against abortion as early as 1865, the end of the Civil War, as did six of the ten territories. Dellapenna, *supra* note 37, at 429.
39. B. Patten, *Human Embryology*, 43 (3rd ed. 1969) (emphasis added). See also L. Arey, *Developmental Anatomy*, 55 (7th ed. 1974); W. Hamilton & H. Mossman, *Human Embryology*, 1, 14 (4th ed. 1972); K. Moore, *The Developing Human: Clinically Oriented Embryology*, 1, 12, 24 (2nd ed. 1977); *Human Reproduction, Conception and Contraception*, 461 (Hafez ed., 2nd ed. 1980); J. Greenhill & E. Friedman, *Biological Principles and Modern Practice of Obstetrics*, 17, 23 (1974); D. Reid, K. Ryan & K. Benirschke, *Principles and Management of Human Reproduction*, 176 (1972).
40. See, e.g., Estrich & Sullivan, *supra* note 35, at 128–29. While a complete discussion of cell biology, genetics and fetology is beyond the scope of this brief writing, the standard reference works cited by Estrich & Sullivan verify the fact that individual human life begins at conception.
41. *Supra*, note 39.
42. *Id.*
43. By its etymology (*contra* + *conception*, i.e., against conception) and traditional and common usage, the term *"contraception"* properly refers to "[t]he prevention of conception or impregnation," Dorland's *Illustrated Medical Dictionary*, 339 (24th ed. 1965), or a "deliberate prevention of conception or impregnation," *Webster's Ninth New Collegiate Dictionary*, 284 (1985).
44. Estrich & Sullivan, *supra* note 35, at 1.
45. Planned Parenthood International, *Plan Your Children* (1963).
46. Estrich & Sullivan, *supra* note 35, at 129.

47. At oral arguments in *Webster v. Reproductive Health Services*, 109 S. Ct. 3040 (1989), Justice Antonin Scalia could see a distinction between contraception and abortion, remarking, "I don't see why a court that can draw that line [between the first, second, and third trimesters of pregnancy] cannot separate abortion from birth control quite readily."

48. For example, the West German Constitutional Court in 1975 set aside a federal abortion statute which was too permissive, for it "did not sufficiently protect unborn life." M. Glendon, *Abortion and Divorce in Western Law*, 33 (1987). The West German court began with the presumption that "at least after the fourteenth day, developing human life is at stake." Id. at 34.

49. B. Nathanson, *Aborting America*, 193 (1979). Nathanson, a former abortionist and early, organizing member of the National Association for the Repeal of Abortion Laws (NARAL, now known as the National Abortion Rights Action League), says:

> In N.A.R.A.L. . . . it was always "5,000 to 10,000 deaths a year [from illegal abortion]." I confess that I knew the figures were totally false. . . . In 1967, with moderate A.L.I.-type laws in three states, the federal government listed only 160 deaths from illegal abortion. In the last year before the [*Roe*] era began, 1972, the total was only 39 deaths. Christopher Tietze estimated 1,000 maternal deaths as the outside possibility in an average year before legalization; the actual total was probably closer to 500.

Id. at 193. Nathanson adds that even this limited "carnage" argument must now be dismissed "because technology has eliminated it." *Id.* at 194 (referring to the fact that even abortions made illegal by more restrictive abortion laws will generally be performed with modern techniques providing greater safety, and antibiotics now resolve most complications).

50. U.S. Dept. of Health and Human Services, *Centers for Disease Control Abortion Surveillance*, 61 (annual summary 1978, issued Nov. 1980) (finding that there were 39 maternal deaths due to illegal abortion in 1972, the last year before *Roe*).

51. Deaths from legally induced abortions were as follows: 1972 = 24, 1973 = 26, 1974 = 26, 1975 = 31, 1976 = 11, 1977 = 17, 1978 = 11. *Id.* During the same period, deaths from illegal abortions continued as follows: 1972 = 39, 1973 = 19, 1974 = 6, 1975 = 4, 1976 = 2, 1977 = 4, 1978 = 7. *Id.*

52. See, e.g., Henshaw, Forrest & Van Vort, "Abortion Services in the United States, 1984 and 1985," 19 *Fam. Plan. Persps.* 64, table 1 (1987) (at the rate of roughly 1.5 million abortions per year for the 18 years from 1973 to 1990, there have been about 27 million abortions in the U.S.A.).

53. Estrich & Sullivan, *supra* note 35, at 152–54.

54. B. Nathanson, *The Abortion Papers: Inside the Abortion Mentality*, 177–209 (1983).

55. Estrich & Sullivan, *supra* note 35, at 152–54.

56. See, e.g., *id.* at 153 n.132.

57. *Harris v. McRae*, 448 U.S. 297, 319 (1980).

58. See generally R. Adamek, *Abortion and Public Opinion in the United States* (1989).

59. These are some of the radical positions urged by abortion rights partisans in cases such as *Roe v. Wade*, 410 U.S. 113, *Planned Parenthood of Central Missouri v. Danforth*, 428 U.S. 52 (1976), and *Thornburgh v. American College of Obstetricians and Gynecologists*, 476 U.S. 747 (1986).

60. "Most in US favor ban on majority of abortions, poll finds," *Boston Globe*, March 31, 1989, at 1, col. 2–4.

61. *Id.*

62. Torres & Forrest, "Why Do Women Have Abortions?" 20 *Fam. Plan. Persps.*, 169 (1988). Table 1 of this article reveals the following reasons and percentages of women giving their most important reason for choosing abortion: 16% said they were concerned about how having a baby would change their life; 21% said they couldn't afford a baby now; 12% said they had problems with a relationship and wanted to avoid single parenthood; 21% said they were unready for responsibility; 1% said they didn't want others to know they had sex or were pregnant; 11% said they were not mature enough or were too young to have a child; 8% said they had all the children they wanted or had all grown-up children; 1% said their husband wanted them to have an abortion; 3% said the fetus had possible health problems; 3% said they had a health problem; less than .5% said their parents wanted them to have an abortion; 1% said they were a victim of rape or incest; and 3% gave another, unspecified reason. (Figures total more than 100% due to rounding off of numbers.) It is significant to note, also, that 39% of all abortions are repeat abortions. Henshaw, "Characteristics of U.S. Women Having Abortions, 1982–1983," 19 *Fam. Plan. Persps.* 1, 6 (1987).

63. *Roe* held that a state may prohibit abortion after fetal viability, but that it may not do so where the mother's "life or health" would be at risk. 410 U.S. at 165. In the companion case to *Roe*, *Doe v. Bolton*, the Supreme Court construed "health" in an extremely broad fashion to include "all factors—physical, emotional, psychological, familial, and the woman's age—relevant to the well-being of the patient." 410 U.S. 179, 195 (1973). The breadth of these factors makes a "health" reason for an abortion extremely easy to establish, so that we have virtual abortion on demand for all nine months of pregnancy in America. Moreover, there are physicians who declare that if a woman simply seeks an abortion she *ipso facto* has a "health" reason and the abortion may be performed. *McRae v. Califano*, No. 76-C-1804 (E.D.N.Y. Transcript, August 3, 1977, pp. 99–101) (Testimony of Dr. Jane Hodgson) (Dr. Hodgson testified that she felt that there was a medical indication to abort a pregnancy if it "is not wanted by the patient.").

64. J. Mill, *On Liberty* (Atlantic Monthly Press edition 1921).

65. *Id.* at 13. It should be noted that Mill's contention that society should never use its power to protect the individual from the actions of himself or herself is hotly disputed. See, e.g., J. Stephen, *Liberty, Equality, Fraternity* (R. White ed. 1967) (the 1873 classic response to Mill); P. Devlin, *The Enforcement of Morals* (1974).

66. *Roe*, 410 U.S. at 159 ("We need not resolve the difficult question of when life begins.").

67. H. Liley, *Modern Motherhood* 207 (1969).

68. "Technology for Improving Fetal Therapy Advancing Exponentially," *Ob. Gyn. News,* Aug. 1–14, 1987, at 31.

69. P. Williams, "Medical and Surgical Treatment for the Unborn Child," in *Human Life and Health Care Ethics,* 77 (J. Bopp ed. 1985).

70. Estrich & Sullivan, *supra* note 35, at 152–54. In legal terms, this argument is an equal protection one. See *id.* at 124 n.10. However, equal protection of the laws is only constitutionally guaranteed to those who are equally situated, and the Supreme Court has held that treating pregnancy differently from other matters does not constitute gender-based discrimination. *Geduldig v. Aiello,* 417 U.S. 484, 496–97 n.20 (1974). For a further discussion of this point, see Bopp, "Will There Be a Constitutional Right to Abortion After the Reconsideration of *Roe v. Wade*?" 15 *J. Contemp.* L. 131, 136–41 (1989). See also Smolin, "Why Abortion Rights Are Not Justified by Reference to Gender Equality: A Response to Professor Tribe," 23 *John Marshall L. Rev.* 621 (1990).

71. *Rostker v. Goldberg,* 453 U.S. 57 (1981).

72. *Schlesinger v. Ballard,* 419 U.S. 498 (1975).

73. *Id.* at 508.

74. Bopp, "Is Equal Protection a Shelter for the Right to Abortion?" in *Abortion, Medicine and the Law* (4th ed. 1991).

75. *Jacobson v. Massachusetts,* 197 U.S. 11 (1905).

76. *The Selective Service Draft Law Cases,* 245 U.S. 366 (1918).

77. See, e.g., *Sistare v. Sistare,* 218 U.S. 1 (1910). All states have recognized this obligation by passage of the Uniform Reciprocal Enforcement of Support Act. See Fox, "The Uniform Reciprocal Enforcement of Support Act," 12 *Fam. L.Q.* 113, 113–14 (1978).

Internet Resources

Visit our website at http://www.mhhe.com/diclerico for links and resources relating to Civil Rights.